/595

The Science of the Soul

EXPLAINING THE SPIRITUAL UNIVERSE

The Sacred Science Chronicles • Volume III

ROBERT SIBLERUD

Sacred Science Publications
9435 Olsen Court
Wellington, Colorado 80549
(970) 568-7323
E-mail address: SacScience@aol.com

Other Sacred Science Chronicles
In the Beginning: Mysteries of Ancient Civilizations • Volume I
Keepers of the Secrets: Unveiling the Mystical Societies • Volume II

The Science of the Soul: Explaining the Spiritual Universe
Copyright © 2000 by Robert Siblerud
All rights reserved

Printed and bound in the United States of America.

Published by
Sacred Science Publications
9435 Olsen Court
Wellington, Colorado 80549

ISBN: 0-9666856-2-8

Library of Congress Catalog Card Number: 00 091684

Acknowledgements:

Cover Art: **Ron Russell** (Copyright © 1998, Ron Russell)
Editing: **Margaret Shaw**
Copy Editing: **Betty Taylor**
Proof Editing: **Shirley Parrish**
Typesetting and Layout: **Pat Alles**
An Enlightened Scholar: **Leo Sprinkle, Ph.D.**
Reference Material: **Franklin and Carolyn Carter**
Libraries: **Colorado State University, University of Colorado**
Permission: **The Urantia Foundation**
Permission: **Omi Lange**
Suggestions: **Phil Porter**

TABLE OF CONTENTS

Foreword by Leo Sprinkle, Ph.D.   V

Preface   VII

Chapter One   The Soul and Religion   1

Chapter Two   Involution and Evolution of the Soul   28

Chapter Three   The Spiritual Planes   45

Chapter Four   Rebirth   75

Chapter Five   Destiny and Free Will   105

Chapter Six   Celestial Inhabitants   141

Chapter Seven   The Spiritual Hierarchy   165

Chapter Eight   The Soul After Death   199

Chapter Nine   Spirit Communication   225

Chapter Ten   Electronic Spirit Communication   249

Chapter Eleven   The Sacred Science of Spirit and Matter   266

References   303

Index   311

OTHER SACRED SCIENCE CHRONICLES

In the Beginning, Volume I of *The Sacred Science Chronicles,* is a unique book that provides a new perspective to the role that ancient civilizations have played in shaping society over the millennia. It begins with the most ancient of civilizations, Lemuria, the lost continent of the Pacific, and explains why ancients call it the "mother of civilization." Lemuria's seeds spread to civilizations of Atlantis, Egypt, the Mediterranean, and the Americas. Ancient prehistoric civilizations of Lemuria, Atlantis, Sumer, Egypt, Central America, South America, North America, the Mediterranean, and Europe are discussed. The book gives evidence that the Celts, Egyptians, Libyans, and Phoenicians inhabited North America long before Columbus.

The gods of these ancient civilizations played an important role in their development. *In the Beginning* explains who the gods were and where they came from, suggesting they may have been of extraterrestrial origin. It gives a new perspective to Genesis.

Keepers of the Secrets is Volume II of the *Sacred Science Chronicles* providing a synopsis of the mystical societies' influence throughout civilization. It summarizes the history and spiritual philosophy of the shamans, Druids, Essenes, Gnostics, Hermetics, Kabbalists, alchemists, magicians, witches, Sufis, Rosicrucians, and Freemasons.

These mystical societies shared many spiritual truths that contradicted orthodox beliefs. As a result, the Church and state tried to suppress most of these societies, forcing them to become secret, as humanity was not ready for many of these truths.

To update your set of the Sacred Science Chronicles, please contact your local bookstore or Sacred Science Publications.

FOREWORD

R. Leo Sprinkle, Ph.D*

Welcome reader to the *Science of the Soul* by Robert Siblerud. I am honored to introduce you to Dr. Robert Siblerud because he has provided much knowledge on the efforts of many scientists to explore the relationships of science and spirit. He has done an excellent job of summarizing complex topics that allow the reader to feel comfortable in "knowing" the topic.

I use the word "scientist" in the original meaning of "science": "to know," "to discern." Thus, in my opinion, one who continues to seek knowledge is a scientist. However, in recent human history, the word "scientist" has been used more often to acknowledge those who seek formalized knowledge of nature, or the physical world. Our society seems to be comfortable in describing physicists and biologists as scientists. However, we are less certain if historians are scientists, although we may accept psychologists and sociologists as "behavioral scientists." If so, then we may accept historians as "social scientists." But "spiritual scientists?" Scientists of the soul? The reader may recall that the original meaning of "psychologist" was "psych-ology," "the study of the soul." Over the years, however, the definition of psychology was changed from the "study of the soul" to "study of the mind," to "study of consciousness," and finally to the "study of behavior." One humorist observed that this progression could be summarized as follows: "First psychology lost its soul, then lost its mind, and then lost consciousness. Finally it became a behavior problem!"

Of course, Western civilizations as well as Eastern civilizations have a long history of philosophers who focused on spirit as well as matter. For example, old world astronomers also were astrologers who viewed themselves as exploring a material world that reflected the handiwork of a Creator God. Earlier religious traditions spoke of God and Goddess, for example, Native American traditions of Mother Earth and Father Sky.

In Western civilization, there has been an increasing emphasis on a male God, and a patriarchal hierarchy of authority, not only in religion but in science and government, as well.

But now, humanity seems to be at a crossroads: the emphasis upon exploration and exploitation of Mother Earth has led us to a polluted and pained planet. The emphasis on domination by men over women and children has been associated with despotic leaders and oppressive governments.

Now, many observers are calling not only for democratic governments but also a renewed focus on spirit and matter, ethics and technology, feminine and masculine, goddess and god. Thus, science can be viewed both as a body of knowledge and a method for seeking knowledge. That method can be used at various levels: nature, body, mind, and soul. Many scientists, and indeed members of the general public, claim that "science" can be used to focus on the environment as well as the extraction of resources; using energies other than fossil fuels for industry and travel; "zeropoint energy" and "cold fusion," rather than fission; and so forth. I n d e e d , other than the usual concerns about greed and controlling the marketplace, the current knowledge of technology promises a bright future for the material wellbeing of humankind–and a healthier planet.

Thus, it is important for us, as individuals as well as members of our human society, to be clear about who we are. Are we humans on a spiritual journey? Or are we spirits on a human journey? Robert Siblerud provides us with a "map" to assist us in our quest.

He has described various systems of knowledge in his earlier volumes, *In the Beginning* and *Keepers of the Secrets*. Now he turns his attention to these perspectives on the questions of the soul. Not only does he compare various systems, but he also provides the empirical "scientific" evidence that supports some of these traditions about our inner selves.

So, welcome, dear reader. Prepare yourself for some thoughtful emotions and emotional thoughts as you accompany Robert Siblerud on his journey of the sacred science of spirit and matter.

*R. Leo Sprinkle, Ph.D.
Counseling Psychologist
Professor Emeritus, Counseling Services, University of Wyoming
Author of *Soul Samples*

PREFACE

The *Sacred Science Chronicles* are based on the axiom of a spiritual realm, with an underlying supposition that the spiritual world follows laws of the universe that we are just beginning to understand. Sacred science subscribes to a holistic approach that incorporates legends, history, experiential evidence, and traditional science to explore various hypotheses regarding the nature of reality. Spiritual science falls under an entirely different paradigm than physical science, a difference that explains why traditional science has not yet investigated the spiritual realm. Because science cannot define this realm in physical terms, it has chosen to ignore the world of spirit, often critical of those who investigate it. Scientists are reluctant to study spirit, and spiritualists are reluctant to apply science to spirit. The principle underlying sacred science is that no separation exists between spirit and science. Spiritual principles should undergo scientific inquiry, and spiritual integrity should underlie scientific investigation.

Fortunately, a few pioneer scientists have applied scientific rigor to help establish the new paradigm for spirit reality. As we will see, this rigor has supported some spiritual hypotheses that will be presented in the book, strongly suggesting the existence of a spiritual world.

Each religion has incorporated a part of the spiritual truth into its doctrine, but dogma seems to override truth in religion. No judgment on the author's part is intended, because religion has well served its purpose for many people on the spiritual path. The *Science of the Soul* is dedicated to those truth seekers who believe additional answers to the spiritual universe lie outside the realm of religion. The book explores these areas and sheds light on truths underlying religious dogma. For example, as we look into this spiritual science, the reader will have a better understanding of Heaven and Hell and the spiritual life of departed souls. Certain religious dogma is confirmed, but the book expands on the reality that lies behind some of these doctrines. The book also disagrees with many religious doctrines and provides a different view, one supported by science.

What would the world be like if everyone understood and believed in spiritual truths? We would become a world taking responsibility for our actions. Humanity would be more compassionate, more forgiving, and less judgmental. These principles are taught by all the great masters. Humans have adulterated great spiritual truths by translating them into dogma, with the hope of gaining control over their followers, often using fear and guilt to accomplish their objective. Religion has been a vehicle to disseminate many of these partial truths, and religious fathers have purposely withheld important truths from their followers. Members of every religion claim they have the answers to the spiritual world, but each religion differs, resulting in mass confusion if one tries to find spiritual truth in religion. Many religious leaders teach that they are serving as a liaison between God and their converts. Gnostics, during the early Christian era, claimed that the individual was responsible for finding God, and that going through a third person, such as a priest, was unnecessary. They became very critical of the early Church and became known as the original heretics.

The Science of the Soul examines religious doctrine underlying the soul and looks at the science that either supports or contradicts the dogma. For those readers who are religious, the intent of the book is not to change your view, but to help you understand the spiritual doctrines underlying your beliefs. For those who are seeking spiritual answers beyond religion, hopefully the book will be a stimulus to further investigate the mysteries of the spiritual universe. *The Science of the Soul* lays a foundation for the soul's purpose and journey in the early chapters, and the following chapters provide scientific evidence that supports these underlying hypotheses. The final chapter provides a new scientific paradigm, a unified theory of reality that helps to explain the spiritual world and journey of the soul.

Hopefully, the book will serve as an inspiration for future research into the spiritual realm. As we will see, many inhabitants in the spiritual realm are souls like ourselves, gaining experience to perfect themselves on their sojourn back to the Absolute. The soul is who we are, as represented by our actions and thoughts, and we are here on the earthly plane to gather experience for its evolution. Thank you for joining me in discovering the nature and path of the human soul. I hope you enjoy the book.

Robert Siblerud

Chapter One

THE SOUL AND RELIGION
Immortality, a Common Thread

Who are we? What is our life purpose? What is our destiny? All these questions can be answered by understanding the soul. The soul is the most important aspect of a human being, but few people understand the nature and purpose of the soul. Institutionalized religion has claimed dominion over knowledge about the soul, and religious dogma tells followers to accept the soul's existence based only on faith. Most religions teach that the soul is the nonphysical support of the corporeal body and survives after physical death, taking for granted the soul is immortal. Except for Hinduism, religions have not experimented with the nature of the soul, and the average person is left in ignorance of the soul's true nature. Traditional science refuses to approach the science of the soul because the soul lies outside its narrow paradigm of reality. If the soul exists, and it does, what clues give scientific evidence of its existence? The goal of this book is to define the soul and its purpose, to examine different belief systems regarding the soul, and to look at evidence supporting the soul's existence as discovered by pioneer scientists.

A soul is an individualized, nonphysical entity. When embodied, it provides the nucleus of the rational, mental, and physical aspects of human personality. An individuated soul establishes contact with the physical world through mind, intellect, and body, but it also maintains contact with the spiritual realm that lies beyond space, time and causality. The embodied soul of an individual human is an integrated whole of body, mind, and intellect. However, the soul as activator can be independent of mind, intellect, and body.

The soul is an invisible, activating, psychic force that provides direction to the human personality. Personality results as a natural force of the soul and does not act independently. Each personality is unique because the makeup of the soul that forms it is unique. A soul's persona has interaction with physical matter. Gary Zukav writes in *The Seat of the Soul*, "The conflicts of a human life are directly proportional to the distance at which an energy of personality exists separated from the soul."

The soul is the center, entity, or force that makes a person alive and capable of action. It animates. When it leaves, a person is dead or dying. The soul force differentiates one person from another and maintains its specific character, even after death. It usually maintains a spirit form after discarding the physical body and can sometimes be recognized as a ghost. Often the soul is the medium through which discarnate spirits contact the living. A soul's consciousness extends from the physical world into another dimension that spirits occupy.

Often people confuse the spirit with the soul. The soul is not spirit, but is that by which the spirit is known. In other words, we understand the soul by the nature and power of the spirit. Neither soul nor spirit is perceptible without the presence of the other. They cannot exist without each other. The soul is formless and intangible, shown by the attributes of spirit.

As we will discover, some religions and most mystical societies believe that the spiritual ego, a scintillating atom point of the soul, or spark, evolved from the Divine Soul of the Deity. Soul is therefore an attribute of the Divine Ego or Deity. Deity is defined as Absolute Potentiality, pure, formless spirit with unlimited, unconditional intelligence. This eternal, scintillating atom of Deity, the seed of the soul, is beyond human conception. It rests in serenity and peace, tabulating and using all the knowledge and experience that the soul continually receives during its various cycles. As it gathers knowledge and experience for its unfoldment and development, the soul receives all knowledge from within or without the universe of external life. Each person must discover the special development required for his or her soul. The presence of an embodied soul has a purpose realized through the relationship of the individual soul with God.

The Fall of humankind, as described in the Bible, refers to the descent of the soul into matter. A soul longs to return home to the Deity and must evolve out of matter into the spiritual realm and ascend back to the Absolute. In various guises, each religion teaches humanity about a path back to God. The highest purpose of religion is to bring about the realization of this transcendental soul.

Because each soul contains an atom of the Divine Ego, mystics believe a human is a miniature universe or image of God. A human is the microcosm of the macrocosm. Human functions parallel God's manifestation as the cosmic center. The core of one's personality controls the periphery of intellect and body. It is the soul center that contacts the Universal Mind. The souls of humans cannot transcend the earthly limitations of time and space in the material world unless they attune through spiritual discipline to the Cosmic Consciousness. To activate this contact with God, all true religions advocate a selfless attitude of service and love. An enlightened mind sees unity in diversity and sees harmony in discord. This person recognizes the light of God in all people different from him– or herself. There are many paths to God, but some are faster and straighter.

THE SOUL AND NATIVE PEOPLE

Native people around the world have always believed in a soul that survived death. Their spiritual leader, the shaman, is the specialist of the soul. Shamans have the ability to see the soul, know its form, and foresee its destiny. Though they are continents apart, the shamans of North America, South America, Australia, and Asia have similar practices. A shaman changes states of consciousness at will and can then travel to a nonordinary state of consciousness to contact lost souls, spirit helpers, and teachers. Through trance, a shaman can leave the body and ascend to the Sky or Lower World, the abodes of the gods and spirits, respectively.

Shamans believe a life essence or soul inhabits all natural phenomena such as animals, rocks, and plants. Each plant and animal specie is guided by a spirit master. Shamans believe humans have no superiority over the rest of nature, but depend on nature and the goodwill of the spirits who rule it.

The shaman's primary gift is the ability to enter nonphysical worlds to communicate with spirits. During the journey to the nonphysical world, the shaman encounters souls of the dead, guardian spirits, power animals, and evil spirits. Spirits act as intermediaries between cosmic power and the humans who receive that power.

After death, the soul of the dead enters the spiritual world and often becomes confused. The shamans believe that evil spirits provoke death through disease, and these spirits lead the deceased into the Lower World, often resulting in confusion. Sometimes the dead do not accept their place in the Lower World. The shaman's duty is to enter the spiritual world, capture the wayward soul, and lead it to its new dwelling. Some indigenous societies believe a man possesses from three to seven souls. At death, one soul remains in the grave, one descends to the Lower World, and a third ascends to the Sky.

Shamans often have helpers in the spiritual world to guide lost souls to their proper destination. Each shaman has at least one guardian spirit that serves him or her. Frequently the guardian spirit is a power animal. In the altered state, the shaman actively uses the guardian spirit, consults it, and travels with it on the journey. North American Indian shamans often obtain through vision quests the guardian spirit that assists them in healing. Helping spirits could be collected almost anywhere, according to Professor Mircea Eliade, the foremost researcher on native spirituality.

Shamans believe that many illnesses are caused by the soul leaving the body. In times of sickness, shamans are called upon to retrieve the soul from the Lower World. Once the soul has been retrieved, the patient is expected to improve and recover. Several things may cause the flight of a patient's soul. Fearful experience, such as a bad dream, may have frightened it away. Often dead souls want companionship and take a loved one's soul to the Lower World. On occasion, the soul has strayed away from the body and becomes lost in the Lower World. Soul loss is always the shaman's business, and the shaman must find the soul and restore it to the patient.

Primitive cultures share a similar cosmology. A central axis connects the realms of Sky, Earth, and Lower World. Shamans possess the knowledge and techniques to pass among the three planes, communicating among these regions. Along this axis, the gods descended to the lower worlds. Through this axis or tunnel, the soul of the shaman flies up or down in the course of its celestial or infernal journey.

The cosmic tree, called the Tree of Life, symbolizes the connection of the three cosmic regions. This cosmic tree has seven branches that correspond to the seven planetary heavens. Shamans have direct knowledge of all these heavens and of the gods and demigods that inhabit them. The underworld has the same number of levels. Those who have transgressed in their previous lives dwell in the

Lower World, as do unskilled hunters. Inhabitants of the Sky lead a happy existence and find pleasure and prosperity. The privileged, including chiefs, shamans, and initiates, go to the Sky.

Legend describes a Golden Age when people traveled with ease among the three regions, with no rigid division between wakefulness and dreams. If someone could imagine a dream or event, it would manifest. Indigenous myths also taught that a Fall took place, which manifested after an arrogant act. The bridge between the three worlds collapsed, and travel between the three cosmic worlds became the exclusive privilege of the deities, spirits, and shamans.

A soul, according to the Mexica (Aztec) Indians of Mexico, provided animation to the body and conferred highly individual characteristics of personality, aptitudes, abilities, and desires. It also provided consciousness. If the deceased was filled with great emotion at the time of death, such as anger, the soul would wander throughout the world as a restless wind spirit. Some tribes believed that if a person died prematurely, the soul would wander until the person's time of destined death or that it might try to enter the body of a newborn child. Dead infants and young children did not journey to Mictlan, the Aztec underworld, but instead went to the Sky to join the deity who gave life to each person. These young souls went to a garden paradise where they drank nectar from flowers.

The Mexica called one aspect of the soul *tonalli*. It had a will of its own and followed its desires, whatever they may be, which could cause a person to become socially unacceptable. It could escape the body before death. Some believed the soul traveled during sleep to other worlds and that it might become lost at that time. If it did not return within several weeks, a person became tired, warm, and sleepy.

A religious belief in both a divine origin and destiny of the human soul is found among African peoples. They believe the soul, which they called *orka*, preexists a physical embodiment and survives in an incorporeal state after physical death. The two-way interaction between the living and the dead is significant in the religion and culture of the Africans. Although they believe in divine judgement, seldom do they believe in Heaven or Hell. Rather, the soul is a spiritual substance that returns to the divine source following death.

After death, the deceased reunites with dead relatives. In the afterlife, the soul preserves its earthly identity in name, social status, and religious status. Physical features of the deceased are also maintained in the afterlife.

African myths suggest that God gave humans a choice between mortality and immortality. If they chose to procreate, mortality was the result. This is not unlike the biblical story of Adam and Eve and the forbidden fruit of carnal knowledge.

In African belief, a synergistic relationship exists between body and soul. What happens to the soul of a person affects the body, and what happens to the body affects the soul.

Some tribes believe that the dead will come back to life, reborn into their families. Though a person has been reincarnated in his or her grandchildren, the deceased person continues to live in the afterlife, maintaining his or her identity. The dominant characteristic of the ancestor reincarnates, not the soul. Sometimes described as a partial reincarnation, each soul remains distinct and each birth represents a new soul. Other tribes believe that if the soul does not complete its destiny, it is sent back to Earth to complete it. Those who have good characters and have lived a good life will have a good sojourn in a return incarnation on Earth. They are allowed to be reborn into their families. According to some traditions, a bad life on Earth results in an afterlife in a hot and dry environment, where the entity is destined to eat centipedes and earthworms.

THE EARLY EGYPTIAN CONCEPT OF THE SOUL

Early Egyptians believed an individual had nine souls, or that one soul was composed of nine aspects. Much of ancient Egypt's culture was centered around the immortality of the soul, evidenced by the fact that most of the pyramids were constructed to ensure the immortality of the pharaoh's soul.

The first aspect of the soul is the *khu*, the primordial life spirit that resides in the blood. Khu represents the inspirational aspect of life, considered the consciousness in the body.

Ab resides in the heart and is the seat of wisdom, knowledge, and understanding. It is the source of good when conscious, and evil when unconscious. Guilt and innocence reside in the a*b*.

The *ba* is related to the universal or spiritual being that resides in the *ab* of the heart, being both eternal and fixed. It is the aspect of the soul that joins the gods after death, described by Egyptians as flying to Ra, the sun, to reside with Osiris. The *ba* can take on human form and can become material, depending on its will. Today it would be called a ghost or spiritual aberration. *Ba* has the ability to fly like a bird. It is that part of the soul that leaves the body at sleep and comes back whenever it desires. When one undergoes a near-death experience, the *ba* is the consciousness involved.

Ka is the ethereal double that is commonly associated with the emotional body of a human. An abstract personality, it can assume form without matter to resemble the person it inhabits. *Ka* is creative, giving rise to movement and the ability to wander at will. Known today as the astral body, it can project into the mental realm and act as a vehicle for exploring more subtle planes of consciousness.

Khaibut is literally related to the shadow of a person, according to the ancient Egyptians. It can exist outside the body. People, who practice black magic, often use the *khaibut* as a model of an individual over whom they wish to gain power. For example, in witchcraft, pins are stuck into a doll representing the *khaibut* of the individual. In tribal societies not familiar with photographs, individuals may become frightened if their shadows are captured on film, believing they may die.

Khat is the sixth aspect of the soul, which is the physical body animated by the *ba*. It is the consciousness associated with bodily functions, such as elimination, breathing, heartbeat, and so forth.

Sekham is the incorporeal form manifested by a spiritual body. It represents the vital forces of a human being and is the power that a person possesses to become incarnate. The *sekham* maintains vital power to the body.

Ren is the eighth aspect of the soul, the person's name, which is powerful and holy. Often parents would not reveal the birth name until the person reached adulthood. Egyptians believed that as a person's name goes, so does his or her destiny in the afterlife. Names were very important. As souls moved through the nether world attempting to return to Osiris, the soul at various times on the death journey was asked to name the various gods that guarded various chambers and passageways before it could enter. Correct pronunciation of a name gave one power over the god.

Sahu, the ninth soul aspect, is the spiritual body that departs the material body at death. Within it, mental and spiritual attributes of the natural body were united and given new power. It took on the same body form as the *khat* but was itself nonmaterial and contained within the other soul bodies or aspects. The *sahu* traveled to higher worlds.

In ancient Egypt, a person such as the pharaoh was composed of two elements, the body and the spirit. The latter was composed of three components, the *ka*, the *ba* and the *akh*. *Ka* was considered part of the divine spirit, the divine omniscience of the creator. *Ba* was the immortal soul, the being's personification. *Akh* was described as the power that generates and receives waves, the energy and spirit connected to the life of the perishable body. *Ba* is one of the oldest references to an inner being of light, or soul image of man. It was regarded as man's spiritual double. Two things were essential upon the king's death: Keeping the body latently alive was necessary so that his *akh* might allow him to remain in contact with his soul (*ba*), which had joined the solar *barque* (boat) that would carry him to join the sun god Ra and bypass the cycle of rebirths. The divine *ka* must also remain connected to the Earth by being forced to pass into the body of the king's successor. These were the goals of the royal *Isial* funerary rites. Mummification of the royal body followed the magical operation of the transferral of the *ka* to the new king.

GREEK PHILOSOPHY OF THE SOUL

Some of the greatest thinkers humanity has ever known came from Greece. These great philosophers wrote volumes about the soul. Many of their thoughts originated from the study of Egyptian and Chaldean religions. Similar to believers of all religions, the Greeks also believed the soul was immortal, and these philosophers tried to provide understanding of the nature of the soul.

Diogenes (third century A.D.) wrote that the soul is air composed of the finest particles. He taught that the soul was the ultimate principle that both knows and causes movement. Heracleitus also describes the soul as the first principle, believing it was the emanation from which things are constructed. He believed it was an incorporeal entity in ceaseless flux with all things that exist in motion. Alcmaeon described the soul as immortal because it resembles immortal things, and that its characteristic is due to perpetual motion. All three of these Greek thinkers distinguished the soul by three attributes: movement, sensation, and incorporeality.

Aristotle was a biologist who received his education in the school of Plato and believed experimentation was a means of collecting evidence that applied to the soul. Aristotle (384-322 B.C.)

believed the soul contains an element that produces movement and an element that produces knowledge. He described the soul as a living entity, as distinguished by two functions. It has the capacity to judge, a function of intellect and sensation. The soul also has the capacity for exciting movement in space. Aristotle also believed the soul was the cause and first principle of the living body, from which motion is derived. He writes that the soul is a harmony of some kind, being a "blend and composition of contraries from which the body is composed."

Homer (700 B.C.), the early Greek, described the soul as immortal. The "free soul" of the living continued as the soul of the dead, known as the psyche by Homer. The psyche represented the individual free of psychological attributes. A person could not survive without the psyche, which at death fled to Hades, the abode of the dead. Dependent upon the psyche was the body that could become ill and die if the psyche disappeared. Psyche, or the free soul, was the individual's nonphysical mode that existed in death, dreams, trance, and other forms of unconsciousness. It was always active outside the body but was not bound to it. The psyche represents only the individual, having no physical or psychological attributes. It represents the complete identity of a person. Because the psyche cannot continue in a worldly existence after death, it has to pursue an afterlife.

The free soul, or psyche, was known to leave the body temporarily and experience adventure, being visible during the sojourn outside the body. Today, this phenomenon is called bilocation. This explains how Pythagoras was seen in Croton and Metapontum at the same hour on the same day. St. Francis was seen simultaneously blessing the brethren in Arles and sitting on the mountain in Laverna.

Homer describes three other souls associated with the body: the *noos*, associated with the mind; the *menos*, a momentary impulse directed toward a specific activity; and the *thymos*, the soul of emotions. The *thymos* resides mainly in the chest, a location called the *phrenes*, where the seat of emotion, such as joy, grief, fear, and anger, is found. *Thymos*, identified with breath, expresses hope and urges people on, but during trance it leaves its original seat. In summary, the ancient Greek soul belief was dualistic, composed of two elements: the psyche and three body souls.

NEOPLATONISM AND THE SOUL

Plato's teaching was related to the sacred traditions of the Egyptians, Chaldeans, and Assyrians. He acknowledged that his teachings were a deeper mystery of Egyptian thought. Plato's view of the soul was so influential that centuries after his death, a movement was born called Neoplatonism. It flourished between the third and sixth century A.D., and synthesized Greek thought and oriental mysticism. Founded in Alexandria by Ammonius Saccas, its leading proponents included Plontinus, Iamblichus, and Porphyry. Emanation, the belief that the human spirit can participate in the divine, was the central doctrine of Neoplatonism. All material and spiritual existence emanated from the Absolute, the transcendent Godhead, through the actions of the divine mind, or logos, and the world soul. Emperor Justinian I banned Neoplatonism in A.D. 529, but it was later revived by the mystics Picodella Mirandola and Marsilio Ficino. Iamblichus (A.D. 240-325), the leader of the movement to repaganize the Roman Empire, was considered the foremost Platonist of his time and was designated the savior of Hellenic culture. The practice of theurgy followed the canon of the Platonic tradition. Theurgy is defined as a "work of the gods" capable of transforming man to a divine status.

Plato said that in man's golden age, a divine hierarchy ruled man and ensured the well-being of all. Society was governed by daimons. The Greek word "daimon" means spirit, a term to describe beings that are between God and people. Guided by these daimons, humans enjoyed peace, prosperity, and justice, until people usurped the daimons' authority. Humanity began to rule themselves, ignoring the hierarchial law that demands each species must obey its superior order. Plato believed humanity should reinstate the hierarchy of the golden age. Iamblichus writes that the soul was completely descended into matter. He referred to matter as a pollution from which souls must be cleansed. Matter was the obstacle that kept souls from communion with the gods. Gods were free from the pollution of matter, and to reach them the souls had to break away from the material bonds. Matter is opposed to the gods, and the body is the prison from which souls are to be freed. However, matter was an impediment only for individual souls, but not for the World Soul or Celestial Soul (stars).

According to the teachings of Iamblichus, the daimons lead

souls down into matter and not up to the gods. They were agents of the Demiurge (creators of the world) and were powers that defiled the soul by bringing it to matter. The task of the daimons was to externalize specific aspects of the divine into matter. They were the personified powers of matter.

To free the souls from the bonds of generation (rebirth), theurgic sacrifices had to overcome the daimonic bonds that tied souls to their bodies. By fulfilling the commands of a theurgic rite, the soul began to share in the continuity that extended from the gods to matter.

Iamblichus taught that the soul is contained in the order of fate. It needed to take its place in this order, fulfill its requirements, and make proper use of it. Once the soul developed pure reason, was self-substantiated, self-moved, and acting from itself, it had developed perfection and was liberated from the bonds of the material world. However, if the soul identified with the body and material world, it remained within the physical realm.

Each soul was symbolized by an astrological portrait given to it by the cosmos. This astrological influence tested the soul in the material world and measured the soul's ability to integrate corporeal existence into a divine pattern. Failure to fulfill the conditions of the body resulted in the subsequent suffering of fate. Only by proper care of the body and right actions in the physical world could the soul be freed from its body.

The human soul was the lowest aspect of divinity. Because it identified with only certain aspects of the cosmos, it lost its perspective of the whole and became absorbed into the flow of the mortal life. The body was inborn with the soul, the soul innate with the intellect, and the intellect with God. Theurgy limited and redirected daimonic attractions and transformed humans into the soul's receptacle of salvation.

According to Iamblichus, if the soul directed excessive attention to the body, it became subject to rules governing corporeal action. In theurgic terms, this demanded that the soul be reconciled with the daimon who ruled the realm of nature governing this activity. Until the soul achieved a proper relation with the daimon, it remained subject to the daimons' punishment. Objects such as stones, herbs, animals, and aromatics served as receptacles for the gods and bore their signature in the manifest world. Gods preserved an intimate relationship with them. Through appropriate use of the gods in nature, souls could awaken in themselves the power of their corresponding symbols. This would realign the soul with the manifesting energies of a deity and free it from servitude to the daimons. Theurgic knowledge was gained only through practical experience. In theurgy, anything that received the god and mediated its presence functioned as a sacred receptacle.

By means of appropriate rites, the theurgist directed the power of its particular soul into alignment with the power of the World Soul, which gave the theurgist direct participation in the whole. Plato said that individual souls must also make their contribution. Souls moved from the experience of embodiment, as an isolated prison, to participation in the World Soul, where they were reestablished in the unity of the whole. In theurgy, the soul gradually transformed the chaos of its embodied experience into a perfect measure of the cosmos. By mediation of the gods, the soul became its own demiurge.

Matter was the mirror that reflected the condition of the soul, measuring the degree of divinity. The intensity of the soul's contact with the gods was in direct proportion to its receptive capacity. Perfection of the soul was realized only by first assimilating oneself into the physical world. The highest condition of the soul was achieved only when it was conscious of being of lowest divinity. Only then did the soul realize its place in the divine hierarchy. A perfect theurgist then became an embodied demiurge whose presence created harmony out of discord and drove evil away. The body of the perfect theurgist became a vehicle through which the god appeared to the physical world and through which the god received communion.

Iamblichus said the celestial gods (souls) mediated between the World Soul and individual souls. Celestial gods serve as a link between the unity of the World Soul and the multiplicity of individual souls. Perfection of an individual soul occurred only through its return to the celestial orders and through them to the Demiurge.

Each soul, claims Iamblichus, began its corporeal life in a fallen and separated state because of the weakened consistency of human souls. Each human soul carried a part of the Divine as established by the Demiurge, but the human measures of coherence were broken apart into the divisions of time. Iamblichus categorized eight tiers in the hierarchy of souls: (1) gods, (2) archangels, (3) angels, (4) daimons, (5) heroes, (6) archons-sublunar, (7) archons-material, and (8) humans.

The acts of embodied souls were separated from their essences and completed within the cycles of rebirth. The body reflected the activity of the soul and indicated the kind of soul that animated it. Each incarnation produced an entirely new identity.

Although the gods were everywhere, their powers could not affect souls that lacked an appropriate receptacle. Only when the vehicle was prepared could divine possession occur. Iamblichus said, "The time one spends in prayer nourishes the intuitive mind and greatly enlarges the soul's receptacle for gods."

Souls descended into bodies, either voluntarily or involuntarily, for one of three reasons: (1) to save, purify, and protect the cosmos, (2) to correct and exercise their character, or (3) to undergo punishment and judgment. The soul type that entered the corporeal world to preserve the cosmos was already free and thus entered voluntarily. Most entered the physical world to work toward perfection, and most of these embodied involuntarily.

Each soul had a personal daimon that guided it during an incarnation. A soul progressed furthest at the rare moment it received a god as a guardian to replace the personal daimon. A guardian was assigned to a soul according to its astrological profile.

Even before a soul descended into rebirth, the personal daimon was established with it. The soul would select the daimon as its leader, which would immediately attend to the task of fulfilling the lives of the soul. The daimon would bind the soul to the body when the soul descended and would coordinate the soul's descent into the material world. A ruling daimon mixed the soul's immortal logos with the mortal life to meet the particular demands of the incarnation. Each soul's goal was to align itself and its activities with the ruling god. After this was achieved, the guardian daimon gave way to a higher guide. The daimon oversaw the composite life of a soul and body, along with the individual life of the soul. It was a rare privilege to have a god become a guardian, but first the soul needed to prepare the proper receptacle. This happened when the soul became resonant with the World Soul and when it began to live for the entire world. The soul must see itself in all things before it entered the immortal body.

MATHEMATICS OF THE SOUL

The Greek Pythagoras spent twenty-two years studying Egyptian mysteries such as astronomy and sacred geometry and was initiated into all the mystic rites of the gods. He was also instructed by the magi of Babylonia, where he perfected worship of the gods and reached the highest level in knowledge of numbers, justice, and other mathematical disciplines. Pythagoras passed down these mathematical initiations in symbolic, obscure forms.

Mathematical mysteries of Pythagoras purified the mind and allowed it to participate with the gods. Pythagoras proclaimed he had been given the purification rites of the gods through mystic initiations. These sacred rites allowed one to discern and obey the will of the gods.

Platonic and Pythagorean philosophers identified the soul with different branches of mathematics. The soul, according to Iamblichus, existed in ratios common with all mathematics. The soul possessed the power of discerning their own sacred ratios and of generating and producing the incorporeal measures themselves. Mathematics recapitulated the soul's descent and return and allowed one to see clearly the soul's process.

Seven numbers divide the World Soul, according to Plato's *Timeaus.* They include the numbers 1, 2, 3, 4, 8, 9, and 27. These numbers have metaphysical functions. The Demiurge had created the World Soul out of geometric, harmonic, and arithmetic proportions. The mathematical essence of a soul can be identified as a geometric figure, as a number, and as a harmony. One represents sameness and unity. Two stands for duality. Three means the return to God. Four represents communication of the primary order to its secondary manifestations. Eight symbolized the Ogdoad, the sphere beyond the seven planets, the home of the soul. Nine symbolized perfection and functioned as a new monad.

The Greek philosopher Proclus (A.D. 410-485) refers to numbers as the temporal measure of the cosmos and speaks of the power of time to perfect souls. Time proceeds according to number, and by number it measures the existence of all souls. By performing rituals at precise times according to proper constellations, the soul could be united with the gods. According to Proclus, mathematics are used for recollection of divine principles, and numbers and shapes are consecrated to the gods. To each god, an appropriate symbol and shape is assigned. Acute angles lead the soul down into fate and rebirth, and obtuse angles provide the soul a connection with the god's above fate. The soul contains all the mathematical and geometric figures that it consecrates, resulting in a schematic of the entire process of separation and return to the gods. Pythagoreans also claim that physical things are determined by number and are concrete manifestations of number. The variety and vitality of nature are simply the concrete manifestations of numerical powers. Soul and body are not produced from the same number, but soul forms cubic numbers, for example, (6 X 6 X 6 = 216), and body forms irregular numbers (5 X 6 X 7 = 210). As a numerical number, the soul eventually has to undergo a numerical transformation in its evolution.

RELIGIONS OF RESURRECTION

Three religions, Judaism, Christianity, and Islam, teach that the physical body and soul both are resurrected after death. The Jewish concept of the soul has changed over the millennia that began with a vague notion of a shadowy world of the dead called the *sheol*. A *sheol* was a vast tomb where all people, good and evil, were at rest. It was the abode for the ghostly double of the living. The early books of the Hebrew Bible contain no promise of physical life after death and are emphatic that a body does not survive death. Later, the Jewish doctrine regarding life after death included resurrection of the body. For most Jews the idea of physical resurrection was inconceivable in light of their scientific understanding of the nature of the world. In modern times the idea of physical resurrection was replaced in both orthodox and nonorthodox Judaism by the belief in the soul's immortality and resurrection of the spirit.

No explicit belief in eternal salvation is found in the Old Testament. Rabbis of the postbiblical period had a difficult time proving that the resurrection of the dead was contained in scripture. However, Daniel 12:2 does partly address resurrection, "And many of those who sleep in the dust of the Earth shall awake, some to everlasting life, and some to shame and everlasting contempt." Jews today believe that to enter Heaven, one needs to lead a good life in accordance with God's law. Disobeying God's Torah and Mosaic Law results in confinement to Hell.

Christians believe in the doctrine of resurrection of the body and immortality of the soul. A life after death is taken for granted in all the New Testament documents. Heaven is mentioned two hundred forty times, and the original Christians thought of Heaven as their true home. St. Paul's writings of the New Testament popularized the concept of resurrection. Paul said that if the dead are not raised, our gospel is null and void. Some scholars believed that Paul was not referring to the mortal body's resurrection but to the re-creation of the body as a spiritual body. However, Church Fathers believed resurrection meant physical resurrection of the body (the flesh) as stated in the Apostle's Creed, which affirms the "resurrection of the flesh," and in the Nicene Creed which affirms the "upstanding of the dead bodies." Church Fathers were adamant that the resurrection was definitely a physical reconstruction. Catholic orthodoxy states, "The same person he was in the same flesh made living by the same spirit." Protestants also believe in the physical resurrection.

Many early Church Fathers agreed with their pagan predecessors that humans possessed multiple souls. They believed a soul had parts or functions, with some aspects that could be stolen or lost: Clement of Alexandria (A.D. 200-266) taught of five divisions of the soul that each provides speech, reproduction, thought, and regulation of physical processes. Those who accepted the faith were given part of the Holy Spirit. Church Fathers of Saint Augustine (A.D. 354-430) asserted that the soul was indivisible, immaterial, and was similar but not identical to the substance of God. Over the next millennium, the church reduced the number of souls from many to one. The soul was described as one, an infragmented entity without multiple parts. The church finally declared the soul to be newly formed at the time of conception. They rejected any idea that the soul was recycled, as taught in Eastern religions.

Christians taught the souls who would be saved are those who believe in Jesus Christ. No person earns salvation, but it comes only through Jesus, mediated through baptism, grace, and a life of holiness. Christians believe there will be a day of judgement for souls at the time of Christ's return and that this is when the soul will be resurrected. The souls who earn salvation will go to Heaven, and souls who love self, sin, and evil will go to Hell. Soul is mentioned thirty-six times in the Old Testament and fourteen in the New Testament. Very little understanding about the soul is provided in the Bible.

Of the three major Abrahamic religions, Islam talks most about the life in the hereafter. The resurrection and judgment occupy a large and important place in the Koran. Islam, along with Judaism and Christianity, teaches that a human lives only a single life. At death, the soul survives in a disembodied state. At some unpredictable future date, every soul will be reembodied and undergo the last judgment. According to God's verdict, the soul will enjoy physical bliss in Heaven or physical anguish in Hell.

The Koran teaches that humans are given life on Earth so that they may serve their creator and be rewarded by God in the hereafter. Only through faithful practice of the Koranic teachings can a person become a full-fledged Muslim. Islam teaches that the prophet Muhammad was sent as a warner and guide to humanity and not as a savior. To prepare properly for the life hereafter, certain functions of Islam were required. One should say five daily prayers, perform the fast, give the Zakat, and make a pilgrimage to the holy city of Mecca to perform the Hajj.

The Koran does not offer many clues regarding soul, spirit, day of judgment, nor the life hereafter, but it does say Allah identifies the soul as it leaves the dying body. Humans are created for a purpose and are responsible for all deeds on Earth. The human body is only a vehicle by which the soul must develop itself. Before entering Heaven, a soul develops from a level of simple consciousness to a level of spirituality. Death is a gateway for entering into a new life, a life of unlimited progress. A person's state of mind at the moment of death is very important, because change is not possible thereafter. After death, the soul is suspended in the ethereal world called *Barzakh* until the hour of resurrection, after which it will be sent either to Heaven or Hell.

RELIGIONS OF REINCARNATION

Two of the most ancient religions, Hinduism and Buddhism, teach the doctrine of reincarnation. Only Hinduism, of all major religions, has elaborated on the nature of the soul. Contrary to Western religion, Hindus believe immortality applies to the soul and not the body, that is, survival of the spiritual self and not the physical self.

Five thousand years ago the Hindus taught and practiced the *Bhagavad Gita*, and it continues to be practiced today. It accepts God, both as immanent and transcendant, as a Being beyond personality. Humans are the highest divine manifestation in the visible form. They are in constant quest of their source and God.

The purpose of human life is to seek God though the path of true knowledge, love, and service regardless of occupation, caste, creed, or culture. The *Bhagavad Gita* encourages every individual to use earthly existence to evolve his or her soul to its greatest potential. This is done by subordinating all thoughts, feelings, and actions to the love of God and man. Once this stage is reached, in which humans are completely dedicated to God and in which the light of God is seen reflected in all creatures, humans will perform their life duties without indulgence or attachment and with full consciousness of God. This stage of development is termed spiritual liberation or self-discovery and foreshadows the soul's eternal life that will be attained after death. To reach this stage, the soul passes through numberless incarnations, progressing toward perfection until it receives the highest grace of God.

The highest stage described in the *Bhagavad Gita* is difficult to attain. All souls have the same potential and are destined eventually to attain it, some earlier than others. Freedom of will, granted to all individuals, influences the progression of the soul. The choices made may accelerate the progress, hinder, or actually regress its evolution. Some advanced souls have reached the stage of eternal life but have chosen to reincarnate to help others along the path.

True liberation means freedom from the bonds of rebirth and realization of Brahman, the Supreme Reality and ineffable Truth, which transcend all boundaries. According to the *Gita*, the liberated person attains the state of Brahman by casting off all selfish desires and by renouncing the claims of "mine" and "I." Liberation infers the realization of God's mode of being. By the love of God, the liberated man realizes God's nature. Here, the soul participates in the total being of God. Self realizes itself as it externally exists, in perfect identity with the Absolute.

The Sanskrit term for self is *atman*, the soul, or the essence of a human being. Atman is none other than Brahman. The self (soul) alone is real and immortal. Everything else that we know and experience, the objects of the external world, are unreal and mortal. This includes body, mind, and senses. Spirit is self; material is not-self.

Avidya means ignorance and is the cause of human bondage. It is the causal form of humans. Along with the gross body and subtle body, it makes up the components of matter. Only knowledge can remove *avidya*. When a person attains self-realization, *avidya* ceases to be.

As long as the self (soul) is embodied, it is in bondage and not free. It is called the empirical self and individual self. Man consists of the soul and the body. The nature of the soul or self is transmitted to the mind so that the mind is credited with the power of comprehension. The body is external to the soul, and nothing in the nature of the soul requires it to be related to the body. When a person attains liberation through the right knowledge of self, *avidya*, the causal form, ceases to be.

A liberated human is in the state of peace, which is bliss par excellence, free from desires, moving without attachment, without selfishness, and without vanity. This liberated person is free from all three bodies, gross, subtle, and causal. Once all desires that dwell in the mind and heart are gone, a person having been mortal becomes immortal, and attains Brahman in the very body. The soul (self) then becomes disembodied and immortal. Immortality can be attained in the present life itself. However, it often takes many lives to break the bondage to the physical world.

In Hinduism, the present life is determined by the past, and in turn it determines the future life. The subtle body, with which the self (soul) is associated, serves as the link between one life and another. The inner life of man is dependent on the subtle body, composed of intellect and mind. After death of the gross external body, the subtle body, which is the physical vesture of the soul, departs to form a new life. It carries the impression left over by knowledge, work, and past experience. A soul associated with the subtle body has a particular consciousness at the time of death, and it goes to the body related to that consciousness. The future life is decided upon even at the time that the empirical self departs from the present life.

When a person dies, his karma remains attached to his self (soul). Karma's force decides the nature of the next birth, where one reaps the fruit of the past life. The cycle of rebirth is governed by the law of karma. Without love of God, continued birth and rebirth follow for the person who has no faith in God and relies only on oneself. The law of karma demands that a person be reborn to reap the fruits of his action. Every good act meets with reward, and every bad act meets with punishment. Only through higher wisdom can one be freed from the bondage of the cycle of rebirth. Rebirth follows the penalty of Hell or rewards of Heaven. After death, the spirit passes to the world of spirits. The full personality of the departed is believed to remain after death. Yam, the judge of the dead, passes judgment. Good spirits go to a paradise of bliss and happiness, and wicked spirits go to an abode of Hell, a place of darkness and demons.

The *Upanishads* distinguish three classes of souls: (1) Those who rely on faith in the eternity of the atman are released from the cycle of rebirth. (2) Those who perform Vedic duties of sacrifices, alms giving, and austerities return to the world in human form after being in the world of the fathers (the ancestors who have passed through death and attained life in the third heaven). (3) Those who do not know either of these ways are condemned to the life of an insect or a reptile. The doctrine of transmigration is taught as part of the law of action or karma. Transmigration is the passing of individual souls at death into new bodies or different forms of life.

A soul in its pure form is a core that is unaffected by mental, biological, and physical changes. The *Bhagavad Gita* (17-20 and 20-24) says, "The bodies which this eternal soul puts on are terminable; but the soul is imperishable and external . . . The soul neither kills nor is it killed . . . The soul is neither born nor does it die in time . . . It does not come into being nor has it any future time to become again . . . It is unborn, permanent, ever existent, ancient and is not destroyed in the perishable body . . . The soul puts on a new body after laying aside the old one . . . It is invisible and is incorruptible in itself."

The concept of reincarnation differs in Buddhism from that of Hinduism. Buddhists deny both the immortal body and immortal soul. They believe in a life span that flows on and on until it expires at Nirvana.

Death marks the beginning of the waning phase of the life process. The connecting psyche is the unit of mental energy produced at death. This mental energy leaves the dead body and travels to a new body in a mother's womb, if it is to be reborn as a human. It is the seed of a new life. This linking psyche joins the embryo within the womb. From the moment of birth, old age begins, and the waxing phase of life ends when conventional death occurs.

Death marks only the waxing phase of the life stream. As long as karmic disposition and ignorance remain, the linking psyche will produce a start to a new waxing phase. No one lives forever, because the life stream is an integrated phenomena, and every integrated thing must disintegrate.

At the moment of death, the linking psyche will be attracted to rebirth in any of eight classes of beings, according to karmic disposition. A linking psyche with positive karmic force will be drawn to a higher world of beings. A negative karmic force will be reborn in a lower realm. Buddhists also believe in transmigration of the soul, and humans can be reborn into any species of animal.

The life stream is regarded as semi eternal, for it is a very long process. Death is the change of only status and location. Each being wanders back and forth through five realms, which include human, animal, spirit, devil, and eventually a god.

The life process can be terminated by a noble eightfold path, which begins with a right view of life. This involves realization of the truth of suffering as the result of repeated births. The life stream will continue to flow automatically as long as ignorance and desire exist.

Once the person learns the most precious lesson of life, of repeated births and suffering, the individual will do something to liberate himself or herself from the cycle of rebirth. By developing the right view, an aspirant will develop right speech, right action, and right livelihood. One will then develop right effort to rid the mind of ignorance, desire, and attachment. Right insight is then developed, which is accomplished by proper breathing techniques. This is helpful in understanding the basic truths of the life process. In a passive state, the mind gradually becomes perfect and stronger than in an active state by performing outward active work. A person then has no desire to know, speculate, or to possess.

At the moment of right insight, the three fundamental truths of impermanence, suffering, and egolessness will be understood. Then comes final deliverance from the life stream. The mind becomes liberated when intuitive insight is experienced and ignorance is eliminated. A liberated mind has four noble qualities: enlightenment, purity, peace, and compassion. The person has become a worthy one, released from karma and experiences into Nirvana, the deathless state. Here, the individualized nature is extinguished. The enlightened mind and self merge and become identical with the cosmic Nirvana, the supreme spirit.

MYSTICAL SOCIETIES' DEEP KNOWLEDGE
OF THE SOUL

Many consider mystical societies and mystery schools to be the most knowledgeable about the spiritual realm. This knowledge ran deep. Because their teachings contradicted church doctrine, and because not all people were ready for these truths, many such societies and schools were secretive and passed their hidden knowledge onto dedicated aspirants through initiations. Most of these mystical societies taught that humans have an immortal soul whose purpose is to return to God. To accomplish this goal, one needs to develop perfection, and to reach perfection usually takes more than one lifetime. Heavenly planets influenced the lessons to be learned in each lifetime. Mystical societies provided guidance and knowledge to their initiates on how they could achieve perfection and bypass the rebirth cycle. They tried to shorten the soul's journey back to the creator God.

One of these mystical societies was the Gnostics, whose name meant the knowledge of God. They appeared shortly after the birth of Christ, claiming the church was not teaching the true teachings of Jesus. They rivaled the early church and became the first heretics whom the Church Fathers denounced. After several centuries, the anti-heretical writings of the church eventually caused the demise of the Gnostics. Gnostics tolerated independent thought and non-conformism. Various religions and philosophies influenced Gnosticism, but much of the knowledge came from the spiritual realm, some from apostles such as Mark, some from John the Baptist, and some from the inner circle of Jesus.

Dualism dominated most of their cosmology in relation to creation. Gnostics taught that the kingdoms of light and dark were brought together almost by accident, resulting in the world we know. Light became entrapped in the dark, and once the dark tasted light, it was unwilling to relinquish it. The Supreme God lay in the realm of light and was unknown to humans. The realm of darkness was inhabited by the creator of the world, known as the Demiurge, the god of Israel. Gnostics considered the Demiurge evil and subordinate to God the Father.

When light met dark, the soul descended into darkness and evil. The soul became imprisoned in the darkness, and the Demiurge confined it to the body, preventing it from ascending to the light. It was controlled by the planets and signs of the zodiac. In the unawakened state, it was entrapped in a cycle of rebirths. A messenger from God the Father was sent to humankind to reveal the path out of entrapment. The messenger was Jesus.

The Gnostic doctrine of redemption referred to the ascent of the soul to its origin. Gnostics taught about the awakening of humanity to its true origin and to the worthlessness of the Demiurge. Jesus brought knowledge that the soul was imprisoned by evil powers, and he taught that we could escape their confines by love, faith, perfection, patience, and wisdom. It was the Gnostic goal to release the soul from the bond of the world and to assist its return to its original home, the kingdom of light. Once the soul was awakened, humans could not only save themselves, but could join the gods to save all souls bonded to matter.

Gnostics believed that humans possessed a divine spark that was part of the soul, known as the *pneuma* or spirit. This spark had fallen from the divine world into a world of destiny. The pneuma was immersed in the soul and flesh and was unconscious of itself while imprisoned in the world. The spark needed to be reawakened to restore it to the divine world.

Archons created humans for the purpose of keeping the soul captive in the cosmic world. Archons were planetary rulers who guarded the world collectively and were assigned to certain planetary spheres. The soul was the food and power of the archons, and without souls, the archon could not live.

As the soul descended, it was partially controlled by planetary powers and influenced by discarnate beings. Astrological influences helped humanity on its earthly sojourn. Astrology was true for every natural human in the cosmic universe, but it did not hold true for the spiritual human.

On its downward sojourn into matter, the soul gathered discarnate entities that developed layers around the terrestrial soul. These entities battled for the soul's possession. Only by receiving Christ could one expel these demons and overcome astrological influences.

Some Gnostic writings describe two souls of man. One was from the first mind and shared the power of the Demiurge, and the other soul was God seeking. Rebirth and transmigration of the soul were an integral part of Gnostic doctrine. For these souls to become free, they had to experience every kind of life and action, that is, to be free of the Demiurge. Souls needed to be reincarnated until they experienced every deed there was in the world. Once this occurred, they were released from the power of the Demiurge to the Supreme God and saved; their karmic debt had been paid. The Gnostics said that humans were superior to the Demiurge, their creator, because unlike the Demiurge, earthly humans contained the divine spark of the Supreme God and had knowledge about returning to the Supreme God.

At death the soul was liberated from the body. The ascent of the soul occurred at that time and was rarely accomplished without assistance. The ruling archon tried to impede the soul's return to the world of light. For this return, the soul needed Gnostic knowledge and magic, taught by most Gnostic schools. These schools taught them protective signs, symbols, magical sayings, and death ceremonies to assist in the ascension. As the ascending soul crossed the evil barrier, called the firmament, it needed to find favor from the archons at each of the seven planetary stations. Seven angelic archons and angels of light surrounded each departed soul. Secret archon names had to be known to gain control of the archon, as this was vital for passage. This knowledge presents one meaning of the term *gnosis*.

Gnostics believed liberation of the soul from this world could be attained only gradually with the aid of a divine messenger and redeemer. It could occur only in death of the body or at the end of the world itself. Gnosticism was a religion of redemption. The awakening of the soul by the act of self-recognition through knowledge guaranteed salvation. Only at death could the process of bringing back the particles of light occur. The end of the world would come when all the particles of light had returned to the light realm, and the conditions that prevailed at the beginning would recur. This would happen when all that was spiritual was perfected through knowledge, and when the educational process was completed on Earth. The spirits would detach from their souls and enter the *pleroma*. At the end, the impure souls would be punished until they were purified and their imprisonment ended. At this time, all forms of nature and all the demons would be eliminated.

Gnostic philosophy was influenced by Hermeticism, based on the teachings of Thoth (Hermes in Greek lore) who was the god/man of ancient Egypt. He was god of knowledge and preserved the knowledge of humankind before the Great Flood. Egyptians knew Thoth as the personification of God's mind and supreme master of wisdom. His will and power kept the forces of Heaven and Earth in equilibrium. The Greeks thought of Thoth as synonymous with their god Hermes, and in Greek writings Thoth became known as Hermes Trismegistus. His teachings and writings formed the foundation of many religions, as well as of magic and alchemy.

Thoth taught that the elements of nature arose from the will and word of God, the *nous*. The Supreme God of life and light brought forth a second god, called the Demiurge. They fashioned seven governors, or spheres, that enveloped the sensible world, the planet Earth. God brought forth a man similar to himself whom he loved as his own child. Man saw the creation that the Demiurge had fashioned and asked permission also to produce a work. Man entered the Demiurge spheres in which man had full power over mortal beings and over the animate, and the Demiurge fell in love with man. Man desired to know the physical nature below the beautiful form of God. In doing so, man broke through the seven spheres. Nature smiled with love, and man wished to dwell with her. At the moment he wished this, it was accomplished, and man took on a mortal body, but still maintained his immortal sense. Once he entered the mortal world, he fell under destiny and the governing spheres of the Demiurge.

The seven governing spheres are the rulers of destiny and fate. Each sphere is ruled by a Demiurge and a planet. These spheres are of psychic nature and are forms of subtle matter endowed with reason. Constituting the cosmic energy that fashions and transforms souls, these spheres are energies of fate that determine the ordered sequence of cause and effect. Until the soul falls into matter, it has no fate or karma. Once in matter, it is under the domain of fate, which is the result of time and manifestation. The desire of the soul to be released from the entrapment of the material world underlies all human action and thought. Its release is the salvation of the soul. The only useful knowledge is the path of immortality. This is the way of Hermes, who said fate was to be overcome so that the soul could be free of the bodily prison.

To reach salvation, the soul must reach perfection on the physical, intellectual, moral, and spiritual planes. When one reaches purity, one has full perception of God. To reach purity, according to Hermetic writings, the soul must undergo multiple rebirths into physical bodies. One must overcome the tendency that keeps bringing the soul to a body. Hermes affirms those who know God are protected from evil and are not subject to destiny. The seven spheres are the regions of purification of the lower energies of the human soul. Perfection makes one an instrument of perception, capable of seeing God.

Between Earth and Heaven are seven spheres where souls dwell after they are freed from their bodies. The station that they occupy between physical lives corresponds with their level of evolution. If they have transgressed God, they descend to the lower regions. Each soul knows where to go after death. The pure soul ascends to the eighth sphere. Gnostics called this pure sphere Ogdoad, the Jerusalem above.

Corpus Hermetica states that the experience of rebirth can take place within the span of mortal life, whereas the Hermetic *Poimandres* holds that it can occur only after death. Hermes taught that when purity was reached, the soul was absorbed into God, and the purified person could then be called a god.

Humans, according to Hermetic thought, are divine beings who are above the gods of the Demiurge, or who are at least their equal. None of the celestial gods would leave their heavenly abode to descend to Earth, yet humanity ascends into Heaven and measures them. Virtuous souls are rewarded in future lives. Once purified, virtuous souls become free from destiny and reside in the eighth sphere. Punishment is dispensed to those who have erred, accompanied by ignorance, sadness, and injustice. Twelve signs of the zodiac and the influence of the planets govern punishment and rewards. A soul descends to Earth to pay the debts of transgressions committed in past lives. Guardian angels assist the soul on its earthly sojourn. If the guardian is warlike, the soul assumes those characteristics. If the guide is gentle, the soul follows a quiet path.

According to the law of equity, the two energies of memory and experience preside over the souls. Memory directs the preservation of all the soul's past happenings. Experience provides every descending soul with a body appropriate for the Earth lessons. The soul adjusts to the body destined to it. It causes the body to live by the laws of nature governed by the planets.

Hermes said every human soul is immortal, but immortality is not uniform. The emotional part of the soul is mortal, and the rational part is immortal. Hermes asserted that everything that suffers and enjoys is a mortal creature. Everything that enjoys and does not suffer is an immortal being.

A soul is an eternal and intelligent essence of perpetual movement. The soul is the spontaneous movement of thought. A soul controls its reasons and confers onto the entity a movement that is analogous to its own thought. One property of the soul is to assimilate other things into its own character.

The Hermetics told of four types of souls: (1) A divine soul abides in divine form and it moves and acts. (2) A human soul also has divinity, but is bound to irrational elements, such as desire and passion. These are energies of the mortal body removed from the divine part of the soul. When the divine soul enters a mortal body, it becomes a human soul. (3) The soul of an animal is composed of passion and desire, and is devoid of reason. (4) Souls of inanimate creatures are found outside their bodies. These souls move in divine form and passively impel inanimate bodies.

Destiny is the result of Necessity that causes all things to happen. It is the chain that binds all events together. Providence is the free will of the Supreme God. Nothing is void of Providence, and Destiny is subject to both Providence and Necessity. The position of the stars and planets determine Destiny, which no person can escape. The planets accomplish the will of Destiny throughout all nature and human existence. Destiny occurs because there is Necessity. Destiny produces the beginning of all things, whereas Necessity enforces the effect. This causes Order, which is the sequence of things accomplished in time. Nothing occurs without Order. Necessity, Destiny, and Order all depend on the will of God, because they have no will in themselves. This is the universal law according to Hermes.

The art of determining fate by the planets is known as astrology and was extensively mentioned in the Hermetic literature. Astrology presupposes a direct, calculable connection between planetary movement and human action. By knowing the exact time and place of birth, astrologers can foretell the future and fate of each individual according to the position of the planets.

Chapter Two

INVOLUTION AND EVOLUTION
OF THE SOUL
From Spirit to Matter to Spirit

Most religions teach about the Fall of humankind which falls from a state of innocence to a state of knowing evil. Mystery schools describe the Fall as the involution of the soul from a state of oneness with God into the material world, and an evolution of the soul back to God. Hermetic adept Thomas Burgoyne, one of the guardians of "the wisdom of the ages," wrote an outstanding treatise regarding the nature of the soul. Written for members of the exterior circle of the Hermetic Brotherhood of Luxor, the text is found in the book entitled *The Light of Egypt*.

Burgoyne describes pure spirit as "diffusive, nonatomic, uncreated, formless, and self-existent." It exists in a divine state of silent unconsciousness without motion. Spirit resides in a realm of unmanifested being. The first action of Divinity, which was of the unconscious mind, was a thought that implied vibration or motion. At the moment the divine Mind vibrated with thought, the act of creation began. This one primal force of divine thought contained unlimited potential within itself.

Mystery schools teach that the whole universe is filled with the spirit of Divinity. This universe is boundless, with an unlimited circumference and without a center. Its nature is dual, the manifest and unmanifest. Deity has infinite plans for spiritual unfoldment. From the spiritual center of the manifested universe emanate divine life principles. These spiritual rays of the Creator vibrate with divine activity and become alive with an infinite number of subordinate universes. The Divine brings rays to focus at various points in space to form spiritual centers of smaller universes. The divine purpose of creation is to differentiate the unconscious formless Divine into deific intelligences.

28

These separate minds reflect the idea of the universal mind. The conscious individualized minds possess immortal souls that eternally progress. As differentiated life atoms of the creation, they will become secondary creators and arbitrators of the destinies of worlds.

INVOLUTION

The dual process of creation consists of involution and evolution, which are inseparable. Involution begins from without and goes to within, that is, from the infinite to the infinitely small. From the spiritual center of the universe emanates a pure white light, a deific ray, the formless one. This spiritual center constitutes a realm of limitless potential, with divine beings that are infinitely higher than the highest archangels. When the first creative pulsation of thought vibrated, the whole sphere of motionless, formless, white light flashed with living energy. The white light was replaced with rays of enormous force that radiated in every conceivable direction and differed in velocity, color, and potentiality. Essentially the Deity had become refracted into seven rays, and a portion of the Infinite Soul decomposed. Its original, unlimited potential resolved into a series of active but limited attributes.

From the divine spiritual center, seven subcenters called the seven principles of nature were formed. From these seven worlds came angelic life forms from whose matrix issued all the life atoms of the universe. When any universe commences, the pure, formless essence is indrawn from the realms of the unmanifested. The universe enters into the sphere of creative life by the angelic will and an immediate change transpires. It is formless no longer, but atomic and endowed with an attribute it did not have prior, polarity.

This polarity evolves into a sort of partnership from which it divides the formless substance into two parts. Each part is necessary for the other, one being positive and the other negative. The positive ray, straight and penetrating, constitutes the spiritual force of all things, with infinitely fine atoms. Atoms in the negative ray, which is round and unfolding, are coarse and loose, tending toward a state of repose or inertia. Substances formed by the negative ray constitute every species of matter. This ranges from the extremely fine etherealized substance that composes divine archangels of the universe's spiritual center, down to the densest mineral of the Earth. What is called spirit is not pure spirit but only the positive ray or active attribute of that which is matter. Matter, considered unreal, is an appearance produced by the negative ray through an interaction with the positive ray, known as mode of motion.

From the seven angelic states, spiritual involution begins. Each of the seven spheres, or principles of nature, reflects one of the seven refractive principles, which constitute the divine mind of the angelic creator. From these seven reflections originate the seven angelic races, second only in mental power and potentiality to their creator. Lower states are produced from these seven angelic spheres that correspond in nature, color, and attributes to the sphere from which they originate. Each state in descending order is similar by correspondence, but becomes smaller and more material. Spiritual potency of angelic spheres is weaker and less active as the spheres become more involved and descended within matter. This process of involution descends from one state into another, forming a spiral on its descent until it reaches its lowest point. At this stage, motion is impossible and the infinitely great has become infinitely small. This is the polarizing point that reflects the material world. From this lowest spiritual state of life, the first ethereal race of human beings was formed.

An archangel who corresponds to a Sephiroth of the Jewish mystical Kabbalah, a planet, a color, and an attribute rules each of the seven angelic realms. The seven spheres receive their creation from the spiritual center of pure white light which is represented by the Crown Sephiroth of the Kabbalistic Tree of Life signifying Love and Wisdom. Surrounding this spiritual center are seven angelic spheres. One sphere corresponds to the Sephiroth Splendor, ruled by archangel Raphael, the planet Mercury, the color violet, and the attribute of intelligence. Other angelic spheres and respective characteristics include the following:
- Mercy Sephiroth, archangel Zacharial, Jupiter, indigo, and greatness.
- Justice Sephiroth, archangel Cassiel, Saturn, blue, and patience.
- Foundation Sephiroth, archangel Gabriel, moon, green, and prolific.
- Beauty Sephiroth, archangel Anael, Venus, yellow, and love.
- Power Sephiroth, archangel Michael, sun, orange, and purging.
- Victory Sephiroth, archangel Samuel, Mars, red, and strength.

Matter is the polar opposite of manifested spirit in which force and motion are in an exact state of equilibrium. In solidified spirit, spirit becomes matter and its refinement or density depends upon its degree of etherealization. The potential of spirit to expand its infinite possibility must evolve because it has become incarnated by the process of unfoldment. Spirit has fallen in space into the crystallizing point, and its only possible means of return to the original spiritual state is through the progressive cyclic pathways of material unfoldment. Matter is the negative ray externalized in a state of crystallized inertia. It is the first offspring of spirit. Matter and spirit, when combined, comprise everything in the universe, including Deity itself.

An infinite Creator cannot get beyond his creation and exist apart from Itself because of polar opposites, which are the direct emanations from Its own divine nature. The same laws and principles that control Its creative activities must also govern the Deity. Traced to the source of pure white light are the primal laws of Wisdom and Love, as well as the polar opposites of positive and negative, activity and repose, and male and female. The idea of polar opposites can sum up one law and principle of the infinite universe.

Seven principles govern nature's processes in the unfolding of matter as it fulfills the creative design. From the seven angelic worlds, the laws of harmony intelligently direct the seven powers or principles. Mother Nature has made every known thing dependent upon something else, and all things are mutually dependent upon each other. For instance, evolution is dependent on involution, the objective is dependent on the subjective, and humans are dependent on the Earth. All these dependencies contain the same seven eternal principles. The objective world contains the latent attributes of the worlds of cause. If this were not so, the evolution of matter would not be possible. The celestial worlds find the perfect expression for their souls. In other words, humans are microcosms of the macrocosm, a universe within themselves.

The seven principles of nature correspond to their chemical affinities to the seven prismatic light rays of the solar spectrum. They present a perfect correspondence to the seven progressive states of manifestation called "life waves." These waves of cosmic life energies carry out the ascending side of material evolution. When a wave commences, it sets in motion evolutionary activities. These forces produce a responsive vibration within the realm of force that form their material correspondence. They act and react upon each other, producing another scene in the drama of external life.

These seven waves of cosmic life energies succeed each other in the following order:

1. Spiritual, realm of creation, symbol of the word.
2. Astral, realm of design, symbol of ideas.
3. Gaseous, realm of force, symbol of power.
4. Mineral, realm of phenomenon, symbol of justice.
5. Vegetable, realm of life, symbol of beauty.
6. Animal, realm of consciousness, symbol of love.
7. Humans, realm of mind, symbol of glory.

In the world of mind, the mind again begins to assert its supremacy over matter, and here life conquers death. Involution is the original action and evolution is the reaction, a consequence of the forces.

According to Hermes, the atom is the first component of physical creation. When two equal forces come from opposite directions and meet each other, both become polarized. A material atom is the physical product of this change of energy. From the infinite network of rays produced by vibration of the pure white light, an evolution of unlimited rays of opposing force occurs. This process is summarized as the first act in biblical creation, the creation of light. Genesis 1:3 says, "And God said, let there be light, and there was light."

Solid dimensional matter requires six equal forces that meet at an atomic or impenetrable point. These forces may exceed six, but must approach in pairs from opposite directions. This will produce different forms of crystals. The atomic point can be made by forces from all possible angles, resulting in an infinite number of possible crystals. All forces, when balanced, make crystals, but no motion. Crystallization is the negation of motion. The law of crystallization concerns minimum action in the activities of force.

Scientists have recognized three external spacial dimensions, but the Hermetics teach there are seven dimensions in all. A solid is not solid on a submicroscopic level. A molecule consists of a group of atoms with electrons revolving around their primary nucleus, which forms the impenetrable point of every crystal. Space exists between every atomic component. The Hermetics assert these unoccupied spaces form the fourth dimension of matter.

To dematerialize matter and resolve it into its original element requires the application of an external force, powerful enough to polarize the cohesive affinity of the atoms. If electricity is the force used, it destroys the form and releases atomic energy. If the force is magnetic, it etherealizes the object. In this state, matter can be made to pass through matter. The instant the magnetic force is withdrawn, the object will resume its original physical state. According to the Hermetics, this is the secret principle of the spirit materializing phenomenon and the foundation for all magical manifestations in a physical universe.

The involution and the reactive evolution of matter are based upon absolute laws. In the soul state both realms of cause and effect unite; hence there is neither cause nor effect, but where the two are one.

A genesis of life must be viewed from the seven planes of its manifestations. The seven planes include: (1) celestial, (2) spiritual, (3) astral, (4) mineral, (5) vegetable, (6) animal, and (7) human. The complete cycle of necessity is composed of ten great cycles that correspond to the ten Sephiroth of the Kabbalah. The soul, or life atom, involutes from the celestial, to the spiritual, to the astral, and finally to the mineral state. The evolution cycle then begins from mineral to vegetable, to animal, to human, to astral, to spiritual, and finally it returns to the celestial.

In the celestial state, the diffusive intelligence of the Infinite Spirit becomes differentiated and atomic. The divine soul of the human soul is absolutely atomic. It self-exists as an absolute atom of the Divine, which is impossible to alter, and is as eternal and immortal as the Deity from whence it came.

The process of differentiation of the divine soul of the human soul occurs within the celestial matrix of the angelic world. Here the divine soul is formed into twin souls, a male and female. They have alternate cycles of activity and repose. Their angelic vibrations transform formless intelligence into active eternal souls. The divine activities of the soul results from the creative attributes of the angelic progenitors of the celestial worlds. The soul (ego, self) is not created in the angelic state, but is only differentiated from the divine soul. Celestial vibrations endow it with spiritual activity. Aroused from an unconscious state, it is propelled forward with the motion of eternal life.

The newly differentiated atom remains within the celestial sphere until the vibrations have ceased. Then it becomes attracted by the angelic energy, is withdrawn from the celestial matrix, and carried into the spiritual sphere to the embryonic state of the

Seraphs (the highest of the nine orders of angels). The next descent is to the world of the Cherubs, a lower order of angels, where the bisexual soul becomes the biblical Adam and Eve. Here, the pure twin souls unconsciously obey the internal impulse of their evolutionary tempters. They become attracted toward matter. At this stage, completely innocent, they know neither good nor evil.

Divine soul can descend into matter. It projects the twin souls outward as spiritual monads into the vortex of cosmic evolution. Theosophists define the monad as the universal life force that animates all matter at an atomic level. Here, the twin souls become separated and eventually incarnate in the mineral realm. During the descent, each monad passes through every state of the soul world. It descends through each realm of the astral kingdom before it appears in the external mineral plane.

As discussed earlier, it takes a minimum of six equal forces to form a crystal in the physical world. If one of these forces is not equal to its opposite, the two do not balance. When three of the opposing forces are not equal to their opposing forces, a spiral forms, the spiral of life. If half the force makes an impenetrable point of matter that is less than its opposite, an essential idea of life forms.

The spiral of life varies in magnitude from the infinitely great to the infinitely small. The spiral will be almost infinite in its sweep and curve and will almost require eternity to reach its culmination point. The greater the diversity in forces, the tighter the curve will become, until an infinitely small spiral culminates almost instantly. Between these two extremes we have every phenomenon of life, from the tiniest amoeba to an astral universe cosmic life.

EVOLUTION

Within the mineral state lies the potential for an immortal being. When all the forces balance, they produce a crystal and motion ends. Motion is the life of matter, and the first step of evolution on the spiral is the motion of life. This step of evolution brings us to the vegetable state, where the motion of life can be measured.

The phyllotaxy of plants, or the study of leaves in relation to one another, proves that the plant kingdom uses the spiral of life. On the stems of plants, the leaves are so arranged that a line wound around the stem, and touching the petiole of each leaf, is a spiral. If the leaves form two rows, the space between the two opposite leaves is just half the circumference of the stem, if three rows, it is one third the circumference of the stem, and so on. It continues to a regular successive series in different plants that expresses the ratios of 1:2, 2:5, 3:8, 5:13, 8:21, 13:34, and 21:55. The vital force is represented in plants, and the phi ratios that form the spiral are the sacred geometry ratio, the Fibonacci numbers of 0, 1, 2, 3, 5, 8, 13, 21, 34, and 55. Dividing the adjacent number into the next leads to the phi ratio of 1.6189. This ratio is found in ancient Egyptian architecture, such as the Great Pyramid and the Luxor Temple, and in the spiral ratio of the Milky Way.

The various changes of atomic polarity must be comprehended to understand how the vegetable evolves from the mineral. For example, a mixture of oxygen and hydrogen atoms in a certain combination produces water. When this happens, both atoms become polarized to form a substance that is the polar opposite of their original state. Atoms of the mineral state evolve into the vegetable state. When the vegetable product has served its purpose and decays, the liberated atoms arise in the spiral and become attracted to atoms of air, to which they have a natural affinity. The same process of polarization repeats, with some slight variation, and a higher germ of vegetable life evolves. For example, the lichen is the lowest form of plant life. The liberated atom of the lichen springs forth to a higher type of the same family. This atom has a higher and more ethereal attraction, and the polarized germs bring forth the next higher form of vegetable life. As time passes, this original form develops species, classes, and families of vegetation. From these, through the medium of water, evolves a still higher round of being: insect, reptile, animal, and finally human.

The Hermetics, according to the writings of Thomas Burgoyne, taught that the Deity, a unity, manifests itself as duality. Each function of the deific soul, through action and reaction, differentials for all eternity as the primary fundamental principle of manifested being. The Kabbalists describe this spirit as Love and Wisdom. Love, the negative or feminine ray, reflects contentment and is always seeking to enfold. Wisdom, the positive or masculine ray, is always restless and in pursuit. Feminine forces are striving to encircle the atom, whereas the masculine force strives to propel it in a straight line. From dual energy of spiritual potential is born the spiral, which is the motion of life and the symbol of eternal progression.

The human soul is a deific atom of life. In its primal state, the spiritual atom has latent potential. Wisdom of the soul is latent because it possesses no means of arriving at true knowledge of its various surroundings. No love resides in the soul because it has never experienced the various contrary conditions which distinguish love. In the primal state, neither love nor wisdom manifest within the soul. In other words, these attributes are subject to the requisite for their evolution. The divine soul must penetrate the various states to evolve its soul sphere. Internal potentials must be awakened.

Once awakened, the divine soul becomes pregnant with the dual forms of its own organic life. The twin souls are born, and at this stage the innocent male and female elements know neither good nor evil. These souls are the absolute expression of the masculine and feminine, the feminine ray contains some masculine qualities and the masculine ray contains feminine elements.

When differentiated, they are as eternal and immortal as the divine soul that called them into existence. They can be absorbed by neither time nor eternity. They become the divine expression of Love and Wisdom upon the Earth.

To attain the full development of its internal attributes of the soul, each of the twin souls is projected outward upon the spiral arc of the great cycle. The souls pass through the innumerable spheres and states of life, each finally reaching the polarizing point of creation in the mineral. Then they evolve from the lowest mineral form to its highest material form, the human. Each of the twin souls is conscious of itself and is a perfect expression of the positive and negative forces of its being. Each portion of the dual soul maintains forever the perfect symbol of its internal qualities and always gives expression, in the outward form, of its internal nature. The function of the soul is to awaken its latent qualities and attributes. Twin souls relate to each other originally as brother and sister and finally as husband and wife. The true meeting place is in the plane that embodies humanity. In this human cycle, few spiritual unions of twin souls occur. Whenever the twin souls of the same divine soul meet, love is the natural result. This love is not the physical sensation but the deep, silent emotion of the soul. The soul never makes a mistake when claiming its own.

Both female and male souls possess the necessary qualities to perfectly subjugate the material form. When the twin souls descend into matter, they travel upon divergent paths along the subjective arcs of the soul's evolution. The male soul is positive and aggressive and explores nature to seek wisdom. His will is electric, penetrating, and disruptive. His counterpart, the female is negative and passive. Her will is magnetic, attractive, and formative. The twin souls express the polar opposites of nature's forces.

The great objective, which the divine soul seeks to realize in the evolution process, is the complete differentiation of its latent attributes. Each soul must express the true nature of the binary spirit and express both its qualities. Therefore, male and female evolution results. Each soul refines and completes its own position of the divine soul. In doing so, it individualizes as a complete expression of one ray of the divine idea and becomes a perfect identity with its source. Both male and female souls complete the whole. Their spiritual identity is forever preserved with the united and separate consciousness.

THE LAW OF ACTION AND REACTION

The Egyptian Hermetics speak of the law of action and reaction. Eastern religions call it karma, but the Rosicrucian Order, a Christian mystical society, may describe the science of the law better than anybody. Max Heindel, a Rosicrucian Mystic, writes about the principle of rebirth and consequence in *The Rosicrucian Cosmo-Conception*. Heindel successfully combined science and spirituality to explain this important concept.

Rosicrucians taught that the higher worlds of the cosmos are the worlds of causes, of forces that we cannot comprehend. These forces cause all material things. They taught that seven different worlds compose the universe: (1) world of God, (2) world of virgin spirits, (3) world of divine spirits, (4) world of life spirits, (5) world of thought, (6) world of desire, and (7) world of the physical. Solids, liquids, and gases comprise the chemical realm of the material world. Four ethers are found in the physical world that impart vitality to the forms in the chemical regions. Some scientists believe there is a substance of this kind, called ether, that cannot be measured with current instrumentation. Likewise, the trained clairvoyant believes ether is as tangible as any of the chemical constituents.

Rosicrucians, like most other mystical societies, believe one universal spirit is expressed in the physical world through varying stages of development. This molds chemical matter into the four kingdoms: (1) mineral, (2) plant, (3) animal, and (4) human. The vital force that gives life to these kingdoms flows by means of four states of ether: (1) chemical ether is the force that causes assimilation and excretion; (2) life ether is the force that maintains the species; (3) light ether generates blood of animal and man, and makes the individual a source of light; and (4) reflecting ether is the reflection of the memory of nature, as everything that has happened has left a picture in the reflecting ether. (Mediums obtain their knowledge through the reflecting ether, called the astral world, which will be discussed later). Thought makes an impression upon the brain through ether.

The desire world provides incentive to the physical world. Here, the forces of animals and humans interact with forces of spiritual beings from many hierarchies that are not manifested in the physical worlds. The desire world is the world of feelings, desires, and emotions. It is responsible for the growth and evolution of the kingdoms' inhabitants. Four regions comprise the desire world: (1) the region of passion and sensual desire; (2) the region of impressionability; (3) the region of wishes; and (4) the region of feeling (the highest). Desire world causes everything in the physical world, as its countless spiritual inhabitants permeate the physical world.

Spirit and thought meet in the world of thought, which is the highest of the three worlds (physical, desire, and thought) and carries human evolution forward. The region of concrete thought provides the mind information, and ideas are generated in the region of abstract thought. Concrete thought regulates the impulses from the desire world by impacts from the phenomenal world.

The forces that work through the etheric region are archetypes, models that fashion forms of the physical world in their likeness. In the etheric world are archetypes of passions, wishes, feelings, and emotions. The region of archetype force directs the archetype in the region of concrete thought, from which spirit helps form matter. Only when the archetype model changes can the intelligence that we call the "laws of nature" cause physical conditions that alter the physical features of the Earth, according to the plan designed by spiritual hierarchies in charge of evolution.

Each plant and animal has three bodies: (1) vital body (etheric body), (2) desire body (astral body), and (3) dense body (physical body). A soul's vital body extends beyond the dense body by one and one-half inches. It builds and restores the dense forms. After death, it leaves the dense body. The desire body interpenetrates the dense body. Its luminous ovoid extends twelve to sixteen inches beyond the dense body. As humans evolve, the desire body will become as organized as the vital and dense body, and humans will be able to function in the desire body as they do in the dense body.

Humanity's threefold spirit, divine spirit, life spirit, and human spirit, works on the threefold body during a lifetime. It is connected to the body by mind, and this brings into being the threefold soul (conscious soul, intellectual soul, and emotional soul). These souls are the spiritualized product of the body, according to the Rosicrucians. The growth of the conscious soul results from activity of the spirit in the dense body to create right action. Memory of actions performed in the dense body causes growth of the intellectual soul. The emotional soul grows from the highest desires of the desire body.

Consciousness of the human spirit becomes more conscious through the emotional soul. The intellectual soul gives consciousness to the life spirit, and the conscious soul increases the consciousness of the divine spirit. In summary,

Spirit Consciousness	Soul	Body
Human	Emotional	Desire
Life	Intellectual	Vital
Divine	Conscious	Dense

When death occurs, the vital body, desire body, and mind leave the dense body in a spiral movement. It takes with them the threefold soul incorporated in one dense atom. All past-life experiences of the dense body are imprinted on this atom, which has been part of every dense body the ego (soul) has used. It reawakens each time a new body enters into another lifetime. The same ego builds around the nucleus of the new dense body. Called the "seed atom," the nucleus lies in the apex of the left ventricle of the heart. A silver cord connects the vital body and desire body to the "seed atom." Only when the panorama of the past life contained in the vital body has been reviewed will the cord snap. It is important that the body, whether cremated or embalmed, remain intact until three days after death, enabling the panorama of the past life to be etched into the desire body. Research by Professor Twining at the Los Angeles Polytechnic School found that all animals lost weight at death. Mouse subjects weighing 12.9 grams suddenly lost 3.1 milligrams at death. Some speculate that the departing etheric body accounts for this weight loss.

At the time of death, the whole of the past life passes one's vision in reverse order. Everything in the past life is remembered, but no feeling is evoked. This happens in the desire world. The panorama can last from several hours to a few days. The vital body remains floating over the grave and decays with the dense body. Ancient spiritual masters recommend that bodies be cremated to restore elements to their primordial condition. Most who die retain their desires and keep the desire body. If one maintains desire connected to the Earth, one must stay in the desire body. To ascend to a higher region, called Heaven, the existence in the desire world must be purged to purify one from binding desires. This is purgatory. Our individual evil habits and acts make purgatory a hell for us. The intensity of desires determines the time and suffering endured in their purging.

The law of action and reaction, or cause and effect, rules everything in the world of nature, be it physical, moral, or mental. The New Testament verse holds true: "Whatsoever a man soweth, that shall he also reap." It works everywhere, adjusting to restore equilibrium that operates on the principle of polarity. The results may manifest immediately or may be delayed for years or future lives. The working of the law is absolutely impersonal. It is the law of consequences. It operates in the desire world by purging desires and corrects weaknesses and vices that hinder progression. The law makes one suffer in a manner adapted to the purpose. Spirit has etched a clear record into the desire body, and the mistakes of the past will be realized. These deep feelings stamped into the "seed atom" of the soul are imported into future lives. Experiences may be forgotten, but the feelings remain. Purgatory eradicates the harmful habits by making their gratification impossible. One suffers exactly as much as one makes others suffer. One learns to act kindly and honestly toward others in the future. When reborn, one is free from evil habits. Evil acts occur because of free will, and the tendency to do evil acts remains.

The Rosicrucian desire world consists of seven regions that correspond to seven astral levels of other mystical societies. Purgatory constitutes the three lower regions of the desire world (astral world). The first heaven constitutes the upper region of the desire world. The central region, between purgatory and the first heaven, is called a borderland. Here reside honest and upright people who have wronged no one. They were deeply immersed in business and worldly things, thinking nothing of the higher life. They find themselves in neither Heaven nor Hell. These people did not believe in the afterlife and thought death ended all consciousness.

When the experience in purgatory is complete, the purified spirit ascends to the first heaven. Its suffering is incorporated into the "seed atom," and again the panorama is unveiled backward. One has learned to appreciate the fairness of others though gratitude, which makes for soul growth. Service is considered a thousand times better than giving money. The first heaven is a place of joy without bitterness. Here the spirit is beyond the material influence. It is a place of rest. The more difficult the past life, the more one enjoys the rest. In the first heaven, the thoughts of Christians have built the New Jerusalem. Thought originating in the subtle desire realm builds beautiful homes, gardens, and natural beauty. Everything here is just as real and tangible as in the physical wold. Souls of all children who die under the age of fourteen inhabit the first heaven. Children live a beautiful life, because they are not held responsible for their actions. The desire body and mind of children remain with them until a new birth, which occurs from one to twenty years after death. For that reason, children often remember a previous life. This heaven is a place of progression for the studious, artistic, or altruistic. They have access to all the libraries of the world.

The desire world, where the first heaven and purgatory are located, is the world of color, whereas the physical world is the world of form. The world of thought, where the second and third heaven are located, is the world of tone.

A time comes when the pain and suffering incident to purgatory, together with the joys and actions of the past life, are built into the "seed atom" of the desire body. Together they constitute the conscience. This force warns us against evil as a source of pain and directs us toward good, which is a source of happiness and joy. This seed atom is the nucleus atom of future desire bodies.

After completing the rest in first heaven, one proceeds to second heaven. The human soul and its threefold spirit enter this new realm clad in the sheath of mind with the three "seed atoms." The second heaven lies in the region of concrete thought where one discards the desire body. Souls are perfectly conscious and enter a great stillness where thought itself rests, a state of peace without fear. The awakening state follows this great silence and the spirit then hears the sound of music and realizes that it is in its home world, Heaven.

Both color and sound are present, but the tone is the sound of color. Tone builds all forms in the physical world. These tones make a whole that is the keynote of the Earth tone. The forms we see in the physical are the crystallized sound figures of the archetypal forces. Matter is spirit crystallized, whereas force is the same spirit not crystallized.

Humans' work in the heavens is most important as it prepares them for the next life. The threefold spirit is built from the quintessence of the three bodies. Much of the desire body worked upon in the previous life will be incorporated into human spirit, depending on the degree of purging of desires and emotions. This also applies to the vital body and dense body. Heindel writes that the spiritualization of these bodies is accompanied "by cultivating the faculties of observation, discrimination, memory, devotion to high ideals, prayer, concentration, persistence, and right use of forms."

The real home of human soul is the second heaven, a place of reflection. Many centuries may be spent here, with the soul contemplating the fruits of the previous life and preparing for the next. One's instrument is the tone that pervades this realm. The tone vibrates into the threefold spirit, the essence of the threefold body, which depends on it for growth. A different environment has been prepared in the physical world whereby new experiences can be gained. Humans actively engage in fashioning new bodies that will best facilitate their new growth. The teacher of the higher creative hierarchies directs them. Human destinies are to become creative intelligences. A law of the universe says that one cannot inhabit a more efficient body than one is capable of building. As one advances in evolution, the bodies will eventually be immortal.

A human's individual spirit ascends to the third heaven once the work of the second heaven has been accomplished. The third heaven also resides in the region of thought. With harmony from the higher world, the soul is strengthened for its next journey into physical matter. The time comes when the soul desires new experiences and a new birth. This conjures up a panorama awaiting the new life that contains only the principal events. Free will ensures the spirit freedom to fill in the details. The picture begins at birth and ends at death, and shows the returning soul the relationship of cause and effect. At death, the panorama reverses, showing how each event was the effect of some cause. Experience is the purpose of life, not happiness. The most benevolent teachers are sorrow and pain, whereas the joys of life are but fleeting distractions. Experience, which is the object of life, gives us knowledge of effects that follow acts. Another purpose is the development of will. These objectives can be gained by following the hard path of personal experience or by observing the result of peoples' acts. We must return to the physical until we have learned all there is to learn in the world. The law that works for the good brings humans back to the physical world to benefit themselves and others. Their acquired growth and experience of past lives are not wasted in Heaven where everyone is happy.

In preparing for the new rebirth, the mind of the last life awakens from the latent "seed atom." Material is attracted from the region of concrete thought, and the new body forms around the nucleus of the last life's exact counterpart. Built without the evil that has been purged, the new body incorporates the good into the "seed atom" awakened in the vital body. Our Lords of Destiny direct the building of the new vital body and select a proper environment for it. Pictures of the coming life are impressed into the reflecting ether of the vital body. The inhabitants of the heavens along with elemental spirits build the vital body to form a particular type of brain. The quintessence of former vital bodies is incorporated, and the soul adds a little work. This gives freedom for original and individual expression that is not predetermined by past action. An influx of new and original causes form the foundation of evolution.

The law of consequence is complex. It involves association with souls in and out of physical incarnation. Those living in the material realm may not reside in the same locale, making it impossible to work out destinies with everyone in one lifetime. The soul chooses an environment and family. Once the soul has been placed, the Lords of Destiny watch unseen and make sure that no amount of free will hinders the working out of fate selected. Human beings have complete control of future action but are hindered by past actions. They cause their own sorrow or joy.

The vital body created by the lords of destiny gives form to the dense body. The matrix of the vital body, or mold, is placed into the womb of the future mother. A dense body cannot be built without a vital body. Heredity helps the dense body, whereas the soul plays a minor role, incorporating the essence of past physical qualities. The soul has much leeway in building the desire body, little in the vital body, and almost none in the dense body. Eighteen to twenty-one days following impregnation, the soul enters the body.

History of the progression of the soul is called evolution. Its cyclic path is spiral. The theory of rebirth teaches that repeated incarnations evolve to improve bodies. The law of rebirth and consequences is the only law that can satisfactorily make sense of justice. It explains why individuals are born into wealth or poverty, health or disease, joy or sorrow, or peace or conflict. Genius is often the hallmark of the advanced soul. Each body is only an instrument whose work depends on the soul guiding it. Souls typically gravitate toward the most congenial associations. Eventually hate must be transformed into love, and enemies must eventually become friends. Souls are here to gain experience to overcome the lower self and attain self-mastery. Eventually, humans will evolve to be released from the wheel of birth and death and enter the motionless world of Nirvana at the end of evolution.

The laws of rebirth and consequence are associated with the motions of the cosmic, including the sun, planets, and signs of the zodiac. Each of these radiate subtle vibrations that determine the fate of individuals. Humans are born at a time when planetary bodies are in position to facilitate the conditions necessary for the experience and advancement in the school of life. This placement shows accurately the time in a human's life when the debts of past lives are due. Astrology, according to the Rosicrucians, is an exact science, though it may be misinterpreted.

Rosicrucians differ from the Hermetics regarding the bisexuality of the soul. Both agree the soul is bisexual, but the Rosicrucians believe that the soul alternates incarnations between male and female, whereas the Hermetics teach that the masculine ray of the twin soul incarnates only in a male body and the female ray only in a female body.

Among other great mysteries, Rosicrucians have secretly taught for all ages the laws of rebirth and consequence. Before Christianity, religion taught these laws, but Christ, according to the Rosicrucians, requested that the laws not be taught publicly for two thousand years, although he taught the laws privately to his disciples. He believed the knowledge of these laws was not conducive to human advancement at the time. Heindel's writings leave a legacy of intricate interactions between the physical and spiritual, enfolding and unfolding from one another in a continual spiral upward to perfection. Such is the path of the soul's evolution, according to the Rosicrucians.

Chapter Three

THE SPIRITUAL PLANES
Heaven, Hell, and Purgatory

As we explore the spiritual worlds described by the ancients, mystical societies, and spiritual masters, we find a world of hierarchies regarding both spiritual worlds and spiritual beings. The axiom "as above, so below" carries forward when comparing the spiritual world with the physical world. Both are worlds of evolution for the soul where the soul gathers experience in the physical realm and processes this experience in the spiritual world.

When a soul departs the physical world at death, it enters the astral world embodied in the astral body. In this realm the soul becomes purified, purged of evil and selfish characteristics. This realm of desire and emotion consists of seven subdivisions. If the desires and evil actions were severe, they are purged in the lowest level of the astral world. This is the Christian Hell, a hell that is not eternal. Following the purging of desires and selfish traits, the soul progresses through the remaining subplanes of the astral plane to the Christians' material Heaven, located in the upper levels of the astral plane. After spending time in this heaven, the soul sheds the astral body, enters the mental plane, and functions in the mental body.

The mental world, the realm of thought, consists also of seven subdivisions. The four lower levels of the mental world encumber the world of concrete thought, which is the realm of form. Abstract thought resides in the upper three levels, the realm of the formless, where the soul sheds the mental body and then functions in the causal body on the causal plane. This is the real home of the soul, the real Heaven. Only good attributes of the soul are allowed in the causal plane, where evil attributes exist only as germs. A time comes when the soul decides to incarnate again, to gain experience, and to purify its essence so it can return to its God source. After the soul becomes an adept following many incarnations, it no longer must incarnate in the physical world. Beyond the mental plane, it progresses through four additional planes before returning to the Absolute.

The evolutionary process of the soul is similar in the teachings of many religions, mystical societies, and mystery schools such as Hinduism, Rosicrucians (Christian mysticism), the Hermetics, and Theosophists. Eastern and Western mysticism are nearly alike, with only terminology differing. This chapter on spiritual planes is largely based on the teachings of the Theosophical Society, a mystical organization founded in 1875 by Madame Helena Blavatsky and Colonel Henry S. Olcott. The society has three basic purposes: (1) the brotherhood of man, without distinction of race, color, religion, or social position; (2) the serious study of the ancient world religions for purposes of comparison and the selection of universal ethics; and (3) the study and development of the latent divine powers in people. Much of the society's knowledge came from masters who revealed divine wisdom. Dr. Annie Besant and Charles Leadbeatter were two of the society's leading contributors regarding spiritual knowledge.

GOD AND CREATION

Beyond the creator God is the Absolute, which we know nothing about except that it is. Each solar system is the expression of a mighty Being, called creator God, Logos, Word of God, or Solar Deity. This Deity permeates the whole universe with one fragment of Himself. With apologies to the feminine gender, God will be referred to as the traditional masculine, knowing that God is both feminine and masculine. Even though we cannot see God, we see the Deity through his power at work. There is nothing in the universe that is not part of God. The mystics believe we are an evolving fragment of God's life. We do not know the purpose of creation or why God has sent us forth. The Solar Deity is God, which is the ultimate of all our thought and imagination. He is the only God that we can conceive because we ourselves are he and none other. Action by the Solar Deity is to nourish us until we grow into Individuality, which is a fraction of his Individuality. Activity of the Solar Deity radiates from the sun to the farthest planet. As the cycle of evolution passes, more of his plan is revealed to us. Eventually all that comes forth from him will return to him. Judaism calls God Yahweh or Jehovah, the Greeks called him Zeus, the Romans knew him as Jupiter, the Egyptians as Ra, the Scandinavians as Odin, and the Muslims as Allah.

God energizes the universe as a trinity of three fundamental modes of manifestations. Christianity refers to the trinity as God the Father, God the Son, and God the Holy Spirit. Hinduism describes the trinity as Brahma the Creator, Vishnu the Preserver, and Shiva the Destroyer. The mystics call God the Logos, the manifested Deity. Logos means the Word. In the book of John (1:1) it is written, "In the beginning was the Word, and the Word was with God, and the Word was God . . . all things were made through Him and without Him was not anything that was made." In the Jewish Kabbalah, the world is said to have been formed by the utterance of the sacred name of God, an extension of the Tetragrammaton, which is the sacred four-lettered name of God, rendered as YHVH transcribed as Yahweh.

The Logos also exists as a trinity: the first Logos refers to the root of all being; the second Logos is the manifestation of two aspects, life and form, which is the primal duality, the two poles of nature; and the third Logos is the Universal Mind in which all archetypes exist. The Logos works through these three aspects: first Logos, divinity-humanity; second Logos, life-form; and third Logos, force-matter. Logos is the source of all beings, the fashioning of energies, the fruits of past universes, and seeds of the present. All three aspects of God are concerned in the evolution of the solar system and the evolution of man, which is God's will.

Below the creator God come his seven ministers, sometimes called the seven cosmic planetary logi, which are the seven embodiments of nature. The Gnostics called them the Demiurge. All evolution comes forth from God, through one of these planetary logi. In Hebrew and Christian tradition, they are called the "seven spirits before the throne of God." The energies of these seven control and direct all that takes place within the solar system. They are seven expressions of God's nature. Each of the seven logi contributes to his unique nature as a vibratory response, down to each atom. They are rulers of hierarchies of creative entities who work under their direction in the building and sustaining of the solar system. These entities are the devas and angelic hosts. In Christian tradition they are called angels, archangels, thrones, dominations, principalities, virtues, powers, Cherubim, and Seraphim.

Before God began the work of the solar system, he created on his plane of the Divine Mind the blueprint of creation as it was to be, from its beginning to its end. He created the archetype of forces, forms, emotions, thoughts, and intuitions. God determined by what stages in civilization each should be realized in the evolutionary scheme of his plan, and he began his work through the third aspect of the Logos, force-matter.

In the beginning, the vast sphere in space from which the sun and its planets were to arise, contained no substance similar to matter. It was called root matter in this primordial ether of space. Matter was created out of "holes" in the primordial ether. Into this primordial ether, the cosmic logos pressed back the ether from innumerable points within it. Where there is no primordial ether, points of light exist. Each point of light in reality is a point of consciousness of the third aspect of the Cosmic Logos, the Universal Mind, which exists only when the Logos wishes to keep back the envelope of ether.

At the next stage, the creative God through his third aspect, the Universal Mind, swept seven points of light into a spiral formation. These spirals of the first order are held by the will of the Logos. Great lengths of these first order spirals were made into still larger loops with seven spirals comprising the second order spiral. This process was repeated until he had created lengths of spirals of the sixth order. Ten parallel strands were twisted from lengthy spirals of the sixth order to make the fundamental of physical matter.

Charles Leadbeater describes these holes in ether as tiny spherical bubbles, which we have referred to as points of light. This infinite mass of bubbles is the ultimate composition of matter. The creator God sets up a kind of gigantic vortex, a motion that sweeps the bubbles into a vast central mass. In this vast revolving sphere, the creator God sends forth his successive impulses of force that gather the bubbles into an ever more complex aggregation. This produces seven gigantic interpenetrating worlds of matter of different degrees of density, all concentric spheres occupying the same space.

The third aspect of the Logos establishes a vast number of tiny vortices throughout the sphere, drawing into itself forty-nine bubbles arranged in a certain shape. The grouping of bubbles so formed are the atoms of the second interpenetrating worlds. Another impulse arises from the third Logos that establishes another set of vortices that hold within itself forty-nine squared bubbles that form atoms of the third world. A third impulse arrives for the third plane, and the process is repeated until the sixth of these successive impulses has built the atoms of the seventh sphere of the lowest world. This contains forty-nine to the sixth of the original bubbles. The atom of the seventh world is the ultimate atom of the physical world. A vast whirling sphere now contains seven types of matter, with the heavier atoms gravitating toward the center. The seventh impulse sent out from the third aspect of the Logos makes many protoelements formed together into a chemical element. After time, the matter of these interpenetrating worlds concentrates into the newly formed planets. The Earth, which is built of atoms of the lowest world, has attached to it matter from the sixth, fifth, fourth, third, and second worlds.

Particles of matter actually never touch one another, with the space between them always greater than their own size. This leaves ample room for all other kinds of atoms of another world to lie between the atoms of the dense matter. The Earth upon which we live is not one world but seven interpenetrating worlds that all occupy the same space, with the finer type of matter extending from the center.

No name has been given to the first world because humans have not yet connected with it. The second world is the monadic because in it exists those sparks of the Divine life called human monads. In the third sphere is the spiritual world within which functions the highest spirit in man. This is followed by the intuitional world, called the buddhic plane by the Theosophists because from it comes the highest intuition. The fifth sphere is the mental world where matter of this world is shaped from the mind of humans. Emotions of people cause undulations of matter in the sixth sphere, called the astral world or emotional world. The last sphere is the physical world, the densest of the seven concentric spheres.

Matter in all these interpenetrating spheres is essentially the same but arranged in different degrees of density with different rates of vibration. Physical matter has the lowest octave and each succeeding sphere has a higher octave. Each world has its unique substance arranged in seven classes according to the rate their molecules vibrate. Slower oscillations involve larger molecules. Each world contains inhabitants whose senses are normally capable of responding to vibrations in only their own world. A being living in the astral world may occupy the very same space as a being who lives in the physical, yet each world would be entirely unconscious of the other.

Our physical atom is not matter but, in reality, the many points of consciousness of the third Cosmic Logos. The Solar Logos holds the physical atom in a particular formation to do a specific work, that of building the physical plane, which is preceded by building the super-physical planes. The third aspect of the Logos also accomplishes this. Points of light form the seven planes of the solar system, and each plane contains seven subplanes.

On the physical plane, the highest subplane is composed of physical atom units of two varieties, positive and negative atoms. From these come the remaining subplanes called subatomic, superetheric, etheric, gaseous, liquids, and solids. Building these subplanes of the physical world produces the chemical elements.

During the next stage, the work of the second Logos, described as life-form, appears. With this energy is ensouled matter of the seven planes. This produces forms that have the unique quality called life. This life force builds the matter of the planes into varying forms, each persisting as long as the life of the second Logos holds the matter in that form. Now for the first time the phenomena of birth, growth, decay, death, and rebirth appear. Decay occurs because the second Logos slowly withdraws life from the form, and the form dies when all the life has been withdrawn. During rebirth, the second Logos sends life back to build a new and better form, which can give the evolving life new experience for further growth and self-revelation.

On the physical plane, the expression of the force of the second Logos is vitality, called *prana* by Eastern religion. When this force is manifested in the four highest planes of the solar system, the life of the second Logos is called monadic essence, which descends stage by stage, gaining at each stage the growth required in the Great Plan. At the beginning of the fifth cycle, the second Logos begins to ensoul the matter of the higher mental plane. Until this stage, monadic essence was not limited for its experience to one scheme of evolution. However, it is now restricted to the Earth plane of evolution. In the mental plane it is called elemental essence. The second Logos continues its descent into the lower mental matter and then astral matter. This ensouling life provided by the second Logos gives mental matter and then gives astral matter a peculiar living quality. The faintest vibration caused by thought in the mental plane and the vibrations caused by desire in the astral plane give rise to shape and form. Finally, the second Logos ensouls physical matter.

The third Logos now enters the picture, where it can create

atoms such as oxygen and hydrogen in the physical world. Only when the energy of the second Logos appears can atoms form molecules that result in physical matter, such as oxygen and hydrogen forming water. Physical matter results through the work of the second Logos.

Action of the second Logos guides the ascent from mineral to vegetable to animal. When the animal group soul has been built, and a particular animal is ready for individualization, then the work of the first Logos begins. He sends a fragment of himself, a monad, to make an individual in a causal body. The soul of a human is made in the image of the Maker. Then evolution begins, which is to discover the Divinity in oneself, in fellow people, and in all nature that surrounds them. On the physical plane we find the expression of the first Logos' force as the immortal soul in a mortal body.

The phrase of "spirit matter" infers that all matter is living, meaning even the tiniest particles are lives. No force exists without matter and no matter exists without force. All form expresses life. Spirit is life. There is no life that a form does not limit. The Logos, or creator God, manifests in the form of the universe down to the smallest atom. Every particle in the universe is ensouled by the Logos. The materials of each plane have in them a latent condition, one of all the form and force possibilities as well their own. These two facts make evolution possible. In other words, evolution is latent potentiality becoming active power.

Through all seven planes, matter exists whose combinations are derived from a particular set of atoms. These atoms are units possessing organization, whose life is the life of the Logos veiled in fewer or in more coverings, according to the plane. Countless hosts of entities, called the builders, take part in building form out of spirit-matter combinations. All forms exist as ideas in the mind of the Logos, who becomes the organizing force of his universe.

THE PHYSICAL PLANE

The physical world gives the soul an environment in which it can perfect itself on its sojourn back to God. In this world, the soul is tested to learn lessons that enable its godlike qualities to manifest. The physical world has a great official in the spiritual realm who represents the creator God, and who is in absolute control of all evolution that takes place upon this planet. Under this administration lies a hierarchy of ministers, with different departments, involved with the evolution of humanity. One minister oversees the development of the various Earth races while another oversees religion and another education. The official in charge of religion comes himself or sends a pupil to found a new religion when one is needed. Religions help guide individuals on their path to perfection. All religions, at the time of their first presentation to the world, have stated a fundamental truth. This truth has always been the same, but presentation of it has varied according to the various races of humanity. The source of the truth is always the same but appears externally different within different religions.

A teacher is always sent by the great brotherhood of adepts, called the Great White Brotherhood. Their ethical and moral principles remain the same, a body of truth that lies behind all the religions founded by the teachers. Often the religions lose the message of the teacher and do not adequately answer the truth about God, life after death, and life purpose. However, those who have the will to find these answers can because the truth is obtainable.

To hold a high office in the ministers of the hierarchy, a person must evolve to a very high level and become an adept. An adept exhibits goodness, power, and wisdom so great that he or she towers above ordinary humanity. An adept has reached the summit of evolution when he or she no longer has to incarnate on the earth plane.

Many souls have attained the adept level and choose to remain in touch as hierarchy members with the planet Earth. This body, the Great White Brotherhood, is in charge of the administration of the world affairs and of humanity's spiritual evolution. Members do not live together as a community, but constantly communicate with one another and the head of the Brotherhood. Their knowledge of higher forces is so great that they can communicate without meeting in the physical world. Those not masters on the spiritual planes may live in various countries unsuspected by those who live nearby. A few of these great adepts, who work for the good of the world, take on an apprentice to help serve humankind. These adepts, called masters, live selflessly for the good of the world. To this stage of evolution the soul aspires.

The first step of soul evolution on the physical plane begins in the mineral kingdom. On its descent into physical matter, the soul becomes part of the group soul. It takes up residence upon the lower mental plane to ensoul bodies in the astral sphere. This is called the third elemental kingdom. At this stage the soul can ensoul the etheric part of the mineral, vegetable, and animal kingdoms. Included in the mineral kingdom are liquids, gases, and etheric substances unknown to Western science. Here the soul begins its upward sojourn. After mineral evolution has been completed, the life force withdraws itself into the astral world, keeping with it the experience of the mineral kingdom. Next, it ensouls the vegetable kingdom and then the animal kingdom.

The group soul passes an extremely long period of time in each kingdom as it goes through a definite course of evolution, beginning with the lowest manifestation and progressing to the highest of that kingdom. For example in the animal kingdom, the group soul may begin as an insect and end as a highly developed mammal.

Each human is an individual soul, but each animal and each plant is not an individual soul. Humans as souls can manifest in the physical world through only one body at a time. One animal soul can manifest simultaneously through a number of animal bodies, and one plant soul through a number of separate plants. For example, when a tiger dies, the separate soul of the individual tiger goes back to the group soul from which it came. The group soul provides souls for many other tigers. A group soul may embody one hundred tigers, so that each tiger may have one-hundredth part of a group soul. A tiger is an individual during the physical life, but not a permanent individual. The identical tiger soul cannot be separated again from the group soul. The qualities gained by the experience of the tiger attached to the group soul are shared with the entire group soul. This explains instinct. Qualities developed will become common property.

As one goes down the evolution of animal life, an enormous number of bodies are attached to a single group soul. Countless millions of small insects are attached to their group soul. When a certain stage of evolution has been reached, the group soul splits into two. The smaller group soul inhabits more advanced animal life. At the highest point of animal evolution, after many divisions in animals, the soul will arrive in man as an individual soul, which no longer returns to the group after death. Not every group soul passes through the whole of that nature kingdom. For example, in the vegetable kingdom, if a group soul has ensouled trees, it can pass into the animal kingdom, bypassing the lower stages of the animal kingdom, and perhaps even enter as a low mammal. The insects and reptiles will be ensouled by souls that have left the vegetable kingdom at a much lower level than that of the tree. A group soul that has reached the highest level of the animal kingdom will not incarnate into a primitive man, but into someone more advanced. A primitive man may be ensouled by a group soul that has left a lower level in the animal kingdom.

Group souls at any level arrange themselves into seven great types, according to the ministry of one of the seven cosmic planetary Logi. Species of animals, vegetables, and minerals are arranged within one of these great groups. When a soul of mineral passes into vegetable and then animal, it will remain in the type it originated. In man, it will inhabit that type as well.

Individualization of souls is possible only for certain kinds of domestic animals. One domestic animal kind stands at the head of each of the seven types, including, dog, cat, monkey, and elephant. Wild animals such as the fox and wolf will line up with the dog. A group soul of one hundred foxes may divide into five group souls animating twenty dogs.

The animal if kindly treated will develop affection for humans and intellectual power by trying to understand them and anticipate their wishes. Human thoughts and emotions act constantly upon the animals and tend to raise their emotions and intellect to another level. If conditions are favorable, this development may proceed to raise the animal beyond the group soul to which it belongs, and the animal becomes capable of responding to the third Logos aspect. This outpouring may result in an ego forming in the higher mental world, and permanent individuality results. To make this ego, the fragment of the group soul becomes ensouled with a divine spark from above. That spark may have been hovering in the monadic world over the group soul until its corresponding fragment of the group soul had developed sufficiently to permit it to join the separate ego. The breaking away from the group soul marks the distinction between the highest animal and human. Once the soul has individualized, this does not mean the former animal soul has to embody the most primitive of humans. It can enter a more developed human.

In summary, when humanity has been reached, we find that the one vast soul has broken into millions of comparatively little souls of individual humans. Thus begins the sojourn of a person's individualized soul.

The dense body and etheric double exists in humans, with the latter being the exact duplicate of the dense body, particle for particle. It is etheric because it consists of ether. Three subdivisions comprise the physical plane, including solids, liquids, and gas that make up the dense body. Atomic, subatomic, superetheric, and etheric are the four ether subdivisions that comprise the etheric double. Any portion of matter is capable of passing into one of these states. Theosophists assert that every chemical atom can lead an independent life. Each combination of atoms becomes a more complex living thing.

Electric action accompanies all bodily changes, and whenever electric action occurs, ether must be present. The etheric double gives rise to magnetic and electric action, which pass onto the astral body when they reach the mind. Action in the physical matter gives rise to chemical and physical energies. Ether penetrates all and surrounds all. No particle of physical matter makes contact with another physical particle, but each is encompassed in a field of an ether envelope. The etheric double, perfectly visible to those trained to see it, appears violet-gray in color. The four ethers enter a dense body and can exist in coarser or finer combinations as do the dense constituents. As an aspirant refines the dense body by proper diet, and abstinence from meat, smoking, and alcohol, the etheric double follows without the aspirant's consciousness.

Through the etheric double, the life force of *prana* (vitality) runs along the nerves of the body. This enables the nerves to act as carriers of motor force and to become sensitive to external impacts. Vitality comes originally from the sun. When clothed in matter, it appears as a definite element. When a physical atom is charged with vitality, it draws around itself six other atoms and makes for itself an etheric element. The original force of vitality subdivides into seven, with each atom carrying a separate charge. An etheric element thus made is absorbed into the human body through the etheric part of the spleen or through one of six other force centers. It circulates along the nerves, and an interruption of absorption affects the physical body. (Acupuncture works on blockages in the etheric and facilitates flow). This etheric element splits into its component parts and flows to various assigned parts of the body. The *prana,* as it runs along the nerves and nerve cells, can express on the physical plane the activities of the soul, working through the inner bodies. This is the active energy of self. The etheric double becomes the vehicle for *prana.*

The seven force centers appear as shallow vortices. Here force from the higher bodies enters the lowest, from the astral to the etheric, from the etheric to the physical. The seven center locations include (1) the base of the spine, (2) the solar plexus, (3) the spleen, (4) the heart, (5) the throat, (6), between the eye brows, and (7) the top of the head. These correspond to the major chakra centers that some trained aspirants can see.

In sleep, the thinking ego slips out of both the dense body and etheric double. Upon death, the dense body takes with it the etheric double, but in less than thirty-six hours, a person draws out of the etheric body. If the dense body is buried, the etheric double floats over the grave and slowly disintegrates. If cremated, it breaks up immediately. The etheric double cannot pass on to the next plane, the astral realm. Sometimes it may appear immediately after death to a friend or family, but shows little consciousness. It is also responsible for ghosts. When the time comes for rebirth, the etheric double is built prior to the dense body and the latter follows exactly in its prenatal development.

THE ASTRAL PLANE

The astral world surrounds and interpenetrates the physical world but is not perceptible to ordinary observation because it is composed of a different order of matter. All physical atoms have astral envelopes and astral matter forms the matrix of the physical world. The physical body is embedded in a current of astral matter that sustains and nourishes every particle of physical matter. These astral currents or vital forces give rise to all electrical, magnetic, chemical, attraction, cohesion, and repulsion forces. From the astral world, vitality passes to the ether of the physical that becomes the vehicle of all these vital forces. Without the general action through the astral body, there would be no connection between the external world and the mind of man. An impact in the physical becomes a sensation in the astral body and is perceived by the mind.

The astral plane is the home of emotion, of desire, and of lower thoughts. Desire is a far greater force in the astral life compared with the physical. Astral life results from all feelings that have given rise to the element of self. Selfish feelings give rise to a condition of great unpleasantness in the astral world, whereas selfless feelings bring a pleasant but more limited time on the astral plane. Astral life corresponds to what Christians call purgatory, whereas the lower mental plane corresponds to heaven where people are always happy. People make for themselves their own purgatory and heaven, as they are but states of consciousness. Neither is eternal. Theosophy writings teach that an average small business person in the lower middle class would spend an average of forty years in the astral world, and a life in the mental world, the plane above the astral plane, would last almost two hundred years. A spiritual man may spend twenty years in the astral world and one-thousand years in the mental world. Of course, the conditions vary depending on the person. The length of time a person spends in a subplane is precisely proportional to the amount of astral matter of that subplane found in the astral body. This is determined by the type of life one has lived, one's desires, one's indulgences, and the class of matter attracted.

The astral world is more real than the physical world. All people constantly work through the astral body in the physical world, but few work in it separated from the physical. Dead people who wake up in the lower regions of the astral world are unconscious of any difference in their surroundings. They believe themselves still be to living in the physical world.

Life is more active in the astral plane than in the physical, and form is more plastic and can change rapidly. Scenery in the astral world resembles that of Earth and is made of astral duplicates of physical objects. Everything is transparent. Forms can change outlines very quickly, as an astral entity can change its appearance almost instantaneously. Astral matter takes form under every impulse of thought, swiftly remolding the form with a new expression. Duration of the form depends on the strength of the thought that has created it. Clearness of the outline depends on the precision of thinking, and color depends on the intellect, devotion, and passion of the thought. Most astral forms have greater brightness compared with forms on the physical. Figures shaped by sound vibrations have a longer and more active lifetime on the astral plane. Forms created by feelings and desires are more vigorous and definite than those created by thought. An outburst of anger will create a definite outline and a flash of red. Love creates a beautiful form in a soft hue of rose.

People's thoughts in the physical can also affect others. These thoughts enter the astral world and if directed toward another can cause harm or good to that person. Thoughts of hate, jealousy, revenge, and bitterness go out by the millions and crowd the astral plane with artificial elementals whose whole life contains these feelings. These thoughts create a hostile environment on the astral plane and affect our own astral bodies by a feeling of dread.

The astral body is a vehicle in which humans function, and it influences the physical body. Within the astral plane are seven divisions of astral matter ranging from coarse to fine. The astral body is the vehicle of man's desire-body consciousness, the seat of all passions and desires. It is the center where all sensations arise, changing color continually and vibrating under thought impacts. High and noble thoughts create a fine astral matter. An evil thought will create coarse astral matter. Being susceptible to thought, the astral body matter responds more rapidly than the physical body to every impulse from the world of mind.

Improvement of the astral body depends on one aspect on the purification of the physical body and on the purification and development of the mind. A well-formed astral body means that a person has reached a higher degree of intellectual, cultural, and spiritual growth. Its appearance signifies the progress made by the owner, as manifested by definition of outline, luminosity, and perfection of its organization. Thus the stage of evolution reached by the soul using the body can be judged. A man who has low thoughts and animal passions has a gross, thick astral body, dark in color. An advanced person is fine, clear, luminous, and bright in color. All good desires and emotions strengthen the finer parts of the astral body and eliminate the coarser parts.

Astral bodies responding to the habitual evil thoughts of its owner attract similar thought forms, whereas a pure astral body repulses such thoughts. By purifying the physical body by proper eating and exercise, one improves the physical world of consciousness and purifies the astral body. Shaping the astral body when alive carries over to the astral body after death and into the next life. We are not only living in an astral body now, but are fashioning the type of astral body that will be ours in another birth, linking all of our lives, past and future. The process of purification and development is continuous and carried out in successive Earth-lives to break the bonds of captivity.

The astral world has a large population beyond those human entities who have lost their physical bodies by death. Included are the nature spirits or natural elementals divided into five classes: the ether, the fire, the air, the water, and the earth. The last four groups include, respectively, the salamanders, sylphs, undines, and gnomes, which are the true elementals. They carry out the activities concerned with their own element. There are also nature spirits concerned with building the animal and human astral bodies, and are called desire-elementals. Desires of all kinds strongly animate them. Nature spirits concerned with building form in the mineral, vegetable, animal, and human kingdoms are also found in the astral world. They guide the vital energies into plants, form the bodies of animals, and help make up their astral bodies. Included are the fairies and elves.

Many initiates of varying degrees who live in the physical body have also learned to leave the physical body at will. Shamans, while still embodied, function in full consciousness in the astral. Disciples who have just died also inhabit the astral plane, and they await immediate reincarnation under the direction of their master. Buddhists believe in this immediate reincarnation, thus explaining the Dalai Lamas' immediate reincarnations. Also passing through the astral plane are human souls on their way to rebirth. They descend from the mental plane and have desire-elementals around them that assist in building an astral body for the upcoming earth-life. Not only do the dead inhabit the astral world but also one-third of living people, who have temporarily left behind in their sleep their physical bodies. During sleep, the astral body floats just above the physical body and is held there by its strong attractions. In sleep, a well-developed astral body can slip from the physical body. A person can gain knowledge when out of the body that may be impressed on the brain through a vivid dream or vision.

Angels also inhabit the astral world. They are more highly evolved than humans, and only the lower fringe of the angelic realm touches the astral world.

Purifying the astral body during one's journey on Earth is important because after death one cannot roam the astral world at will. The astral plane is divided into seven subplanes, and people are confined to the subplane to which the matter of their external astral shell belongs. A spiritually undeveloped person with animal-like tendencies has an astral body composed of coarse-dense astral matter. A person remains imprisoned in the subplane corresponding to that astral matter. Only when the outermost shell sufficiently disintegrates can the person escape that subplane and pass to the next level. The greater the quantity of gross astral matter, the longer a person stays on that astral plane level. Each ascending level of the astral world contains finer and finer astral matter.

The astral world of the Earth extends nearly to the mean distance of the moon orbit. This whole realm is open to any of its inhabitants who have not permitted the redistribution of their astral matter. After death, if the matter has not been rearranged from coarser to finer, the person will notice little difference from physical life. One can float about in any direction at will and move to any part of the astral realm. The person can also see the astral bodies of the living. Once the astral matter has been rearranged, the person will go to the subplane that has the specific gravity of the astral body's heaviest matter. The majority who permit rearrangement do so because they can sense clearly a certain part of the astral world. A person who has permitted rearrangement has to progress through all the subplanes, and the decision for arrangement is a conscious decision.

Kamaloka is the Sanskrit term used to describe the process of astral bodies gradually shedding the astral matter, referring to the habitat of desire in the astral plane, separated by the conditions of consciousness of the entities belonging to it. It is the purification process of humans who have died before they can pass on to a happy and peaceful life known as Heaven.

The astral plane of humans is a temporary dwelling place after they leave the body and before they reach Heaven, as described by all great religions. It is purgatory and the various hells, not eternal torture or an endless hell. However, the lower astral plane does include conditions of suffering that are temporary and purifying in their nature. Humanity lives in a world of universal law and for every cause there is an effect. Here people learn the effects of their actions, as every seed must grow up after its kind. Death makes no difference in a person's moral and mental nature, but leaves a person as he was when alive.

The Kamalokic condition exists on each of the seven subplanes of the astral world. Materials from each of the seven regions enter the composition of the astral body. Its arrangement separates souls from one region to another. Each region differs in matter density, and this difference acts as a barrier between subplanes.

At the time of death, the etheric body carrying *prana* (vitality) withdraws from the dense body. All the outgoing life energies draw themselves inward and are gathered by the *prana*. The panorama of the past life unrolls before the person in the death hour. One relives all events, triumphs, failures, loves, and hates. The ruling thought of the life asserts itself and stamps itself into the soul, determining where the astral habitat of the postmortem existence will begin. The person briefly sees oneself as he or she is, sees the purpose of that life, and knows the law is just and good. Ties between the dense and etheric break, and the person sinks into a peaceful unconsciousness. Within thirty-six hours after death, the person withdraws from the etheric body, leaving it as an abandoned corpse that will disintegrate. The *prana* withdrawn from it is returned to the great reservoir of the life universe.

The person now passes into Kamaloka (purgatory) and undergoes a rearrangement of the astral body that readies it for submission for purification, which is necessary for its freedom. Astral matter arranges according to densities in a series of seven concentric shells, with the finest within and the coarsest on the exterior. Sets of seven superimposed shells now comprise the astral body that imprisons the person. Only when each layer is disintegrated can the person escape to the next subplane.

A spiritually developed person rapidly passes through Kamaloka, the astral body disintegrating with extreme swiftness. Less-developed persons who have been pure and temperate will spend more time in Kamaloka and will dream peacefully, not conscious of their surroundings as they pass through the lower subplanes. After passing through this lower region they will become conscious in the region connected with the active working of the consciousness during the earth-life. A lowly developed person with animal passions will awaken to his or her appropriate region in the lower astral plane.

People, who suddenly die by accident, suicide, murder, or sudden death, differ from those who die by failure of life energies caused by disease or old age. If they are pure and spiritually minded, they are specially guarded and sleep out the term of their natural life. In less-developed cases, these souls remain conscious and for a time are often entangled in the final scene of earth-life. A murdered person may repeatedly relive the scene of a murder, and a suicide victim may relive the feelings of despair and fear that preceded the suicide. Often people remain unaware that they have lost the physical body and that they now reside in whatever region related to the outermost layer of the astral body. Death by accident is a disadvantage, because possession of full consciousness in the lower Kamalokic regions is closely related to Earth with more inconvenience and per-ils. A person who was full of plans and interests remains conscious of people and things connected with them. This person's longing usually irresistibly impels him or her to try to influence the affairs to which passions and feelings still cling. The only hope of peace is to turn from Earth and fix the mind on higher things. Some do not want to give up the etheric body and struggle to keep it, not realiz-ing they are in the astral world. They may go through a difficult struggle. Occasionally they grasp at other bodies and try to enter them, and occasionally they are successful. They may enter a baby and oust the personality for whom it was intended.

Vitality in any given shell of the astral body depends on the type of energy spent during earth-life and the kind of matter of which the shell consists. During earth-life a person can foresee the future he or she is preparing for immediately after death.

The lowest subplane contains conditions of religious hell. People who arrive here have evil passions and desires that remain part of their character. A gloomy, heavy, dreary, and depressing atmosphere pervades this region. A bestial desire shapes the astral body into a bestial form. Repulsive human-animal shapes appropriately clothe these brutalized human souls. All souls appear in their proper like-ness, because no man is a hypocrite in the astral world. Inhabitants of this lowest region consist of murderers, violent criminals, ruffi-ans, and drunkards.

Each person inhabiting this astral region immediately creates his or her own miseries. They have indulgences but no physical organs to enjoy them. Alcoholics become earth-bound astral entities and may gather around bars on the physical plane. An alcoholic's appetite may be one hundred times stronger because the craving cannot be satisfied. Such life is pure hell for drunkards, yet no one is really punishing them. They reap the natural results of their own actions. These earth-bound entities seek to obsess the living and can drive them into extreme excesses and influence them into shame and violence. These astral entities often create a sickening atmos-phere around bars. Their suffering is only temporary and gives a much needed lesson for the addicted soul. Learning the law of nature, they reap what they sow. Not able to learn these lessons in the earth-life, the torments of lust and desire are pressed onto the soul. In future lives, they must overcome these desires. The lessons are hard, but necessary for the evolution of the soul. The passions and desires that led a person here are not eliminated, but remain part of one's character. They become a latent germ to be expressed in a return birth in the physical world. As one progresses through the seven successive subplanes, each outer layer is purged until the last shell is shed in the seventh subplane.

The second subplane is the astral double of the physical world where the astral bodies of all physical things are found. Most people are composed of astral matter belonging to this division. This region is in close touch with the physical world, more than any other part of the astral realm. A great majority spend time here after death, with most souls consciously aware of it. These people were bound up with the trivial things of life. They died with an appetite still active and desirous of physical enjoyment. On this subplane, these people are mostly dissatisfied, uneasy, restless, and suffer according to the strength of the desire they cannot satisfy. Many lengthen their stay unnecessarily by trying to communicate with Earth friends and relatives through mediums. Others may try to communicate in an effort to arrange earthly affairs, impressing their desire upon a friend through a dream. Other souls may remain attached to friends and family they have left behind.

The third and fourth subplanes differ little from the second, but are etherealized copies of it. More progressed souls reside here, as determined by the astral shell they have built by their actions on Earth. Somewhat susceptible to earthly stimuli, their weakened interest may be reawakened. Large numbers of educated and thoughtful people, mainly occupied with world affairs, are conscious in this level. It must be pointed out that spiritual illumination does not come from Kamaloka.

One finds many new characteristics in the fifth subplane, including a more luminous and radiant appearance. Here lie all the materialized heavens that play an important role in popular religion, including the Paradise of Muslims and the New Jerusalem of Christians. Here are the literal satisfactions of their cravings that were unconsciously created in astral matter by the powers of imagination, mainly fed by world scripture. This home of religions has astral churches, schools, and houses. People of the same religion flock together and cooperate with one another in a variety of ways. Communities form largely based on religion and language, which remains a barrier. Spirit guides come, for the most part, from this region and the one above it. Souls on this plane take an interest in attempting to establish communication between this subplane and the next world above. They are aware that they will pass onto a higher life where communication with Earth is not possible.

The sixth Kamalokic region of the astral plane resembles the fifth, but is far more refined, largely inhabited by advanced souls. Their souls have refined the astral body by the work they did for humanity in the physical body. The time spent here is due largely to the selfishness of their intellectual or artistic life spent on the earth-plane. Surroundings on the subplane are the best of any Kamaloka region. Creative thought fashions the luminous astral material into beautiful homes, exquisite landscapes, oceans, mountains, and beauty one can only imagine.

Highest of the subplanes is the seventh, occupied almost entirely by advanced intellectual men and women. They reside in this region because they were materialistic on Earth or attached to the ways knowledge was gained in the physical body. Students may live there for many years or even centuries, studying in the astral libraries that specialize in their favorite subjects. Diplomats and scientists dwell in the region as they slowly disentangle themselves from the astral body.

A time comes when the bonds of the astral body are shaken off. Only a small minority who, while on the Earth plane, expressed unselfish love, intellectual aspirations, and a spiritual sense escape the astral purgatory. Each shell disintegrates, and after the seventh disintegration, the person escapes the prison of the astral world. The remaining magnetism of the soul holds together the astral corpse and drifts away in the astral current. After shedding the astral body, the soul sinks into brief unconsciousness of its surroundings. It awakens to a sense of bliss in the real heaven world, the world to which its own nature belongs. The soul has entered the mental world where astral matter cannot exist. Disintegration of astral matter yields a mass of mental matter of the coarsest kind.

THE MENTAL PLANE

The third great plane, the mental plane, belongs to consciousness working as thought. This land of the gods is known as the happy or blessed land. Nothing in this plane can cause pain or sorrow, and evil cannot penetrate this plane. It is one of three concentric spheres that comprise humanity's schoolhouse: physical, astral, and mental. Through these three spheres people work out their development and evolution. Our birthplace and home are in the mental plane. Divided into seven subplanes, it has two main divisions. The lowest four subplanes comprise the mental body, the realm of form. Formlessness helps describe the causal plane, the three highest mental subplanes that consist of extremely subtle mental matter. People function with two levels of consciousness from the mental plane. The causal body is the permanent body of the soul. Surviving after death, the mental body passes through the mental subplanes and disintegrates after passing through the lowest four subplanes.

The mental body forms from mental matter of the four lower levels of Devachan, the term used by the Theosophists to describe the mental plane. Called mind in ordinary waking consciousness, the mental body influences the astral and physical bodies in all their manifestations. This body is the vehicle of the soul for all reasoning that is poorly organized and helpless during early life. Mind/body is composed of a rare, subtle matter found in the third subplane that manifests itself as mind, and as sensation in the astral world. The soul manifests this vehicle as intellect, and it grows in proportion to the intellectual development. It literally grows in size with man's advancing evolution.

These two divisions of the mental plane relate in consciousness to the divisions in the mind. In the mental body, comprising the four lower subplanes, consciousness gives rise to forms, images, or pictures. Every thought appears as a living shape, called concrete thought. In the upper three subplanes, the causal body gives rise to abstract thought. These thoughts have no form but produce ideas that enter the mental body, which then gives form to them with different shapes. The formless region of the causal plane belongs to pure reason, which does not work within the confines of language. Words, the symbols of language, operate from the mental body.

The Universal Mind of nature is reflected in the mental plane and corresponds to the Great Mind of the Cosmos. This storehouse gives materials to the mental body, giving rise to every kind of vibration that varies in quality and power. All the archetypal ideas that are so much involved in our evolution exist in this high region. In the lower regions these ideas are adapted into successive forms, reproduced in the astral and physical worlds.

Vibrations from a single thought produce form, color, and sound. These vibrations on the mental plane cause exquisite colors, unknown on Earth, that constantly change. Thought constantly stimulates matter of the mental world into vibrations, giving rise to form, color, and sound. Complete thoughts are conveyed as colored and musical pictures. A thought produced in the mental body passes to the astral world and then to the physical world. When we think, we think with our mental body. The mind is the self in the mental body. Our thoughts are the materials built into the mental body, and the mental body grows by thought. Only by exercising the mind can the mental body develop.

If one does not exercise mental abilities, one becomes a receptacle instead of a creator. Much thinking is not our own thinking but thoughts of other people. A mind full of good and useful thought attracts similar thoughts, and repels evil thoughts. Particles in the mind body constantly change, as happens with the physical body. Mental matter can be shaped into thought forms that help or injure. Older particles are thrown out and replaced by others that respond to the new vibrations. Mind can also change its character by attracting the good and repelling evil. At first, changing is difficult, but with an increase in right thinking, the old form changes and eventually the mental body changes. Concentration also helps change the mental body, as does the good practice of following a consecutive line of reasoning, where one thought grows naturally out of previous thought. Thoughts become sequential and rational, giving strength and growth to the mental body.

As the higher intellectual qualities develop, the forms in the mental plane show very sharply defined outlines. Perfected geometric figures appear, accompanied by an equally singular purity of luminous color. Mental matter can combine under the impulse of thought vibrations into any combination that thought can construct.

Many intelligences occupy both divisions of the mental planes. Beings of vast knowledge and great power, called the Shining Ones, guide the process of natural order. Most of them appear splendid, multicolored, and very radiant. They rule the vast number of elementals in the astral world. On the lower mental planes, many spiritual gurus work in their mental bodies, for a time freed from their physical vesture. In deep sleep, a true person or self may escape from the physical body and work in these higher regions. Such people can aid fellow humans, suggest helpful thoughts, or give noble ideas. Masters sometimes appear in the lower levels of the mental plane, but are more frequently in the upper formless division. From this upper region, masters help humanity by impressing noble ideas, inspiring thoughts and devotional aspirations, along with giving spiritual and intellectual help. The purest souls on Earth receive these impressions. A scientist may receive a scientific breakthrough or a musician a new melody from a master. The vast majority of lives in the lowest mental subplanes are in various stages of evolution. Communications between intelligences occur practically instantaneously, especially if the souls share the same stage of evolution. Whole thoughts flash from one to another, with each soul having its own mental atmosphere.

The mental body of the undeveloped person is hardly perceptible. Closely intertwined with the astral body, they act as a single body. Mind wants to serve the senses, and the mental body begins to stimulate the astral body, arousing in it the desires of an animal. Mind becomes the slave to passions.

A person of average development possesses a larger mental body, with a certain amount of organization, and draws a greater amount of thought matter from the second, third, and fourth sub-planes of the mental plane. Mental exercise increases the mental body and disuse atrophies it. Although difficult to change thought patterns in the beginning, if persistent, one may shake off the coarser mental matter and replace it with finer constituents.

The spiritually developed man has eliminated all the coarse matter and contains only finer combinations from the lower subplanes. The mental body responds to all the higher intellectual influences and no longer dwells on objects of the senses. This allows a person's divine self to express itself more fully in the lower mental, astral, and physical worlds.

Devachan, the land of the gods, is the Theosophists' name for Heaven found in the mental plane. Spiritual intelligences specially guard and oversee that part of evolution that excludes all sorrow and evil. Devachanic life consists of two stages: The first stage is in the lower four subplanes where the divine self still wears the mental body and is conditioned by it. Here earth-life experiences gathered by the soul are assimilated. The second stage is the formless world where the divine self has escaped from the mental body and entered the causal body. Here the divine self lives an unencumbered life with full self-consciousness and the knowledge it has attained.

The time spent in Devachan depends upon the number of experiences for the Devachanic life that the soul brought from its life on earth. The harvest includes all the intellect, moral efforts, aspirations, and all the memories of useful work and plans for human service. Selfish passions and all past life evil cannot enter. A scanty harvest may render a brief Devachan life. In past ages, when people focused their lives on Heaven, they spent a long time on Devachan, sometimes thousands of years. Today, fewer thoughts are directed to the higher life.

Eventually, all souls will pass through these seven heavens. The latter three heavens will be discussed in the next section regarding the causal body. The apportioned time spent in the three worlds of astral, mental, and causal depends on the soul's evolution. A more advanced soul spends more time in the mental life and less time in the astral life.

Thoughts belonging to the higher mind, the region of abstract impersonal thinking, are worked out in the formless Devachanic region of the causal plane. Thoughts of personal self, such as ambition, hopes, and fears, originate in the lower Devachanic region, where forms are found. Most people enter the higher Devachanic region, after spending much time in the lower regions, only to pass through it swiftly. A small minority, very advanced souls, may spend most of their Devachanic life in this lofty region.

Mental life is far more intense and vivid in this sphere than in the life of the physical senses, being nearer to reality. Physical reality has two veils of illusion around it, compared with mental life. We know nothing of people or things, because we know them by our impressions and senses, often being erroneous. In Heaven, all thought is reproduced in form because the rare and subtle matter found here is mind stuff. When free from passion, every mental impulse takes shape. As the soul develops its power, Heaven grows increasingly subtle and exquisite. With the expansion of the soul, Heaven expands deeper. An evolved man in Devachan has a fuller and more real life. The good work on Earth is rewarded in Heaven.

Mental impressions of friends dominate in Devachan, and around each soul gathers those he loved in his life. Every image of loved ones lives in the heart and becomes a living companion of the soul in heaven. No barrier between soul and soul exists on the mental plane, yet no enemy can enter into our Devachan. We meet souls in forms we loved on Earth, with perfect memory of our earthly relationship. It is a world of joy and bliss.

All that was valuable in the mental and moral experience of the soul during its previous life is gradually transmitted to definite and moral impressions that will be taken into the next rebirth. Past experiences work into mental capacity. A person who has given great depth to a study or interest in the past life will receive a special faculty to master that subject again when first presented with it in another incarnation. The person will have an aptitude for that line of study or interest. Every past life aspiration works into the power of the soul. Life in Heaven is no dream, but is the realm where mind and heart develop without hindrance by dense matter. When the higher self has consumed all the fruits of the mental body that belong to the earth-life, it shakes off the mental body. The mental body, last of the temporary vestures of the true person, as with the etheric and astral bodies, disintegrates and its materials return to the general matter of the mental plane. The causal body alone remains as the receptacle of all that has been assimilated.

Of the four levels in Devachan, the lowest level is the heaven of the least progressed souls. Perhaps their highest emotion was an unselfish love for family and friends, or an admiration for someone they met on Earth. They will be reborn with a somewhat improved emotional nature. Men and women of every religious faith who have devoted their hearts to loving their God compose the second heaven. They have lost themselves in the rapture of devotion. These souls grow in purity and devotion and these qualities intensify. Those noble souls who have devoted themselves to service of humanity while on Earth achieve the third heaven. They poured out their love to God in the form of works for humankind. Their reward is greater power in service and increased wisdom. The next life will be of greater benevolence, for example the life of a great philanthropist who possesses innate power and unselfish love. On the fourth level of heaven reside the most advanced souls, masters of art, literature, and music. Scientists who searched into the secrets of nature come to the fourth level and will return to Earth to discover the mysterious ways of nature. Students of deeper thought are also found here. Those who sought out the great spiritual teachers will return to Earth and themselves be teachers and light bringers. The time arrives when the soul chooses to leave Heaven in the lower Devachanic world and shed the mental body. It now finds itself functioning in the permanent body, the causal body.

THE CAUSAL PLANE

At the end of the Devachanic period, the mental body will pass on to the permanent causal body, the good characteristics thus fashioned to be carried into the next incarnation. In the causal body, the second mind-body, all causes reside that have manifested themselves as effect on the lower planes. Described as the receptacle in which all people's treasures are stored for eternity, it grows as the lower nature passes on all that is worthy. This body is the form-aspect of the individual.

No true person exists until growth through the physical and astral planes has been accomplished, and matter of the mental world begins to show itself within the evolved lower bodies. This formless aspect of a true person is like a delicate film of subtlest matter, which is the body that lasts through the whole of human evolution. The receptacle of all that is in accordance with the law, its every attribute is noble and harmonious and therefore enduring. The causal body marks the stage of evolution to which a soul has attained. Every noble thought, every pure emotion, is carried up and incorporated into this substance.

Only the causal body, a storehouse of evil and good, remains after the lower bodies have all dissipated. Good traits work into the texture of the body and aid its growth, while evil remains but a germ. Evil actions in a person's life do great injury to the causal body, and when persistent can retard it. If one continuously follows evil, the mental body becomes so entangled with the astral realm that after death it cannot free itself entirely. Ambition, pride, and power of the intellect used for selfish purposes are far more dangerous than the tangible faults of the lower nature, and they retard evolution. Everything evil has within itself the germ of our destruction, whereas everything good contains the seed of immortality. Good woven into the texture of the causal body is never lost, for it becomes the true person who lives forever. Good harmonizes with the cosmic law, and it moves forward to become part of the evolutionary stream that can never be destroyed.

Death holds no power over the causal body. All causes that effect future incarnation reside in the causal body. The germ sown by the causal body can grow only after its kind, attracting to itself the grade of matter that belongs to it and arranging that matter in its characteristic form. It produces the replica of the quality the person made in the past life. Karma helps build the body that results from the harvest of the seeds sown in the past.

The permanent causal body grows very slowly. Results of all experiences act as causes and mold the future life. With the mental, astral, and physical all perishing, the harvests of these experiences are stored in the permanent causal body.

The fifth subplane of the mental plane, the lowest region of the formless region, is the habitat of the divine self or eternal person. Comprising the self of the causal body are the mind, the higher mind or higher self, and the divine self which are all one. It is the source of innumerable energies and vibrations, with the finest expressed in the matter of the causal body. They form pure reason, think abstractly, and gain knowledge through intuition.

Less subtle vibrations attract matter of the lower mental region. This is the lower mind expressed in dense matter. We call this intellect, which comprises reason, judgment, imagination, and comparison. It thinks concretely and uses logic. It argues, reasons, and infers. These vibrations act on the etheric brain through astral matter, and through the etheric brain, acts on the physical brain. This is how consciousness works, being the only medium to harvest experience. As the soul develops, it becomes more conscious of its inherent powers and of the working of energies on the lower planes. Memory of the past guides the soul's will and these past impressions develop the conscious, which deals with morals and intuition that enlighten the intellect. All these past-life memories are stored in the treasure-house of the causal body to determine the future life. Each person becomes exactly what they have made themselves to be during the past life.

Those souls who are deep thinkers and who lived noble lives have sown much seed. The harvest leads them to the fifth Devachanic region, the lowest of the three heavens in the formless world. They have risen above the bondage of flesh and passion and begin to experience the real life of a human, unfettered by the attributes of the lower worlds. These souls have learned truths by direct vision and see the fundamental causes of which all concrete objects are the results. They understand the underlying unities, the presence of which is masked in the lower worlds, and they develop deep knowledge of the cosmic law and understand how it works below. By studying their past, they understand the interactions between cause and effect. They know what deficiencies need to be worked out in future lives.

More advanced souls reach the sixth heaven. They have devoted all their energies to the higher intellectual and moral life during the Earth sojourn. No veil of the past exists in this region, because their memory is perfect and unbroken. Here they can study the archetype of all forms that gradually evolve in the lower worlds and can foresee the problems connected with the development of these archetype forms. In the sixth heaven, the soul is in immediate presence and communion with the greater souls that have evolved in humanity, who have escaped the bonds of Earth. They enjoy the rapture of these great souls and grow more like them in character. Here they plan for the next life to infuse energies that will neutralize forces that hinder the soul's evolution. They plan actions that need to be performed and actions that need to be avoided, and make certain to exclude evil from the next life. Being born into the world with high and noble qualities, they render an evil life impossible.

The highest level of the Devachanic world is the seventh heaven where masters and initiates reside. No soul can dwell here unless it has passed the narrow gateway of initiation while on Earth. From this region come the strongest intellectual and moral impulses that flow down to Earth. Here the intellectual life of Earth has its roots. The will of God becomes the will of the soul who now sees the good of the world. All separateness is eliminated in those who have reached this final emancipation. At this stage of evolution, the soul does not have to be reborn on Earth.

Death is the greatest of Earth's illusions and is merely a change that gives the soul a partial liberation. There is no "death" but only a change in life conditions. Life is continuous, unbroken, unborn, eternal, ancient, and constant, according to the teachings of the great masters of this universe.

The consciousness of past lives, carried through the processes of all the lower worlds, exists on the high plane of causes in the causal body. People do not remember these past lives because they are not conscious yet of their causal body, which has not developed functional activity of its own. It is the essence of past lives that lives. Until fully conscious, memory cannot pass from plane to plane, and from life to life. As a person advances, flashes of consciousness come forward to illuminate fragments of the past.

THE HIGHER PLANES

The causal plane is not the highest plane to which the soul evolves. After reaching the seventh subplane of the mental world, the soul leaves the wheel of birth and death, and enters the next plane called "Buddhi" by the Theosophists, which is a Sanskrit word for wisdom. Here, a soul realizes its own consciousness and the underlying unity of the universe, where separateness belongs to the three lower worlds. The spiritual body is the vehicle of consciousness, the body of bliss. This becomes a fact of experience and no longer an intellectual belief. In the spiritual body, a soul becomes one with all the lower worlds and its consciousness can expand to embrace the consciousness of others to become one with them.

Although the Buddhic plane has duality, there is no separation, being a state that cannot be approached in the lower planes. This state is similar to two people in love who feel they are one person, without barriers between them.

In this bliss, the self begins to send outward its vibrations, which draws around them matter on the plane below, and this helps form the buddhic body known as the blissful body. Man can contribute only to the building of this glorious form by cultivating pure, unselfish, and beneficent love that is neither partial nor seeks return for its out flowing. This spontaneous outpouring of love, the most significant of the divine attributes, gives everything. Pure love brought the universe into being, maintains it, and draws it up toward perfection. Through unconditional love, humans develop the bliss aspect of God within them. They prepare that body of beauty and joy into which the divine self will rise. All limits disappear and souls find themselves one with all that lives.

The Nirvanic plane is the plane of the highest aspect of the God within us. Called *atma* by the Theosophists, it means self. Divine powers in their fullest manifestations reside in this plane of pure existence. Those who have completed the cycles of evolution and have become masters attain this Nirvanic consciousness. These wise souls have solved in themselves the problems of uniting the essence of individuality with nonseparateness. They possess a live immortal intelligence, perfect in wisdom, bliss, and power. The Nirvanic consciousness is the antithesis of annihilation.

Limits of earthly consciousness have dropped. Those who dwell here have accomplished their own evolution in past universes. They have come forth with the Logos when he manifested himself to bring this universe into existence. Lords of all God's hierarchies and ministers working on the lower planes abide in Nirvana. All life currents issue from Nirvana, the heart of the universe.

Evolution of the Buddhic plane and Nirvanic plane belongs to a future period of our race. Those who choose the more difficult path of rapid progress may travel that path even now. They attain unity when they reach the Buddhic plane. Here a soul feels the brotherhood of humanity and serves those in need. They see all beings as themselves. Bliss comes when a person knows the absence of separating barriers, and wisdom flows when one transcends the limits of intellect. When this is achieved, the soul escapes from the binds of the lower world. The last of the seven planes of the universe, the sixth and seventh, can only generate conjecture from mere mortals about what happens within them.

The stage in evolution that humans and nonhumans reach depends on the age of the soul. Some individualized souls are younger than others, and therefore not as evolved. We are all one in origin, evolution, and goals, but differ in age. A wise person rises above the petty differences of race, religion, class, and country, knowing that he or she is one with all. The wise soul does not judge, knowing that the younger soul is learning lessons that at one time the wise soul had to learn.

Chapter Four

REBIRTH
Until We Are Perfect

Millions of people throughout the world believe in the universal law of rebirth, even those in Western countries where religion does not teach reincarnation. This sacred law helps answer some of the most important questions about the nature of humanity and can explain the most complex human problems. Traces of rebirth can be found in all religions and in the myths of most primitive people. Thus far we have presented knowledge about the nature of the soul handed down by the masters and by some religions. Some of these beliefs are difficult to prove within the current scientific paradigm. These concepts of the soul have led to the doctrine of rebirth. As we will see, traditional scientific evidence strongly supports this universal law of reincarnation.

Evidence suggests that more people in the world believe in reincarnation than do not. Of course, the millions of Hindus and Buddhists found in Southeast Asia learn this from their religions. Surprisingly, 18 percent of people in eight Western European countries also believed in reincarnation, according to a 1968 Gallop poll. A similar poll, one year later, found 20 percent of Americans and 26 percent of Canadians believed in reincarnation. In 1982, this figure rose to 23 percent in America. These figures are surprising considering that traditional Christianity and Judaism do not hold reincarnation as a tenet in their faith. An ironic aberration arises when we examine the mystical offshoots of these major religions. All believe in reincarnation! The Sufis of the Islam faith, the Kabbalists of the Jewish religion, and Rosicrucians of the Christian faith all believe in the rebirth concept. These mystical societies have preserved the mystical truths upon which these religions were founded.

Reincarnation was the major belief of people long before Christianity. In early Europe, the natives of Finland, Iceland, and Lapland were all believers, as were the early Norwegians, Danes, and

Swedes. Old Prussians and Lithuanians taught this concept as did the Celts of Ireland, Britain, Scotland, and France. Early Greeks, Romans, and Egyptians believed in reincarnation, which was also a cornerstone for the Gauls of France, Italy, Belgium, Netherlands, and Switzerland.

Indigenous people of Africa, the aborigines of Australia, and natives of the South Pacific accept the principle of rebirth. The Huna religion of Polynesia and later Hawaii taught that evolution of the soul occurred through a series of incarnations. In North America, the Hopi, Zuni, Pueblos, Sioux, and many other tribal nations are believers in reincarnation. Margaret Mead stated that the Eskimo (Inuit) culture is based on reincarnation.

Christians frequently object to the concept of reincarnation because it provides an excuse to postpone one's salvation to the next life. However, passages in the New Testament suggest the people at the time of Jesus believed in the concept of rebirth, as did Jesus and the disciples. John 9:23 states, "(As Jesus) passed by, he saw a man blind from his birth, and his disciples asked him, 'Rabbi, who sinned, this man or his parents, that he was born blind?'" The disciples suggest the man had lived previously, and perhaps his parents had a karmic debt. In Matthew 11:2-15, Jesus says, "Truly, I say to you, among those born of women there has risen no one greater than John the Baptist . . . and if you are willing to accept it, he is Elijah who is to come. He who has ears to hear, let him hear." In Matthew 17:10-13 and Mark 9:9-13, Christ replied, "Elijah does come, and he is to restore all things: but I tell you that Elijah has already come, and they did not know him, but to him whatever they pleased. [John was beheaded.] So also the son of man will suffer at their hands." The New Testament has fourteen texts that suggest a belief in reincarnation.

Gnostics, an early Christian mystical society, also believed in reincarnation and believed knowledge was the key to salvation. They had become very critical of the church, accusing the church of teaching lies. The battle between the Gnostics and the church took place over several centuries and the church branded the Gnostics as heretics. The Gnostics acquired much of their knowledge from Jesus, friends of Jesus, some disciples, and disciples of John the Baptist. Finally the church ordered the writings of the Gnostics destroyed. In 1945, some Gnostic gospels were discovered buried near Nag Hammadi in Egypt. References to reincarnation were found in these gospels and include the *Pistis Sophia* text in which Christ says, "A person who curses others will in the new life be continually troubled in the heart." He also said, "Prior to incarnation, such a person, as do most people, drink of the water of forgetfulness, and therefore do not remember what transpired during the time between incarnations." Jesus warns Mary Magdalene about a time limit for attainment of perfection in any world. "When the number of perfect souls shall be at hand, I will shut the gates of light and no one from that time onwards will enter nor will anyone hereafter go forth into (incarnation again) for the number of the perfect souls is completed, for the sake of which the universe has arisen."

The Bible confirms that Jesus confided truths to the disciples that he withheld from the masses. Mark 4:33-34 states, ". . . but privately to his own disciples, he explained everything." In Mark 4:11, "To you has been given the secret of the Kingdom of God, but for those outside, everything in parables, so that they may indeed see but not perceive, and may indeed hear but not understand."

The Church forced the Gnostics to go underground. Most prominent among their "heresies" was the belief in reincarnation. Cranston and Williams write, "Medieval history reveals that all over Europe were hundreds of thousands of Christian reincarnation believers who were eventually crushed through holy wars and inquisitions. They were charged with the crime of succeeding the early Gnostics." Included were the Cathars of southeast France, a peace-loving sect who did not believe in war, of which representatives of the Roman Catholic Church killed more than 20,000 in 1209. Because the Cathars practiced esoteric Christianity and dispensed with the institutional aspects of the Christian way, the Church felt threatened. Cathars wanted to control their own destiny and not be controlled by the Church, which refused to relinquish its power.

Early Jewish sects also believed in reincarnation. Josephus, the early Jewish historian, writes that both the Essenes and the Pharisees believed in reincarnation. The Essenes have been linked with the early education of Jesus and John the Baptist. The Pharisees taught that virtuous souls have the power to revive and live again on Earth. A collection of Jewish laws and tradition, the *Talmud*, compiled before the time of Christ, states that God created a limited number of souls whose destiny was to reincarnate until they were purified for the Day of Judgement. Likewise, the Jewish *Kabbalah* states that no man is perfect who has not kept 613 precepts of the law, and they who fail to do this are doomed to undergo transmigration as many times as necessary, until they have observed everything they neglected in their former existences. It also states that repeated lives are a blessing because they give humanity an opportunity to develop all the perfections of which the germ was planted. The soul eventually becomes fit to reenter the absolute substance from which it came and attain reunion with God.

In the early days of Islam, a widespread belief in reincarnation came about in three forms: First, periodic incarnation of the perfect man, such as Jesus and Muhammad; incarnation of a spiritual leader after death; and reincarnation of the soul of the ordinary man. Leaders of Islam who succeeded the Prophet Muhammad taught rebirth to a select inner circle. Sufis preserved this esoteric doctrine of Islam. They linked rebirth with conscience evolution in the process of perfecting man.

Why, if reincarnation is a universal law, is it not part of the Christian, Jewish, or Islamic traditional doctrine? One can only speculate. Some believe that without the concept of reincarnation, the religious fathers could control people. Perhaps the teachings were unintentionally misinterpreted. Perhaps one could perfect the soul in one lifetime, if one practiced faithfully the teachings of these religions. Perhaps it may be, as the Rosicrucians teach, that Jesus requested the concept of reincarnation not be taught to the masses for two thousand years, as he felt humanity would progress faster. One must have faith in the spiritual hierarchy's master plan for humanity's evolution. Perhaps the hierarchy experimented to see how humanity progressed without these major religions' belief in reincarnation. There are no accidents. We have completed two millennia since Christ, and if the Rosicrucians were right, it is time to begin talking about this sacred law.

THE CONCEPT OF REBIRTH

As we have seen, evolution consists of an evolving soul that passes from form to form, storing in itself the experiences gained through each form. According to the writing of Annie Besant in *The Ancient Wisdom,* reincarnation is the adaptation of the universal principle to meet the conditions rendered necessary by the individualization of the continuously evolving soul. In each person lies hidden all the divine powers of our Creator. They are latent, neither manifest nor functioning. Through evolution, they are gradually awakened by external experiences. All possibilities of vibrations exist in the self. Any vibration touching it will arouse a corresponding vibrating power. In this way, one force after another will pass from the latent state to the active.

When the form perishes, the life keeps the record of those experiences in the increased energies aroused by them. The life force pours itself into new forms derived from the old, carrying this accumulated experience with it. The soul is the receptacle of all results and becomes the storehouse in which all experiences accumulate as an increasingly active power. In other words, these experiences give power to the soul. The ever flowing stream of life force from the Creator supplies new life forces to form on the higher levels, so that involution and evolution proceeds continuously. As the more evolved souls incarnate into the lower worlds, newly energized souls in the higher realms take their places. As involution proceeds, the group soul attains the attributes of power through the forms in which it is incarnated. By the repeated process of group soul reincarnation in the mental world, and then the astral world, the souls are ready to respond to experience from physical matter. Once the group soul descends to the physical plane, it begins to incarnate itself in a filmy physical form, an etheric double of the dense physical matter. After the group soul evolves through the mineral, plant, and animal incarnations, it then individualizes and finally receives the human monad. Three aspects of the human monad include the spirit, the spiritual soul, and the human soul.

In summarizing the Theosophical view, from the higher planes the spirit descends and veils itself in the spiritual soul. The third aspect, the human soul, first shows itself in the higher subplanes of the mental (formless) world. A germ from the causal body fructifies, and the union forms an embryonic causal body. The spirit individualizes and is encased in form in the causal body. This is considered the birth hour of the individualization of the spirit into the human soul, which is the real human. The human soul essence is eternal, unborn, and undying. Its birth in time as an individual is definite. Spiritual intermediaries, called the Sons of Mind, help the life force (divine spark) reach individuals of the human race, needed for the formation of the embryonic soul.

Sons of Mind have completed their own evolution in other worlds and have come to Earth to aid in evolution of the human race. They are our spiritual fathers and some of these great ones actually incarnated into human form to become guides and teachers of infant humanity. Ancient records called them Sons of Mind and gods, for they possessed a mind more developed than the embryonic souls of most of humanity. These souls of other world races, by way of their evolved intelligence, became the leaders of ancient worlds. Because of their higher mentality and power of acquiring knowledge, they dominated the masses of less-developed people in antiquity. As a result, there developed in our world an enormous difference between mental and moral capacity of souls, separation of the most highly evolved from the least evolved races, and from the highest philosophical thinker to the primitive human. These differences are only differences in the stage of evolution as measured by the age of the soul that has existed throughout the history of humanity. The most highly developed soul had its childhood and infancy in previous worlds, as documented in the cuneiform writings of ancient Sumer in Mesopotamia. Eventually, the infant soul will mature and new souls take its place. Nature brings to all souls infancy, childhood, and maturity.

An infant human soul will have radical experiences impressed upon it. This soul will experience riotous pleasures and excruciating pain. Recognition of the difference between pleasure and pain is a preliminary essential for awakening the unthinking soul. The immature soul gradually recognizes and perceives as it experiences the hard knocks of life. Countless repetitions of lives awaken the soul and eventually it makes gains. After many lives, perceptions are formed in the mental body and inferences are drawn from certain actions. This inference, the beginning of reasoning, is the germ of logic that begins to evolve in the humans intellect. Early experiences lead the desire-nature to increase pleasure and lessen pain. Each experience stimulates the mental body into a more ready function. At this stage, a person has no knowledge of good or evil. Good is in accordance with Divine Will and evil retards evolution.

By experience, a person learns that moderation balances pain and pleasure. Each new birth brings a mental faculty influenced by the past lives. After dying, the young soul spends most of its time in purgatory of the astral world (Kamaloka) and sleeps through a brief mental plane period (Devachanic) of unconscious assimilation of minute mental experience. It is not yet sufficiently developed for the active heavenly life that lies before it. The enduring causal body is the receptacle of the soul's good qualities, and it carries the soul on for future development into the next life on Earth. In the earlier stages of evolution, the causal body allows evolution to proceed. Without it, the accumulation of mental and moral experiences shown as faculties would be impossible.

Eventually all souls will develop all their powers, but the order in which they are developed depends on the circumstances in which the soul is placed. The soul must conquer every region of nature. Striking differences may be seen among same aged souls because they have had different experiences. Once perfected, the soul will possess all powers and energies.

After death, a person loses his or her physical, mental, and astral bodies. The germs of the faculties and qualities are stored in the causal body and include the seeds for the next astral and mental bodies. A new life dawns when the mental germ is activated to grow into a mental body, representing exactly the mental state of a person. Only past life experience exists as an essence. After the soul has created a new mental body, it vivifies the astral germ that provides a new astral body. This body represents the desire-nature evolved in the past lives. A physical body external to the soul is then planned which will be suitable for the experience of its qualities.

During past lives, a soul makes ties with other souls, which may create liabilities. Some of these liabilities may determine the place of birth. Whether the soul has been a source of happiness or unhappiness to others in past lives will determine the conditions for the next life. The development of certain mental powers, such as those of a musician, will determine physical heredity. All these conditions are determined by spiritual intelligences called the Lords of Karma. They function to supervise the working out of cause, continuously determined by thoughts, desires, and actions of the soul. They determine the soul's destiny which it has created.

The Lords of Karma guide the reincarnating person to the new environment as determined by his or her past. They establish the race, nation, family, and physical body that best suits the qualities of a soul. A class of elemental spirits builds a new etheric double within the mother's womb. Elementals build the dense body into the etheric double, molecule by molecule, following the etheric template. Physical heredity is provided to the incarnating soul. Thoughts and passions of the mother and father influence the elementals in the creation of the etheric double. At an early stage, the new astral body connects with the new etheric double and influences its formation. Through it, the mental body works on the nervous organization. When an infant is born, the brain reveals the mental and moral qualities of the soul. The building of the brain continues to the age of seven. Until this age, the conscious soul lives more on the astral plane than upon the physical plane. During this time, a child may see invisible friends, hear voices inaudible to elders, and perhaps remember a past life.

As a soul evolves, a conflict develops between memory and desire, and the mind grows more active through this conflict. At this stage, a germ of will begins to manifest. Desire and will guide a person's actions. Desire is outgoing energy determined by attraction of external objects. Will is outgoing energy as determined by reason gained from past experience or from intuition. Desire is guided from without and will from within. At the end of evolution, desire has been eliminated and will rules. Will is guided through reason based on past experience. Suffering occurs from mistaken actions. From this, wisdom develops. A person will no longer desire objects that bring pain, a choice learned from lessons repeated many times. Reincarnation provides these lesson opportunities until desire dies out and the object is rejected. Choice by the soul begins to harmonize with universal law. An infant soul begins its earthly sojourn by rebelling against these laws, but eventually the soul evolves to a harmonious condition based on knowledge and memory of past disobedience. Will is the domain of morality, which is entitled conscience. If consequences are connected with certain actions, the conscience speaks with conviction. With unfamiliar conditions, conscience has no experience and often decides wrongly.

Laws of morality are based on enlightened reason, which discerns the laws of nature. They bring human conduct in alignment with Divine Will. The roots of obedience of these natural laws are found in love, the hidden divinity of humanity. Morality begins in the infant soul, when as an adult, it is moved by love of spouse or child, without thoughts of self-gain. This is the soul's first conquest of lower nature on the path to moral perfection. It is often easier to purify than to create love, according to ancient wisdom.

The next step of consciousness involves the development of higher intellectual powers. Here, the mind no longer dwells in mental images originating from sensations. At this stage, an image of an abstract idea without form originates from the higher mental planes. This provides the soul material from which it can work. Consciousness spreading out to embrace the world involves the next level. A soul sees all things in itself and as parts of itself. It considers itself as a ray of the Creator and as one with him. The soul has now become conscious.

In summary, the physical body is the lowest vehicle of consciousness, the astral body the next highest, followed by the mental body, and the causal body is the fourth highest vehicle of consciousness. Here, the soul possesses memory of the past and can trace its growth through the long succession of incarnations. Strength, calm, and wisdom come to those who use the causal body as a vehicle of consciousness. The predominant element of consciousness in the causal body is knowledge and ultimate wisdom. At the next higher level of consciousness is the Buddhic body in which bliss and love abide. A soul recognizes its nonseparateness and its unity with all. The aspiring soul learns to hold all its power for the service of humanity and to share with lower consciousness the knowledge of the highest.

Reincarnation is necessary for the evolution of the soul, so it can eventually reach the higher states of consciousness enabling it to free itself from the body. *Ancient Wisdom* teaches that the soul is born again and again in each of these worlds of consciousness, until it has completed the evolution possible in that world. Further evolution lies before us in the other worlds, but according to Divine Law they are not open to us until we have mastered the lessons our current world has to teach. Some lessons are learned quickly because the soul is recovering past knowledge. Other lessons are learned slowly because the soul is acquiring experience for the first time.

KARMA

Karma is another of the great laws of the universe, the law of causation under which rebirths function. It is a Sanskrit word meaning action. All actions are effects flowing from preceding causes, and each effect becomes a cause of the future karma. Karma is the unbroken linked series of cause and effect that make up all human activity. Every event is linked to a preceding cause and to a following effect. According to karmic law, there is no such thing as chance or accident. All thoughts, deeds, and circumstances according to *Ancient Wisdom* relate to the past and will causally influence the future. Natural laws lay down the conditions under which all experiences must occur, but do not prescribe the experience. Humans remain free at the center of their activities, but external activity is limited by conditions of the plane on which these activities occur.

Humans can become the masters of their own destiny because destiny lies in a realm of universal law. Knowledge of the law can build the science of the soul and place in individuals' hands the power of controlling their futures. Their choices can determine their future characters and their future circumstances. "For whatsoever a man soweth that shall he also reap."

Humans send out three classes of energy. Mental energies lead to the causes called thoughts. Desire energies on the astral plane cause desires. Physical energies aroused by desires and mental energies give rise to causes called actions. Every force works on its own plane and reacts on the plane below it, proportioned by its intensity. The motive that generated the activity determines the plane to which the force belongs.

The ancients describe three types of karma: (1) Ripe karma is ready to manifest itself as inevitable events in the present life. (2) Karma of character manifests itself in tendencies that are the outcome of accumulated experiences, which can be modified in the present. (3) Now karma refers to the current actions causing future events and future character. A person is also connected to family karma, national karma, racial karma, and, of course, individual karma.

Thought is the most potent factor in the creation of human karma. The energies of self in thought work in mental matter. Vibrations called thought give rise to forms and mental images that shape and mold the mental body. Each thought modifies the mental body, and mental faculties in each successive life are made by the thinking of the previous life. No created mental image is lost, but remains as material for faculty.

People affect others by their thoughts. These mental images reproduce themselves in secondary forms. Thoughts set up karmic links between the soul and others and influence the future environment. These thoughts draw people, good or evil, to later lives and tie us to relatives, friends, and enemies. They attract entities who help or hinder us, benefit or injure us, and love or hate us. Therefore, thought produces mental and moral characteristics that help determine our future human associations.

Desires are outgoing energies that attract themselves to objects and an environment where they can be gratified. Humans are born according to their desires, which also determine the place of birth. Desires can affect others, and they are linked with other souls, often by the strongest ties of love and hate. An ordinary person's desires are generally stronger and more sustained than his or her thoughts. Desires attract people, influences, and connections of which the person is totally unconscious.

The energy of actions generates karma by its effect on others. Karma results from past thinking and desires. If actions are repeated, they set up a habit of the body that limits the experience of the soul in the outer world. The effects of action, happiness, or unhappiness on others also determine future human associations. Past actions chiefly determine our nonhuman environment.

Every force works on its own plane. For example, if a person sows happiness for others on the physical plane, he or she will reap conditions favorable for happiness on that plane. The motive for sowing does not affect the results. Motive is a mental or astral force and arises from will or desire, reacting on moral and desire characteristics. A sacrifice of physical wealth will bring due reward in the future. Happiness derived from wealth depends chiefly on one's character. A good person cannot escape physical suffering if he or she caused physical misery, even by mistaken action. The misery one caused will bring misery. One good motive that has improved character will provide a source of happiness within oneself. As a result, the soul may be patient and content amid its self-created troubles. Motive is far more important than action. A mistaken action with a good motive produces more good than a well-chosen action with a bad motive. High motive builds character. If the motive is gaining objects, it attaches the person to the physical plane. A motive of divine service sets one free on the spiritual plane. It cannot attach an individual to the physical because the individual is asking for nothing.

A certain amount of karma can be exhausted in a single life. Various types of karma require a different type of body for the experience and need to be paid in another life. Some liabilities are contracted with other souls who may not be in incarnation at the same time. Some types of karma may require a different nation, social situation, or environment in a future life. The part of karma to be worked out is determined by the Lords of Karma who guide the soul to family and location. The aggregate of causes will fix the length of that particular life. To learn the lessons, a body is given its characteristic powers and limitations. A competent astrologer can sketch out in a horoscope all the ripe karma. Choices the soul made in the past determine the liabilities of the current life. The physical, astral, and mental bodies are important in ripe karma and limit the soul on each side. A wise person cheerfully accepts these limitations and diligently works out his or her improvement.

Every action is the final expression of a series of thoughts. A persistent repetition of thought of the same kind, such as revenge, reaches a point when the thought solidifies into action and a crime may result. Habitual thought forms, such as individual or national prejudices, limit thinking capacity. These thoughts cannot be suddenly transcended. However, a freedom of will remains. The exercise of free will can gradually create necessities for oneself.

Evil habits imprison a person and will create an evil life resulting from past evil thinking. If the soul has been growing and developing noble qualities, opportunities can throw out this past evil in one life.

Accumulated karma is subject to modification, unlike ripe karma. It consists of strong or weak tendencies according to the thought force. This karma can be strengthened or weakened by new thoughts to work with or against it. A person who wants to change these tendencies can free himself or herself by proper thought.

Collective karma involves a group of people. Karmic forces upon each member of the group introduce a new karmic factor upon an individual. The karma of a group results from the interaction of individual forces composing the group. For example, in a plane crash, those who have accumulated karma, but not a ripe karma, have the incurred debt of a shortened life. An individual may be allowed to drift into the accident to pay back this past life debt. Another intending to go on the plane but who has no debt, may be providentially saved by arriving late for the plane. Collective karma may throw a man into a war. He may discharge debts of his past that are not necessary within a ripe karma. A man can never suffer for what he does not deserve. If an unforeseen opportunity occurs to fulfill a past obligation, it is best to pay it off and get rid of it. The Lords of Karma can adjust the complicated working of karmic law. The karmic recorder knows the karmic record of each person, and omniscient wisdom selects part of that past record to plan for a single life.

A life plan includes physical heredity. A soul with a peculiar attribute is guided to parents who enable it to meet that requirement.

For example, a person devoted to singing would be guided to take a physical body in a musical family and would inherit the nervous system and body necessary for singing. An evil soul would be guided to a vicious family whose bodies are coarse. An alcoholic would be drawn to a family whose nervous system is weakened by addictions, whose parents might also be alcoholics. The soul receives a body suited to karmic possession of faculties and desires. A soul must return to Earth until it discharges all liabilities.

As long as the soul attaches to any object, it must be drawn to the place where the object can be enjoyed. Good karma binds the soul as much as bad. Desire is the binding element in karma. When the soul no longer desires any object on Earth or in Heaven, his or her tie to the wheel of reincarnation breaks. Until man approaches divinity, he needs the purging of desires. The desires grow purer and less selfish as the soul evolves. When the soul achieves perfection, it neither desires nor dislikes any object.

Knowledge is necessary to break the chains of karma. Strong thoughts of love will negate a cause of past hatred, which will cause an otherwise inevitable event. People may send out thoughts of goodwill and forgiveness to those who have wronged them. They may pour out thoughts of love and service to those people they have injured. One can also unconsciously discharge karmic liabilities by following the great teachers.

All teachings of the great teachers are based on these precepts. In countries that believe in reincarnation, a person with misfortunes does not blame others or God, but regards misfortune as the result of a past mistake. Such a person escapes worry and anxiety, compared with one who does not know the law. The law that brings pain to one will bring joy to another, if he or she sows the seeds of good. Those who understand the laws will eliminate feelings of impatience and hopelessness, which strength and patience replace.

Consciousness of man is not dependent upon the brain for existence. The mind is not the brain. Human consciousness exists before birth and conception, being a fundamental fact of reincarnation. Growth of the soul is an evolution of consciousness measured over thousands of years through the embodiment of various bodies. The process is painfully slow. Evolution of consciousness matches the evolution of form, which is an automatic process of nature. Consciousness is immortal, but nature destroys forms. The consciousness retains all memories and faculties.

The chief purpose of reincarnation is education, as the whole universe is a great school. It is the only school that offers the entire curriculum. Power, wisdom, and character develop during the soul's sojourn on Earth. A soul's thirst for experience and desire for knowledge is the driving power behind reincarnation. At the end of an incarnation, one has little desire for rebirth. However, the deeper self realizes the need for growth and the conscience is anxious to return.

Memories of experiences build recognition of relationships, which constitute knowledge. Selfishness, the longing to possess things and people for ourselves, causes much of our sorrow. Pain comes because of ignorance and willful disobedience. Wisdom comes with the realization of the inner meaning of experience and understanding the spiritual purpose.

The interval between incarnations varies and depends on three factors. A lengthy life is followed by a long stay in the unseen world, and conversely, a shorter life has a shorter interval. If an Earth life has been quite intense, with a great amount of experience gained, the interval between lives is greater. More advanced souls will often spend a longer time in the heaven worlds. Studies by the Theosophists found the interval between incarnations usually ranges from five to three thousand years, with the average interval being around five hundred years.

Grace also plays a role in the soul's evolution. The prison of karma cannot be broken without grace, and grace is not a gift. Virtuous karma with the will of love can set the soul free. Only those who express the will of unselfish love earn the right to enter the heaven worlds. A person needs to experience the state of spiritual perfection while the soul is in the physical body. Only at the highest stage of spiritual perfection in the physical body do the faculties of telepathy and clairvoyance occur. When the soul has completed its development, grace descends upon all the accumulated karma and annihilates it. The grace of God results from the soul always loving God, loving fellow humans, performing selfless service, and gaining inner knowledge of the soul's unity with God. After this has been achieved, the soul will finally be liberated.

SCIENTIFIC EVIDENCE FOR REINCARNATION

Until this point in the book, knowledge about the soul and rebirth cycle has mostly come from masters and enlightened teachers. Various cultures and religions around the world teach slight variations in the concept of reincarnation, but have one underlying theme, the perfection of the soul. Is there any evidence for reincarnation and how does one prove it? The person who has come closest to this remarkable achievement is Ian Stevenson, M.D., the former chair of the psychiatry department at the University of Virginia Medical School. Stevenson grew dissatisfied with psychiatry's methods for helping people. Often he found that human personality was not the product of genetics and environment. He believed that reincarnation might explain some mysteries of the personality. Stevenson was a meticulous scientist, often interviewing up to twenty-five people about one case of reincarnation. During an eleven-year period, from 1966 to 1977, Stevenson traveled over 600,000 miles to investigate cases, usually of children who remembered past lives. Some of his research was published in scientific journals, and much of it he published in a series of books. Stevenson, being a cautious researcher, said that he could not prove the existence of reincarnation, but his goal was to make plausible the idea of reincarnation.

So how does one gather knowledge regarding the possibility of reincarnation? Stevenson lists a number of methods, but believes only using past life memories of children is of value. The weakest evidence, according to Stevenson, is a past life reading, often by a psychic. A past life reading is of little scientific value, but if the information is correct, could explain events in a person's present life. Hypnotic regression provides stronger evidence, but can vary from person to person in quality of detail. The best evidence is found in the famous book *In Search for Bridey Murphy,* written by Morey Bernstein, an amateur American hypnotist, in the 1950s. Bernstein's life changed forever when he regressed Ruth Mills Simmons, a pseudonym for Ruth Mills Tighe. Under hypnosis, Mrs. Tighe began to speak in an Irish accent and said she was born December, 1798, in Ireland. Ruth had never been to Ireland, but described in great detail her life in Ireland as Bridey (Bridget) Murphy. She went on to describe many physical landmarks of her past life. Later research verified a number of facts; however, many statements could not be verified.

A number of cases by other hypnotherapists have been reported of people under hypnosis speaking in foreign languages, a phenomenon called xenoglossy. Most subjects had never been to the country from which the language originated nor were they familiar with the language they were speaking. Stevenson described two young twins who spoke to each other in an unrecognizable language. By accident, a college professor heard the twins speak and recognized it as Aramaic, the language spoken during the time of Jesus. Often people can speak the language responsively and engage in a sensible conversation with others speaking the same language. Stevenson spent sixteen years studying one case and wrote several hundred pages about a subject who spoke in a two hundred-year-old Swedish language.

Déjà vu also suggests a previous life. Stevenson describes some children of the "reincarnation type experience" who went to villages and claim they lived previous lives there. Within the village, these kids would remark on detail changes in rooms, doors, trees, local building features, and grounds. Recognition, says Stevenson, is greater than recall.

Some individuals have dreams in which they see themselves in another place wearing clothes from a different era. Often the dreams are recurrent and unpleasant. The dreams seem to relive events. Stevenson believes some vivid and recurrent dreams may stem from actual memories of previous lives. One girl dreamed of dying in a landslide, and further research showed a landslide did kill a young girl as described in the dream.

Other stimuli such as illness and drugs like LSD have caused people to relive a portion of a previous life. Stevenson found that occasionally during an illness a child would have a vivid memory of a past life. During meditation, some individuals have memories of past lives. Spiritual aspirants in Hinduism and Buddhism are said to remember previous lives. Strong emotions such as grief have been known to cause some adults to remember a previous life.

By the time a person has reached adulthood, he or she has filled the mind with a variety of information from many sources. Some of this information could only be a fantasy of previous lives. Stevenson places greater value on utterances by children when they speak of a past life. Children usually speak of their own volition, and their minds have not been contaminated. Parents often question the accuracy of events talked about in their children's memories. Often the case attracts attention in the community and a newspaper occasionally reports on it. These were the leads that Stevenson researched. For over twenty-five years, he concentrated his research on young children, feeling this is the best evidence suggestive of reincarnation.

Stevenson has studied over two thousand cases of reincarnation in India, Sri Lanka, Burma, Thailand, Turkey, Lebanon, Syria, West Africa, Europe, and North America. A higher correlation was found between remembering past lives and geographic location and belief in reincarnation. A study in 1978 found nineteen cases in one thousand inhabitants who remembered a past life in Padresh, India. In Asia, most of the cases were among poorer villagers who had little education. Cases from the United States usually came from individuals living in smaller towns with little education and a Christian background.

Five major features were recurrent in the cases Stevenson studied. (1) A person, usually elderly, predicted he would be reborn after he died. (2) The person died, and someone dreamed about his return to a particular family. (3) A baby was born, and a birthmark corresponded to a wound, scar, or other mark of the deceased person. (4) Shortly after, the baby begins to speak, rudimentarily at first, about the deceased person's past life. (5) The child behaved in ways that were unusual in the family but matched the behavior of the deceased person. Few cases showed all these characteristics.

Stevenson found ten of forty-six (22 percent) Tlingit Indians in northwest North America, whose previous personalities had stated before death their choice of parents in the next incarnation. The individuals in these verified cases sometimes predicted the appearance of birthmarks on their next bodies. The birthmarks helped identify them as having reincarnated.

Lamas of Tibet often make predictions about their next lives that are more subtle and allusive than the Tlingits. When trying to determine the reincarnation of the Dalai Lama, a lama may have a vision of the family from which the Dalai Lama reincarnated. After the child had been identified and after the age of two, he would be presented objects important in the Dalai Lama's previous life. Passing the identification test indicated the youngster possessed the soul of the previous Dalai Lama.

Announcing dreams about a soul before its birth has occurred in all of the countries that Stevenson researched. The dreamer is usually a married woman and potential mother of the next incarnation of the person to be reborn. The dreams occur before birth and often before conception of the subject. In Burma, the dreams occur before conception, and the personality petitions the dreamer to let it incarnate. Among the Tlingits, the disincarnate personality announces its intention to incarnate. Occasionally, a member of a deceased person's family dreams of the family to which the deceased will incarnate. In most announcing dreams, the dreamer recognizes the person who appears to communicate his or her intentions of rebirth.

Many subjects have birthmarks or birth defects that correspond to those on the body of the previous personality. Stevenson verified this in thirty cases by obtaining autopsy records detailing the wounds of the deceased. These autopsies were written before the new personality was born. These birthmarks and birth defects provide some of the strongest evidence in favor of reincarnation. In one case, two people decapitated a boy, and the reborn boy had a linear mark encircling his neck. Other subjects who died by gunshot or knife blade had corresponding marks on the new body. In another case, a person committed suicide with a muzzle rifle and both the entrance wound and exit wound showed up as marks on the new body. Another example involved a set of twins whose sisters had been killed in an auto accident prior to their birth. Birthmarks on one twin were identical to one of the deceased sisters. A mark on the other twin also matched a scar on a deceased sister. The twins recognized objects such as toys that their sisters had owned, and they could remember schools and swings that the deceased sisters had known about. Their behavior also matched that of the deceased sisters.

A child, when referring to a previous life, does so between the ages of two and five. In India, the average age of 235 subjects was thirty-eight months, the same average as of seventy-nine American cases. The children varied widely in the detail included in their memories. Some children spoke in the present tense of their wife and children from the previous life. Most children had a continued strong involvement with the remembered people and events. Some wept about past lives and others were angry about the way they died. Children nearly always stop talking about previous lives between ages five and eight, which usually coincides with increased activity outside the immediate family. Children with verified previous lives continue talking about them until about seven and one-half years, and children with unverified memories speak about the past life until just about six. If the child's statement cannot be verified by the family, the child tends to lose interest. Most memories are visual images.

The child's memories tend to be about events that happened in the last year and days of the previous life. About 75 percent remember how the person of the previous life died. Subjects may recall a variety of people and objects with which the previous personality had been familiar. Names of the previous personality and some family and friend's names are remembered. American children do not make as many verified statements as children of India.

Few subjects remembered anything of what happened between incarnations. Occasionally some remembered being involved in poltergeist activity. One child's memories of the disincarnate life included wearing elegant clothes that did not need washing. Another child could have food when he wished for it, though it was not required. Other subjects remembered a sage-like man who guided them to their new family.

Frequently, subjects wanted someone to take them to a village or town of the previous life. Reports of recognition frequently occurred when visiting the previous family. Stevenson gives credence only to spontaneous recognitions of someone from the previous life when a child's emotions toward the previous family were appropriate for the past-life memories. In the majority of these cases, the two families saw each other for several years and then gradually ceased to meet.

Other evidence consisted of traits like fears, dislikes, likes, interests, and skills that were unusual in the child's family, but corresponded to traits of the previous personality. Phobias related to the previous mode of death frequently occurred. Stevenson found that among 252 cases in which the previous personality had died violently, 127 (50 percent) had some type of phobia in the present life. If a subject died of drowning in the previous life, the subject was likely to show a phobia of water. Among 47 drowning cases, 30 (64 percent) had phobias to water in the present life. One case Stevenson cites is of a person who remembered being murdered by a barber, and who in the present life showed a phobia to all barbers. A phobia of snakes occurred in 9 (39 percent) of 23 cases in which the previous personalities had died of snakebite. If one had been shot, the subject was likely to have a phobia of firearms.

Often subjects who remembered their adult status appeared to their elders as more mature than other children of their age. They often adopted an adult demeanor.

Many children claimed they were members of the opposite sex

in the previous life. Most of these children showed, to varying degrees, habits of dressing, ways of speaking, and other behavior typical for the sex of the previous life.

Stevenson found the interval between the previous personality's death and the subject's birth was usually less than three years. The median interval of 616 cases from ten different countries was fifteen months. They ranged from six months in Lebanon to forty-eight months among Tlingit cases. Stevenson's research supports the belief that those who died violent deaths were led to a more rapid reincarnation than those who died natural deaths.

Of 1,095 cases studied, 62 percent were males and 38 percent females in the present life. In the previous life, 66 percent had been males and 34 percent females. Among 725 cases from six different cultures, 61 percent remembered lives that ended in violent death. The research found that violent deaths were more memorable than natural deaths. Far more boys had died violent deaths than had girls, perhaps explaining the higher number of boys who reported past life memories. In solved cases (where Stevenson confirmed the facts of a previous life), 94 percent of the subjects remembered the manner of death if it had been violent. If a natural death, 52 percent of the subjects mentioned the manner of death. Among solved cases, 76 percent of the subjects remembered the previous personality's name. Knowing the previous name makes solving the case much easier.

Stevenson found four basic characteristics in those who had died naturally and remembered past lives: (1) sudden death; (2) death at a young age; (3) unfinished business, as with a mother who left young children; or (4) engagement in a continuous business. At the time of death, for varying reasons, individuals felt entitled to a longer life than the one they had. They craved for a rebirth, perhaps leading to a quicker reincarnation than for those who led a complete life.

Of the two thousand subjects studied, twenty-three subjects remember killing themselves. Of those who committed suicide, most had phobias of the instrument of suicide, for example, of guns. Memory of the suicide did not necessarily eliminate the inclination to suicide. Three of the subjects, when children, had made threats to their parents of committing suicide. A fourth committed suicide in midlife, and a fifth said that he would commit suicide in an intolerable situation. This discredits the belief that suicide victims live in eternal hell.

Stevenson found no evidence that moral character in one life had external circumstances in the next. The vicious were not demoted in socioeconomic status nor the virtuous promoted. He found only a few cases of the process of retributive karma. He is quick to point out this does not mean that conduct in one life cannot have effect in another. Such effects would not occur externally, but internally in the joys and sorrows of experiences. Subjects frequently carried over interests, aptitudes, and attitude to the next life. However, Stevenson saw an evolution of attitude and an inner growth of the new personality compared with the previous personality. Stevenson concludes there is no external judge of one's conduct, but that we are makers of our own soul.

PAST LIVES

During the latter half of the twentieth century, a small segment of psychotherapists has reported great success in treating mental health patients with past life therapy. These therapists used hypnotherapy to regress patients to a previous life. They often found the current mental health problem was seeded in a former life. By reliving and understanding the root cause, the present problem often dissipated. They found these phobias were often associated with traumas in a former life. Deep-seated phobias, such as a fear of water frequently being associated with drowning in a past life, often disappeared. Helen Wambach, Ph.D., psychologist and former college professor, undertook an ambitious research project to investigate past life regressions. Her results on 850 subjects, which were quite surprising, were replicated in a second study on 350 subjects.

Wambach's research in the 1970s provided a method of collecting a large amount of data from many subjects, ruling out the subject's prior knowledge of the past and any fantasies. Group regressions were used to accomplish her goal. In her research, Wambach asked a series of identical questions for each of the regression groups. Questions included color of skin, color of hair, landscape, climate, food, eating utensils, architecture, clothing, footwear, and finally the death experience itself. Wambach asked her subjects to regress to five time periods, one of which was explored in detail. She asked them after they had died in that life to "flash on the year they died in modern time" and to "flash on the modern geographical name of the area after they had died." She found 70 percent of the subjects vividly recalled past-life experiences when they were hypnotized in the group situation.

Wambach's research discovered the group hypnotic technique was more effective than a one-on-one situation because the subject did not have to talk. She believed this relaxed the ego's fear of saying embarrassing things and allowed privacy of thought and experience recorded directly after the regression on a standardized data sheet. The left side of the brain that holds the speech center did not have to be activated. Wambach said the ego controlled the left brain, and in hypnosis it relinquishes temporary control of the "tuning knob" in the right brain. Normally, the right brain responds to commands from the left brain, the language-orientated ego. In hypnotic states, when subjects enter the rapid eye movement stage, the ego goes along on the trip, monitoring the experiences and judging whether to continue the experience. By using a hypnotic technique which enlists the ego's cooperation, the hypnotist shares control of the right brain with the subject's left brain ego. Essentially, the right brain functions as an amplifier or tuner. In this state of consciousness, Wambach found a telepathy phenomenon that helped explain past-life recall. In almost all subjects, they were able to foresee the question before Wambach asked it, suggesting they were in a state of consciousness beyond space and time. Telepathic communication is more than hearing words, claimed Wambach. She concluded that the past-life recall came from the right side of the brain, substantiated by the fact that her subjects reported feelings (also seated primarily on the right side of the brain) they had experienced in past lives. Subjects believed these emotions from past-life recall came from a deeper level than from the source of the visual image.

The best way to check past-life recall, decided Wambach, was to relate it to historical reality. She used references to verify architecture, culture, clothing, and landscape. Surprisingly, only 11 data sheets out of 1,088 (less than 1 percent), showed clear evidence of discrepancies between historical reality and reported facts in the hypnotic recall. Part of Wambach's research protocol included three "trips." The first trip took the subject on a preview of five different time periods; the second trip took them to a period where they would not likely have had previous knowledge; and the third trip to geographical areas around the world. This trip checked known particulars of the time period against the experience. By using three trips, she also controlled for fantasy. If past-life recall is fantasy, personality dynamics of the subject would be reflected in each of the past-life recalls.

In support of the idea that the subjects' experiences were not fantasies, Wambach discovered that most subjects reported a very mundane past life. She found that less than 10 percent reported being in the upper class in all periods. Between 60 and 77 percent said they were from the lower class and between 18 and 38 percent said they were from the middle class, depending on the period. For example, in 2000 B.C., the upper class was 5 percent, middle class was 28 percent, and lower class 67 percent. In A.D. 1850, 7 percent was upper class, 34 percent middle class, and 59 percent from the lower class. None of the subjects reported a past life as a historical figure. The 7 percent in the upper class did not find life pleasant because of all the responsibilities. Most of the happy lives were reported by the peasant lives. These percentages of classes presumably correspond to the class percentage in those eras.

Most subjects were not Caucasian in previous lives, but in the present life almost all subjects were. In 2000 B.C., 20 percent were Caucasian and 40 percent were black or Near Eastern with most living in North Africa across to Mesopotamia. By A.D. 400, one third were Caucasian, one third Asian, and one third black and Near Eastern. By 1850, 69 percent were white. Only 45 subjects reported a past life in the twentieth century, and most of them had died a violent death. The nineteenth century found 318 subjects living during that period.

Wambach believed that if past-life recall was a fantasy, she would expect more subjects to have been males in their past live as surveys have indicated most people would prefer to be males. The first research group consisted of 78 percent females, with 50.3 percent of the subjects reporting being males and 49.7 percent females in past lives. A similar percentage was found in the second study. Over the years of Wambach's research, more than 2,000 of her subjects had experienced past lives in the opposite sex.

Past-life clothing correlated closely to historical accounts, being classified as sewn garments, draped cloths, and animal hides or woven tunics. Subjects who reported being from the lower class of Egypt in 1000 B.C. reported wearing a strange kind of diaper arrangement from the waist to the mid-thigh. Egyptian drawings confirmed this type of clothing. By A.D. 1200, pants began to appear in the data. They wore short pants or knickers from 1200 to 1700, and long pants showed up in the 1850s. Before A.D. 1700, the great majority of subjects walked barefoot or wore crude sandals or hides around their feet. In China, cloth slippers went back to 2000 B.C. and made their appearance in Europe around A.D. 1400, during Marco Polo's time.

Food products reported also correlated with historical documentation. Until 1850, half of the subjects were eating grains as their primary food. Meat eaten between 500 B.C. and 1 A.D. was either domesticated fowl or some kind of lamb. During the Dark Ages (A D. 25 to 1200), cereal grain consumption increased. No one reported eating beef until late A.D. 1500. Spoiled food was reported by 8 percent of the subjects, especially concerning meat.

The great majority reported eating the evening meal with their fingers. From 500 B.C. to 400 A.D., 35 percent reported eating with a shallow wooden spoon. Forks changed appearance over time, beginning with two prongs, then three, and finally four by 1500. Most subjects reported using wooden plates, leaves, or gourds, and some reported eating directly from a community pot. By 1700, more people were using china plates, and before then metal plates were more common.

Population of the world doubled from A.D. 25 to 1500, and then doubled again by 1800. This was reflected in past lives reported by the subjects, which paralleled the population curve.

When asked about the death experience, most had a positive comment about it with 49 percent feeling a deep calm, accepting death with no difficulty. Thirty percent experienced positive feelings of joy and release, and 20 percent reported seeing their bodies after death. Some reported dying and being released and going back home. Following the regression, many reported losing the fear of death. Only 10 percent felt upset and sorrow at death. Natural death was experienced 62 percent of the time and 18 percent died a violent death. Many subjects reported to Wambach that their phobias had dissipated because of the regression.

As reported in *Life Before Life*, Wambach conducted another research project based on hypnotic regression where 750 subjects were taken to the consciousness before birth. Ninety percent of these subjects had reported the previous death process as being pleasant. When asked if they chose to be born again, 81 percent said it was their choice, but many were reluctant to do so and consented only after consulting with advisors. Subjects reported they had the right to refuse to be reborn but felt they had a duty to do so, as it was necessary. Only 28 percent felt enthusiastic about being alive again, but felt they had planned the new life carefully. One typical response was, "Yes, I chose to be born, and there were others around teaching and guiding me. But I felt very depressed at the prospect of living another lifetime. I did not want to, but I knew I needed the experience."

Most chose the sex they were to experience the next life. Eighteen percent reported their purpose was to be with one or several other people they had known in past lives to work out relationships. A large percentage, 87 percent, reported they had known parents, lovers, relatives, and friends before in their past lives. One subject said, "My mother was a close male friend from a past life. My father was my wife whom I used to treat cruelly in a past life." Most subjects told the same story, that they came back with the same souls, but in different relationships. We live again not only with those we love, but also with those we hate and fear. Subjects reported that when they feel compassion and affection, they are then freed from living over and over again with the same souls, who are forced to live with them.

Of the 750 subjects, 89 percent said they did not become part of the fetus or involved with the fetus until six months after gestation. This same percentage said their consciousness was separate from the fetus. One third said they joined the fetus and experienced being inside the fetus just before or during the birth process. Under hypnosis, 84 percent went through the birth process, with most reporting a sense of sorrow pervading the experience. They felt the soul in the newborn life felt cut off and alone compared with the between-life state.

Helen Wambach's research gives great credibility to past life regression. The potential for treatment of mental health problems that is totally ignored by traditional psychotherapy is enormous.

EDGAR CAYCE

Perhaps the person who raised most awareness about reincarnation in Western society was the American clairvoyant, Edgar Cayce, sometimes called the sleeping prophet. Cayce, born in 1877 in Kentucky, came from a family of uneducated farmers. While working as an insurance salesman, Cayce lost his voice for a year. The cure came from self-hypnosis after Cayce had diagnosed his own case. He found he could also diagnose the illnesses of others when in a self-induced trance. Even though Cayce had only a ninth-grade education and had never read a medical text, while in a trance he could give medical counsel. One anecdote describes him speaking in flawless Italian while giving medical advice, even though he did not speak Italian in the waking state. In 1910, the *New York Times* ran a two-page article on Cayce's ability to heal while in trance. Shortly afterward, people worldwide sought Cayce's help. He could give a distant reading by knowing the person's name and location. For twenty years Cayce gave medical readings.

One day in October 1923, a man named Arthur Lammers, who had no medical problem, asked Cayce to give a reading about the nature of the soul and purpose of life. Thinking that to do so was sacrilegious, Cayce was reluctant to give such a reading. Cayce was a devout Christian who taught Sunday school and read the entire Bible once a year. However, Cayce proceeded with the reading, and when in trance told Lammers that he had been a monk in a past life. Upon awakening, Cayce was shocked at what he had said and remembered nothing while in trance. He seriously doubted the validity of the past-life reading. After much searching in the Bible, Cayce reconciled himself to the concept of reincarnation. In fact, he found the fundamental principle of Christianity could not be made without the theory of reincarnation and karma. Following this fortunate decision, Cayce subsequently gave thousands of past-life readings in which he traced present tendencies of people to past-life incarnations. Cayce believed the law of karma explained the Christian verse, "as you sow, so shall you reap."

Following this milestone event, Cayce took measures in his readings to encourage the client to change attitudes toward conditions and fellow humans, which would help heal the physical body. The readings would explain the karmic condition that caused life problems.

Cayce's past life readings were divided into three categories: (1) boomerang karma, (2) organismic karma, and (3) symbolic karma. Boomerang karma was exemplified in a reading for a college professor who had been born totally blind. Cayce said that as a member of a tribe in a past life, the entity would blind his enemies with a red-hot iron. Now he was paying back that karmic debt. Organismic karma involved the misuse of the organism in one life, resulting in another life's appropriate affliction. A reading given to a man suffering from digestive weakness since infancy revealed that the affliction was a result of gluttony in a previous life. Symbolic karma was reflected in a reading for a congenitally deaf person who had turned a deaf ear to a person's plea for help in another life.

Edgar Cayce's source of information came from Cayce's subconscious, thought to have been tapped into the Universal Mind. The second source came from the Akashic record. Cayce explained it as follows: *Akasha* is a Sanskrit word that refers to the fundamental etheric substance of the universe whose composition is electro-spiritual. Upon the Akasha is impressed an indelible record of every sound, light, movement, or thought the universe has manifested. The impressions are registered on the Akasha as on a sensitive plate, somewhat like a huge candid camera of the universe. Cayce said we all have the ability to read this vibratory record, depending on our sensitivity. This sensitivity consists of tuning in to the proper consciousness similar to tuning in to a proper radio wavelength. He called the Akashic record "the universal memory of nature" or the "book of life." The Akashic record traces the life of individual souls who have incarnated in the world.

Cayce's readings revealed how the physical, mental, ethereal, metaphysical, and spiritual realms are interdependent and ultimately united. Many consider Edgar Cayce the father of holistic medicine. Cayce, as did the ancients, claimed the goal of the individual was its reunion with God. He referred to God as the universal, all-pervasive Cosmic Being. The soul is self and the image of God. Cayce connected individual suffering with the soul and the soul with God. Each soul, he said, enters the material world for a purpose, to gain experience for soul growth. However, Cayce said, "But let it be understood here: no action of any planet or the phase of the sun, the moon, or any of the heavenly bodies, surpasses the rule of man's own willpower: the power given by the creator to man in the beginning when he became a living soul with the power of choosing for himself." In other words, people have free will that enables them to overcome astrological influences. The Cayce readings say that people are not the innocent victims of their environment but are simply meeting self. Meeting self is actually meeting the consequences of our actions and attitudes, including previous thoughts and emotions. We reincarnate to face the results we have caused. We are free to choose, but must realize that within each choice are future choices.

The entity is the sum of what it has done about creative and ideal forces in its experience on the Earth. Latent or manifest urges are expressions in the varied phases of consciousness.

The Cayce readings do not teach about the transmigration of souls to lower levels of beings as does the Buddha religion. Stevenson had found in 30 of 2,000 cases that the previous personality was an animal.

Cayce said we should learn well our lessons on Earth, for reincarnation is a spiritual truth. He said, "Criticize not unless ye wish to be criticized: For with what measures ye mete, it is measured to thee again. It may be in the same way, but ye cannot even think bad of another without it affecting thee in a manner of destructive nature. Think well of others, and if ye cannot speak well of them, do not speak at all–but do not think it either! Try to see self in the other's place. All ye may know of God must be manifested through thyself."

Cayce emphasized in all his readings that people practice love, tolerance, and patience to bring back the primeval glory of God. The sole purpose of life is to reunite with God. He stated, "Know that the body, thy mind, thy soul is a manifestation of God in the Earth–as is every soul: and that the body is indeed the temple of the living God." Cayce is perhaps the first Westerner who attempted to clarify the concept of the soul and its relationship to God in a way similar to Eastern Indian philosophy.

OTHER EVIDENCE FOR REINCARNATION

Reincarnation answers so many questions that traditional Christianity has poorly addressed. Perhaps the biggest enigma of Christianity is explaining the concept of justice, as there is little evidence of justice on this planet. If all souls are equal at birth, why are human destinies so unequal? Human equality is a myth, because every soul is not given the same chance to develop its power. People are unequal physically, mentally, morally, and spiritually. Some people are healthy and some are diseased. Some are rich and some are poor. Some are smart and some are not. Why can some people work hard and end with nothing, and others not work and end up with a large inheritance? Why can one person develop into a great leader and another grows into a beggar? Christianity has addressed these dilemmas along two avenues, original sin and the will of God. Neither satisfactorily explains these inequalities for an intelligent mind. Reincarnation very clearly answers these questions and provides evidence to back it up.

Irving Cooper writes in *Reincarnation, The Hope of the Future* about evidence of reincarnation. He asserts that living only one life on Earth is purposeless, whereas reincarnation allows one to attain perfection over many lives. This conforms with the economy of nature and explains the purpose of good and evil. Reincarnation explains the rise and fall of nations, the reappearance of characteristics of earlier races, and explains the appearance of great men in groups. It explains enigmas of heredity and the mental and moral differences among people. Reincarnation provides an explanation for the purpose of life.

Reincarnation can explain innate faculties of children and maternal extinct, the ability to see a truth, to generalize from a single experience, and to understand certain situations. Rebirth explains unaccountable fears, sudden friendships, and the feeling of having known someone before, as well as the propensity for vice or virtue, masculine women, and feminine men.

Ian Stevenson found that interest in vocations may derive from interests of previous lives. Often, a subject expresses the vocation of a previous personality when playing. At times a child has been given a doll and then names it after his or her child in a previous life.

Reincarnation explains unusual aptitudes or untaught skills. Several subjects in India recited lengthy passages of scriptural verses that they had never been taught. These children remembered the lives of devoutly religious, previous personalities who had learned the scripture in a former life. Child prodigies may have studied and learned their skills in previous lives.

Other subjects may have a craving for tobacco or alcohol that developed in a previous life and see no reason why they should not resume the vice in this life. Stevenson found the temperament of a previous life carried into the present life, regardless of particular circumstances. The level of activity, persistence in an undertaking, and irritability were often similar in both lives.

Some children have an overt sexual interest in the wife, mistress, or girlfriend of a previous personality. Others make sexual advances toward members of the opposite sex who resembled their partners from the previous life. Children who switched sex in the new incarnation show traits characteristic of the former life sex. Sometimes a girl will assert she is a boy and dress in boys' clothes, play boy's games, and become a regular "tomboy." Eventually the majority accept their new sex and become normal in all respects. Some remain fixed on the previous sex and are usually unhappy. Stevenson suggests homosexuality and gender identity confusion often arise from the entity being of the opposite sex in the previous life.

Child psychologists recognize that children differ in their responses toward parents at birth. Stevenson found a strong conviction among some subjects that the previous parents were better than the current parents. Friction between a parent and child may have developed from their relationship in a previous life. One girl claimed to have been the mother's first husband in a past life. This child attempted to rid the family of her father, believing that she and her mother did not need him.

Reincarnation can explain irrational behavior as well. Some of Stevenson's subjects developed an irrational, antagonistic behavior toward a person or group of people. Several children have spoken openly about revenging themselves on their assailants of the previous life when they became old enough to do so. Usually the vengefulness disappeared over time and they developed a more tolerant attitude. Sometime a vengefulness by children developed toward a whole group, like policemen, Jews, or Moslems. In a previous life, one of Stevenson's subjects had been killed by the police and hated all police in the present.

Hand preference carries over from one life to another. Stevenson verified ten cases where subjects were left-handed in the previous life and also left-handed in the present life.

A small number of Stevenson's subjects claimed to remember more lives than just the previous life. In only one case could both lives be verified. In several cases, the subject was born before the person, whose previous life he remembered, had died. The interval varied from several days to several years. Stevenson thinks this may indicate a possession and cites ten cases of this type with accurate dates.

Evidence has been presented strongly suggesting the possibility of reincarnation. Evidence has also been given that suggests the soul is to learn certain lessons on its Earthly sojourn to help in its growth and evolution. How can the soul be sure it will find situations in which to learn these lessons? As we shall see, the stars, or what we call astrology, help determine fate and destiny.

Chapter Five

DESTINY AND FREE WILL
A Road Map for Life

If the ancient mystics are correct, the purpose of physical rein-carnation is to perfect oneself by learning certain Earth lessons decided upon while in the spiritual state. Through certain challenges in life, the soul gains experiences through choices it makes while encountering life dilemmas. The choices are made with free will, but circumstances are part of the soul's destiny. A soul, aided by spiritu-al helpers, plans its earth journey, and chooses parents, geographical location, race, religion, and other attributes to learn lessons from its sojourn. When encountering circumstances, there needs to be some influence that ensures the soul will be put into situations to make choices. The ancients said the planets caused this influence, what we today call astrology. If there is an astrological influence, applying scientific principles to astrology would be very easy for science. However, many variables, such as planet location and zodiac sign of the sun at birth can influence an astrological chart.

Destiny is governed by universal law that is often beyond the understanding and skills of an experienced astrologer. A skilled astrologer often amazes people with the accuracy of a horoscope reading. Unfortunately, astrologers are not scientists and scientists are not astrologers. If one could prove scientifically that planet posi-tions correlate with certain life situations, one could prove that plan-ets help govern destiny. Such scientific evidence has come forward.

HISTORY

Sumer, Earth's first recorded civilization, has five thousand-year-old cuneiform writings that show this ancient civilization practiced astrology. They knew that planets, invisible to the eye, circled fixed stars. The land of Sumer, in present day Iraq, later became known as

105

Babylonia. Discoveries in this Mesopotamian land set the pattern for the development of astronomy and the zodiac system of astrology. Located on the Persian Gulf, the area has extremely clear skies. Babylonians built towers on flat areas of the country where they could view the entire horizon. Priests lived secluded in monasteries, usually adjacent to the towers. Here, they discovered the laws that governed the movement of the stars and planets, which in turn influenced events on Earth. Observers presented reports to the king, who preserved them in the royal library. Later, these reports were gathered in a collection of writings, named after Sumerian gods, called the *Enuma Anu Enlil,* which the Assyrians preserved after they conquered Babylonia.

During the early stages of their religion, Babylonians believed the stars and planets were actual gods. Later they believed the gods ruled the corresponding planets. According to the Babylonians, stars formed a background against which the planets moved. The background moved in a yearly cycle. Planets were not fixed and each took a different length of time to complete its cycle. Because the solar system had approximately twelve lunar cycles in the solar year, the year was divided into twelve parts, or months, identified with twelve different constellations along the ecliptic. Seventy clay tablets containing astrological horoscopes, known as the *Illumination of Bel,* were unearthed in an ancient library at Ninevah, Assyria in A.D.1851. Astrology reached its peak in Babylonia between 625 and 538 B.C. Several centuries later, a Babylonian priest named Berossus established a school of astrology on the island of Cos from where the art spread to Greece.

Assyrian-Babylonian astrologers, known later as the Chaldeans, influenced the Jewish people. A star led the three wise men from the East to Jesus. This was part of an ancient Chaldean legend. In Chaldean astrology, the constellation of Cassiopeia presided over Syria and Palestine. Chaldean's knew it as "the woman with child" because every 300 years it brought forth an unusually bright star. Astrologers interpreted it as the Queen of Palestine bringing forth an heir to the throne. Astronomers have calculated that the star appeared just after the birth of Christ.

Egyptian astrology came from Persia in the sixth century B.C. and was not fully developed until the Hellenistic period. Egyptians developed the decans, a further division of each zodiac into equal parts of ten degrees each. Under Greek influence, the decans were incorporated into the Babylonian zodiac so that each sign was divided into three decans of ten degrees each.

The Greek philosophers believed that a series of seven concentric spheres surrounded the Earth, each enveloping the other. A planet ruled each of the seven spheres. After the fourth century B.C., names of Greek gods replaced names of the planets who bore a certain resemblance to the Babylonian deities thought to govern the planets. Aristotle believed a number of lesser gods ruled using the planetary spheres.

Greek philosophers believed in a relationship between music and the motion of the planets. Discovering that the musical scale depended on the relationship of numbers, the Greeks tried to prove that the motions of the heavenly bodies related to music in the same way as did numbers to harmony.

Believing that the motion of a body was a measure of the quantity of its soul, the Greeks determined the relative degrees of velocity (and therefore of soul) of the planets. They imagined a straight line drawn from the Earth to the outermost sphere, and then divided it according to the proportions of the musical scale. On this scale they placed various planets with Saturn, the outermost planet, corresponding to the 36th tone. The Earth corresponded to the first tone, and between Earth and Saturn the other planets were set at varying harmonic distances. Plato wrote in *The Republic* about musical harmony between the planets. He said each of the seven spheres (planets) carried within it a certain vibration, and when the vibrations sounded together, with each emitting a different tone, they formed a sublime celestial concert.

Stoicism was a Greek school of thought that was affected by Babylonian astrology. Seeing the world as an organism of sympathetic forces, the Stoics believed the forces acted and reacted incessantly upon one another, and they attributed a predominating influence to the heavenly bodies. Stoic philosophy spread throughout the Semitic world.

When astrology passed from Greece to Rome, the Babylonian, Egyptian, and Greek influence crystallized into a single unified system. The system explained how the planets and signs of the zodiac fit into the system. Astrologers developed the concept of the twelve houses, which were imaginary divisions of the Earth's surface projected into the sky. They established the ascendant, descendant, midheaven, and lower midheaven. The seven planets, including the

Sun and Moon, represented the basic forces that affected a person's character. Signs of the zodiac indicate the ways in which these forces are modified, the same way that rays of light are modified when they pass through colored panes of stained glass. Houses show the earthly departments of everyday life in which the modified forces operate. Each planet ruled one or two of the signs. Planets were divided into friendly and unfriendly, Sun, Moon, Jupiter, and Venus were beneficial, and Mars and Saturn were malefics. Mercury could be either. At this time, it was determined that the angle of planets to one another modified the planetary influence. Planets opposite each other produced a negative effect, as did planets which were square or 90 degrees apart. Planets trine, or 120 degrees apart, produced a positive effect, and those sextile, or 60 degrees apart, were also positive. The relationship between planets reveals the areas of personality in which a person could attain full positive expression and other areas in which one may experience psychological stress and strain. A distinction was made between fatalistic astrology, which claimed a person's life was predetermined, and catarchic astrology, which claimed the planets influenced only certain parts of a person's life. Since the time of Alexander the Great, the Greeks practiced astrology extensively and believed the planets governed human fate.

The Greek astronomer Hipparchus made a discovery contrary to astrological theory and alarmed practicing astrologers. He discovered the spring equinox was not fixed in relation to the ecliptic, but that it moved at the rate of nearly one zodiac sign every two thousand years. This gradual slippage backward is called the precession of the equinoxes. For the past two thousand years, the spring equinox has been in Pisces and is now about to enter Aquarius.

During the first century A.D., a group of loosely connected Christian sects called the Gnostics arose. This century, researchers discovered buried in Upper Egypt a Gnostic text, known as the *Pistis Sophia*, which survived the early church's purging of Gnostic literature. The text details a conversation between Jesus and his disciples after the crucifixion. In describing his heavenly sojourn, Jesus tells of the terror experienced by the archons, rulers of the seven planetary spheres, as Jesus passed through their region. Jesus told the disciples that he had weakened fate by introducing irregularity into the operation of the planets. He had not done away with their power altogether, but arranged it so that any caster of horoscopes would have a diminished chance of being accurate in their predictions.

Mary Magdalene asked Jesus whether astrology would continue to be effective, since he had not taken away the power of the planets, but had merely confused them. Mary said, "My Lord, will not then the horoscope casters and consulters from now on declare unto men what will come to pass for them." Jesus replied, "If the horoscope casters find the fate and sphere turned towards the left, according to their first extension, their world will come to pass, and they will say what is to take place. But if they chance on the fate or the sphere turned to the right, they are bound to say nothing true . . ." Jesus explained that the only planet that exercised great influence was Zeus (Jupiter). He said the Creator arranged it that way because the planets "needed a helm to steer the world and the aeons of the spheres, so that they might not wreck it [the world] in their wickedness."

Jesus explained to his disciples that the Creator arranged planets and their influences. "He bound 1,800 rulers in every aeon, and set 360 over them [i.e., 360 degrees of the zodiac] and he set five other great rulers as lords over the 360 and over all the bound rulers, who in the world of mankind are called with names: the first is called Kronus (Saturn), the second is Ares (Mars), the third Hermes (Mercury), the fourth Aphrodite (Venus), the fifth Zeus (Jupiter)."

Most Gnostics did not approve of astrology for divination, but recognized it as effective. Gnostic thinking was deeply embedded with astrological symbolism.

Neoplatonists such as Plotinus (born A.D. 203) criticized the Gnostics for believing the planets and spheres ruled with tyranny over men. Neoplatonists both rivaled and fertilized Christianity in its early development. As did Plato, Plotinus believed the stars were living beings. He said that heavenly bodies affected the disposition of the soul, and he believed that celestial movements were signs rather than the cause of the future. Carl Jung later argued something very similar in his theory of synchronicity.

Historians believe astrological principles of Mesopotamia influenced Chinese and Indian astrology. A population movement from Sumer to India and China occurred about the third millennium B.C. Similarities were found between Sumerian cuneiform writings and ancient Chinese script and folklore. A sophisticated astronomical/astrological system became an integral part of Chinese ethics and religion.

Around the fourth century B.C., when the Greek influences began to affect the country, the modern system of horoscope astrology appeared in India. According to Hindu teachings, the original source of religious wisdom came from the seven ancient sages known as the Rishis. They preserved the teachings of a civilization (thought by many to have been Atlantis) that lived prior to the Great Flood. The seven Rishis were identified with the seven stars of the constellation Ursa Major, which the Aryans revered. It was to the Rishis that the sacred hymns, known as the *Vedas*, were revealed. The concept of lunar mansions emerged from India. According to this concept, the ecliptic was divided into twenty-eight parts, each corresponding to a day of the lunar month and possessed a special significance. These twenty-eight lunar stations were used similarly as the twelve zodiac signs. Today, Indian astrologers use in conjunction both the lunar and solar zodiacs.

Around A.D. 300, astrology flourished in India, and this was the time most of Hindu astrology was set down. The Hindus widely used astrology to determine the stage of soul evolvement. They believed a mixture of free will, karma, and fate conditioned the progress of the soul from one incarnation to another and was reflected in astrology. Hindu karma consisted of three aspects: It was (1) the sum of results of acts committed in previous incarnations, (2) acts in the previous incarnation that were subject to the influence of the previous life and the exercise of free will in the present, and (3) future unrealized acts.

The early Christian church vacillated between tolerance and violent opposition to astrology. Early church scholars believed that heavenly bodies influenced people's lives. However, a sufficient exercise of will could always resist this influence. As time evolved, the general trend of Christianity was against astrology. The church violently attacked all systems of thought with any pagan association. As a result, the church's oppressive actions contributed to suppressing astrology.

In general, Christianity maintained that all divinatory arts, especially astrology, were inventions of the devil. They could be carried on only with the aid of demons. This theory arose early and persisted throughout the Middle Ages, as it became the argument of last resort. One only needs to ask how could even demons read the future in the stars if it were not written there? How does one distinguish between predictions through the help of evil spirits and those sanctioned by God? Genesis 1:14 states that the heavenly bodies were placed in the sky for the express purpose of serving as signs. Examples found in biblical history tell of God making use of astrological predictions. Examples include the miracle of Hezekiah's pillars, the star of the Magi, the darkness at Christ's death, and the celestial signs to announce his return. All divinatory arts had been permitted until the coming of Christ. At this time, the rule of demons ended, according to the Church Fathers. Unsubstantiated rumors claim that the Vatican library has one of the largest collections of astrological writings in the world. Although astrology was suppressed in Europe, it was kept alive in the Moslem world. From here, astrology later returned to Europe in a reinvigorated manner.

St. Thomas Aquinas later tried to reconcile Christianity and astrology. He taught that the stars influenced human affairs, but that the will remained sovereign. He said, "The stars governed the bodily appetites and desires, which condition most human affairs, since few can resist them." Aquinas claimed that astrology was capable of correct predictions about the great mass of humanity. Free will could rise above this influence. For several centuries Christianity and astrology existed in reasonable harmony.

During the Renaissance, kings, popes, generals, and physicians all made use of the astrologer's services. The *Amicus Medicorum* (1434), written by Jean Ganivet, showed how maladies could be cured by relating the ailment to its astrological causes, and how a person could guard against weaknesses shown in his or her horoscope.

In 1472, a comet appeared that caused astrologer Perre le Lorrain to predict the death of Pope Paul II. After this prediction, Lorrain was imprisoned and told he would be put to death if his prediction proved wrong. In the afternoon of that fateful day, the Pope was still in good health. Before day's end the Pope was dead, and Lorrain was released with great honors.

The Church revitalized its violent opposition to the science and art of astrology, especially during the years of the witch hunts. Adherents of astrology were forced underground to study this forbidden practice, which they did secretly in the lodges of the Freemasons and Rosicrucians.

THE PRINCIPLES OF ASTROLOGY

Free will means that a person's destiny is subject to his or her choices or will. All actions that we make are the result of previous causes already set in motion. Every new act brings into being chains of new causes, which in turn determine other actions. Tightly bound to the wheel of destiny by chains of necessity, no one can escape fate, according to many ancient teachings. Life experiences include many situations that cannot be controlled, dictating the need for actions independent of a person's will. On the other hand, many choices in life do not seem to be predestined. Pretty women can choose among many suitors, and scientists can choose among many research projects, all examples of free will.

People have within themselves a Higher Self in varying degrees of development. Higher Self is also known as the soul, spirit, spiritual ego, Divine Spark, and monad. This is who we really are. Our personality, or psyche, is merely a reflection of this Higher Self, astrologically symbolized by the sun sign. This is our immortal soul that sheds bodies and personalities on its evolution. The soul incarnates for the purpose of gaining experiences to develop new aptitudes and abilities, necessary for further growth. The Higher Self looks at lessons not learned, weaknesses and abilities not acquired, and assesses them for correction in the next incarnation. A physical body and personality are selected that can best aid in learning those lessons. All these factors ensure that certain experiences will be attracted to the life of the personality, experiences that have tremendous impact on the development of personality.

People react differently to their predestined handicap, resulting in different destinies. Our inner states, attitudes, and qualities determine what happens to us. A person who is chaotic and negative inside will attract like a magnet those kinds of events. By changing the inner state, one changes his or her destiny. A horoscope maps out these lessons and attitudes that a soul has chosen to experience.

A horoscope is a map of the heavens, encompassing 360 degrees, for a specific moment in time and identifies the positions of the planets and sun in different signs of the zodiac. Astrologers interpret the relationships or aspects between the planets and Earth as favorable or unfavorable influences that pertain to the specific moment for which the horoscope is cast. The most significant moment in a person's life is the moment a person is born and takes his or her first breath. Horoscopes can be cast for other occasions, such as discovering favorable conditions for marriage, birth of a new company, travel, or the future of a nation.

A natal horoscope, cast at the moment of birth, is a blueprint that outlines the basic structure of a person. It shows the ingredients and relationships that have gone into the makeup of that person. These factors are predestined and outside one's control. However, the province of will can modify and improve the basic structure established by astrology. One of astrology's greatest attributes is that it outlines basic structure and shows limits. It shows what things you must accept about yourself and what areas you can change. People have free will, but yet are predestined. We are born into a certain predestined set of outside circumstances that we can master by exercising will over our inner selves. A person's inner development and growth are subject to free will. Proper inner attitude is the first step in mastering outside events. We all have free will to handle negative predestined events, especially our inner reactions.

Most problems in life arise from trying to be something we are not and from not being what we could and should be. Whatever sun sign we happen to be of, we can strive to express its highest form, as each sign has many levels of expression. Here, will plays a role. Signs of the zodiac symbolize different stages of natural processes. Each sign represents a different phase in the cycle. Everything in nature begins with an Aries stage and progresses through each of the twelve signs as it develops. Astrological symbolism can be applied to all disciplines. The sun sign represents the psychological attitude toward life. Many astrologers suggest that reaching the highest expression of the sun sign is impossible for a person unless one also learns the lessons of its opposite sign. The Aries must be like the Libra, the Scorpio like the Taurus.

Astrology is the science of time, the synchronization of astronomical time with biological time. Genethlical astrology is used to analyze and predict the future of individuals. Astrology used to determine the answers to a question based upon the horoscope is called horary astrology.

The Planets

In Western astrology, the position of Sun, Moon, and planets in the zodiac sign determine the character of the individual. Their relationship by angle to each other and what house they reside in indicates destiny, circumstances, and relationships. The planets symbolize the character of people as determined by their position in the zodiac sign and symbolize specific cosmic functions.

The Sun reveals the nature of the individual will that motivates the force behind all action. It is the most powerful source, and vitality is the Sun's key word. The Moon rules emotions and moods that influence the will of the sun.

Mercury symbolizes channels of communication, understanding, translation, and intelligence. It rules the logical process. Venus reflects individual capacity for affection, warmth, and love. Artistic expression, aesthetics, beauty, harmony, and luxuries are associated with Venus. On the other hand, Mars symbolizes the principle of assertive energy expressed in aggression and sex. Aspects of it are associated with anger and sexuality.

Jupiter is the planet of expansion, the great benefactor. It is the planet of luck, good fortune, and unearned opportunity. Associated with it are happiness, laughter, and generosity. Jupiter is considered the planet of knowledge, wisdom, and strong spirituality. Next comes Saturn, considered the teacher and taskmaster of the zodiac. Saturn can bring constant trials or creative challenges. Saturn slows things with delays, obstacles, anxiety, and depression. It also provides discipline, tenacity, and inner strength by teaching patience and perseverance.

Uranus is the planet of sudden disruption and surprises, and possesses qualities of originality, genius, innovation, and eccentricity. Neptune, the planet of illusion, symbolizes mysticism, deception, and escape. It represents the principle of divine unity through self-sacrifice, empathy, and intuition. Neptune causes confusion, deceit, drug addiction, alcoholism, and suicide. Pluto, the outermost planet, influences the unfolding of major social changes and mass occurrences.

The Signs

Signs of the zodiac represent the relatively eternal or unchanging feature in a person's character. There are twelve signs of the zodiac and each sign is symbolized by a human figure, living thing, or an image. A planet rules each sign and is also associated with a house in the horoscope. The ruling planet expresses many of the same qualities as the sign it rules. For example, Mercury rules Gemini, and both have similar attributes. Zodiac signs correlate with certain qualities divided into positive and negative aspects.

Aries (22 March to 20 April, key word is pioneer, ruled by Mars)
     Positive: outgoing, original, dynamic
     Negative: foolhardy, impatient, deceitful
Taurus (21 April to 21 May, key word is builder, ruled by Venus)
     Positive: loyal, dependable, patient
     Negative: excess pride, self-indulgent, greedy, stubborn

Gemini (22 May to 22 June, key word is communicator,
  ruled by Mercury)
  Positive: versatile, talkative, creative
  Negative: two-faced, superficial, unstable
Cancer (23 June to 23 July, key word is nourisher,
  ruled by Moon)
  Positive: Nurturing, love of home, protective
  Negative: possessive, retiring, moody
Leo (24 July to 23 August, key word is dramatizer,
  ruled by Sun)
  Positive: regal, entertaining, commanding
  Negative: pompous, domineering, conceited
Virgo (24 August to 23 September, key word is analyzer,
  ruled by Mercury)
  Positive: practical, analytical, intellectual
  Negative: critical, hypochondriac, worrier
Libra (24 September to 23 October, key word is conciliator,
  ruled by Venus)
  Positive: romantic, aesthetic, fair
  Negative: lazy, temperamental, indecisive
Scorpio (24 October to 22 November, key word is investigator,
  ruled by Pluto)
  Positive: scientific, passionate, dedicated
  Negative: secretive, revengeful, cold-blooded
Sagittarius (23 November to 22 December, key word is
  philosophizer, ruled by Jupiter)
  Positive: jovial, freedom-loving, logical
  Negative: blunt, fanatical, intolerant
Capricorn (23 December to 19 January, key word is director,
  ruled by Saturn):
  Positive: executive, conservative, ambitious
  Negative; depressive, miserly, pessimistic
Aquarius (20 January to 19 February, key word is humanizer,
  ruled by Uranus)
  Positive: diplomatic, altruistic, inventive
  Negative: selfish, eccentric, impulsive
Pisces (20 February to 21 March, key word is harmonizer,
  ruled by Neptune)
  Positive: intuitive, sympathetic, artistic
  Negative: martyr, indecisive, melancholy

The Houses

The ecliptic, which is a circle of 360 degrees, represents the horoscope. It is divided into twelve equal pie-shaped segments, or houses, of 30 degrees each. Each house covers two hours in time as the Earth rotates under the constellations. The First House is the degree of the zodiac rising on the eastern horizon. At the specific moment for which a horoscope is cast, the first house signifies the outward personality, the behavior that we show to the world. This ascendant relates to "I" and rules the physical body.

The Second House is associated with money, possessions, and self-value. Learning, teaching, and writing are associated with the Third House, the house of communication. The house of the soul is the Fourth House, which concerns real estate, home, and family.

In the Fifth House is pleasure associated with sports, talents, romance, and children. Routine work is found in the Sixth House, the house of health, service, pets, and hygiene. The Seventh House is the house of marriage, partnership, and legal matters. The Eighth House symbolizes occult forces, the house of birth, death, sex, and unearned income.

The Ninth House is the house of travel, religion, philosophy, and higher education. Mental expansion is found there. Tenth House attributes represent the professions, reputation, aspirations, and rewards. In the Eleventh House are found hopes, wishes, friendships, and associations. The Twelfth House is the house of self-imposed limitations, secrets, confinements, and large institutions. It also involves mysticism, karma, and spiritual retreat.

Planets and zodiac signs fall within a house's sphere of activity according to the chart position. Their influences will be felt in their house position, or departments of life. For example, if a planet falls in the Seventh House, its influence will be focused in the area linked with the Seventh House, that is, in relationships of an emotional and business nature. A planet placed in a particular house on the birth chart affects the area of life represented by that house in a fashion typical of the planet.

Elements, Gender, Qualities, and Progression

Four elements compose the universe: fire, air, earth, and water. In combination, these elements make up our total experience, with each element having specific properties. Each of the twelve signs has characteristics of one of these elements.

Fire symbolizes aggression, energy, enthusiasm, courage, vitality, passion, willfulness, and leadership. Fire signs include Aries, Leo, and Sagittarius. These challenging, loving people are impulsive, self-reliant, and goal-oriented.

Air represents intellect, logic, communication, changeability, sociability, enthusiasm, and adaptability. Gemini, Libra, and Aquarius are air signs, operating from the mental plane rather than the emotional plane. Often they are talkative, amusing, and sociable, but become easily bored and seek stimulation.

Earth symbolizes practicality, materialism, structure, conservatism, caution, stability, and strength. Taurus, Virgo, and Capricorn are the Earth signs. Earth individuals are usually practical, patient, purposeful, and well-grounded.

Water represents emotion, love, feelings, psychic ability, sensitivity, jealousy, manipulation, and creativity. The water signs are Cancer, Scorpio, and Pisces. Water people are emotional and search for the most satisfactory kind of emotional outlet. Good at sensing and perceiving, they know how to control and influence others.

Signs are either masculine or feminine, feminine being receptive and masculine more direct. Often masculine signs suggest extroverted attributes and feminine signs suggest introverted attributes. Masculine signs include Aries, Gemini, Leo, Libra, Sagittarius, and Aquarius. Feminine signs are Taurus, Cancer, Virgo, Scorpio, Capricorn, and Pisces.

Cardinal, fixed, and mutable describe qualities of the signs. Enterprising and outgoing describe the cardinal signs of Aries, Cancer, Libra, and Capricorn. Fixed signs are resistant to changes and include Taurus, Leo, Scorpio, and Aquarius. The mutable signs of Gemini, Virgo, Sagittarius, and Pisces are adaptable to change.

Astrologers use progressions of planets to assess, rather than predict, trends in the lives of clients. They do so by calculating the planet positions for the day in question. Positions of planets and their aspects to one another help determine the trends an individual will have on his or her earthly sojourn.

Chinese Astrology

Many differences are found between Chinese astrology and Western astrology. Chinese view their environment in terms of numbers and like to arrange their ideas into numerical groups. Numbers up to twelve are associated with groups of concepts important to the Chinese mind. Two primary units are essential to this numerical scheme: the Yang and the Yin, which are aspects of the universal life force Chi. Chinese see the world as a series of combinations of numbers based on Yang and Yin. Yang is associated with masculinity, brightness, and motion, and Yin with femininity, darkness, and rest. Those who understood the system were thought to possess the key to all knowledge.

The Chinese lunar calendar is the longest chronological record in history, dating from 2637 B.C. A complete cycle takes sixty years and is made up of five cycles of twelve years. Twelve animals are each assigned to one of the twelve years. According to legend, the Lord Buddha summoned all the animals to come to him before he departed from Earth, and only twelve came to bid him farewell. As a reward, he named a year after each of these twelve animals. First came the Rat, then the Ox, the Tiger, Rabbit, Dragon, Snake, Horse, Sheep, Monkey, Rooster, Dog, and Boar. Many attributes of the ruling animal correspond to the character of the person born during that year.

During the complete sixty-year cycle, each of the animal signs combines with the five main elements: Wood is ruled by the planet Jupiter, fire by Mars, earth by Saturn, metal by Venus, and water by Mercury. The five elements further split into magnetic poles, the Yin and Yang, the positive and negative.

The day begins at 11:00 p.m. in the lunar calendar, and the twenty-four hours of the day are divided into twelve sections of two hours apiece. One of the animal signs rules each division. As in Western astrology, the sign which rules the time of birth is the ascendant and strongly influences the personality.

The Yin aspect of a planet signifies the element in its raw material state, and the Yang aspect of a planet signifies the corresponding element in its man-modified state. In addition to the twelve zodiac signs, the Chinese have ten planetary signs, five under Yang and five under Yin.

THEORIES ON HOW ASTROLOGY WORKS

On first thought, it is almost impossible to conceive that a planet millions of miles away can influence actions of people on Earth. However, as one examines the scientific evidence, one clearly sees a correlation between planetary bodies and behavior.

Duke University researcher Dr. Leonard J. Ravitz plotted the change in electrical potential emitted in normal and in mentally ill people. His research found marked changes coinciding with the phases of the moon and seasons. The more disturbed the patient, the more the electrical potentials were affected. Ravitz could successfully predict the emotional state of his patients by noting the phases of the moon.

Abram Hoffer, M.D., found depressed patients reacted most strongly in March. Neurotic patients' symptoms peaked in January and July.

Studies of 33,000 births in 1938 by Japanese researcher Dr. Yamahaki showed a significantly higher frequency of births during the full and new moons. An American study of one-half million births replicated the study.

Eugene Jonas, M.D., a Czech physician, discovered that the ability of a woman to conceive is stronger under the phase of the moon (full, gibbous, or new) that prevailed when she was born. At the time of conception, he found the gender of the child depended on whether the moon was in a positive (masculine) or negative (feminine) sign of the zodiac. Jonas' predictions of sex were correct 87 percent of the time on 250 birth charts. Other independent studies found his methods of predicting gender to be 94 percent and 83 percent correct.

Electrical engineer John H. Nelson discovered most magnetic storms that cause radio disturbances occur when two or more planets are in conjunction or in 180 degree and 90 degree aspects to the sun. He could predict disturbances in the atmosphere with 80 percent accuracy and radio disturbances with 93 percent accuracy. He also discovered that he could make good predictions when a number of planets lined up in 60 degree and 120 degree angles to the sun. These angles correspond to the sextile and trine of traditional astrology, the beneficial aspects. Nelson also found the harmonics of the squares and oppositions produce detectable effects such as all multiples of 15 degrees and 7.5 degrees.

Rudolf Tomaschek, Ph.D., a well-known physicist and astrologer, carried out a statistical analysis of 134 major earthquakes. His research found that Uranus, Pluto, and Jupiter were positioned in statistically significant aspects, but that the Sun and Moon played no role in earthquake prediction.

Statistical studies have also found a correlation between road accidents and solar activity. Accidents were sometimes four times higher than average after a solar flare. Research has also shown that increased sunspot activity parallels an abnormal increase in blood lymphocytes.

Harvard professor Ellsworth Huntington, Ph.D., discovered inexplicable cyclical data everywhere he looked. He discovered the cycles usually fell into time slots of 3.4 years, 9.6 years, 11.2 years, and 18 years. Sunspot activity is on a 11.1 year cycle. Cycle studies infer that, on a large scale, cyclical factors affect human and animal psychology. After one studies the cycles of life, it is difficult not to conclude that rhythms have some functional significance, are set in motion by some external source, and driven by some kind of timing device.

Cycles occur throughout all nature. The sun's celestial clock sets the migratory patterns of birds. A small Pacific worm, called the *Palolo Viridis*, has an annual swarming date that corresponds to a particular new moon of the year. Rhythmic behavior of fireflies, grasshoppers, and locusts cause them to swarm according to an unidentified stimulus. The daily cycle of sleep and wakefulness is triggered by light and dark. The Moon's recurring phases trigger ocean tides. Plankton yields in Lake Michigan occur on four-year cycles.

Cycles also occur outside nature. Four-year cycles have been found in U.S. commodity prices and pork prices in Germany. Ten-year cycles occur in cigarette production, cotton prices, and U.S. Post Office revenue. Cyclic forces determine booms and recessions, prosperity and depression. Prices of commodities have cycles, as do political views. Scientists concur that cycles occur in single living organisms as well as social and historical events.

Biorhythms have been a popular concept over the past several decades. Research by Herman Swoboda, Wilhelm Fleisss, and Alfred Teltscher shows that everyone is affected throughout life by three internal cycles: physical, emotional, and intellectual. The physical cycle takes twenty-three days to complete and affects resistance to disease, strength, coordination, and other body functions. The emotional cycle includes factors of sensitivity, mood, perception, and mental well-being, and takes twenty-eight days to complete a cycle. Lasting thirty-three days, the intellectual cycle includes memory, alertness, and logical aspects of intelligence. The cycles begin at the time of birth and pass through a positive or high phase and decline through a negative phase. Biorhythms relate cyclic behavior patterns, and some countries, such as Japan, take these cycles very seriously.

Our bodies seem to be governed by a whole series of internal clocks that change our body chemistry. Our clocks are not always synchronized with everyone else's, and this explains morning and night people. Some people experience extreme cycles in which hormones vary by 50 percent during the day. A woman is on a twenty-eight-day cycle. Japanese studies show that body weight changes correspond to an annual cycle, with a high point in the summer. Research shows blood is thinner in the summer. Hormones that control water content appear to be on an annual cycle. Babies conceived in January will have brains that are influenced by the mother's body chemistry in March. A mother's body chemistry changes according to the seasons, thereby changing the chemical message transmitted to the unborn infant. Scientists are beginning to understand how personality and behavior are in one sense predetermined. Physical conditions on Earth may be associated with cycles caused by an unknown source. The evidence strongly suggests that subtle energy from planetary bodies may affect behavior. Several theories propose how this subtle energy may be associated with astrology.

Research by English astrologer John Addey found that astrological events are based on the harmonics of cosmic periods. Waveforms characterize certain things, perhaps a particular profession, and reflect their harmonious relationship with distant planetary events. Addey believed the universe at the cosmic, biological, and molecular level is a complex of waveforms whose periodicity may range from nanoseconds to millions of years. He asserts that objects, events, people, nations, and planetary systems may be linked in incomprehensible ways according to principles of physics and astronomy. These principles were explicitly discovered through astrology. Addey theorized that different clocks, whether molecular or cosmic, drive and set in motion different aspects of life on Earth.

Prague researcher, Johann Kepler (1571 - 1630), provided empirical confirmation of the harmony of spheres. With a Neoplatonist outlook, Kepler was both an astronomer and astrologer. His research uncovered the elliptical orbit of the planets and a ratio of their distances. Kepler literally provided physical proof of the Pythagorean concept of the harmony of spheres. He tried to demonstrate that the distances between the planets could be related to perfect solids, which in turn bore harmonic relationships to one another. He believed these relationships were not coincidental, but key to the meaning of shapes and forms.

Kepler tried to calculate the literal sounds emitted by the planets, maintaining this music could be heard only by the sun, which embodied the Divine Principle. Thinking he had rediscovered the Egyptian secret, Kepler tried to show this as the principle behind the facts of astrology. His astronomy was astrology. Astrology was explained by Kepler in terms of the principle of musical resonance. The soul, he said, vibrates to the music of the spheres. He asserted the harmonic basis of the planetary aspects should be expanded. For example, if the 90 degree angle (corresponding to the fourth harmonic, one-fourth of 360 degrees) was operative, then its harmonic fractions and multiples of those fractions, the 45 degree and 135 degree angles, should also be sensitive and incorporated into interpretation. Astrologers do not know how astrology works, though they know that it does. Kepler tried to explain it with harmonics.

Frank A. Brown, Ph.D., professor of biology at Northwestern University, proved that under constant conditions, all living things have continuously imposed upon them environmental rhythms of natural geophysical frequencies such as tides and weather patterns. He performed his rhythmic research on rats, potatoes, beans, flies, crabs, and so forth. Kepler would have disagreed with the word "impose" but would have maintained that Brown's natural geophysical frequency was Pythagoras' harmony of spheres. Brown had a difficult time explaining how minute differences of energy levels could cause such dramatic changes in the entire organism. He hypothesized that a minute application of energy sets off a chain reaction that culminates in the vast amount of energy expended in the organism.

Astrology researcher Jeff Mayo hypothesizes in *The Planets and Human Behavior* that astrology may be the result of magnetic fields. Each planet has its own magnetic field and a gravitational effect on every other planet. A continuous harmonic counterbalancing interplay of gravitational forces exists among every body in the solar system. Mayo writes that the galactic system bounded by the Milky Way is one of 10,000 million galaxies in the observable universe. Life is one great energy system in an ever-decreasing scale, from galaxy to solar system, from star to planet, from Earth to man, and from man to atom. Each energy system is seen as separate cell, yet is dependent upon and maintained by other cells. Each cell is an organized energy system centered upon itself but functioning interdependently with other energy systems.

Some researchers speculate that the genetic code is the response of the united sperm and ovum to the complex of cosmic frequencies prevailing at the moment of conception. However, character is determined at the moment of birth, not conception.

The universe contains energy in the form of cosmic rays, which are essentially streams of particles. Gravity, another force, is a weak vital force. Scientists know how it acts, but do not know why. Outer galaxies recede at very high velocities due to cosmic repulsion, another force we do not understand. Humanity has much to learn about the forces of the universe. However, just because we cannot understand them, does not mean they are not real. This also applies to astrology. At this time we can only speculate on how it works, but as we will see, scientific evidence strongly suggests planets do affect our lives and character.

THE SCIENCE OF ASTROLOGY

According to traditional scientists, to be valid, astrology should stand up to scientific rigor. However, few scientists are willing to investigate astrology, and few astrologers are scientists. Astrologers claim there are too many variables in a horoscope, making it difficult to research. A few pioneer scientists have applied statistics to astrology and have proven beyond a reasonable doubt that there is a correlation between planetary position and behavior, suggesting that planets do affect behavior.

Paul Choisnard, a French astrologer/scientist, was the first to apply statistical methods for testing the validity of horoscopes. Choisnard said, "The occultists, on the one hand, are reluctant to admit that positive science is by itself capable of reconstituting a knowledge which they believe to be of a priestly nature, a knowledge to which they hold the key. The scientists, on the other hand, find it more difficult to retract their scepticism and admit that astrology is valid."

Choisnard proved significant astrological factors were involved in early mortalities regarding the Sun-Mars relationship. He also found a significant Moon-Mercury relationship in the chart of philosophers, a favorable Sun-Moon aspect with celebrities, and certain aspects of Mars in soldiers' charts. Swiss astrologer Karl Ernst Krafft, who became a victim of Hitler's purge, continued Choisnard's attempt to prove astrology by statistical means.

French astrologer Alexandre Volquire was an outspoken critic of the scientific method. He said, "Whether one likes it or not, it [astrology] is the open door to the sacred domain which transcends present day science and where there is no place for statistics. It is the science of the soul, and the soul will always escape the scalpel of arithmetic."

In 1975, 192 leading scientists, including 19 Nobel Prize winners such as Linus Pauling, signed a manifesto against astrology in an American journal, *The Humanist.* It was intended as the death sentence for astrology. The manifesto concludes, "It has been proven that astrology has no scientific base and that there is well-established proof of its nonexistence." Instigating the article was Professor Bart J. Bok, who admitted he at one time thought about doing statistical studies of astrology but later decided it was a waste of time. Carl Sagan refused to sign the manifesto because it had the tone of scientific authority. These elitist scientists totally ignored the scientific research of a particular French scientist/astrologer, Michael Gauquelin, who has provided the best scientific evidence for astrology.

Gauquelin believed that in proper astrological research, the specific birth hour is of crucial significance because it fixes the position of the planets in their daily movement, that is, in their houses. Luckily for him, in 1793, the French passed a law requiring the hour of birth be included on all birth registrations.

In 1951, after gathering names and birth times of 576 French doctors from the register offices in France, Gauquelin came across some interesting findings. He pinpointed two important aspects in a chart, the rising (Ascendant) and the culmination (Midheaven). He discovered these French doctors were born at the rise or culmination of two planets, Mars and Saturn. None were born at the rise and culmination of Jupiter. He then replicated the study on 508 famous doctors, with the same results. Both studies were compared with a control group.

In less than three years he acquired more than six thousand birth dates of famous French figures distributed over ten professional groups. Guaquelin discovered the rise or culmination of Mars favored the success of sports champions and exceptional leaders. Actors and politicians had Jupiter significantly more in the rising or culmination sector of the horoscope than any other. For scientists, Saturn was either rising or culminating. Artists, painters, and musicians were not born when Saturn was rising or culminating.

Guaquelin then applied his research outside France and acquired 7,000 birth dates and birth times in Italy, 3,000 in West Germany, 3,000 in Belgium, and 2,000 in the Netherlands. He attempted thirteen repetitions of the French study and in each case the results correlated with the French experiment.

For two thousand years astrology has included the idea of astral heredity. Kepler asserted that people's horoscope resembled those of their parents because the souls are in sympathy. Guaquelin wanted to research this hypothesis and gathered 30,000 dates and hours of birth for parents and their children, with the potential for 15,000 comparisons. He found that children tend to be born when a certain planet has risen or culminated, the same planet in the same region of the sky as the birth of their parents. The probability of this happening by chance was less than one million to one. This related to planets that are most massive and closest to earth, including the Moon, Venus, Mars, Jupiter, and Saturn. Heredity similarities were found between father and child, mother and child, and were distributed equally between boys and girls. Planetary heredity became weaker over generations and less marked from grandparent to grandchildren. All planetary effects on heredity disappeared in children whose birth did not occur naturally but was caused by surgery or drug intervention. Guaquelin hypothesized that parents transmitted some genetic factor influenced by the similarity of the natal position of a planet.

Guaquelin decided next to research personality characteristics by collecting 5,000 biographical documents of 2,000 famous people with known birth dates and birth times. He extracted 50,000 personality traits from the biographies, including 6,000 traits for sporting champions, 10,000 traits for scientists, 18,000 for actors, and 16,000 for writers.

He found that sporting champions were energetic, courageous, and obstinate, characteristic of traditional Mars traits. Successful actors were elegant, vain, funny, talkative, and eccentric, which often characterized many of the traditional Jupiter traits. Famous scientists were quiet, methodical, and scrupulous, attributes often associated with Saturn. Famous writers were sensitive, witty, subtle, dreamers, and imaginative, attributes often associated with the Moon. This correlation between character attributes and profession would happen by chance one time in one hundred thousand.

Guaquelin published a study in the *British Journal of Social and Clinical Psychology* reporting that introverts were born significantly more often when Saturn was in the section of rise or culmination. Extroverts were born more often when Mars and Jupiter were in rise or culmination, and when Saturn was not in those positions.

Next, Guaquelin studied 6,400 mentally ill people and 623 murderers. He found no related planetary aspects and concluded that planetary effects do not affect abnormal psychology. He also found no planetary effect with suicides. Guaquelin found it difficult to research ordinary people because they had no written biographies. Guaquelin could not scientifically prove zodiac symbolism of Sun signs, but he did prove that the traits (symbolism) of Mars, Moon, Jupiter, and Saturn corresponded to scientifically observable and measurable reality.

The number of hereditary similarities between a child and parent were two times greater when a child was born on a day with disturbed geomagnetism compared with a quiet day. Guaquelin's findings found a significant relationship between planetary effects and geomagnetism.

Trying to explain astrology, Guaquelin said the Sun acted as a motor, and the solar field as the medium. The Moon and closest massive planets cause a disturbance in this field. The stronger the disturbance, the more intense the child feels it at birth.

Astrologers assert that part of each person's character is predetermined at birth. Educators have found a correlation between the season of birth and IQ of their students. Observers of professional people have found that each profession seems to have a stereotypical personality. For example, a doctor has a different personality from a professional athlete, even though there is a range of personalities in each profession. With this background information, Edmund Van Deusen conducted a study correlating birthdays with various professions. He started with the assumption that the season of birth does not affect a person's choice of profession. If true, this would mean that the birth dates of all doctors, writers, professional athletes, politicians, and so forth would be evenly distributed throughout the year. Van Deusen's results were quite startling as he proved convincingly that personality, as determined by birth date, did contribute to choice of profession. He hypothesized that the personality pattern revealed by the surveys was a function of chemical changes in the mother's body during the period between conception and birth. Something happened to affect our lives that was directly related to the season of birth. Van Deusen hypothesizes in his book *Astro-Genetics* why particular sun sign personalities are drawn to certain professions. A brief summary of Van Deusen's findings follows. Only the sun signs are reported here, but Van Deusen found that many of the profession's birthdays were grouped together in adjacent months or similar seasons.

Profession	Number	Most Frequent	Odds*	Least Frequent	Odds*
Journalists & Editors	2,088	Scorpio +20.9%	1:200	Capricorn -19.3%	1:200
Librarians	5,111	Libra +21.6%	1:200	Capricorn -34.2%	1:200
Authors	2,931	Virgo +13.5%	1:50	Gemini -9.5%	1:20
University Scholars	13,183	Sagittarius +4.9%	1:20	Scorpio -8.4%	1:200
College Athletes	4,006	Leo +10.8%	1:40	Aries -6.8 %	1:10
Prof. Baseball Players	8,024	Libra +10.6%	1:200	Gemini -14.1%	1:200
Businessmen	5,047	Cancer +7.5%	1:15	Sagittarius -13.5%	1:200
Young Women Achievers	7,694	Leo +10.9%	1:200	Gemini -10.4%	1:200
Singers	1,055	Aquarius +15.6%	1:10	Virgo -30.7%	1:200
Composers	4,698	Capricorn +17.8%	1:200	Virgo -21.2%	1:200
Musicians	2,616	Pisces +22.9%	1:200	Cancer -14.3%	1:100
Actors	1,552	Taurus +14.1%	1:15	Cancer -17.3%	1:50
Celebrities	1,515	Taurus +18.4%	1:40	Scorpio -21.2%	1:50
Scientists	10,123	Capricorn +5.4%	1:20	Leo -7.9%	1:100
Lawyers	5,477	Gemini +17.0%	1:200	Pisces -10.4%	1:100
Clergymen	8,762	Gemini +5.7%	1:20	Capricorn -9.6%	1:200
Elementary Teachers	5,056	Leo +8.7%	1:50	Capricorn -10.6%	1:200
Physicians	5,000	Leo +12.3%	1:200	Aries -8.8%	1:50
Psychiatrists	5,015	Scorpio +9.2%	1:30	Leo -15.7%	1:200
Bankers	2,696	Virgo +27.2%	1:200	Taurus -29.8%	1:200
Labor Leaders	432	Leo +43.2%	1:100	Capricorn -40.1%	1:200
Community Leaders	4,651	Aries +20.0%	1:200	Gemini -10.5%	1:100
Politicians	5,022	Libra +9.4%	1:40	Aries -8.0%	1:40
Government Officials	5,013	Gemini +9.0%	1:40	Taurus -10.0%	1:100
Congressmen	4,985	Capricorn +13.6%	1:200	Cancer -14.2%	1:200

(*means the odds of it occurring by chance. Odds of one in twenty are scientifically significant)

At the time of the study there had been twenty-nine men elected as first-term presidents. Ten were born during the winter and eleven during the fall. Only eight were born during the half-year represented by spring and summer.

Van Deusen hypothesized these significant findings are due to changes in the mothers caused by the seasons. Changes in the chemical message were transmitted to the unborn infant. The genetic expression of our brains, the basic structure and organization, is directly affected by our mother's body chemistry, asserts Van Deusen. This may give the first clue in the search for a scientific explanation of personality patterns as revealed by birthday surveys.

Other scientific studies have validated astrology. Psychiatrist Carl Jung studied 500 marriages using one thousand horoscopes. He found a highly significant tendency for the woman's Moon to be in conjunction with the man's Sun. Leon Lasson found scientific significance in the horoscopes of 134 politicians when Mars aspected the ascendants and descendants. Venus aspected the ascendants of

190 artists, and mercury aspected the ascendant and descendant of 209 actors and writers.

John Addey researched the charts of 970 nonagenarians (people in their nineties) taken from *Who's Who*. He found no significant difference in sun signs accounting for their longevity. However, he found significant separative planetary aspects in the charts of 970 nonagenarians. He concluded this preponderance of widening planetary aspects made astrological sense because nonagenarians might typically be expected to share an ability and propensity to conserve energy, and not waste or play havoc with their physical resources, as is noted with separating planets.

Addey followed this research with a study on polio victims. It was a medical fact that polio victims present a recognizable type: bright, nervous, and active. Addey hypothesized that polio victims might show a preponderance of applying aspects. His scientific study supported this hypothesis as polio victims were clearly linked by astrological factors. Addey explained there was created a waveform corresponding to a harmonic of a year that significantly occurred. Polio victims tended to be born in the 12th harmonic, with the strongest being the 120th harmonic. His research showed that a child born every third degree (irrespective of the zodiac division) is 37 percent more likely to contract polio than a child born in the two intermediary degrees. This occurred by chance one time in one thousand.

Don Bradley, an astrologer statistician, also proved the concept of harmonics. His study of 2,593 clergymen found they were born on days corresponding to the 7th harmonic, occurring by chance one time in one hundred.

Vernon Clark, an American psychologist, studied the abilities of twenty astrologers. The astrologers were given charts of ten people in well-defined professions, such as teachers or doctors. He asked the astrologers to match the professions with the astrological charts. Seventeen of the twenty astrologers correctly matched the charts, this result occurring by chance one time in one hundred. They also significantly matched ten pairs of horoscopes with histories, correctly matching the horoscopes of ten cerebral palsy patients with a control group of ten non-cerebral palsy subjects. Clark's experiments were subjected to the scrutiny of statisticians and could not be faulted. Science can validate astrology.

NUMEROLOGY

Numerology also plays a role in the character and destiny of a person. According to the Pythagoreans, numbers are the first principles of all things in nature, the basis of all things. Pythagoras used numbers to synthesize cosmic knowledge. He taught that all of Heaven is a musical scale and number. The number one, the monad, was the principle of all numbers and contained all the properties of other numbers.

Pythagoreans treated numbers geometrically. By taking their geometric properties as the properties of solids (being of three dimensions), everyday objects were actually made up of their theoretical geometric shape.

Pythagoras was the first to state that mathematical ratios were involved in musical harmonic relationships. He studied those intervals most important in the tuning of the Greek scales. Impressed by the harmonic discovery, he believed he had come across the basic laws of the universe.

Simplicity of ratios and their containment within the important and powerful decad (ten), brought all things back to the unity they revered (1+2+3+4 = 10). Pythagoreans used this principle in the generation of figures. He generalized this knowledge of the relationship between music and numbers, making it the basis of any true knowledge of the soul and cosmos.

Pythagoras became most famous for his concept of the "music of the spheres," and with this concept, he attempted to explain the whole plan of the universe. He believed the physical bodies in the heavens moved so rapidly that they emitted a sound (as when swishing a stick in the air). Spatial intervals between the seven planets and the spheres of the fixed stars corresponded to the mathematical ratios for the notes of the octave in the diatonic scale (diatonic scale relates to a major or minor musical scale comprising intervals of five whole steps and two half-steps). The sounds emitted by the planets would also correspond to the mathematical ratios of the notes of the octave in the diatonic scale. Pythagoras said both the cosmos and soul are ordained according to number, and the soul itself is harmony.

The Pythagorean's reverence for numbers led them to endow individual numbers with symbols. For example, the number four symbolized justice. Justice essentially involved a reciprocal relationship between persons, and reciprocity was embodied in a square number. The most scared numbers were one, two, three, and four. These four numbers became known as the tetraktys that made up the decad. Tetraktys symbolized the magnitude of point, line, surface, and solid; they symbolized the bodies of fire, air, water, and earth; the seasons of spring, summer, fall and winter; the ages of infancy, youth, manhood, and old age; and symbolized societies such as man, village, city, and nation. Philolaus (460 B.C.) writes, "for it [the tetraktys] is great, complete, all achieving, and the origin of divine and human life and its leader . . ."

Pythagoreans believed the nature of number is the cause of recognition, giving guidance and teaching to every man about the unknown. All things by themselves or their relationship to one another is made clear by the essence of numbers. Numbers allow all things to be perceived through sense perception and make them recognizable and comparable with one another. Truth, the Pythagoreans taught, is related and in close natural union with the numbers.

Plato also believed numbers were the keys to understanding the soul and universe. He said the soul of the world could be partitioned into a particular series of numbers consisting of 1, 2, 3, 4, 8, 9, and 27, forming the Platonic lambda. These numbers defined a musical scale with the world soul consisting of a harmonica. Later this series of numbers defined the actual sizes of the planetary orbits. The inner life of man could be made into music, according to Plato, and the attainment of a moral life occurred when the man's soul tuned in harmony with the universe. In Plato's *Timaeus*, the world soul (a religious concept), world harmony (a musical concept), the regulation of the cosmos (a concept of physics), and the soul of man (a psychological concept) are fused. The concept of the world soul is a mathematically ordered creation, according to Plato.

Kepler differed from Pythagoras and Plato in that he insisted that speed and not distance of the planets from the sun determines the musical celestial harmony. He believed God had put his mathematical signature on all things, and that the soul generates and corresponds to the harmony of the universe. According to Kepler, the geometrically formed soul becomes excited when the heavenly bodies that are traveling in the zodiac form certain angles with one another, the basis for astrology. Kepler agreed with Plato that mathematics draws the soul upward, and musical harmony provides the clue to the structure of the universe.

With this historical background, numerology is based upon the sacred science of numbers. It is an offshoot of the melodious rhythm of the mathematical precision that controls all creation. As in astrology, numerology is an indicator. A study of man and his relation to the cosmic power, numerology helps answer many questions about the soul of man and his purpose on Earth. Knowledge about numerology remains limited because few scientific studies have been applied to this discipline. However, this does not negate its validity.

The purpose of a soul's development is to lose fear, give love, render service, and seek enlightenment. This leads to cosmic consciousness. Planning this incarnation, each person lays out his or her own path or destiny. This destiny is revealed in the birth date and the letters that constitute the name. Numerology points out to each individual his or her shortcomings and helps give a better understanding of life on Earth. The sacred science of numerology is based on two pieces of information, the name and birth date. The birth date reveals much information regarding the path of life or destiny. This path of life never changes.

In numerology, all numbers are reduced to a single digit, from one to nine. Nine is the ultimate cycle of humanity, as life revolves around a nine-year cycle. All numbers of the birth date need to be added and then reduced to a single digit, with two exceptions. Eleven and twenty-two are never reduced and are called master numbers. A birthday of August 27, 1944, can be reduced to the number 8. The numbers of the birth date ($8 + 2 + 7 + 1 + 9 + 4 + 4 = 35$; $3 + 5 = 8$) add up to 8. Any path of life (birth numbers) will have a positive or negative effect. The positive side enables a person to expand growth and understanding in a positive way. Negative effects present obstacles in achieving full potential of growth. This would be karma attached to the path, which can be overcome. A summary of the number symbology follows:

One (key word, attainment)
   Positive effects: individual action, originality, self-confidence
   Lesson: to fall back on one's own resources
Two (key word, association)
   Positive effects: cooperation, peace, companionship
   Lesson: do not put self before others

Three (key word, pleasant)
    Positive effects: self-expression, harmony, enjoyable activities,
        sociability
    Lesson: to be self-expressive
Four (key word, limitation)
    Positive effects: hard work, loyal, good organizer
    Lesson: overcoming hatred
Five (key word, freedom)
    Positive effects: frequent changes, travel, unattached
    Lesson: to overcome indulgences
Six (key word, responsibility)
    Positive effects: power and greatness, adjustment, achievement
    Lesson: to serve without using tyranny
Seven (key word, perfection)
    Positive effects: philosopher, wisdom, spirituality, peace
    Lesson: to overcome aloofness and to be humble
Eight (key word is material)
    Positive effects: power, material success, generous, dependable
    Lesson: to control love of power and money
Nine (key word, encompassing)
    Positive effects: intuition, knowledge, traveler, kindness
    Lesson: to overcome immorality and fickleness
Eleven (key word, inspiration)
    Positive effects: super intelligence, idealism, intuition,
    an old soul
    Lesson: to be easy to live with and to relax
Twenty-two (key word, builder)
    Positive effect: universal outlook
    The name is the other key in numerology. One can calculate the
name number from the full name given at birth. Each letter of the
alphabet is assigned a number.

```
1 2 3 4 5 6 7 8 9   Example:
a b c d e f g h i   Name: John Lee Smith
j k l m n o p q r         1685 355 14928  Add numbers: 57
s t u v w x y z     Reduce to single digit 5+7=12, 1+2=3
```

To determine the name number, one needs to add the total letter value of the full name. A person's expression and challenge in
life are the sums of all letter values in the name. This is the total of
what each individual has to work with in life. This number should
help determine what type of life occupation one chooses. The soul

urge can be determined by the numbers associated with the vowels in a name. One's quiet self in life can be determined by finding the value of the consonants.

The life path consists of three subpaths: formative cycle (until maturity), productivity cycle (working years), and harvest cycle (retirement period). Determining the formative cycle is the month number, the productivity cycle is the day number, and the year number determines the harvest cycle.

Each person in their incarnation has a specific life purpose. On a conscious level, many do not know their purpose in life, but on a subconscious level they know through dreams, intuitions, or innermost longings. Often the hidden force behind our personality shapes our careers, relationships, and direction of life. For those who have not discovered their purpose, life can be very frustrating.

Dan Millman believes he has discovered one of the universal laws that can guide us toward our life purpose. In his book *The Life You Were Born to Live*, Millman shows how one can help determine the life purpose from the birth date. According to Millman, each digit of our birth number uncovers hidden meanings related to our life purpose. Energies from the digits that make up our birth number contribute to the attributes of our life. The order of each digit in the birth number determines its degree of influence. Digits to the left have less influence than those on the right. For example, consider a birth date of March 19, 1954 (3+1+9+1+9+5+4 = 32; 3+2 = 5 written as 32/5). The entire birth number 32 (left hand digits) indicates the particular blend of energies that make up the individual's life path. The right-hand digit of the birth number (5) indicates the primary life purpose. Millman calls this number the summit. To reach this summit and experience the fulfillment of our destiny, we must pass through the left most digits 3 and 2, with their associated issues and energies, to bring them to maturity.

Our life purpose is what we are here to do, not what comes the easiest. Life is supposed to be a challenge. Our life purpose represents the summit, and our birth numbers point the way, reflecting the force of predestination, according to Millman. He states that, "No life path is harder or easier, except to the degree we make it." How we pursue this path is up to us, because we all have free will.

According to Millman, each prime number has issues and energies. The numbers reflect inborn promises because accompanying each birth number are deeply rooted psychological drives toward the fulfillment of destiny. Along with this intrinsic drive comes fear. Millman explains that the dynamic tension between our desires and our fear creates the theater of our lives. The energy of

1 is creativity and confidence;
2 is cooperation and balance;
3 is expression and sensitivity;
4 is stability and process;
5 is freedom and discipline;
6 is vision and acceptance;
7 is trust and openness;
8 is abundance and power;
9 is integrity and wisdom.

Once we discover the path, we find the inspiration to strive toward the summit.

THE SEVEN RAYS

Perhaps the least scientific of the energies controlling a person's destiny is the concept of the seven rays, reintroduced to the Western world by Helena Petronna Blavatsky in the late nineteenth century. Founder of the Theosophical Society, Blavatsky received much of her information from ascended masters. The Urantia material substantiates the seven-ray concept guised in somewhat different terminology, stating that each soul is under the influence of one of seven master spirits, which are the sevenfold source of the cosmic mind, the intellectual potential of the Grand Universe. As the Urantia material reveals, the master spirits derive their origin and characteristics from the following likenesses: (1) Universal Father, (2) Eternal Son, (3) Infinite Spirit, (4) Father and Son, (5) Father and Spirit, (6) Son and Spirit, (7) and Father, Son, and Spirit. Through evolution, each ascending mortal exhibits traits which indicate one of these presiding spirits.

Blavatsky writes in the introduction of the *Secret Doctrine* that "the *Secret Doctrine* gives a clue to the sevenfold nature of man, for each principle is correlated to a plane–and the human principles are, on every plane correlated to the sevenfold forces–those of the higher planes being of tremendous power." She continues, "On the seven rays hang the seven worlds of being. These are the seven lights whose reflections are the human immortal monads–the irradiating spirit of every creature of the human family."

There are seven forces in humanity and all nature. Ancient mysticism teaches us that man is divided into seven distinct groups, which have three main subdivisions of mental, spiritual, and physical. *Rig Veda*, the most ancient Hindu text, refers to the rays. The seven wise ones fashion the seven paths, which are primarily beams of light leading to wisdom. In other words, they are the seven rays. *Rig Veda* holds the esoteric tradition of the correspondence between the seven rays, the seven fields of consciousness, and the seven groups of souls of humanity.

According to a Gnostic gospel, the *Pistis Sophia*, the human entity is the septenary ray that comes from the one light. The seven centers of energy are represented by the Sephiroth of the Kabbalah and the seven gifts of the Holy Ghost in Christianity. In Christian theology, there are seven spirits of God. Hermetic philosophy states that nature produces seven men in accordance with the seven natures of the seven spirits. "Nature gives birth to the seven notes, the septenary scale of the creative forces . . . all born from the one white ray of light . . . itself generated in darkness." Blavatsky states that the seven principles are allied to the seven states of matter and the seven forms of force, the seven rays. She emphasizes that the rays are essentially qualities of consciousness, psychological energies.

In 1922, Theosophist Alice Baily, in collaboration with the Tibetan master Djwhal Khul, expounded in more detail about the seven rays. This information is found in Baily's books, including *Initiation, Human and Solar* and *Esoteric Psychology*. She describes the evolutionary path as a series of initiations, each marking a definite expansion of consciousness. She defines a ray as one of seven forces of the Logos, one of seven great lights. Each is an embodiment of a great cosmic entity. The seven rays are divided into three major rays of aspects and four rays of attributes, which are a subdivision of the third aspect ray. The four rays of attribute produce the qualities of the three rays of aspects in greater detail. These seven rays include

1. Ray of Will and Power
2. Ray of Love and Wisdom
3. Ray of Active Intelligence
4. Ray of Harmony
5. Ray of Concrete Knowledge and Science
6. Ray of Devotion and Idealism
7. Ray of Ceremonial Order or Magic

Baily writes in *Esoteric Psychology* that the seven rays are the building forces and sum total of all that is in the manifested universe, but their essential quality and nature remain a mystery.

The soul of each human being exists on one of the seven rays. This ray determines the manner in which the soul becomes integrated with the personality. There are seven processes of integration, one for each ray, with the soul being the integrating factor. The soul is the instrument for abstract thinking, the storehouse for abstracted essence, and wisdom gained from experiences. Because of the soul, a human is capable of having self-consciousness and of developing group consciousness. A soul acquires a personality consisting of the mental, emotional, and physical bodies.

The seven rays produce all states of consciousness in all fields of awareness. Everything in the world belongs to one of the seven rays. A ray is a name for a particular force or energy type, with the emphasis upon the quality that the force exhibits.

The first Ray of Power and Will is characterized by a dynamic will and the power within a human that works on the force of destruction that will produce liberation. Characteristics include independence, courage, ambition, logic, and managing skills.

Embodied in pure love is the second Ray of Love and Wisdom. It is the ray of applied consciousness and works through the creation and development of those forms found throughout the universe. Characteristics include patience, sensitivity, intuition, calmness, understanding, and wise teachings.

The third Ray of Intelligent Activity brings in discrimination through mental activity that causes our evolutionary path. It is the energy of intelligent activity displayed in creative activity. Qualities include clear intellect, articulate speech, ability to handle money, critical attitude, and adaptability.

The Ray of Harmony, Beauty, and Art is also called the fourth Ray of Harmony through Conflict. Its main function is to create beauty through the interplay of life and form. Beauty comes through struggle. Attributes of the fourth ray include sense of beauty, creativity, harmony, intuition, sympathy, and exaggeration.

The fifth Ray of Scientific Knowledge encompasses the principle of knowledge and has produced science. Man, on this ray, learns to use all acquired knowledge to serve the inner life, and the outer form becomes the magnetic expression of the divine life. It is the ray of intelligent love. Qualities include exactitude, analysis, narrowness, true thinking, not seeing the larger issue, and power to master a chosen field.

The sixth Ray of Idealism and Devotion is reflected as a powerful devotion to the intent of the life urge. It embodies the principle of recognition and is the ideal reality lying behind the form. Characteristics of the sixth ray encompass idealism, loyalty, desire for good, reverence, religious instincts, excessive enthusiasm, aspiration, mysticism, and sacrifice.

The coordinating factor unifying the inner quality and outer tangible form is the seventh Ray of Ceremonial Magic. This ray works primarily on etheric levels and involves physical energy that spiritualizes forms. Attributes of this ray include ritual, ceremonial living, order and organization, gift of healing, narrowness, and spiritual judgement.

Consciousness expansion is the result of the activities of these seven rays, which function cyclically in various degrees throughout the universe. In the human, consciousness develops into self-consciousness, then soul consciousness, and finally into God consciousness. The seven rays come through the zodiac and solar system and emanate on cosmic levels from the most high. They are the seven great builders of all that exist, from universe to subatomic structure. The ultimate source is the Absolute, which differentiates into the Trinity of the Father, Son, and Holy Spirit. Ray one of Will and Power reflects the Father aspect; ray two of Love and Wisdom is the Son aspect, the cosmic Christ; and the Holy Spirit is symbolized by ray three or Active Intelligence. These three aspect qualities permeate all that exists.

What responds to these various ray energies is our soul, our true self, which is the Christ consciousness within us. Our sensitivity to these radiation energies determines our consciousness development. We respond according to the state of our own development. Behind each ray stands a great cosmic being, called a Lord of the Ray. The purpose of the seven rays is to bring human consciousness from the fourth kingdom to the fifth kingdom of nature, then to the sixth kingdom of the soul, and finally to the seventh kingdom of the spirit. The first three kingdoms include mineral, vegetable, and animal. Consciousness is synonymous with soul, and the seven rays carry the seven types of souls into light. The seven ray energies reach our sun by way of the twelve constellations of the zodiac.

Influences of the rays are mostly concerned with the stimulation of the soul that brings about changes in consciousness. Humans gradually respond to the soul and unfold latent potentials. Each person is sensitive and responds to ray stimulation according to his or her level of evolution.

All seven rays are always present in everybody, but only one of them is dominant, and the other six are supportive. The dominant soul ray provides the motives of one's living, determines where one's happiness lies, and is the key to one's decisions.

Different rays influence various aspects of a human. One ray may govern the physical body, another the emotional body, yet another ray governs the mental nature and personality aspects of a person. Eventually, the soul ray begins to work and dominate the other rays. Body and soul become integrated, leading to a perfect human. Finally the monadic ray takes control and absorbs the ray of the personality and soul into itself. This technique integrates each of the seven rays, the soul acting as the integrating factor.

A soul operates under the influence of cosmic, solar, and planetary energy force. It is responsible for the type of brain, mental ability, and attributes of a human who enters into an incarnation. The seven main points of focus in the etheric body are called force centers or chakras. All seven chakras are perpetually rotating wheels of energy into which the life stream enters. The subtle energy from the seven rays, planets, and Sun enter the chakras. These seven whirlpools of force swirl etheric, astral, and mental matter into activity. Development of our consciousness directly relates to the activity of these centers within the etheric body. This metaphysically explains how both astrology and the seven rays work. They influence the chakra centers, the spiritual nerve centers, that align with the central nervous column. Here transformation of cosmic subtle energy into a person's life energy takes place.

Different combinations of ray energies influence and help unfold the consciousness of each human. These beneficial energies impel, but do not compel. Ray energies are transmitted through the constellations and transfigured through the planets. The zodiac signs transmit the cosmic ray energies to the chakras.

THE SOUL'S RELATIONSHIP WITH ASTROLOGY AND THE SEVEN RAYS

One of the astrologer's most important tasks, writes astrologer Alan Oken in *Soul-Centered Astrology*, is to observe through the horoscope how the lower-self attributes can be cultivated to eventually harmonize with the energies of the soul. When the ego of the lower-self unites with the soul, the process creates a soul-infused personality capable of co-creating in the personal and collective life. Following soul infusion, a person begins to see life in a much different manner compared with the lower-self view. When the horoscope can be read from the soul's perspective, "the path to the opening of the heart and our 'other' eye becomes clearly revealed," asserts Oken. Following soul infusion, one begins to perceive the world in collective terms and one thinks more of the whole of humanity rather than self. The soul is the middle way as it stands between spirit and matter.

A soul acts as the intermediary between essence and material manifestation, providing the necessary channels through which consciousness may exteriorize and come to know itself. Through this knowing, we come to identify ourselves as Divinity in manifestation. The lower-self should be reformed and refined so that it may eventually correspond vibrationally with the soul's rhythm and life purpose. When one reads the horoscope exoterically from the perspective of the personality and esoterically from the soul, the natal horoscope will reveal the unfolding of the necessary process. Personality is a tool for one's inner creative source, but true creative intelligence comes from the soul, which is used to shape the ego. The material world is essential for our soul evolution. However, negative attachment to the material world inhibits our spiritual growth. Once the personality is infused with the soul's purpose, one's true life work can be prepared for and understood.

Our evolving consciousness links the soul and personality on individual and collective levels. It aligns the path between the lower and higher selves. An esoteric rendering of the natal chart will point out the bridge between the two selves. It helps link the lower and higher mind, the emotional body with intuition, and personal will with the will of the higher self.

Oken describes our solar system that is septenary in nature. Our planet responds to seven cosmic emanating sources called the seven rays, which have specific qualities of vibration and manifestation. The number seven was called "worthy of veneration" by the Pythagoreans in their sacred teachings. It represented the seven spirits before the throne of God who are known as the archangels. Through the seven primary forces, one creates and builds the primary structures of the manifested universe. Each of the seven planets, rays, and chakras corresponds and acts on an endocrine gland of the human body. Nothing happens in the universe that does not have its correspondence on all planes of manifestations. The law of cause and effect interconnects all these structures of planets, rays, chakras, and endocrine glands. Their interplay is vital to the nature of cause and effect and can be analyzed through a horoscope.

The nature of soul astrology concerns itself with karma and the timing of cycles of those relationships that unfold the consciousness of life through all its infinite forms of manifestations. Interplay among the seven rays, the zodiac, and corresponding endocrine glands governs the consciousness unfoldment. Love and wisdom are the primary qualities of consciousness in our solar system and for life on Earth. The energy of love in action is expressed through the forces of the soul, the quality of consciousness on any plane of manifestation. In our solar system, the words of love and consciousness mean the same thing. All problems of humanity are associated with a block in the flow of love consciousness. The Christ consciousness, writes Oken, is the revelation of the soul's reality. A soul does not have religion but is a synthesis of all religions. There is no exclusive path.

The purpose of the solar system is to unfold consciousness on all levels, and the purpose for humanity is the revelation of the soul's reality. Love is the center of all forms and manifestations of life.

Energies of the seven rays interplay with the nature of the twelve zodiac signs. Planets are lenses through which the seven rays focus themselves in the solar system. According to Oken, the seven rays are much closer to the basic energies of life than their expression through the archetypes of the twelve zodiac signs. Our destiny, governed by the planets and seven rays, guides our evolution. We learn through our painful life transformations and through our many rebirths that the quality of consciousness is love itself.

Chapter Six

CELESTIAL INHABITANTS

From Angels to Fairies

Inhabitants of the celestial realm far outnumber those on the physical world, according to many sources. If the axiom "as above, so below" is true, then who are these residents of the spiritual world? According to Genesis, angels have been a part of human history since the time of Adam and Eve. "At the east of Garden of Eden, God placed the Cherubim and a flaming sword which turned everyway to guard the tree of life." The Western ideas of benevolent spirit entities originated from Judeo, Christian, and Islamic lore, which in turn were influenced by ancient Sumerian, Babylonian, Chaldean, Persian, and Greek beliefs. The Bible, Kabbalah, and Koran frequently mention angels, and individuals from secular walks of life speak of angel encounters. People who go through a near-death experience often report seeing angels. Using both traditional religious sources and secular experiential anecdotes, explaining this intriguing phenomenon of celestial beings might be possible.

EARLY CHRONICLES OF ANGELS

For more than three thousand years humanity has believed in the concept of angels. The word "angel" originated from the Greek word "angelous," meaning messenger. Hebrew and Aramaic words for angels were used less frequently in the Bible and translated into English as "mighty," "sons of God," "ministers," "servants," "holy ones," and "watchers." According to the *New Catholic Encyclopedia*, angels are "celestial spirits who serve God in various capacities." In other words, they are nonmaterial divine entities. Angels are mentioned in the Bible almost three hundred times.

141

Angels play an important role in scriptural writings. In the Old Testament angels appear to Abraham, Jacob, Lot, Moses, Daniel, Balaam, Gideon, Joshua, Elijah, and David. The Gospels tell of angels visiting Zechariah (the father of John the Baptist), the Virgin Mary, Joseph, the shepherds near Bethlehem, and Jesus.

During the times of Jesus, angels brought messages at many significant times. Archangel Gabriel was sent by God and told Mary ". . . and behold you will conceive in your womb and bear a son, and you shall call his name Jesus." The birth of Jesus was announced by an "angel of the Lord" who appeared to the shepherds near Bethlehem. When Mary and Mary of Magdalene came to Jesus' tomb to recover the body, an angel said, "Do not be afraid for I know that you seek Jesus who was crucified. He is not here, for he is risen."

Angels gave strength and sustenance to Jesus while alone in the desert for forty days and during his agony in the Garden of Gethsemane. In the book of Acts, angels gave comfort to St. Paul during a terrible storm at sea and reassured Paul that no one onboard the ship would be harmed. An angel protected St. Peter after King Herod imprisoned him during Passover. The angel told Peter to get up quickly, and the chains fell from his hands. The angel led him past the guards and out of prison to freedom.

God tested Abraham's faith by asking him to sacrifice his son Isaac, but an angel appeared and intervened to save his son's life. An angel saved Daniel's life after he was thrown into a den of lions. Daniel told Darius, "My God sent his angels and shut the lion's mouths, and they have not hurt me, because I was found blameless before him . . . "

Biblical angels have acted as ferocious warriors. Three separate books of the Old Testament tell of the night when "the angel of the Lord slew 185,000 in the camp of the Assyrians." Herod met his death at the hands of the "angels of the Lord who smote him, because he did not give God the glory . . ." In Revelations, the archangel Michael and his fellow angels fought and defeated Satan and his rebel forces in the war of Heaven.

The Essenes, a Jewish sect that flourished during the times of Jesus, imposed an oath on those entering the order. Members were never to reveal the names of angels, for knowledge of names was power that could be abused and could distract the spiritual aspirant from the principal reason for being in the Essene community. Evidence provided in *Keepers of the Secrets* suggested that the Essenes had influential roles over both John the Baptist and Jesus.

The Jewish *Testament of Nephtali* says that seventy angels taught humanity seventy different languages. The Archangel Michael taught Hebrew to the Jews. Jewish folklore maintains that an angel led the animals onto Noah's ark, and that Michael taught agriculture to Adam. Tradition also says that angels taught Moses the art of healing. In the Old Testament, the archangel Gabriel instructs Daniel, "O Daniel, I have now come to give you wisdom and understanding." In the *Book of Jubilee,* Gabriel explains the time of creation and events of Genesis to Moses, angels impart the knowledge of herbal medicine to Noah, and they teach the practice of law and justice to all humanity.

Islamic tradition tells of the Archangel Gabriel appearing to Muhammad and commanding him to dictate the Koran. Gabriel also guided Muhammad through the seven Moslem heavens.

During the 15th century, Joan of Arc, the French heroine of Orleans, said she saw angels several times a week. Archangel Michael encouraged her to rise and lead the fight for the king of France against the English.

THE FUNCTIONS AND NATURE OF ANGELS

In his book *In Search of Angels*, David Connolly writes that traditionally the angel's foremost activity is to glorify and praise God. Often art describes and represents angels as musicians who praise and adore God with song and music, frequently depicted as a choir of singers. Scripture depicts angels as playing harps, cymbals, and trumpets. Medieval and Renaissance art portrays angels as playing viols, lutes, and flutes.

A chief function of God's creation is its administration. *The Book of Enoch* places angels over hail, wind, whirlwinds, lightning, thunder, snow, rain, daylight, moon, comets, stars, and planets. Origen, the third century theologian, wrote that angels are placed over the four elements, air, water, earth, and, fire. Some Christian scholars, including Clement of Alexandria of the second century, believed that angels propel the stars and coordinate the intricate movement of the entire cosmos. A nineteenth century Catholic cardinal wrote that angels are "what are called the laws of nature." St. Thomas Aquinas wrote that "Material things are controlled by angels." Connolly quotes Moslem scholar Mirza Ghulum Ahmad, "Whatever is happening in the physical system also does not take place without the mediation of angels. God the Almighty has called angels regulators and distributors, and they are the cause of every change and development. As a part of angels' responsibility for every visible world thing, they are said to directly serve each human being." The Christian and Islamic angels seem to play the same role as that of pagan gods.

The role of the angel as a guardian spirit is the most popular belief among angel believers. St.Thomas Aquinas writes that angelic guardianship begins at the moment of birth and continues without interruption for every moment of human life. Their roles as celestial servants to humans include guardians, guides, teachers, strength-givers, protectors of the righteous, punishers, of the wicked, and many more. Both Origen and Philo of Alexandria thought that two angels, a good and a bad, watch over each person. Scripture examples suggest that angels give comfort and strength to people, and that they protect people from harm and even intercede on certain occasions.

Connolly writes, "Angels are said to be spiritual guides on our life journey. They help to direct our hearts and minds to an understanding of God and ourselves and to finding our way in the world." From the order of God, knowledge is mediated through the angels. They guide humans to choose based on understanding of why a choice is good or bad. Angels are said to watch over national and ethnic groups as a whole. Jewish tradition teaches that an angel prince watches over each of the seventy nations of humanity.

John Wesley, the eighteenth century founder of the Methodist church, wrote, "The angels serve humankind in a thousand ways . . . . They may assist in searching after truth, remove many doubts and difficulties; they may warn us of evil in disguise and place what is good in a clear strong light." Martin Luther wrote, "God rules the world through the agency of his holy angels."

Angelologist Connolly writes that angels make the will and case of God personal and invite us to know God. Angels act as messengers, recorders, and reporters of human behavior. Following death, angels convey human souls to heaven. They carry human messages to God and convey prayers. They oversee the divine equity and karmic balance that explain the seemingly imperfect justice on Earth. The angel records and reports human behavior to higher authorities in heaven.

Gustav Davidson writes in *A Dictionary of Angels* that angels perform a multiplicity of duties and tasks that serve God. They cease-lessly chant glories as they circle the throne of God. Angels also carry out missions from God to man. "Many serve as guardians, coun-selors, guides, judges, interpreters, . . . comforters, and matchmak-ers." In occult tradition, angels are responsive to properly formulated invocations under the right conditions. They are con-jured up to strengthen faith, heal afflictions, find lost articles, increase possessions, increase fertility, protect from and destroy ene-mies, and to help in magic.

Angels, though immaterial and bodiless, are usually depicted as having or inhabiting bodies. Often they are represented as clothed or winged. Angels, like humans, possess free will. However, accord-ing to Davidson, at their creation they were given the choice between turning toward God or away from him. The choice was irrevocable. Those who followed God gained a blissful vision fixed in eternal good. Angels turning from God became eternally fixed in evil. They became demons, not fallen angels. Man continues to enjoy free will and can still choose between good and evil. Like humans, angels each have their own individual character.

Emanuel Swedenborg, an eighteenth century Swedish scientist, mystic, and theologian, believed that angels had physical bodies. For thirty years, Swedenborg experienced angels. Today the New Jerusalem Church follows his teachings. He said, "I have seen a thou-sand times that angels are human form, or men, for I have conversed with them as man to man with one alone, sometimes with many in company." Swedenborg described the angels in a very Earth-like Heaven that portrayed a material lifestyle. Angels wore colorful clothing, married, lived in houses, had gardens, and possessed things similar to those found on Earth.

According to the Roman Catholic Church, the number of angels was fixed at creation. By calculating words into numbers and num-bers into words, fourteenth century Kabbalists claimed there were 301,655,722 angels. The *Zohar* claims 600 million angelic messengers were created on the second day of creation, but also states that angels were also created on other days for other purposes. In contrast, Origen claims angels can multiply like flies. In his vision, Daniel saw 100 million angels standing before him. The Jewish patriarch Enoch, author of the *Book of Enoch,* wrote that on his sojourn to heaven, he "beheld angels innumerable, thousands of thousands, and myriads and myriads." The Koran tells of numerous angels in heaven. If each person has a guardian angel, the total number would be well over five billion. Albert the Great, mentor to St. Thomas Aquinas and a thirteenth century Dominican monk, said there were nine choirs of angels with 66,666 legions. Each legion contained 6,666 angels, bringing the total to over four billion angels. From these various sources, one can conclude billions of angels inhabit the celestial realm.

Justi, the second century Christian theologian, conjectured that angels have an ethereal body. Others speculate angels can assume corporeal forms for an earthly ministry. The Zohar states that angels can turn themselves into different shapes, sometimes female and sometimes male.

Ezekiel described Cherubim in the form of men. They had four faces and four wings with an appearance that sparkled like burnished bronze. In the Old Testament, Isaiah described the Seraphim as having six wings. In Revelations, angels are described as looking like a lion, ox, man, and eagle. These beings also had six wings with many eyes. Ezekiel also described beings as whirling wheels with rims and spokes that were full of eyes that shone. They were construed as a wheel within a wheel. Angelologist, Dr. Moolenburgh, writes that the description is almost like that of a UFO. However, throughout scripture, angels are mostly described in the shape of men. In Genesis 18:2, angels appeared to Abraham in the likeness of man. Also in Genesis, God is presumably speaking to angels, "Let us make man in our image, after our likeness."

Biblical scripture specifically mentions the wings of angelic entities as found in Exodus, Isaiah, Ezekiel, Daniel, and Zechariah. The earliest known image of a winged angel was discovered at Ur in ancient Sumer of Mesopotamia. Angels are often depicted with halos, an emanation of golden light around the head or a bright circle. Halos symbolize sanctity and spiritual brilliance. Some scholars believe the angel's luminosity is an attribute to the emanation of divine light manifested in them.

Angels were known to sin and make mistakes. Peter claimed that it was God's habit to "spare the angels when they sinned." Most scholars portray angels with the ability to distinguish right from wrong. They have free will that enables them to make personal and moral decisions.

Some researchers, such as Zecharia Sitchin, believe that accounts of many biblical angels referred to the ancient gods, such as the Nephilim, who were from the planet Nibiru. They inhabited Sumer and seeded the planet Earth with humans as we know them today.

THE HIERARCHY

The angelic world, as does the human world, functions as a hierarchy in the administration of angelic affairs. A number of hierarchial classifications have been developed over the centuries and surprisingly they all are similar. A first-century Greek named Dionysius organized the long-existing angel hierarchy, which for many centuries has been the standard for the Church. Dionysius was a member of the Athens court of justice that gathered in Areopagite. A number of angelic writings that first became well known in the sixth century are attributed to him. Scholars believe Dionysius committed to writing many angelic traditions that had been passed down orally for centuries. Called the psuedo-Dionysius, the celestial hierarchy consists of nine orders of angelic choirs. They were arranged in three orders of three choirs, and the higher orders are presumed closer in nature to God and function in roles that serve God more directly than the lower orders, which administer the physical universe.

The nine angelic orders include the Seraphim (highest order), Cherubim, Thrones, Dominations, Virtues, Powers, Principalities, Archangels, and Angels. St. Paul wrote of Principalities, Powers, Thrones, Dominions, and Virtues in the New Testament, interpreted as names of the angelic orders. The psuedo-Dionysius order corresponds to the orders established by St. Thomas Aquinas in *Summa Theologia*. Pope Gregory the Great in *Homila* also listed nine orders, but places Powers above Virtues. The Jewish *Zohar* lists ten orders. Other hierarchial orders not listed by the psuedo-Dionysius list includes Hosts, Aeons, Dominions, Martyrs, and Confessions. For the purpose of discussion in this text, we will refer to the psuedo-Dionysius orders.

Seraphim is the highest angelic order, the angels of selfless love and light. They surround God's throne of glory with a constant intone called trisagon, "holy, holy, holy." In *Enoch II*, the Seraphim are described with four faces and six wings. Isaiah, which is the only place they are mentioned in the Old Testament, also describes them this way. The Seraphim are at home in all worlds, as love knows no boundaries. They perpetually call out to one another "holy, holy, holy," the Hebrew words being "kadosh, kadosh, kadosh." Kadosh is literally the song of creation. The first word after kadosh, "Yahweh," is the word a Jew cannot speak aloud. If a person loves selflessly, then he or she is connected with the regions of Seraphim. Miracles happen when one becomes an ally of the Seraphim.

From the highest point of this world starts the creation of Heaven and Earth, the whole essence of which is love. The vibration of the Seraphim goes out into space, and in the Second Heaven, the vibration condenses and transforms into archetypes, the principal blueprint of the universe. Finally the vibrations are condensed one last time to form the world we know. This energy is stored in tiny whirls called atoms, and we perceive this energy as light. The rulers of this order have at various times been Seraphiel, Jehoel, Metatron, Michael, and originally Satan, before the fall. Some of the order defected at the time of the great rebellion.

Cherubim is the second highest angelic order. The word "Cherubim" is of Assyrian or Akkadian origin. Knowledge best describes the order of Cherubim. This order possesses intense awareness called the "logos," meaning the "word." God's awareness formulates this creative word and the Cherubim sing it. People associated with wisdom are associated with the Cherubim. Ezekiel, on his journey to Heaven, described the Cherub with four faces: human, lion, ox, and eagle. They have the likeness of man with four wings. Near each Cherubim were many-colored wheel-like structures, wheels within wheels, according to Ezekiel. Both ancient Hebrews and ancient Christians thought these wheeled forms to be a separate angelic order. The Seraphim send out a carrier wave that vibrates and forms the basic world tone, while the Cherubim modulate this carrier wave and transform it into a symphony or archetype. The Ophanim (Hebrew term for Cherubim) condenses this archetype into a visible creation.

Cherubim is the first angelic order mentioned in the Old Testament. Philo said the Cherubim symbolized God's highest potency, sovereignty, and goodness. Cherub statues stood over palace and temple entrances as guardian spirits. With flaming swords, they guarded the Tree of Life and Eden. In Revelations 4:8, the Cherubs are living creatures who render increasing praise to their Creator. In the Gospel John they are six-winged and "full of eyes within." Two golden Cherubim cover the Ark of the Covenant, the most holy relic of Judaism. Chief rulers of the Cherubim include Ophaniel, Uriel, Raphael, and Gabriel.

Below Seraphim and Cherubim on the celestial hierarchy come the Thrones, which complete the first trilogy. They reside in the

Fourth Heaven. Through the Thrones, says Dionysius, "God brings his justice to bear upon us." Rulers include Oriphiel, Zadkiel, and Zaphkiel. The Throne angels number seven, according to the *Book of the Angel Raziel*. Numbers in other sources range from four angels to seventy. The Kabbalah lists fifteen Throne angels linked in magic art.

The next triad consists of the orders of Dominations, Virtues, and Powers. Some classifications say they compose the Second Heaven. Dominations regulate angels' duties. They perpetually aspire to true lordship, and through them the majesty of God manifests. Mercy and forgiveness are the hallmark attributes of the Dominions. Zadkiel is chief of the order.

Virtues are the chief bestowers of grace and valor. Their principal duty is to work miracles on Earth. Among the ruling princes of the order are Michael, Raphael, Barbiel, and Uzziel.

The principal task of the Powers is to impose order on the heavenly pathways. According to Dionysius, the Powers stop the efforts of demons who would overthrow the world. In Pope Gregory's views, the Powers preside over the demons. Philo Judeus classified the six highest Powers as divine Logos, creative power, sovereign power, mercy, legislation, and positive power. In various epistles, St. Paul suggests that the Powers could be evil. Sammael and Camael are considered the rulers of Power.

According to Moolenburgh's research in *A Handbook of Angels*, the Powers live in the area called harmony, located in a part of Second Heaven bordering the First Heaven. Their task is to recognize opposites. They oversee souls, the territory where the great struggle is fought. The souls consist of pairs of opposites, appearing as a paradox. Good and evil, love and hate, joy and sorrow are choices a person has to make.

Rudolf Steiner sees the Powers as those who create form. Virtues are the angels who get things moving, and Dominions bring wisdom. All angels, from the highest to the lowest, look up to their Creator, and the most they can do is to transmit his will.

Comprising the lowest triad of angelic orders are the Principalities, Archangels, and Angels. Some classify them as belonging to the First Heaven. Principalities protect religion. They also watch over leaders of people, according to Dionysius, and presumably inspire them to make the right decisions. The chief ruling angels include Raquel, Anael, and Cerviel.

Overall, the category of Archangel applies to all angels above the order of Angels. It also designates a specific order of angels in the celestial hierarchy. Some scholars, such as W. O. E. Oesterly in *Angelology and Demonology in Early Judaism*, believe that the proto- types of the seven Archangels were the seven planets represented by Babylonian deities. These in turn were derived from the seven Akkadian elemental spirits known as An (Heaven), Gula (Earth), Ud (Sun), Im (Storm), Istar (Moon), Ea (Ocean), and Enlil (Hell). An, Ea, and Enlil were the three most important gods of ancient Sumer, the earliest recorded civilization. Sumerian cuneiform writings say these gods came from the planet Nibiru, which has a 3,600-year orbit around our sun.

In the New Testament, Archangels are mentioned twice: in Thessalonians and in Jude. In Revelations 8:2, John refers to the "Seven Angels who stand before God," which is commonly interpret- ed to mean the seven Archangels. Only two angels are named in the Old Testament, Michael and Gabriel, also named in Daniel. These are names that originate from Babylonian and Chaldean sources. The seven Archangels, known as the seven Holy Ones, stand before the throne of God and attend him. Sometimes called the Angels of Presence, these seven spirits are always in the presence of God. They also rule over the seven planets.

According to the *Testament of Levi*, the Archangels minister and bring goodwill to the Lord for the sins of the ignorant and of the righteous. Sometimes Archangels are called ruling princes because they rule over cities and nations. For example, Michael rules Israel. Dionysius lists seven Archangels: Michael, Gabriel, Raphael, Uriel, Chamuel, Jophiel, and Zadkiel. Most lists name seven Archangels but names vary. Michael, Gabriel, and Raphael appear on most lists, Uriel is frequently mentioned as well. Only two Archangels, Michael and Gabriel are mentioned in the Old Testament. All other names derive from nonbiblical sources.

Davidson, during his angel research, found a maze of name changes that angels passed through when manuscripts were tran- scribed from one language to another, due to copy mistakes by scribes. For example, Archangel Uriel has eleven different names in the literature. Michael has a mystery name, Sabbathiel, and has been called Shekinah, the Prince of Light, the Logos, Metatron, the Angel of the Lord, and St. Peter. Ancient Persians knew him as Beshter, sus- tainer of humanity.

Guardian Angels comprise the lowest angelic order and dwell on

the border between First Heaven and Earth. They are a class of ministering angels. Tradition asserts that at birth every human is
assigned one or more guardian angels. Matthew 8:10 states that
every child has its protective spirit. The Talmud says that 11,000
guardian angels attend every Jew through life. There are seventy
guardian angels of nations, one in charge of each nation. The
Kabbalah names the four ruling princes of the Guardian Angel
order: Uriel, Raphael, Gabriel, and Michael.

Angels are associated with other cosmic functions. Each planet
has an angelic governor. Twenty-eight angels rule the twenty-eight
phases of the moon. Each day of the week has an archangel and
angel assigned to it, as do the months. Angels rule hours and seconds. The twelve signs of the zodiac have a ruling angel, and each
of the seven heavens is governed by an Archangel. An Archangel is
assigned to each of the ten Sephiroth in the *Kabbalah*. Again, a
strong similarity exists between the function of angels and the
function of pagan gods. Are they one and the same?

CELESTIAL PERSONALITIES

Virtually all angel names, excluding Michael and Gabriel, derive
outside scripture. An early version of the *Book of Enoch* found in
Abyssinia listed names of numerous angels. The early Gnostics possessed angelic names, and the *Kabbalah* also listed celestial personalities. Angelology reached its peak during the eleventh and
thirteenth centuries, when the names of literally thousands of
angels appeared. Many were created by arranging letters of the
Hebrew alphabet or by adding the suffix "el" to certain words.
Ancient mystical societies knew the names of many angels, and correct pronunciation of the name gave one control over the celestial
entity. In early Christian times, the term angel and daimon were
interchanged in the writings of Paul and John. In Greek lore, dae-
mons were benevolent angels. Socrates had a daemon, an attending
spirit. Other sources for angelic names came from the Apocrypha,
Koran, and secular writings.

Michael: Most sources, including the Christian, Jewish, and
Islamic faith, agree that archangel Michael is the greatest of all
angels. Originally derived from the Chaldeans, Michael is considered chief of the order of Virtues and Archangels. He is the angel of
repentance, righteousness, mercy, and sanctification. Often
Michael has been equated with the Holy Ghost, the Logos, God, and

Metatron. Michael is sometimes considered the benevolent angel of death in the sense of deliverance and immortality. He is known for winning his battle with Satan.

Daniel 12:8 called Michael the "great prince" who "standeth for the children of thy people." Michael is prince of Israel and ruler of Fourth Heaven. Considered a superangel, Michael has risen above cities and nations to help those on their pilgrimage to God.

In ancient Egyptian mythology, Michael holds a pair of scales, weighing a man and woman. He weighs souls and is connected to Anubis, where souls arrive after death. Michael is known as the commander of the heavenly legions and patron of the Nile River.

Jewish tradition maintains that in the burning bush, God spoke to Moses through Michael's mouth, and that Michael carried the tablets to Moses on Mount Sinai. The *Book of Enoch* says that Michael presides over Virtues and commands all nations. Islamic lore says Michael dwells in the Seventh Heaven, being the angel of food and knowledge. Michael has appeared twice to Christians, commanding them to build churches in certain locations.

Gabriel: Gabriel is the second highest ranking angel in Judaism, Christianity, and Islamic tradition. He is considered the angel of annunciation, judgment, resurrection, mercy, vengeance, death, and revelation. Gabriel is the ruling prince of the First Heaven and resides in the Seventh Heaven. He presides over Paradise and sits on the left side of God.

Muhammad said Gabriel (known as Jibrilin) dictated the Koran to him. Gabriel was described as having 140 pairs of wings. Moslems describe Gabriel as the angel of truth who delivered the Black Stone of the Kaba to Abraham in Mecca, which is still kissed by pilgrims on their annual sojourn to this sacred city. While riding a white horse, Gabriel fought alongside Muhammad in A.D. 624, helping secure victory in the Battle of Bedr.

Jewish lore says Gabriel dealt death to the sinful cities of Sodom and Gomorrah. Gabriel was unknown to the Jews before their captivity, and he, too, is of Chaldean origin. The Jews consider Gabriel the prince of justice, the chief of angelic guards, and keeper of the celestial treasury.

Known as the messenger angel, Gabriel came to Daniel and prophesied the coming of the Messiah. Five hundred years later he told Mary that she was to give birth to the Messiah and immediately thereafter she became pregnant. He also announced to Zechariah the coming of John the Baptist, and shortly thereafter his elderly wife Elizabeth became pregnant. In apocryphal lore, Gabriel foretells the births of Samson and the Virgin Mary. According to court testimony, Joan of Arc said Gabriel was the angel that inspired her to aid the King of France.

Raphael: Also of Chaldean origin, the Archangel Raphael is the angel of healing and science and knowledge. According to the *Zohar*, he has been charged with healing Earth. Tradition says he healed Abraham and Jacob, and gave a medical book to Noah. In the *Book of Enoch*, Raphael is "set over all the diseases and all the wounds of children of men." He is a patron angel to nurses, physicians, and the blind. Raphael is one of the six angels of repentance and is the angel of prayer, love, joy, and light.

Raphael belongs to many celestial orders including the Seraphim, Cherubim, Thrones, Dominions, Powers, and Archangels. He has been described as a six-winged Seraph, and is considered one of the Apocalypses. Also considered one of seven Angels of Presence, he is an angel to one of the Sephiroth.

In Chaldean lore, Raphael is chief of the guardian angels who protects the young, the innocent, and pilgrims. He is an angel of love, joy, and providence. When Solomon prayed to God for help in constructing the Temple, God responded with a magic ring personally brought to Solomon by Raphael.

Uriel: Uriel, an Archangel associated with light, is the angel of illumination and interpretation. Uriel means "fire of God." Uriel was the messenger sent by God to warn Noah about the impending deluge. He led Abraham out of Ur and disclosed the mysteries of the heavenly arcana to Ezra. The Magi claim alchemy, which is of divine origin, was brought down to Earth by Uriel. Some believe Uriel gave the *Kabbalah* to man, whereas others say Metatron gave it. Jewish and Christian tradition says that Uriel is one of the two angels that God placed "at the east of Eden" to guard the way to the Tree of Life.

Raziel: Raziel is the legendary author of *The Book of the Angel Raziel,* in which celestial and earthly knowledge is set down. This book came into the possession of Enoch, followed by Noah, and finally by Solomon, who acquired great knowledge and power in magic from it. In the middle of the book, a secret writing explained the fifteen hundred keys to the mysteries of the world which, until then, were unrevealed. He is one of the ten Archangels of the Sephiroth and chief of the secret religions and supreme mysteries.

Metatron: Some scholars consider Metatron the greatest of all the heavenly hierarchs. He has been called King of Angels, Chancellor of Heaven, Angel of the Covenant, Chief of the Ministering Angels, and the lesser YHWH (the Tetragrammaton). According to the *Talmud,* he links the human and divine. Metatron is secretary to God and head of the archives and is referred to as the recording angel. Some have identified Metatron with the female aspect, Shekinah, the liberating angel. The *Kabbalah* claims that Metatron led the children of Israel through the wilderness following the Exodus. He is supposed to be the tallest angel in heaven, with the possible exception of Anafiel. Some believe Metatron is mightier than Michael and Gabriel.

Metatron has seventy-two mystical names and resides in the Seventh Heaven, the abode of God. Legend says he controls all hidden wisdom. Prior to the Flood, Raquel transported Enoch, while still alive, directly to Heaven and transformed him into an angel and subsequently into Metatron.

Sandalphon: The twin brother of Metatron is Sandalphon, the master of heavenly song. Elijah, the Jewish prophet, was transformed into the great angel Sandalphon, and Moses sighted Sandalphon in the Third Heaven and called him the tall angel. The *Zohar* describes him as chief of the Seventh Heaven. Legend maintains that Sandalphon carried on an endless battle with the indestructible Sammael (Satan). The *Kabbalah* attributes Sandalphon with differentiating the sex in an embryo.

Melchizedek: Called in the hierarch "most beloved by God", Melchizedek is the famous king of Salem, the ancient name of Jerusalem. It was Melchizedek to whom Abraham gave tithes. Gustav Davidson describes him as a celestial Virtue of great grace, "who does for heavenly angels and Virtues what Christ does for man." Some identify Melchizedek as the Holy Ghost, whereas the *Book of Mormon* refers to him as the Prince of Peace.

Merkabah: Merkabah, in the mystical tradition of the *Kabbalah,* is the throne chariot of God, which could ascend or descend through the heavenly halls of God's palace or seven heavenly planes. Mystics would make an inner journey to the seven planes and use secret names to ensure safe passage through each of these planes. Only recently have the mystical procedures and formulae been published in an important book titled *Meditation and Kabbalah* (1982) by Aryeh Kaplan. The Merkabah has six classes of angels that guard the throne of glory. Anafiel is chief of the eight great angels of the Merkabah and keeps the keys of the heavenly halls.

Watchers: Watchers are a high order of sleepless angels called the *grigori*. According to the *Book of Jubilees*, God sent the Watchers to instruct the children of men. After descending to Earth, they fell and began cohabiting with mortal man. In *Enoch I*, seven Watchers fell because they failed to appear on time for certain tasks. In a recently discovered text, *A Genesis Apocryphan*, Lamech (father of Noah) suspected his wife, Bar-Enosh, of having an affair with one of the Watchers. He became suspicious when Noah was born because Noah immediately started conversing with the "Lord of Righteousness," and the likeness of Noah was similar to the "Angels of Heaven." In Daniel 4:13-17, Daniel tells of seeing Watchers in a vision coming down from the heavens with a decree.

The Nephilim were giants of primeval time and known as the fallen angels (sons of God) who produced offspring from their cohabitation with the daughters of men. Zecharia Sitchin provides evidence that, according to ancient Sumerian cuneiform writings, they were the Annunaki, space travelers from the planet Nibiru.

THE FALLEN ANGELS

The concept of fallen angels did not appear in the Old Testament. In the book of Job, it describes a God-appointed adversary called "ha-satan," which meant "adversary," the title of an office and not the designation of an angel. The notion of fallen angels appears in the New Testament and is described in Revelations 12:7-9,12: "And there was war in heaven: Michael and his angels fought against the dragon: And the dragon fought and his angels, and prevailed not: neither was their place found any more in heaven. And the great dragon was cast out, that old serpent, called the Devil, and Satan, which deceiveth the whole world: he was cast out into the Earth, and his angels were cast out with him . . . Therefore rejoice, ye heavens, and ye that dwell in them. Woe to the inhabitors of the earth and of the seal for the Devil is come down unto you, having great wrath. . . ."

Having fallen from Heaven, Lucifer was no more, but now had a new name, Satan, which is the Hebrew name for adversary. His new dominion was Hell. The angels who had fallen with him were his demons, as determined by the Fourth Lataren Council in A.D. 1215.

Davidson claims that Lucifer was erroneously equated with the fallen angel Satan, due to a misreading of Isaiah 14:12, as Old Testament authors knew nothing of fallen angels. St. Jerome and other Church fathers applied Lucifer's name to Satan. Lucifer signifies a bright star and actually is the name given to Venus, the morning and evening star. Isaiah 14:12 reads: "How art thou fallen from heaven, O Lucifer, son of the morning! How art thou cut down to the ground, which didst weaken the nations!"

Angelologist Robert Marsello disagrees with Davidson and writes about Lucifer in *Fallen Angels and Spirits of the Dark*. He equates Lucifer with Satan. In Heaven, his name was Lucifer (light bearer), and he was God's most beautiful angel. Lucifer took pride in his own angelic nature and was pleased with his supernatural gifts, his immortality, and his closeness to God. However, Lucifer was not content. His pride became so great that he resented having a master at all, even God. Lucifer wanted to control his own destiny, and he rebelled. He raised a banner and recruited an army of equally discontented angels to wage war for supremacy.

Originally Satan (ha-satan) was a great angel, chief of the Seraphim and head of the Virtues angelic order. He was shown to have twelve wings. Pope Gregory paid tribute to Satan in *Moralia*, "He wore all of them [angels] as a garment, transcending all in glory and knowledge." Both Catholics and Kabbalists believe that in time Satan will be reinstated to his pristine splendor and original rank.

Satan is a great angel in the Old Testament, a most glorious one, not evil, with no hint of having fallen. In the Old Testament books of Job, I Chronicles, Psalms, and Zechariah, the term "Satan" represented an office. But in the New Testament, Satan emerges as a prince of evil and enemy of God. John 16:11 describes Satan as "prince of this world" and Ephesians 2:2 as "prince of the power of the air."

Other names for Satan include Azazel, Mastema, Beliel, Duma, Gadreel, Sammael, and Angel of Edom. Iblis is Satan's name in Islamic lore. In *Enoch* I, Azazel is one of the chiefs of the two hundred fallen angels. Church Father Irenaeus calls Azazel "that fallen yet mighty angel." In Jewish lore, Azazel was the angel who refused to bow down before Adam when the first human was presented to God. In rabbinic literature, Sammael was chief of the Satans and the Angel of Death. The *Secrets of Enoch* describe Sammael as the prince of demons and a magician, regarded as both good and evil. One of the greatest and one of the foulest angels in Heaven, Earth, and Hell, Sammael is chief ruler of the Fifth Heaven and is one of the seven regents of the world served by two million angels. Often described as the great serpent with twelve wings, Sammael belongs to the Seraphim order and is an Archangel of the Sephiroth.

Revelations says that about one-third of the heavenly hosts from all the angelic orders fell and defected. After the fall, the fallen angels became demons. Cardinal Bishop of Tusculam (A.D. 1273) and Alphonso de Spina (A.D. 1460) assert that 133,306,668 angels fell and 266,613,336 angels remained loyal. In *Levi* 3 and *Enoch II* 7:1, the fallen angels are found in the Second Heaven.

In Gnostic doctrine, the Aeons were a position in the celestial realm. They were designated as the first created beings, an emanation of God. Before the Dionysian hierarchic system, the Aeons were among the ten angelic orders. Archons, equated with Aeons, were planetary rulers who guarded the world collectively and were assigned to each of the seven spheres. In Manichaeanism (a Gnostic order) they were the "the sons of dark who swallowed the bright elements of primal man." The Gnostics believed the archons inhibited the ascent of souls to God. Demiurge was another term synonymous with archon. Gnostics considered the Demiurge to be the creators of the world and not the Supreme God. A midlevel deity, the Demiurge proposed laws for the world that the initiated could transcend. The Demiurge Iadalbaoth occupies a position immediately below the Supreme God, and the Gnostics believed Iadalbaoth created the seven Elohim.

Enoch I claimed two hundred angels fell and cohabited with the daughters of man. He named nineteen of them, including Azazel, Semyaza, Sariel, and Turel. It is believed they have retained their relative rank in their fallen state. The offspring of these angels were monsters, great giants who killed and ate any unlucky humans they caught. God enlisted Michael to remedy the situation. Michael proceeded to round up all the fallen angels and imprisoned them in Earth valleys until he came for them and hurled them into everlasting fire.

Lilit, in Jewish lore, originated as a female demon. She was an enemy of infants and the bride of the evil angel, Sammael. Tradition holds she predated Eve and had marital relations with Adam.

Little consensus exists about the organization of demons and the hierarchy of Hell. Satan is the Angel of Darkness and Emperor of the Grand Grimoire who was in charge. The demons, a huge and powerful force, included armies, parliaments, aristocrats, and commoners. Satan appointed the unholy aristocrats to rule over the empire. The demons were organized in an inverted ninefold order of angels. When Satan rebelled, he recruited several powerful Seraphim, which included Beelzebub, to fight at his side. While residing in Hell, Beelzebub learned to tempt men with pride, and when summoned by sorcerers, he appeared in the form of a fly. The Gospels describe him as a chief demon and prince of devils. He is known as "lord of flies." Leviathian was another great angel recruited by Satan, and Leviathian is believed to be the serpent who seduced Eve in the Garden of Eden. His duties place him in the maritime regions of the world.

All seven divisions of Hell have a ruler referred to as an Angel of Punishment or an Angel of Hell. Sometimes called Angels of Destruction, they are equated with vengeance, wrath, and death. According to Jewish writings, there are at least a dozen Angels of Death. The Angel of Death is not necessarily a fallen angel, as most remain an agent in God's service. Death angels include Adriel, Apollyon-Abaddon, Azrael, Metatron, and Sammael. Tartatus is the angel who presides over Hell, in charge of the torments of the netherworld. Sometimes Tartarus is identified with Uriel. Over time, descriptions of Hell have included varied landscapes of swamps, ice flows, forests, deserts, lakes, and, in most cases, of burning fire.

Some scholars, such as Peter Binsfield, a German authority on witchcraft, have identified demons with each of the seven mortal sins: Lucifer with pride, Mammon with avarice, Asmodeus with lechery, Satan with anger, Beelzebub with gluttony, Leviathian with envy, and Belphegor with sloth.

The Catholic Church describes demons as "pure" impure spirits that are highly intelligent and self-motivated. Their will is directed toward evil, corruption, and damning humanity. They use singular and often very creative methods.

Davidson cautions that all angels, good and evil, are under God. This includes all those performing deviant acts under the direction of Satan. Evil is an instrument of God who uses it for his own divine end. Overcoming evil is the means for developing perfection on our path to God.

THE SEVEN HEAVENS

Ancient mystics counted seven heavens, each ruled by an angel. Each heaven was an abode to spiritual beings, and one progressed through these heavens on the path to perfection, with the Seventh Heaven being closest to God. The Koran speaks of seven heavens, and the Persians claim that the Almighty lives in the Seventh Heaven. The concept of the seven heavens appears in *The Testament of the Twelve Patriarchs* and other Jewish Apocrypha. Ancient Babylonians told of seven heavens. However, in *Enoch II* the heavens number ten; the Gnostic Basilides claims 365 heavens, and the Jewish *Zohar* tells of 390 heavens with 70,000 worlds. As we will discover, opinions vary and often contradict about what each heaven entails.

In Islamic tradition, the First Heaven is the abode of the stars and each star has a warden. Moslems consider the First Heaven the home of Adam and Eve. The first three heavens, according to *Baruch Apocalypse* "are full of evil looking monsters." Other sources say that evil lodges in the Second, Third, and Fifth heavens. Gabriel is lord of the First Heaven, but sits on the left side of God.

Moslems say Jesus and John the Baptist reside in the Second Heaven. In Jewish tradition, the fallen angels (those who coupled with the daughters of men) are imprisoned here and flogged daily. During his visit to Paradise, Moses encountered the angel Nuriel in the Second Heaven. Admael, one of the seven Archangels who has dominion over Earth, is stationed here. Raphael and Zachariel rule the Second Heaven.

Anahel rules the Third Heaven. According to *Enoch II*, the Garden of Eden and Tree of Life exist here, and the *Book of Jubilees* claims the evil Watchers dwell here. Davidson writes that the Third Heaven is the seat of upper paradise where angels produce and store manna. The *Apocryphal* attributed to James, the brother of Jesus, says the Third Heaven is the dwelling place of John the Baptist. Hell, according to *Enoch II*, the *Testament of Levi*, and other Apocryphal texts, lies in the northern region of the Third Heaven.

The Fourth Heaven is the abode of Michael, who also rules it. Here lies the heavenly Jerusalem. Sandalphon, the angel of tears resides there, and Abel, the judge of souls also dwells there. He is the angel before which every soul must appear for judgment. This will occur after Enoch, the heavenly scribe, fetches the record book of the soul in question. In the Fourth Heaven, Muhammad encountered Enoch.

The Islamic writings say that the Fifth Heaven is the seat of Aaron and the Avenging Angel, who preside over fire. Ptolemy asserts this is the seat of God and his angels. Hebrew tradition asserts that Sandalphon rules here, although others think Michael rules.

In the Sixth Heaven reside the guardian angels of Heaven and Earth, according to Islamic doctrine. The Jews say Zachiel rules it. Kaaishim Angels abide here and praise God in endless hymns of adoration.

Cassiel rules the Seventh Heaven. The angel of solitude and tears, he illuminates the unity of the eternal kingdom. Some sources claim the Seventh Heaven is the abode of human souls waiting to be born. Others claim it is the seat of God and dwelling place of the Seraphim. Zagzagel, the angel who is prince of the Torah and of Wisdom, resides here.

THE SCIENCE OF ANGELS

With all this information about celestial beings, one must ask whether science supports the claim about angels? A Gallup poll found that half of America believes in angels. This includes 75 percent of teenagers, between thirteen and seventeen, who believed in angels in 1992, up from 64 percent in 1978. This is interesting because most Western religions say nothing about angels in their doctrinal canons and tenets of a creed.

In 1982, H. C. Moolenburgh, M.D., a Dutch physician, questioned four hundred of his patients, asking them if they had ever seen or met an angel. Thirty-one (7.75 percent) said yes. Of these, six people (1.5 percent) said the angels had a clear human shape and were not merely a large white light bringing happiness and help. From his pilot study, Moolenburgh concluded that angels do exist and are clearly part of human experience.

Many people who have had a near-death experience report they have seen and communicated with angels. They describe angels as guides, guardians, presences, friends, or companions encountered in a dark tunnel that leads the subjects toward light. To be aware of an angel presence, one must be dead or close to death. Some people describe only one guardian angel and others describe several guides present. Often described as wearing a white belted robe, they radiate serenity. Often bathed in light, the angels reassure and comfort the subjects during the near-death experience.

In a study of twenty-five near-death cases, subjects described the beings as angels (twelve times). Other responses were "a being" (four times), "a presence" (three times), "guardians," "someone," and "a woman" (twice). Children often speak of a very kind lady or gentleman.

Angels generally make themselves known to the subjects after they have gone through the tunnel. In one-third of the cases, they appeared before the tunnel experience, and generally they seek out children who are floating above their body. The study showed that 60 percent of the time, angels spoke with the subjects, always telepathically. Less than one-third of the angels reviewed the subject's past life.

Subjects experiencing near-death describe angels as having gender. Several angels were female, and they often had blond hair. No red-haired or brunette female angels were reported in the study. Male angels were blond or brunette.

Subjects often described the angels as humorous. Many wore golden belts and went barefooted. However, their feet did not touch the ground. Subjects describe angels as made of light that had a powerful attraction for the subject. Their faces might be the faces of handsome young men with supernatural beauty. No one could resist their powers. Angels have been described as moving at the speed of light.

Survivors of the near-death experience came from various religions including, Hindu, Jewish, Catholic, Protestant, and Mormon. Few differences exist among the descriptions of the angels who accompanied the subjects in the tunnel.

William Serdahely, M.D., professor at Montana State University, conducted an in-depth study of eight near-death experience survivors. The study was published in the *Journal of Near Death Studies*. He found help at one's disposal on the other side, help that was loving, warm, and thoughtful. His study also found that after a person died and was brought back to life, he or she reported guardian angels, bright lights, and cures of terminal diseases.

Raymond Moody, M.D., in his book *Life after Life*, concluded from his research that guardian angels are always with us and may intervene to save us from death or dire circumstances. In most cases, the subject heard the words, "It is not your time." Often the person does not want to return to his earthly body but the angels convince him to go back. This is almost a constant report among survivors of near-death. One can conclude that we can die only at a predetermined time, accidents do happen, and that angels see that nothing out of order occurs.

Studies show that supernatural intercessions by angels can be divided into three major groups: (1) angels or beings that arrive and vanish supernaturally; (2) inexplicable intercessions at dramatic moments, such as an audible voice, an unexplainable gesture that forestalls the tragedy, or suspension of time that allows the subject to make a proper decision; and (3) help that arrives and vanishes in the form of human nature, premonitions, dreams, or synchronicities.

People often obey a voice they have heard from within themselves. They later discover they have narrowly escaped death, which changed their lives. Afterward, they realize the voice saved them, but months later they are in denial.

Robert Monroe has been the leading researcher of out-of-body experiences. He developed the hemi-sync system in which frequencies of 200 hertz are introduced to the right ear and 208 hertz to the left. This 8-hertz difference allows the brain to relax in the alpha-brain wave state and enables many people to leave their bodies. At the Monroe Institute since 1981, thousands of people have left their body while lying on a saline waterbed in a soundproof chamber. When out-of-body, subjects encountered entities. Monroe described four attributes of this experience: (1) The beings encountered radiate a love that reassures subjects. (2) Often, the entity presents itself with its face hidden and the subject sees only a light. (3) When a being speaks, it limits itself to the subject's vocabulary. (4) When a being takes possession of a subject's body and uses the voice of the subject, the body of the subject undergoes a variation in voltage.

One conversation between a subject and his angel explained that an angel can give only ideas, and that solving problems is difficult for angels. The angel told the subject about forty-nine different planes of vibrations, and that at the angel's level, synchronizing vibrations with the physical plane was difficult. A good communication link between an angel and human depended on the spiritual evolution reached by the person.

OTHER BEINGS

Fairies: A race of tiny beings called fairies, known as elves, pixies, and sprites, has seldom been seen. In the Middle Ages, Church authorities condemned the fairies as "unmitigated devils." The fairy people in Ireland were considered a part of Lucifer's fallen angels, and were not responsible for their actions. Fairies varied in size, some larger than humans and some only a few inches in height. Fairies enjoyed humans who displayed an open, cheerful disposition, valued hospitality, and showed fondness for lovers. However, fairies could become easily irritated, and they hated stinginess. Iron and steel were a common safeguard against the fairy. Some fairies have been regarded as spirits of the streams, rivers, lakes and woods, as were the elementals and devas.

Goblins: Goblins were fairies famous for their mischief and ugly faces. They meddled in people's affairs and often hung around villages and farms. They delighted in scaring people and were known to steal valuables from their victims. Occasionally, goblins performed routine chores in exchange for a bit of bread, though they went mostly unseen.

Mermaids and Mermen: Half-human and half-fish, these creatures lived in the oceans, lakes, and streams. Mermaids were seductive singers who could lure sailors to leap overboard. Tradition says the mermaid drags her victims to a magnificent underwater kingdom where their souls live forever imprisoned. Near Edam, Holland, in 1407, a mermaid washed up in shallow water. Rescued by the villagers, she was nursed back to health, but never learned to speak. For fifteen years she lived among her rescuers, and they gave her a Christian burial following her death.

Gremlins: The gremlin was not discovered until the twentieth century. In the 1920s pilots of the Royal Air Force first noticed these airy spirits. Navigational controls would malfunction, radios would quit, and engines would stall for no reason. Gremlins lived in underground abodes around the airfield. They were described as green with large fuzzy ears, webbed feet, and stood about a foot high. Their feet provided suction for walking on the aircraft wings and could expand and act as a parachute. Occasionally, the gremlins were seen naked, and sometimes they wore tasteful clothing including spats, top hats, and red jackets. Aircraft fuel was said to be a favorite food. In recent years they have been associated with household gadgets, like televisions and computers.

Incubus: The Church Fathers claimed the incubi were angels who fell from grace because of their insatiable lust for women. Preying on vulnerable women, these demons raped women in their sleep and provoked in them strong sexual desires. These mischievous spirits were clever and could make themselves appear as real people in the form of a husband or neighbor. If a woman freely admitted an incubus to her bed, everyone else in the house would fall into a deep sleep. The sex organ of an incubus was painfully large, freezing cold, and made of iron. Deformed children were suspected to be offspring of an incubus.

Succubus: The female counterpart of the incubus was the succubus. Incubi outnumbered succubi nine to one. Considered alluring and persuasive, they used their considerable charm to seduce men, which would lead to eternal damnation. Some scholars have equated them to descendants of the classical wood nymphs.

Elementals: The elementals, an entity somewhere between a human and a spirit, were neither human nor strictly spiritual. Magicians considered them spirit creatures that personified the qualities of the four elements. Others said they were composed of flesh and blood and moved with the velocity of a spirit. Elementals were mortal and could die of disease. Each category had countless numbers that could never be imprisoned.

Gnomes: Elementals who lived inside the earth were called gnomes. These dwarfish spirits inhabited the underground and guarded hoards of secret treasures. If provoked, they could swell up to become giants. In the symbolism of Western magic, gnomes are spirits of the element earth.

Sylphs: The elementals of air, these airy spirits most resembled humans. Sylphs were friendly and easy to handle.

Salamanders: Named for the mythical lizard-like creatures that could live and breathe inside flames, the salamanders were the elementals of fire.

Undines: The elementals associated with water were undines, female sprites.

A variety of entities inhabit the spiritual world, including the spiritual souls of deceased humans and animals. As we will see, spiritual communications suggest that spiritual entities from other universes and planets also inhabit the spiritual world.

Chapter Seven

THE SPIRITUAL HIERARCHY
Ascending the Celestial Worlds

In 1955, a 2,097-page book appeared on the scene that described the spiritual realm in great detail. The book explained the Deity, the organization and administration of our universe, our planet's relationship to the universe, the genesis and destiny of man's relationship to God, and Jesus and his teachings. Information in the book, entitled *The Urantia Book*, was given by various members of the spiritual hierarchy (including Thought Adjusters and Archangels) to a contact commission led by a Chicago physician in 1934. The technique of transmission has been kept secret because the Chicago-based Urantia Foundation, which subsequently formed, did not want it to distract from the book's message. Spirit has transmitted many great books before, including the *Zohar*, the most important book of the *Kabbalah*, and *The Course in Miracles*, a contemporary book on spirit. This chapter is but a brief summary of the detailed Urantia book, which sheds light on the many mysteries of religion and the spiritual world.

Urantia, the name given to Earth by the spiritual world, is one of the many inhabited planets that make up the local universe called Nebadon. Nebadon and similar local universes comprise a superuniverse known as Orvonton. This is one of seven evolutionary superuniverses of time and space that circle the central universe of Havona, a never-ending and never-beginning creation of divine perfection. Located in the heart of the central universe is the stationary Isle of Paradise, considered the geographic center of infinity and dwelling place of the eternal God. The seven evolving superuniverses, in association with the central universe, compose the Grand Universe.

GOD

"God" is a word symbol that designates all personalization of Deity. The term "God" always denotes personality, and Deity is per-

165

sonalized as God. There are three aspects of God: (1) The Universal Father is God the Father, the creator, controller, and upholder. (2) God the Son is the Eternal Son, who is the coordinate creator, spirit controller, and spiritual administrator. (3) God the Spirit is called the conjoint actor, the universal integrator and mind bestower.

The Universe Father is the secret reality of personality. He bestows personality upon the living and controls the destiny of personality. Personality is one changeless reality in an ever-changing creative experience; it unifies all other associated factors of individuality. Only the Universal Father can bestow personality upon the living.

Universal reality is manifested in humans on the following levels: body, mind, spirit, and soul. Spirit is the divine spirit that indwells the minds of humans. The soul of a human is an experiential acquirement. As mortal entities choose to do the will of the Universal Father, the indwelling spirit becomes the father of a new reality in human experience. Morontia is the substance of their new reality and is neither material nor spirit. This is the emerging immortal soul destined to survive mortal death and begin Paradise ascension. Morontia designates a vast level intervening between the material and spiritual. It may designate personal or impersonal realities, living or nonliving energies.

The Supreme God in Havona is the personal spirit reflection of the Triune Paradise Deity (Father, Son, and Spirit). He coordinates all creature-creator activities. All space-time finite reality lies under the direction of the evolving Supreme God who is engaged in an ever-ascending mobilization and perfecting unification of all phases and values of finite reality.

The Universal Father has established the evolutionary creature's sevenfold approach to Deity: (1) the Paradise Creator Sons, (2) the Ancient of Days, (3) the Seven Master Spirits, (4) the Supreme Being, (5) God the Spirit, (6) God the Son, and (7) God the Father. This sevenfold Deity personalization in time and space and the seven superuniverses enable mortal man to attain the presence of God, who is spirit.

Universal Father is the God of all creation, the source of all things and beings. The highest ambition of all evolving creatures should be to strive for the attainment of the perfection of divinity. Divine perfection is the final and certain destiny of human eternal spiritual progress. God refuses to compel the submission of spiritual free will from his material creatures.

God is the source of truth. He is a personality to all created intelligences and a primal reality in the spirit world. God is a universal spiritual presence, whose existence cannot be proven by scientific experience. In the universes, God the Father is potential who controls matter, mind, and spirit. The minds of the evolutionary creatures originate in the local universe and must gain divine perfection through experiential transformation to spiritual attainment, which results from choosing God's will. The bodies of mortals are the temples of God, and the life sojourn of a creature is a fragment of God.

The Universal Father is an infinite personality who dwells in light that no material creature can approach. He and his creator sons are one. Humans possess the lowest type of personality and God the highest. God also has mercy, which is justice tempered by wisdom. This grows out of perfection of knowledge and recognition of mortal creatures' environmental handicap and natural weaknesses. God is love, and mercy is the offspring of goodness and love. God is present everywhere and rules eternity. He rules the local universe in the presence of his Paradise Creator Sons.

Nebadon, our local universe, was not the personal creation of the Universe Father, but was created by his son Michael. The Father does not personally create the evolutionary universes but does control them. He rules the local universe in the person of his Paradise Creator Son.

THE ETERNAL SON AND INFINITE SPIRIT

The Eternal Son is the original and only begotten Son of God. He is an associate creator of all things, and the spiritual center and divine administrator of the spiritual government of the Grand Universe. The Eternal Son is the spiritual personalization of the Paradise Father's infinite concept of divine reality, considered the eternal word of God. His ministry is devoted to the revelation of the God of love and motivates the spirit level of cosmic reality.

The Infinite Spirit is the third person of the Deity. At the instant that God the Father and God the Son conjointly conceive of an action, the Infinite Spirit instantly springs forward to execute the word. The Eternal Son bestows all possible authority and power on the Infinite Spirit. All knowledge of the Father-Son partnership is transmitted through the Infinite Spirit. It coordinates all existing energies, all universe spirits, and all real universe intellect. Infinite

Spirit is allied with mind, and it brings the universal mind into existence. It personalizes the spirit of the Eternal Son and Universe Father. Infinite Spirit is represented in the Grand Universe by a vast array of ministering spirits, messengers, teachers, adjudicators, helpers, and advisers. These are creator personalities and creature personalities.

ISLE OF PARADISE

The Isle of Paradise is the center of the Grand Universe. This is the abode of the Universal Father, the Eternal Son, the Infinite Spirit, and their divine coordinators and associates. It is the most gigantic organized body of cosmic reality in the master universe. Paradise is a material sphere as well as a spiritual abode. All the intelligent creation of the Universal Father dwells in the material abode. Therefore, the absolute controlling center of the universe must be material. God dwells in Paradise, and he is cosmically focused, spiritually personalized, and a geographical resident at the Isle of Paradise. He is literally present here, and from him flows the stream of life, energy, and personality to all universes.

Paradise is elliptical in shape and essentially flat with three divisions: Upper Paradise, Lower Paradise, and Nether Paradise. Space originates just below Nether Paradise and time just above Upper Paradise.

Upper Paradise has three grand spheres of activity: Deity Presence, Most Holy Sphere, and Holy Area. There are no material structures nor purely intellectual creations in the Deity Presence. This realm is entirely spiritual. The Holy Area has seven concentric zones called Father Paradise Mansions. Each section is exclusively dedicated to the welfare of a single superuniverse, with each of the seven sections subdivided into residential units designed as headquarters for one billion glorified individual working groups.

The central isle ends abruptly at the Peripheral Paradise. In Peripheral Paradise, one finds the landing and dispatching field for various groups of spirit personalities. The Seven Master Spirits have their seats of power and authority here, and certain paradise energy goes forth to the seven superuniverses. Paradise is large enough to accommodate an almost infinite creation.

All physical energy and cosmic current force originates on Nether Paradise. This energy will eventually return, following the completion of its circuit.

All space alternately contracts and expands. This respiration affects the horizontal extension of pervaded space and nonpervaded space, which exists in vast space reservoirs above and below Paradise. Each cycle of space respiration extends in each phase for a little more than one billion Earth years and takes two billion years for an entire cycle. Space does not touch Paradise. Paradise is the nucleus of the relatively latent zone existing between pervaded and nonpervaded space.

The center-focal point of absolute material gravity is the Isle of Paradise. Gravity is the all-powerful presence of Paradise. It is complimented by the dark gravity bodies encircling Havona and equilibrated by the upper and nether space reservoirs. Space is not responsive to gravity and acts as an equilibrant in gravity. Without this space cushion, explosive actions would jerk the surrounding space bodies. Pervaded space causes an antigravity influence upon physical and linear gravity. Local gravity pertains to the electrical stage of energy and matter. Space potency is not under the influence of any form of gravitation. This is the potential that exists within space. It includes all potential that emanates from Paradise and constitutes the space presence of the unqualified Absolute.

Paradise remains the goal for all supermaterial personalities. Not all lower spirit beings of local universes are immediately destined to Paradise. Paradise is the headquarters of all personality activities and the source of all force-space and energy manifestations. All things that have come and will come, come forth from Paradise. It is the center of all creative energy sources and the primal origin of all personalities. The Isle of Paradise is the real and far-distant destiny of the immortal souls of mortal beings, the ascending creatures found in the evolutionary worlds of space and time.

THE MASTER UNIVERSE

The master universe is far from complete. It is a series of elliptical space levels of lessened resistance to motion. It has alternating zones of relative tranquility. All forms of basic energy move around the curved path of the space levels comprising the master universe in obedience to the absolute pull of Paradise gravity. The master universe exists in six concentric ellipses composing the central universe (Havona), the seven superuniverses, and four outer space levels.

Havona contains one billion spheres of sublime perfection surrounded by enormous dark gravity bodies. Located at the center of Havona is the stationary Isle of Paradise. All seven superuniverses and all regions of outer space orbit the Paradise satellites and Havona spheres. Local universes compose each of the seven superuniverses. Nebadon is our local universe, one of the newer creations on the seventh superuniverse, Orvonton. The Grand Universe is the presently organized and inhabited creation, consisting of the seven superuniverses with a potential for seven trillion inhabited planets. These seven superuniverses are not yet completed. All forms of force-energy (material, mind, and spirit) are subject to the universal presence of gravity. Personality is also responsive to gravity, the gravity circuit being the Universal Father, Eternal Son, Infinite Spirit, and Isle of Paradise. The Grand Universe uses only 5 percent of the active functioning of the Paradise absolute gravity grasp, whereas 95 percent of cosmic gravity action of the Isle of Paradise controls the material systems. The guardians of individual destiny are the planets, constellations, universes, and superuniverse that have their rulers and, of course, are under the influence of gravity.

God is spirit, but Paradise is material. The material universe is the arena where upon all spiritual activities transpire. Spirit beings and spirit ascenders live and work on physical spheres called material reality. As the mind of any personality becomes more spiritualized and godlike, it becomes less responsive to material gravity. Physical gravity action is a determinant of nonspirit energy. Spiritual gravity action is a measure of the living energy of divinity. The Infinite Spirit reacts to both material and spiritual realities and inherently becomes the universal minister to all intelligent beings.

Infinite Spirit is to the realm of mind as Paradise is to the physical creation, and as the Eternal Son is to the spiritual universe. Endowment of intelligence is the exclusive domain of Infinite Spirit, which becomes a partner to the spiritual mind. Mind is the technique where spiritual realities become experiential to creative personalities. Mind is organized consciousness not wholly subject to material gravity; it can become truly liberated when modified by spirit. Matter is organized energy, subject to gravity and conditioned by mind.

On the other hand, spirit is the highest personal reality, and not subject to physical gravity if it is true spirit. Eventually it becomes the motivating influence of all evolving energy systems. Spirit is the goal of all personalities. Spirit transcends both mind and matter and is the fundamental reality of the personality experience. Personality is basic to all progressive experience.

THE CENTRAL UNIVERSE

The divine and perfect central universe occupies the center of all creation. Called Havona, this planetary family consists of one billion spheres of unimaginable beauty and grandeur. It is the eternal core of perfection. Around it swirls the endless process of universes that constitutes the great evolutionary experiment. The central universe consists of three circuits of Paradise and seven circuits of the Havona worlds that rotate around the stationary Isle of Paradise. Time is not recognized in Paradise, but each Havona world has its own local time. One Havona day is equal to about one thousand years of Earth time. The surrounding dark gravity bodies hide Havona from nearby inhabited universes of space and time.

Because of Havona's perfection, no intellectual system of government is required. A billion spheres of the central universe are the training worlds of the higher personalities of Paradise and Havona. They also serve as the final proving grounds for ascending creatures from the time's evolutionary worlds. There are real rivers, lakes, and other material attributes on these perfect worlds.

Pilgrims of ascent to Havona freely visit among the world circuits of their previous assignments. They may go back to the planet of those circuits previously transversed. Once the ascending mortals have reached this level, they attain emotional, intellectual, social, and spiritual maturity. These worlds are full of surprises, and monotony is not part of the Havona career.

THE SEVEN SUPERUNIVERSES

To the Universal Father, the universes do not exist, as he deals only with personalities. The universes are localized and individualized under the joint rule of the Eternal Son and Infinite Spirit. Outside Havona, there are seven inhabited universes with Seven Master Spirits radiating their influence from the Isle of Paradise. Earth's local universe presently traverses the periphery of the superuniverse Orvonton. Local universes consist of one hundred constellations and contain about ten million inhabited planets. Each local universe has an architectural headquarter world and is ruled by a creator son of God, from the order of Michael. A representative from the Paradise Trinity is called the Union of Days.

The vast Milky Way represents the superuniverse of Orvonton. At the time of this writing, Earth's astronomers have identified eight of the ten divisions of Orvonton. The headquarters of the superuniverse is provided with every phase of material and spiritual creation. All kinds of material, morontial, and spiritual beings reside in these rendezvous headquarter worlds of the superuniverse. Mortal entities who ascend the universe, passing from material to spiritual realms, never lose their appreciation for their former level of existence as they pass through these higher worlds.

Jerusem is headquarters of our local system of Satania. Satania consists of seven worlds of transitional culture, each encircled by seven spheres that include the seven mansion worlds of morontia. These are the seven heavens and humans' postmortem residence. Uversa is the headquarters of our superuniverse, Orvonton. Seven higher universities of advanced spiritual training for ascending will creatures surround Uversa. Graduating souls are dispatched for Havona from Uversa, and arriving pilgrims from associated worlds replace them. Uversa is the spiritual administration center for countless inhabited worlds.

RULERS OF SUPERUNIVERSES

The headquarters of the superuniverse is the seat of the high spiritual government of time-space domains. One of the Seven Master Spirits directs the executive branch of the supergovernment. Three Ancient of Days, who are the chief executives of the supergovernment, preside over each superuniverse. The executive branch has seven different groups; three of them come from ascendant regions and pass through Havona. After attaining Paradise, they were assigned here. Orvonton is chiefly known for lavishly bestowing a merciful ministry to the ascending mortals. Justice prevails but is tempered by mercy and power and conditioned by patience.

Earth is numbered 606 in the planetary group of Satania, which has 619 inhabited worlds. Another 200 planets are evolving toward becoming inhabited worlds. Jerusem is the headquarters of Satania in the constellation Norlatiadek, which consists of 100 local systems. Edentia is Norlatiadek's headquarters. Nebadon has 100 constellations whose capital is Salvington. The Grand Universe number of Earth is 5,342,482,337,666, which is the registered number on Uversa and Paradise.

THE SEVEN MASTER SPIRITS

The Seven Master Spirits are the primary personalities of the Infinite Spirit, and this explains why the number seven is fundamentally basic in the organization of the universe. Their primary function is supervision of the seven superuniverses. They singly and collectively represent all possible Deity functions. Each creature of every order of intelligent being must bear the characteristic stamp of individuality that represents one of the seven Paradise Master Spirits. The entire morontia career is lived under the influence of this Master Spirit. Master Spirits derive their origin and characteristics from the following likeness: (1) Universal Father, (2) Eternal Son, (3) Infinite Spirit, (4) Father and Son, (5) Father and Spirit, (6) Son and Spirit, (7) Father, Son, and Spirit. Throughout eternity, an ascending mortal exhibits traits that indicate the presiding spirit.

These Master Spirits are the sevenfold source of the cosmic mind, which is the intellectual potential of the Grand Universe. Cosmic mind represents three levels of universe reality: (1) causation - the reality domain of the physical senses; (2) duty - the arena of reason and recognition of right and wrong; (3) worship - the personal realization of divine fellowship. These three realities make it possible for a person to function as a rational and self-conscious personality.

Humans are endowed with a finite-mortal type of personality that functions on the level of an ascending son of God. Personalities may be similar but are never the same. They enable a person to be recognized.

The group of beings who help the Paradise Trinity (Father, Son, Infinite Spirit) is called the Coordinate Trinity, consisting of seven groups: (1) Trinity Teacher Sons - the liaison between Trinity and dual origin personalities: (2) Perfectors of Wisdom - personifying the wisdom of divinity in the superuniverses; (3) Divine Counselors - the counsel of Deity to the realms of seven superuniverses; (4) the Universe Censors - the judgement of the Paradise Trinity; (5) Inspired Trinity Spirit - devoted to the conscious enlightenment of universe creatures; (6) Havona Natives - direct creation of the

Paradise Trinity; and (7) Paradise Citizens - numerous groups concerned with perfecting ascending will creatures.

THE PARADISE SONS OF GOD

The sons of God have three classification heads as they function in the superuniverse Orvonton: (1) Descending Sons of God, (2) Ascending Sons of God, and (3) Trinitized Sons of God. Descending Sons include personalities who are divine creatures. Ascending Sons are mortal creatures who achieve their status by experiential participation. Trinitized Sons have composite origin and are embraced by the Paradise Trinity.

There are three orders of Paradise Sons of God: (1) Creator Sons - the Michaels; (2) Magisterial Sons - the avonals; and (3) Trinity Teacher Sons - the daynals. Four orders comprise the local universe Sons of God: (1) Melchizedek Sons, (2) Vorondadek Sons, (3) Lanonandek Sons, and (4) the Life Carriers. The Universal Father and Eternal Son bring into being the creator sons. Magisterial Sons are children of the Eternal Son and Infinite Spirit. The Trinity Teacher Sons are the offspring of the Father, Son, and Spirit. Melchizedeks are the joint offspring of a local universe creator son, creative spirit, and Father Melchizedek.

Paradise Sons reveal themselves as divine ministers, creators, servers, bestowers, judges, teachers, and truth revealers. The Magisterial Sons judge the destinies of an age and decree the fate of evolutionary races. They constitute the order of avonals, who are planetary ministers and judges. An avonal can appear in a planetary magisterial mission as an adult being by a technique not involving mortal birth. However, on a bestowal mission to an evolutionary world, avonals are born of women. Magisterial Sons are assisted by two orders of local universe entities, the Melchizedeks and the archangels. Even angels in Heaven do not know the time and manner of visitation from a bestowal avonal son. After the mortal incarnation, the avonal bestowal son proceeds to Paradise and is accepted by the Universal Father.

The regular sequence of Paradise Sons on Earth was deranged by the appearance of our Creator Son, Michael (Jesus of Nazareth), two thousand years ago. Michael has promised to return. Ordinarily, a bestowal Creator Son will serve an evolving planet only once. Paradise Sons need to incarnate once to win supreme personal sovereignty of a local universe. They never fail to achieve the goal of their bestowal mission. They do not have offspring on their sojourn, a universal restriction imposed on all orders of Paradise bestowal sons. As teachers, these sons are exclusively devoted to spiritual enlightenment of mortal men. A bestowal son needs to experience death and to experience what mortals encounter.

The Creator Sons are the creators and rulers of local universes of time and space. They are of dual origin, embodying the characteristics of God the Father and God the Son. These Paradise Sons are personalized as Michaels and go forth from Paradise to found their universes. Known as Creator Michaels, the sovereign of our local universe is Christ Michael. It is believed there are more than 700,000 Creator Sons in existence. A Creator Daughter of the Infinite Spirit of a new local universe accompanies each Creator Son. Paradise Trinity gives a Creator Son the range of creation in a universe. Only after bestowal can the Creator Son assume supreme sovereignty. When a Creator has sojourned seven times among the creatures, he finishes the bestowal career, and he is a Master Son. He must experientially penetrate seven creature levels of being through the technique of incarnated bestowal in the very likeness of the creature on the level concerned. The Creator Sons demonstrate their fitness to rule, but they also reveal the nature and attributes of the Paradise Deities. They reveal the Father's loving nature and beneficial authority.

The seven groups of bestowal sons are classified by the number of times they bestow themselves upon the creatures of their realm. Only once in the sevenfold career as a bestowed son is a Paradise Michael born of a woman, as Jesus was. The death of Jesus completed his bestowal career as he attained supreme universe sovereignty. After reaching sovereignty, a Paradise Michael has full control of all other sons of God functioning in his domain.

OTHER CELESTIAL POSITIONS

Trinitized Sons of God: Several divisions compose the Trinitized Sons of God. Trinity Embraced Sons are organized for superuniverse service and include the Mighty Messengers, who are a class of perfected mortals who have been rebellion tested and have passed the test of universe allegiance. They act as defenders of both individuals and planets that come up for adjudication. The second group is those in High Authority, perfected mortals who have exhibited superior administration ability. They foster the execution of justice and the rectification of misadaptation in the evolution universes. Those Without Name and Number comprise the third group of Trinitized Sons of attainment. They are the superior spiritual minds who have developed beyond most others the ability to worship. The Trinitized Custodians, the fourth group, are the faithful seraphic guardians who administer group affairs and foster collective projects. The Trinitized Ambassadors represent groups and assist universe rulers in administering their worlds. Only the Seven Master Spirits have authority to trinitize the union of finaliters and Paradise-Havona personalities.

Solitary Messengers: Acting as ambassadors, they are the only spirit intelligences that can be dispatched from the headquarters of one superuniverse directly to the headquarters of another. Traveling at 841,621,642,000 miles per second, they reveal the interests of mother spirits on a local universe.

Census Directors: Created by the Infinite Spirit, they keep a count of all will creatures. They are competent to give number, nature, and whereabouts of all will creatures. The Census Directors do not function on Paradise, because on Paradise all knowledge is inherent.

Graduate Guides: These entities guide mortal graduates from superuniverses through Havona by counseling and instruction, preparing the pilgrim for admission to Paradise.

Technical Advisers: These are the legal and technical minds of the spirit world. They are devoted to the interpretation of law.

Celestial Recorders: The recording angels of the inhabited planets are the source of all universe records. All records are duplicated, one of which is a spirit recording and the other a semimaterial counterpart available to all class beings. As we ascend, we can consult our records to be conversant with the history tradition of our status. Approximately eight million recorders reside in Uversa.

Universal Conciliators: They are of great value in keeping the universe of universes running smoothly.

The Morontia Companions: Souls will always be given a regular session of rest on their ascent to Paradise. Morontia companions are friendly associates that assist in the last phase of morontia experience.

Paradise Companions: This group is composed of Seraphim, Seconoaphim, Supernaphim, and Omniphim angels. They are dedicated to the service of companionship and are assigned as associates to all classes of beings.

Ministering Spirits: Angels are the ministering spirit associates of the evolutionary and will creatures of all space. There are seven orders.

Mighty Supernaphim: These are the skilled ministers to all types of beings who sojourn on Paradise in the central universe.

Pilgrim Helpers: This group functions on the seventh circle of Havona worlds. A definite requirement needs to be passed before passing from one circle to another. Pilgrim helpers assist the pilgrim in understanding the Paradise Trinity, comprehending the Father-Son partnership, and intellectually recognizing the Infinite Spirit.

Primary Supernaphim: These angels function as supernal servants of the Deities on the Isle of Paradise. On Earth they minister in seven orders of service: worship, philosophy, knowledge, conduct, ethics, chief of assignment, and instigators of rest.

Seconaphim: The Seconaphim are the angelic hosts of the local universe and the ministering spirits of the superuniverse.

Universe Power Directors: This unique group of beings has intelligent regulation of energy throughout the Grand Universe. They operate from Paradise but maintain themselves as effective power centers in all divisions of the Grand Universe.

The Supreme Power Centers: They are the intellect of the power systems of the Grand Universe and possess the secret technique of mind control of the vast network of the master physical controller.

The Corps of the Finality: This corps represents the present known destination of the ascending adjuster-fused mortals of time. There are six groups who represent this unique body of eternal destiny. One or more companies are constantly in service on Earth. They are:

1. *The Havona Natives*: They serve as teachers of the pilgrim training schools of the central universe. Being of divine creation, they greatly assist the mortal Corps of Finality.

2. *Gravity Messengers*: They are a personalized messenger corps able to transcend space and time and are attached to a finaliter company in unlimited number.

3. *Glorified Mortals*: These ascendant mortals have attained Paradise and have been sent back to local universes to administer and supervise affairs. They have found God.

4. *Adopted Seraphim*: Many faithful Seraphim, guardians of mortals, are permitted to pass through the ascendent career as do humans, and share the destiny of human nature.

5. *Glorified Material Sons*: When an evolutionary world attains the age of light and life, the material sons may elect to humanize

and embark on the evolutionary course of universal ascent. This leads to the Corps of Mortal Finaliters.

6. *Glorified Midway Creatures*: They are produced in large numbers and released from permanent citizenship status to start on their ascension path to Paradise. They accompany mortals on their ascension process.

Architects of the Master Universe: Seven groups of master architects total 28,011 beings who plan the universe. At their disposal are numerous groups of assistants and helpers. They contribute technical approval to the creator sons to organize the local universe.

Evolutionary mortals are born on the planets, pass through morontia worlds, ascend the spirit universe, and travel the Havona spheres. They find God and are mustered into the Corps of Finaliters to await their next assignment of universe service. Grandfanda, the first mortal ascender, is the Paradise chief of all six orders of finaliters.

The thirty-one papers published in the Urantia Book regarding the central and superuniverse were sponsored, formulated, and put into English by a high commission of twenty-four Orvonton administrators. This was in accordance with a 1934 (Earth time) mandate issued by the Ancient of Days of Uversa.

THE LOCAL UNIVERSE

A local universe is the creation of a creator son of Paradise Order of Michael. Comprising one hundred constellations, each local universe has one hundred systems of inhabited worlds, and each system has approximately one thousand inhabited spheres. All these universes of space and time are evolutionary. A creative plan follows a path of gradual creature evolution of physical, intellectual, and spiritual capacities. Earth belongs to the local universe Nebadon, whose sovereign is Jesus Christ, also known as Michael of Salvington. The Paradise Trinity, when Michael embarked upon the supreme space adventure, approved all his plans. Paradise architects of the Master Universe planned the material creations.

Only when the Power Directors have effected the mobilization of space energies to provide a material foundation can creation begin. The sun and planets of the emerging universe are created.

When energy-matter has reached a certain stage in mass materialization, a Paradise Creator Son appears upon the scene, accompanied by a Creative Daughter of the Infinite Spirit. Simultaneously, they begin work upon the architecture sphere, which is to become the headquarters world of the projected local universe. In our local universe, the headquarters is called Salvington, the personal headquarters of Michael of Nebadon. An interval of one billion years occurs between the arrival of living staff and the energies that first created the universe.

Following the construction of Salvington came the creation of one hundred headquarter worlds of the projected local systems. When the universe has been completely organized, a Creator Son enters to create mortal man in the divine image of Father and Son. There are 3,840,101 inhabited planets in Nebadon and our local system, Satania, has 619 inhabited worlds. Jerusem, headquarters of Satania, is 200,000 light years from the physical center of the superuniverse Orvonton. Satania is on the periphery of the local universe, toward the edge of Orvonton.

The physical system of time and space is evolutionary in origin. Perfection is progressively attained. All other realms must attain perfection through methods established for the advancement of those particular worlds. Every local universe duplicates the administration of the central universe. The Universal Father literally dwells with the souls of mortals in time and space. All will creatures in the superuniverse are of evolutionary nature, beginning from the lowest nature and ever climbing upward. A highly evolved spiritual personality continues to ascend from life to life, from sphere to sphere. Perfection of the will creature is finally achieved.

In the universe encircling Havona, a sufficient number of perfect creatures meet the need for pattern guides for those who are ascending the evolutionary stations of life. Evolutionary perfected creatures and the divinely perfect creature equal one another in degree of divinity potential, but differ in kind. Each depends on the other to attain supremacy of service. The evolutionary superuniverse depends on perfect Havona to provide the final training for ascending pilgrims.

The Creator Son, who acts for the Universal Father, oversees administration, policy, and conduct of local universes. He rules in all matters concerning ethical associations and creature relationships, whereas the Father is the source of personality. Thought Adjusters indwell human minds and are one of God's separate but unified modes of contact with his created creatures. The Universal

Father lives in the universe and in our hearts through one of the Seven Master Spirits. He has divested himself of every function that another being can perform. God's plan embraces every creature of his vast domain. It is a plan of eternal purpose and unlimited opportunity for an endless life. The goal is eternity, which is achieved by perfection.

ADMINISTRATION OF THE LOCAL UNIVERSE

Matters of the local universe are entrusted to the Creator Son and to the local universe Mother Spirit. The Son and Mother Spirit delegate executive power to Gabriel, who has jurisdiction from the constellation father, system sovereign, and planetary princes.

Michael of Nebadon is our Creator Son, the personification of the Universal Father and Eternal Son, called Christ Michael. He is the only "begotten son" personalizing the universal concept of divinity and infinity. Michael is headquartered in a threefold mansion of light on Salvington. Michael has experienced all three phases of intelligent creature existence: spiritual, Morontial, and material. He is not an Eternal Son nor a member of the Paradise Trinity, but possesses all the divine attributes and powers that the Eternal Son himself manifests. He embodies the personality presence of the Universal Father. To our universe, for all practical purposes, the Creator Son is God, as he personifies all of the Paradise Deities. The creative Mother Spirit is the local representation of the Infinite Spirit and is subordinate to Christ Michael and considered his codirector. Michael spends much of his time visiting constellations, system headquarters, and even individual planes. Sometimes, he journeys to Paradise and often to Uversa, where he counsels with the Ancient of Days. The Ancient of Days and the superuniverse government do limit Michael's power, as do the preexistent gravity circuits centered at Paradise. Michael functions as father of his local universe.

GABRIEL

Gabriel is the chief executive of Nebadon and is the only one of wisdom and majesty that was brought forth for the local universe. When Michael is away from Salvington, Gabriel assumes his place, though he is limited in attributes of divinity compared with Michael. He was created by the Creator Son and Infinite Spirit, and has creature will and imagination. Gabriel is a marvelous administrator, but is not a creator. His great brilliance allows him to arbitrate all executive appeals regarding his administration. He supevises the judicial system. There are seventy branches of the Universe courts. Only the tribunal of Orvonton decides questions of continued existence and life eternal. Father Melchizedek, Gabriel's first assistant, assumes responsibility when Gabriel is gone.

The standard day of Nebadon is equal to about eighteen days of Earth time, and its year equals five Earth years. A Satania day is a little less than three days of Earth time.

Salvington has no true legislative bodies. Legislative assemblies of the local universe meet at the headquarters of the one hundred constellations. The supreme council of the local universe is made up of three members of each system and seven representatives from each constellation. The one hundred councils of supreme sanction are in Salvington, and their presidents constitute the cabinet of Gabriel.

THE MOTHER SPIRIT

In physical creation, the universe sons provide the pattern, whereas the universe spirit initiates the materialization of physical realities. Once a Michael son proclaims that life is to be projected on a newly organized universe, the Deity-embraced Master Spirit creates a new representation of the Infinite Spirit, which is the local universe Mother Spirit. The agency of the creative Mother Spirit produces, administers, and maintains life. The Mother Spirit is independent of space but not of time. Although the Creator Son is not handicapped by time, but is conditioned by space, the universe Mother Spirit never leaves the local universe headquarters.

On the inhabited worlds, the spirit begins the work of evolutionary progress, starting with lifeless realms, then vegetable, next animal, and finally human. All living creatures possess bodily units sensitive to and responsive to directional currents of spirit. The seven adjunct mind spirits in a local universe include: wisdom, worship, counsel, knowledge, courage, understanding, and intuition. They condition the course of organic evolution that explains why evolution is purposeful and not accidental. These adjunct spirits promote, unify, and coordinate spirit-mind of the evolving planets. They lead people toward higher ideas and spiritual ideals. A mind endowed with the ministry of the Holy Spirit can choose the spiritual presence of the Universal Father. Only when a bestowal son has liberated the spirit of truth for planetary ministry to all mortals can minds be prepared for the reception of Thought Adjusters. The goal of the Divine Spirit is to teach truth and to spiritually enlighten the minds of men. It inspires souls of ascending race beings and leads people toward Paradise, the goal of divine destiny. The spirit never drives but only leads. As evolution advances, the spiritual influence on man increases.

SONS OF GOD OF LOCAL UNIVERSES

Only one Creator Son abides on the local universe, Michael, the universe father and sovereign. Of the second order of Paradise Sonships, the avonal or magisterial sons, a full quota of 1,062 dwell on Nebadon. Local sonships are the offspring of a Paradise Creator Son in association with the Mother Spirit. The four orders of sonship include (1) Melchizedek Sons, (2) Vorondadek Sons, (3) Lanonandek Sons, and (4) Life Carrier Sons.

Father Melchizedek: He acts as the first executive associate of Gabriel. Gabriel is more concerned with universe policies, whereas Melchizedek is occupied with practical procedures. Melchizedek oversees the special and emerging commissions and advisory bodies, and Gabriel presides over regularly constituted tribunals and councils of Nebadon. Neither of them is away at the same time. The original Melchizedek is always at liberty to journey to neighboring universes or to Paradise.

Melchizedek Sons: They are the first order of divine sons to approach sufficiently near the lower creatures of life and to function directly in the ministry of mortal uplift. Melchizedek sons serve the evolutionary races without the necessity of incarnation. They are midway between highest Divinity and lowest creature of will endowment. The Seraphic order of angels works with the Melchizedeks and serve as friends, teachers, and counselors to all forms of intelligence. Melchizedeks, a self-governing order, were the first on a local universe to observe the highest type of self-government. They are the hope of every universe that aspires to self-government. All spheres of self-government in Nebadon are patterned and taught by the Melchizedeks. Often these teachers influence whole worlds of advanced life forms to full recognition of the Creator Son and his Paradise Father. Melchizedeks, not always perfect, have been known to make bad judgments. If this happens, the Creator Son purges the Melchizedek of the disharmony.

Melchizedek Worlds: The Melchizedeks occupy a world of their own near Salvington. Called Melchizedek, this is the pilot world of the Salvington circuit of 70 primary spheres, each encircled by six tributary spheres devoted to specialized activities. These marvelous spheres, 70 primary plus 420 tributary spheres, are often spoken of as the Melchizedek University. Ascending mortals from all Nebadon constellations pass through training on all 490 worlds as they acquire residential status on Salvington. The pilot world of Melchizedek is the common meeting ground for all beings who are engaged in education and spiritualizing the ascending mortals of time and space. All evolutionary mortals who are graduated from their constellation training are destined to land on Melchizedek.

The Seraphic ministers conduct much of the training on the Melchizedek world. Besides educating, Melchizedeks function in unique assignments, such as putting down rebellions in Satania. Sometimes they act as temporary custodians on wayward planets. Occasionally a son can make himself visible to mortal beings, and rarely one of the order may incarnate in the likeness of mortal flesh. Seven times in Nebadon a Melchizedek has served on an evolutionary world in the similitude of mortal flesh. The Melchizedek who lived on Earth during Abraham's time was locally known as the Prince of Salem. He presided over a small colony of truth seekers at a place called Salem.

Vorondadek Sons: Approximately one million of them serve Nebadon. They serve as ambassadors to other universes and act as counselors representing constellations within their nature universe. Their work pertains largely to the legislative functions indigenous to the constellation governments.

Lanonandek Sons: They are the continuous rulers of the planets and the rotating sovereign of the systems. The Lanonandek sons serve as administrators of the inhabited worlds and are the Planetary Princes. One now serves on Jerusem. More than seven hundred, including Lucifer and Satan, had rebelled against our local universe, and three of them were local sovereigns. So much of Nebadon's trouble resulted because the order was created with a large degree of personal liberty to choose and plan. A rebellion by a Planetary Prince instantly isolates his planet. Only a bestowal son can reestablish interplanetary lines of communication.

Life Carriers: Life Carriers are entrusted with designing and carrying creature life to the planetary spheres. After life has been established, they remain for long periods to foster its development. The rulers of the superuniverses participate with the Life Carriers in creating life. Life carriers are the offspring of the Creator Son, the Mother Spirit, and the Ancient of Days. Only the Ancient of Days can decree the extinction of intelligent life. A creation of 100 million Life Carriers has been recorded on Nebadon. Gabriel, Father Melchizedek, and Nambia, who is the original born Life Carrier of Nebadon, direct them.

Life Carriers must initiate life on barren planets. They often carry actual life planning to a new world. After the physical patterns have been provided, the Life Carriers catalyze the lifeless material. With a preapproved formula, they organize the life patterns and bestow the vital spirit spark. The spark of life begins the required matter evolution in accordance with the physical, chemical, and electrical specifications of the ordained patterns and plans. Life Carriers are given one-half million years to establish life in a new world. They may manipulate the life environment favorably to direct the biologic evolutionary path. Once creature will has developed, the work of Life Carrier stops. They cannot experiment or interfere with will.

LOCAL UNIVERSE PERSONALITIES

At the head of personality stands the Creator and Master Son who is the universe father and sovereign. He is Michael. Below him resides Gabriel, the Bright and Morning Star, who is chief executive of all Nebadon. He serves as ex officio chairman of most Salvington conclaves, which often have one thousand sessions occurring simultaneously.

Brilliant Evening Stars: This twofold order represents Gabriel, with a superangel corps numbering 13,641. One-third of the corps is created and two thirds are ascending spirits who have attained this goal of exalted service. Many began their career as Seraphim, and others ascended from lower levels of creature life. They serve in many capacities, but are chiefly liaison officers of Gabriel. They customarily work in pairs and accompany the avonal bestowal sons on their planetary mission.

The Archangels: Archangels are the offspring of the Creator Son and Universe Mother Spirit. There are 800,000 Archangels in Nebadon under the direction of Gabriel. Dedicated to the work of creature survival, they function to further the ascending career of mortals in space and time. Our planet Earth has become a divisional headquarters for the universe administration and direction of certain archangel activities concerning Paradise ascension plans. This ensures the revelation of Michael's bestowal on Earth. A corps of one hundred archangels accompanies every bestowal son to an inhabited planet. Archangels usually serve and minister to the avonal order of sonship. The seventh group of worlds that encircle Salvington is assigned to the Archangels. Here the permanent record keeper keeps the record of each mortal birth through its entire universe career. The record ends when the individual leaves Salvington for the superuniverse or is blotted out of existence by the mandate of the Ancient of Days.

MINISTERING SPIRITS OF THE LOCAL UNIVERSE

There are three distinct orders of the Infinite Spirit: Angels are the ministering spirits of time; Authorities are the messenger hosts of space; and Powers are the higher personalities of the Infinite Spirit.

Seraphim: Associated with the Cherubim and Sanobim, the Seraphim are the highest personality of the Infinite Spirit. Found in all universes throughout the superuniverse, all are uniform in design. The universe Mother Spirit creates Seraphim and produces them in unit formation, 41,472 at a time. Periodically, she still creates them. These angelic orders are projected at the time of planning the evolution of mortal will creatures.

Angelic Nature: Angels are of spirit nature and origin without a material body, being definite and discrete entities. Angels can see us in the flesh, without the aid of transformers. Intellectually, they understand the mode of mortal life. Angels love humans and enjoy art, music, and humor. Not being sex-emotion creatures, they are referred to as daughters of God. They have an inherent and automatic power of knowing things, such as knowing the number of hairs on one's head. Superior to humans in spiritual traits, they never accuse or judge us. After death, humans become much like angels. On the mansion worlds we appreciate the Seraphim, on the constellations we enjoy them, and on Salvington we share their place of rest and worship.

Seraphic Worlds: The ninth group of the Salvington primary spheres is the world of the Seraphim. Their headquarters is among the most magnificent realms of Nebadon. Living in pairs, the Seraphim inhabit beautiful homes on vast estates. They are neither positive nor negative, and at least two of these angels are required to accomplish a task. Often they are organized in groups, companies, and battalions.

Seraphic Training: In their first millennium of life, Seraphim live as noncommissioned observers on Salvington and its world schools. During their second millennium, they live in the Seraphic worlds of the Salvington circuit. Melchizedeks play an important role in training all local universe angels, the Seraphim, Cherubim, and Sanobim. After serving as observers with the lowest evolving spirits, they return to associate worlds for advanced study. Seraphim, closely associated with the material creatures of the world, serve lower order spiritual personalities.

Cherubim and Sanobim: In all essential endowments, Cherubim and Sanobim resemble Seraphim. Having a similar origin, they do not share the same destiny. Almost human-like, they are intelligent, efficient, and affectionate. They are the lowest order of angels. Cherubim are positively charged, whereas the Sanobim are negatively charged. Both serve as faithful and efficient aides to the Seraphim and are the routine spirit workers on the individual systems of the worlds. Only Seraphim function as attending angels to humans, a role not afforded the Cherubim and Sanobim. When assigned to a planet, the Cherubim undergo training that includes a course on planetary usages and language. They prove very efficient in their borderland work of the physical, morontial, and spiritual domains. Like Seraphim, the Cherubim and Sanobim engage in self-improvement efforts. They may ascend to the Seraphim state, but most will remain Cherubim and Sanobim. Some are morontia Cherubim with a Paradise possibility.

Midway Creatures: Primary midwayers are the planetary historians. On the system headquarter worlds, they formulate the pageants and design the portrayals of planetary history. Midway creatures remain for long periods of time on an inhabited world and maintain the sovereignty of the creator son.

Seraphic Hosts: These very diverse Seraphic offspring fall into seven groups. They acquire knowledge and experience much as humans do.

Supreme Seraphim: They are associated with service to Paradise avonals, the divine offspring of the Eternal Son and Infinite Spirit.

These Seraphim serve as bestowal attendants, court advisers, universe orientators, teaching counselors, and recorders.

Superior Seraphim: They are in charge of the higher activities of a local universe. Being the intelligence corps of Seraphim, they belong to the personal staff of Gabriel. Superior Seraphim are the real mercy ministers of the local universe, preparing ascendent sojourners on Salvington for their last transition in the local universe. Superior Seraphim serve as helpers and teachers to fellow Seraphim. One faction serves as transporters that carry personalities who are unable themselves to journey from one sphere to another. They serve as space travelers to and from the headquarters of the local universe. When advancing from world to world, ascending mortals must depend upon Seraphim transport. After they become enseraphimed, they go to sleep for a specific time and awaken at the designated moment.

Seraphic Destiny: Seraphington is the destiny sphere for the angels. It is the angelic threshold to Paradise and Deity attainment. Seraphim may attain Paradise in hundreds of ways. Angels are not absolutely sure of their eternal future until they have attained Seraphington. Once the angel's career has been completed, they are forever servants of God. Many completion Seraphim return to their native universe to complement the ministry of divine endowment. On their long journey toward Paradise and attaining divinity and eternity, they remain devoted to the universal plan of assisting mortal evolutionary world creatures. They remain our true friends and unfailing helpers.

THE ASCENDING SONS OF GOD

Mortals represent the last link in the chains of those beings called sons of Gods. The Eternal Son passes down through a series of decreasingly divine and human personalities until he arrives at being much like us. Infinite Spirit down-steps to the expression limit in the angels who guard and guide us. God the Father cannot down-step, but he indwells humans as the indwelling Thought Adjusters. The Thought Adjusters are the only spirits of fusion potential to be identified with man during life in the flesh.

An experiential Adjuster remains with a primitive human throughout his entire lifetime in the flesh. Adjusters contribute much to the advancement of primitive humans but are unable to form eternal union with such mortals. They accomplish two things: Adjusters gain valuable experience as evolutionary intellect, and they prepare mortal subjects for possible spirit fusion (Father-fused). All God-seeking souls of this type, spirit fusion, achieve eternal life through the spiritual embrace of the Mother Spirit of the local universe, thus becoming ascending mortals of the local universe regime.

Mortal races stand as the lowest order of intelligent and personal creation. Once fusion takes place, one is recognized as an ascending son. Earth mortals may regard themselves as the sons of Gods for several reasons: (1) We are sons of a spiritual promise. (2) A Creator Son of God became one of us. (3) The spirit of the son has been poured out onto us. (4) The Universal Father has given us creature personalities. (5) A fragment of the Universal Father dwells within us.

FATHER-FUSED MORTALS

The sending of Adjusters remains a mystery of God, the Father. Fragments of the divine nature of the Universe Father carry the potential for creature immortality. Adjusters are immortal spirits, and union with them confers eternal life upon the soul of the fused mortal. When we and our Adjusters finally fuse, we become one. Once the Father has bestowed himself upon us, he demands ultimate perfection of us. Fusion with a fragment of the Universal Father is equivalent to divine validation of eventually attaining Paradise. Adjuster-fused mortals are the only class of humans who traverse Havona circuits and find God on Paradise.

Practically all surviving mortals fuse with their Adjusters on one of the mansion worlds. After their arrival on the higher morontia sphere, some do not experience this final surety of survival until they have reached the last educational world of the universe headquarters. Occasionally, an ascending mortal cannot fuse and is not guilty of failure as determined by the Ancient of Days. The morontial mortal is then immediately fused with the spirit of the Creator Son.

Adjuster-fused finaliters enjoy the widest opportunity of all. Once fused, they are not restricted to one universe or superuniverse. They can serve in all seven segments of the Grand Universe. Father-fused mortals are destined to live with the Universal Father. When a mortal finaliter is trinity embraced, the being becomes a trinitized son, such as a Mighty Messenger, and reaches his destiny, at least for the present universal age.

THE LOCAL SYSTEM ADMINISTRATION

Jerusem is the headquarters of Satania, an average capital of a local system. The sphere has seven major capitals and seventy minor administrative centers. A standard day on Jerusem is equivalent to three Earth days. Its energy source comes from space that circulates about the sphere. The full-light temperature is maintained at about 70 degrees and falls to 50 degrees during light recession. Several near-by suns give light, but Jerusem is not dependent on them. Jerusem has no high mountain ranges, but it has beautiful highlands and a unique landscape. Mount Seraph is the highest elevation at 15,000 feet. It has thousands of small lakes, but no raging rivers nor oceans. This first world of detention is far more material than spiritual.

Jerusem experiences no rainfalls, storms, or blizzards. However, it enjoys daily precipitation or condensation of moisture during the low temperature of light recession. Its atmosphere is composed of a three-gas mixture, similar to that of Earth.

At ten-mile intervals, main energy currents flow to make up the transportation system. Physical beings ride on these currents and can travel from 200 to 500 miles per hour. Material and morontia beings must use mechanical means of transportation. Spiritual beings on Jerusem proceed by liaison with superior forces and special sources of energy.

Jerusem has no organic evolution, so it has no conflicting forms of life, no struggle for existence nor survival of the fittest. An amazing intermingling of physical and morontia life dwell here.

Jerusem is a taste of Paradise to come. Its glory and grandeur are composed of beautiful architectural worlds. An intricate material economy is associated with this unique world. Perfection of mechanical technique and physical achievement is a hallmark of Jerusem.

Mount Seraph is the point of departure for all transport Seraphim. They depart every three seconds throughout the light period. Transports take off at twenty-five miles per second and reach a speed of several thousand miles per second away from Jerusem. Transports arrive on a crystal field called the "sea of glass." This area is the receiving station for various orders of beings who travel by Seraphic transport.

Superuniverse and Paradise-Havona broadcasts are received on Jerusam in liaison with Salvington. This involves a technique with a polar crystal, the "sea of glass." Three distinct receiving stations adjust to the reception of broadcasts from the local worlds, constellation headquarters, and capital of the local universe.

A considerable portion of Jerusem is assigned as residential areas. Great buildings of both material and morontia type are found there. The purely spiritual zone is very exquisite. Jerusem is unique because it is home to material, morontia, and spiritual personalities. Residential sites, assigned to major groups of universe life, are called Jerusem circles. They include residences for (1) Sons of God, (2) angels and higher spirits, (3) universe aides, (4) master physical controllers, (5) assigned ascending mortals, (6) courtesy colonies, and (7) Corps of Finaliters. Fashioned from differing materials, the residential grouping consists of seven concentric successive elevated circles constructed along the same lines.

Located in one thousand transparent department squares is the executive administration of the system. Ten administrative departments are found there, which include: (1) Physical Maintenance, (2) Arbitration and Ethics, (3) Planetary and Local Affairs, (4) Education and Melchizedek Activities, (5) Constellation and Universe Affairs, (6) Scientific Domains, (7) Morontia Affairs, (8) Pure Spirit Activities, (9) Ascending Ministry, and (10) Grand Universe Philosophy.

The sporangia compose the lower native life of Jerusem. They occupy the one thousand rectangles of Jerusem. Agricultural excellence is a hallmark of the sporangia, and they maintain all the landscape gardens in Jerusem. Sporangia do not possess a surviving soul, but they do live a long life, up to 50,000 years. These bisexual sporangia beings procreate as required, and they do experience reincarnation. Described as beautiful, faithful, and affectionate, the sporangia are also intellectual.

THE SEVEN MANSION WORLDS

The Creator Son, during his sojourn to Earth, spoke of the "many mansions in the Father Universe." All fifty-six of the encircling worlds of Jerusem are devoted to the transitional culture of ascending mortals. The seven satellites of world number one are more specifically known as the mansion worlds. World number one is exclusively devoted to ascendant activities, which are headquarters of the Finaliters Corps assigned to Satania. These seven morontia worlds supervise morontia and the Melchizedeks. An acting governor on each world is directly responsible to the Jerusem rulers.

First Mansion World: On this mansion world, the resurrected mortal survivors resume their lives just where they left off when overtaken by death. All activities center in the resurrection hall. Here the morontia soul trust of the Seraphim and spiritual trust of the Adjusters reunite and reassemble the creature's personality and resurrect the sleeping survivor. Nearly the entire experience of mansion world one pertains to deficiency ministry. Primary activities in this realm are concerned with the correction and cure of the defects and creature character deficiencies portrayed in the physical world. Beings with no deficiency will enter a transition sleep after ten days and will proceed to world number two. Morontia companions and personal guides are assigned to ascending mortals in mansion one. These beautiful and charming companions help develop personality factors of mind and spirit within the morontia body. They are free to accompany individuals or select groups to any transition-culture sphere.

Second Mansion World: Here, the groupings of the morontia life began to take form. Working groups and social groups start to function, and community forms. Spirit-fused survivors occupy the mansion worlds in common with the Adjuster-fused ascending mortals. The Adjuster memory remains fully intact as one ascends the morontia life; this includes all worthwhile memory. One also remains personally intact after passing from the evolutionary world to mansion worlds. Through all seven mansion worlds, one continues to eat, drink, and rest, partaking of mortal food. As an entity ascends the mansion worlds, one becomes less material, more intellectual, and more spiritual. Spiritual progress is greatest on the last three worlds. Mansion world number two removes all phases of intellectual conflict and cures all mental disharmony.

Third World Mansion: After arriving here, one may visit the headquarters of the angelic orders and the various training schools. Instruction in positive education work begins on this level. The chief purpose is to enhance understanding of the correlation of morontia and mortal logic and to coordinate morontia and human philosophy. Ascendants are introduced to the intelligent comprehension of cosmic meaning and universe interrelationships.

Fourth Mansion World: This is the headquarters of the superangels. Ascenders find their place in the group working and class functions of morontia life. Here, they are introduced to the demands and delights of the true social life of morontia creatures. Social order is based on unselfish love, mutual service, and the Paradise goal of worship and divine perfection. Ascenders become self-conscious of God.

Fifth Mansion World: A real birth of cosmic consciousness takes place on the fifth world. Study becomes voluntary, unselfish service is natural, and worship is spontaneous. The study of divine worship is emphasized. One begins to taste what life will be like on Jerusem. One devotes much time to perfecting the Uversa language because all ascending mortals from the system headquarters up to Havona are bilingual.

Sixth Mansion World: On this world, the perfect fusion of the human mind with the divine Adjusters takes place, though it may have occurred previously. After fusion, a simple ceremony marks the entrance of an ascending mortal upon the eternal career of Paradise service. The being remains more or less material and far from being a true spirit. At this level, the ascendant learns about the high spirits of the universe, and begins instruction on the techniques of universe administration. One begins to learn the first lessons of a prospective spirit career.

Seventh Mansion World: Many teachers on this world will prepare the ascendant for residence on Jerusem. Here, one is purged of all the remnants of unfortunate heredity, an unwholesome environment, and unpleasant planetary tendencies. Graduates depart for Jerusem in groups, though they may have previously visited Jerusem a thousand times. They bid farewell to their whole mansion career as an ascending mortal.

These seven mansion worlds are seven dematerialization spheres. At the time of adjuster fusion, one passes from the mortal state to the immortal state. By the time one finishes the Jerusem career, one becomes a full-fledged morontian.

Jerusem Citizenship: Those who have completed the planetary experience and have graduated from the mansion world progression are welcomed to Jerusem. No more literal resurrection will transpire, once Jerusem is attained. Seven times the ascendant in the mansion worlds has experienced the adjustment sleep and the resurrection reawakening. The morontia form granted on departing the mansion world will be with the being until the end of the local universe. Mansion experience through the seven worlds of corrective training and cultural education represents the introduction of the mortal survivors to the morontia career. This transition life exists between the evolutionary material existence and the higher spirit attainment of the ascenders of time who are destined to achieve eternity.

THE MORONTIA LIFE

Morontia life is the only possible avenue through which material mortals can attain the threshold of the spiritual world. Perfection requires many steps. The morontia transition intervenes between the mortal state and the subsequent spirit status of surviving human beings. Morontia realms serve as the local universe liaison spheres between the material and spiritual levels of creature existence. These spheres are the transition phases of mortal ascension through the progression worlds of the local universe. Only seven worlds surround the finaliters sphere of the local universe and are called the mansion worlds. However, all fifty-six systemic transition abodes are called morontia worlds. These creations have the physical beauty of the local universe headquarters sphere. Early morontia life in the local system is similar to that of the present material world, but becomes less physical and more morontial as one progresses.

As we progress to the Salvington sphere, we attain a higher spiritual level. When one traverses the morontia life of Nebadon, the Morontia Power Supervisors provide a being with 570 morontia bodies on each phase of progression transformation. From the time one leaves the material world, one undergoes 570 separate ascending morontia changes. Eight occur in the local system, 71 in the constellations, and 491 during the Salvington sojourn. Through these transformations, one ascends from the material to the spiritual status of creature life.

Morontia passage becomes the evolutionary portal to spirit life and the eventual attainment of creature perfection, when the ascendant being finds God on Paradise. Morontia life is an elaborate universe training school for ascending creatures. It allows the creature of time gradually to master the operations and administrations of the Grand Universe. One actually lives every possible phase and stage of perfected creatures. It encompasses everything presently possible to the living orders of intelligent perfected beings. The future destiny of the Paradise finaliters is service in new universes now in the making.

THE LUCIFER REBELLION

Because of the Lucifer rebellion, for 200,000 years all the worlds of Satania have rested under the spiritual ban of Norlatiadek. Earth's isolation renders it impossible to undertake the life and environment of our Satania neighbors. Earth has been spiritually isolated, and it will require ages to recover from the resultant handicap of sin and secession. Our world has been greatly retarded in all phases of intellectual and spiritual attainment. Because of the rebellion, we have been quarantined. But for ascending mortals, this may be a blessing in disguise. Very clearly, they are entrusted with numerous special assignments of cosmic undertakings that require unquestioned faith and sublime confidence. On Jerusem, the ascenders, known as *agondonters,* occupy a certain residential section by themselves. They can believe without seeing, persevere when isolated, and triumph over extreme difficulties, even when alone.

A most brilliant being, Lucifer was a Lanonandek Son of Nebadon. Distinguished for his wisdom and efficiency, he had experienced service in many systems. The Melchizedeks had commissioned him and designated him as one of the hundred most able and brilliant personalities of more than 700,000 of his kind.

Lucifer was not an ascendant being but a Created Son of a local universe. He was the chief executive of a great system of 607 inhabited worlds, reigning upon the holy mountain of God in Jerusem. Satan was the first lieutenant of Lucifer.

Lucifer and Satan reigned over Jerusem for more than 500,000 years. They began to align themselves against their Universal Father, and his ruling son, Michael. Lucifer became a strong advocate of self-assertion and liberty. Becoming increasingly critical of the entire plan of universe administration, he did maintain a professed loyalty to Michael.

In time, Lucifer rebelled, and he persuaded himself that the rebellion was for the good of the system and universe. At some point in the rebellion, Lucifer became insincere and evil, which evolved into deliberate and willful sin. Lucifer assigned Satan to advocate the cause on our planet. Satan, though a member of the same primary group of Lanonandek Sons, had never functioned as a system sovereign. Another rebel, Caligasta, was known as the devil who was the son of a secondary order of Lanonandeks. He was the deposed Planetary Prince of Earth. Abaddon was the chief of staff of Caligasta and was the chief executive of the Earth rebels. Beelzebub led the disloyal midway creatures who made an alliance with the forces of Caligasta.

Under three headings, Lucifer spelled out the cause of the rebellion in a manifesto:

One: Lucifer claimed that the Universal Father did not exist, and that physical gravity and space energy were inherent in the universe. He asserted that the Father was a myth invented by the Paradise Sons to enable them to rule the universe in the Father's name. Lucifer denied that personality was a gift of the Universal Father.

Two: Believing that the local system should be autonomous, Lucifer protested the right of Michael as sovereign of Nebadon. Lucifer was willing to acknowledge Michael as his creator-father but not as his God and rightful ruler. He criticized the Ancient of Days interference in the affairs of the local system and universe, and denounced them as being tyrants and usurpers. Lucifer asserted that immortality was inherent in system personalities and that resurrection was natural and automatic. All beings, he said, would live eternally if not for the unjust acts of the Ancient of Days.

Three: Lucifer claimed that far too much time and energy were expended upon the scheme of training ascending mortals in universe administration and maintained that the finaliters had encountered a destiny no more glorious than to be returned to a humble sphere similar to their origin. Lucifer believed ascenders should enjoy liberty and individual self-determination. He challenged the entire plan of mortal ascension and believed the scheme was fiction for the mythical eternal destiny of ascending mortals. His declaration of liberty led to the rebellion of darkness and death.

On the "sea of glass" in Jerusem 200,000 years ago, the Lucifer manifesto was issued at the conclave of Satania. Self-assertion became the battle cry of the rebellion. If self-government was good for the Melchizedeks, said Lucifer, it was equally good for all intelligences. Government should be limited to local planets, and the planets should have voluntary consideration into the local systems.

All other supervision should be disallowed. The entire administrative cabinet of Lucifer joined the rebellion and was sworn in publicly as the officers of the liberated world's administration.

The government of the Paradise Son could not stop the rebellion, and the universe rulers allowed Lucifer freedom. Lucifer defied all his superiors. Gabriel, personally present throughout the transition, said that all beings would be left free to make their choices. Lucifer organized his rebel government before Gabriel could contend the right of secession. The Constellation Father continued the activities to the system of Satania.

Michael announced he would pursue the same policy of noninterference characterized by similar upheavals. Because Michael ruled by divine right, he had no absolute and personal sovereign authority. He had not completed his bestowal career. For almost 200,000 years the rebel forces were allowed to run a free course. Michael remained on Salvington while Gabriel established himself on the sphere dedicated to the Father. However, Michael and his angels fought in heaven against Lucifer, Satan, and the rebellious angels. This conflict was fought in terms of eternal life, not of a physical battle.

At the outbreak of the rebellion on Jerusem, the head of the Seraphic Hosts joined the Lucifer cause. Most other Seraphic Hosts followed. The rebellion became system-wide and thirty-seven seceding Planetary Princes joining the archrebels. Caligasta advocated the cause of Lucifer on Earth, and the delusion of self-assertion deceived the young planet. The system circuit supervisors suspended communication between planets. Although a Lanonandek rebellion, the higher order of sonship did not join in the uprising. The Melchizedeks, archangels, and Brilliant Evening Stars remained loyal to Michael. Gabriel valiantly contended for the Father's will and son's rulership.

Not one angel was lost in the supreme order of Seraphim, but a considerable number were lost in the next order, Superior Seraphim. One-third of the Jerusem Cherubim was lost, as was one-third of the planetary angelic helpers. The greatest loss occurred in the angelic ranks, and 95 percent of Material Sons crossed over.

Ascending mortals were vulnerable, but more withstood the rebellion than did the lower angels. Many in lower mansion worlds, who had not attained final fusion with their Adjusters, fell. Not one being who had attained ascendent citizenship on Jerusem participated in the rebellion. The faithful band of mortals numbered 187,432,861.

No local universe could detain or destroy Lucifer. The archrebels were allowed to roam the entire system and perpetuate the doctrine of discontent and self-assertion. No Satania worlds were lost since the fall of the thirty-seven Planetary Princes. Lucifer and Satan roamed the Satania system until the completion of the bestowal mission of Michael (Jesus) on Earth. This terminated the Lucifer rebellion in all Satania. Caligasta was the Prince of Earth, and the last act of Michael before leaving Earth was to offer mercy to Caligasta, but the offer was rejected. Caligasta, still free on Earth, has no power to enter the minds of men. Since Christ, he has been relatively impotent. None of the leaders of the rebellion accepted the mercy offer of Jesus, but thousands of angles and lower orders of celestial beings accepted and received rehabilitation. Faith is an effective armor against sin and iniquity. All evil is not the result of the devil, but much of it is due to people's inherent and debased tendencies.

Since the days Lucifer sought to turn back Michael and prevent him from completing his bestowal to establish himself as unqualified ruler of Nebadon, Lucifer has not been on Earth. Lucifer was taken prisoner by agents of Uversa's Ancient of Days and is currently in satellite number one of the transition sphere of Jerusem. Michael petitioned the Ancient of Days to intern all personalities concerned in the Lucifer rebellion. Permission was granted, except that Satan was allowed to make periodic visits to the defecting princes in the fallen worlds until another son of God should be accepted by the apostate worlds. The Planetary Prince of Earth and Satan are now detained in the Jerusem prison world. The system circuits will not be reinstated while Lucifer lives, though he is wholly inactive.

URANTIA EPILOGUE

True liberty remains the quest of all ages and the reward of evolutionary progress. False liberty is the subtle deception of the error of time and evil of space. Enduring liberty is based on the reality of justice, intelligence, maturity, fraternity, and equity. Liberty becomes suicidal when separated from material justice, intellectual

fairness, moral duty, and spiritual value. Liberty without the conquest of self is not possible. True liberty comes with genuine self-
respect. False liberty is the result of self-admiration. Only true
liberty compares with the reign of love and mercy. Lucifer erred in
attempting to short-circuit time in an experiential universe. What
God had given men and angels, Lucifer would have taken away from
them, that being the divine privilege of participating in the creation
of their own destinies and of the destiny of the local system of the
inhabited world. This completes the summary describing the spiritual universe according to the Urantia material.

Chapter Eight

THE SOUL AFTER DEATH
OOBEs, NDEs, Possessions, and Ghosts

Much evidence has come forward from paranormal phenomena, such as out-of-body experiences (OOBEs), near death experiences (NDEs), spirit possessions, and ghosts, that strongly suggest the soul survives death. Researchers are beginning to investigate these phenomena that support spiritual and metaphysical knowledge regarding the soul. Evidence from these anecdotal happenings strongly suggests that humans possess a second body, sometimes called the etheric double, subtle body, and sometimes the astral body.

OUT-OF- BODY EXPERIENCES

Surveys show that approximately 25 percent of the population has experienced at least one out-of-body experience. An OOBE as defined by Charles Tart, Ph.D., is "an event in which the experiencer (1) seems to perceive some portion of some environment which could not possibly be perceived from where his physical body is known to be at the time: and (2) knows at the time that he is not dreaming or fantasizing." This universal human experience has occurred throughout recorded history. A serious illness sometimes initiates an OOBE, sometimes emotional stress will initiate it, and frequently sleep brings it on. Often an OOBE is one of the most profound experiences in a person's life and frequently alters one's belief about life after death. Afterward, most people say they now know they will survive death. People feel they have directly experienced being alive and conscious without the physical body, and that they possess some kind of soul that survives bodily death. This generally once-in-a-lifetime experience is often joyful, and between 90 and 95 percent of the people who have experienced an OOBE are glad that it occurred. These people who have left their bodies can travel to distant places, and their descriptions of those places are correct and more accurate than would be expected by coincidence.

As suggested in an earlier chapter, a person possesses several bodies in addition to the physical body. One body normally coincides with the physical body and is the body which a person inhabits after death. Some individuals can detach from the physical body at will. Under certain conditions they can spontaneously leave the physical body, such as in sleep, trance, coma, or under the influence of an anesthetic. This astral body is the vehicle of consciousness, the body of desire, emotions, and feeling. Normally it is invisible, intangible, and impalpable to the senses. It constitutes the human double, sometimes called the subtle body that we normally inhabit and use. It is the "spiritual body" St. Paul described in the New Testament.

Proving the existence of this body has been difficult. Many people assert they have on certain occasions found themselves inhabiting such a body and have looked back at their own physical bodies asleep upon the bed. Fully conscious at the time, they no longer function in the material body but in the subtle double, which they can see and handle. Author Sylvan Muldoon describes this experience as astral projection. Muldoon is one of the few people who can voluntarily astral project and has written about OOBEs in *The Phenomena of Astral Projection*.

One theory suggests the second body or astral body is not composed of physical matter, but of subtle elements essentially etheric in nature. Physics has demonstrated that the distance between atoms is enormous, leading one to ask what prevents interatomic elements from occupying such space. There is no reason that intraatomic factors should not exist. Yogis talk about subtle vital centers, the chakras, which are connected with life rather than matter. They teach that living matter in fact depends on three vital etheric centers. Evidence suggests that when the astral body withdraws at death, the material body ceases to function and rapidly disintegrates. If the astral body is independent of the physical body, there is no reason that it should not continue to exist and function in the absence of the other.

Some parts of the scientific community are becoming more open to the idea of an etheric body. W. R. Bousfield writes in *The Basis of Memory* about the etheric brain concept, which would explain the phenomenon of memory. He claims that memory is not based in protoplasmic memory but in an immaterial psychical structure. Engrams, which are hypothetical changes in neural tissue postulated to account for memory, says Bousfield, must be in a substance called psychoplasm. Psychoplasm may be regarded as a modification of the ether. The idea of a psychic brain cooperating with the material brain provides a clue for difficult psychological problems. According to Bousfield, an etheric brain is necessary to account for memory. It could explain why some people who have large parts of their brain missing due to accident, surgery, or disease still have a normal mental life, suggesting that thoughts may be separate from the brain. Sylvan Muldoon asks the question, if an etheric brain is possible, why not an etheric body? Much evidence supports the concept of an etheric body, from the common ghost to astral projection. The astral body may be the body we inhabit at death that separates from the physical body. It appears to be the vehicle of the mind during OOBEs in astral projection.

Bilocation, the apparent ability to be in two places at the same time, may also be explained by an etheric double. Over the centuries many witnesses have testified to seeing an individual in one place while others have testified he was in another place at the identical time. Professor Bozcano studied the phenomenon of bilocation and concluded a human double exists in the form of an etheric body.

Amputee victims also provide evidence for an etheric body. Evidence suggests that amputees have a phantom limb (etheric double) and when the cut-off limb is maltreated in any way, the person will feel the injury. One man claims that he has dug up his buried leg eight times to change its position.

In complete OOBE experiences, the consciousness transfers to the astral body while the physical body is unconscious. As the physical body lies on the bed, mental activities are completely carried over into the astral body, which often hovers over the physical body. The consciousness maintained in astral projection is the same as the waking consciousness.

Spiritual adepts such as the lamas of Tibet, shamans of Siberia, medicine men of Africa, yogis of India, and clairvoyants of the West have all experienced the departure of the astral body from the physical body that occurs at death. All have described it in detail. In ancient Egypt, China, Tibet, India, and throughout the Orient, the idea of astral projection was almost universally accepted. Primitive people held similar views.

The belief that humans possess a second body or spiritual body dates back to antiquity. This idea is fully developed in the *Egyptian Book of the Dead* and illustrated when the *ka* (the soul) returns to its mummified body. Ancient Chinese art illustrates such a body in pictures of victims subject to torture. From the earliest times, this spiritual body has been reported in the form of apparitions or ghosts.

Dr. Zaalberg VanZelst of the Hague published a five-volume treatise regarding astral body research in his laboratory. According to VanZelst, the astral body was capable of contraction and expansion under the person's will, and it weighed approximately two and one-quarter ounces. These findings corresponded with Dr. Duncan McDougall's weighing experiment at the moment of death. McDougall also reported loss of weight by the dying patient of two to two and one-half ounces. Other investigators have replicated these findings in animal studies.

An ethereal cord connects the physical body and the ethereal body. This cord connects to the astral body at the back of the neck, and some report it connects to the physical body at the same location. Others claim it emerges from the forehead of the physical body. As long as the cord remains intact, life is present, and the etheric body eventually returns to reanimate the physical organism. When this cord is severed, as happens in death, the etheric body can no longer return to reanimate the body, which subsequently decomposes. Death is nothing more than the permanent separation of the two bodies, which may have temporarily separated before.

Dr. R. A. Watters attempted to photograph the escaping etheric body of certain smaller animals such as mice, chickens, and frogs. Special forms of vacuum chambers were built and filled with water and oil vapor. At the instant of animal decapitation, a photograph was taken. Dramatic results were obtained in many experiments. Cloudlike masses were often observed hovering over the animal's body and were discernable on the photographic plate. Watters devoted eight years of research to this project, which involved hundreds of ingenious tests. Some results could be explained, and others could not.

Spirit photography and other tests have been used to research the astral body. Hector Durville writes in his book *Le Fairtome des Vivants* that he has obtained positive results in the following ways: (1) by inducing the etheric body to rap at a distance from the entranced subject; (2) asking the etheric body to place its hands upon photographic plates, which produce strange markings upon development; (3) psychic instruments such as the biometer and sthenometer are affected by the etheric body; and (4) a calcium sulphide screen that was caused to glow with added brilliance when the astral body approached it upon request.

People who have OOBEs or astral projections encounter an immaterial world, one described as a mental world distinct from the physical world. Thoughts create in the astral world. Muldoon believes the clothing of the observed spiritual phantom is created by thought, and it is not a counterpart of the physical clothing. Thought governs those in the astral world. On his astral trips, Sylvan Muldoon perceived objects that were not actually there. Time and space on the astral plane are greatly modified, but differ from normal conceptions, according to Muldoon. Neither becomes non-existed. One becomes unaware of the passage of time and has little sense of space. Out-of-body experiences differ from dreams because the experiencer carries full waking consciousness with him or her. One knows it is different from ordinary dream consciousness.

Muldoon reports that in the majority of his OOBEs, he was alone and saw no one. Only rarely did he meet with spirit people who asserted he was in their abode. He sometimes met dead people he had known. Some said their purpose was to greet dead people who had just made the transition. Others were strangers, some helpful, some evil.

Places he visited on his astral excursions were well known to him. Sometimes he was transported to distant lands, but all were on the earth plane. Often his projections carried him along streets and into homes.

Oriental science maintains that a person has a number of bodies, normally coinciding with one another. All except the physical body are invisible to our normal senses. Annie Besant wrote in *Man and His Bodies* that man has (1) a physical body consisting of dense matter and an etheric double, which is still physical and impalpable to the senses; (2) an astral body that dwells on the astral plane and has seven substrates of astral matter; (3) the mental body, which is the vehicle of consciousness; (4) the causal body which is the higher mental body; (5) the spiritual body; and (6) the buddhic body. These six bodies and the physical body make up the seven bodies of man.

Robert Monroe is another rare person who developed the ability to leave his body voluntarily. Believing that he could teach people to have OOBEs, Monroe founded the Monroe Institute to research the phenomenon of OOBE. Monroe wrote several books describing his research including *Far Journeys* and *Journey Out of the Body*. The institute provided controlled holistic environmental chambers that enabled isolation. Here, subjects lay on a waterbed in a darkened eight-foot by ten-foot room that was acoustically and electrically shielded. Electrodes to monitor physiological states were attached to the head, fingers, and body. A microphone hung about four inches from the face and allowed communication between the subject and a monitor in a control room. The monitor introduced a hemi-sync sound into the subject's headphones, a sound of different frequencies to each ear as described in an earlier chapter. This enabled the subject to enter an altered state.

Subjects often reported rapidly traveling through a tunnel and seeing a bright light at its end. When out of body, subjects visited various places around the world, sometimes the moon and other planets. Unlike Sylvan Muldoon, almost every one of Monroe's subjects encountered intelligent beings willing to communicate. Occasionally, a spiritual helper would assist a person to leave his or her body. In hundreds of hours of subject communication, about one-third of the subjects gave permission for friendly entities to take over their physical bodies and speak, using the subject's vocal cords. The other two-thirds of the subjects made contact with the spiritual entities and reported their conversations. In both cases, the monitor in the control room became part of the discussion.

When contact was made with the entities, a certain pattern developed. The spiritual entity often radiated a warmth of friendliness, and spent much time advancing the best mental and physical state of the subject. The being would often appear with face hidden. Once the subject became familiar with the feel of the entity, the hooded robe was discarded and the subject would sense the radiation of the being. When speaking to the subject, the entity would use only the vocabulary in the memory bank of the subject. Often they would hesitate in searching for the correct word. When the entities used the physical body of the subject to speak, there was always a change in body voltage and bio-monitoring data in the subject.

The following is a conversation between a nonphysical entity and a human monitor that helps shed light on the mysteries of the spiritual universe:

Entity: "As I have said to you earlier, plants exist on levels one through seven. They are on a vibrational rate on levels one through seven. It is the same pattern. Animals exist on the level's eight through fourteen, and when a person attains level fourteen, it can no longer go any higher unless it is willing to change its form of consciousness. Levels fifteen through twenty-one are what you call human life on this Earth. When a person progresses to level twenty-one, he then has the choice of going higher or staying within the realm of human form, but he cannot go higher unless he is willing to give up human form."

Entity: "And then once a person is a consciousness (we are talking about consciousness) and reaches level twenty-eight, the bridge is crossed, and from that point on for a consciousness to evolve higher, it would not again assume human form of any kind, not even as a learning experience. I will never incarnate again as a human–another form of life, yes, but not as a human. The words are very hard because your plane of existence is not the same. Perhaps I can explain it by asking you to image seven of the circles, which would give you forty-nine levels. The first three levels are physical matter as you know physical matter. They are your plants, your animals, your humans. The fourth circle is your bridge, your realm, your center for that overall plane. It is the time in which a consciousness can choose to go back into the lower level or to transcend into the higher levels, and many consciousnesses do choose to go back into the lower level in physical form. The upper three circles are the realm that in your consciousness is called the spiritual realm, and here much of the work is done. I could not help someone who was (below) the eighteenth level very much because my plane, my vibrational rate, would be different. That is why it is hard for me to help you with specific problems. I can give you ideas, but I cannot give you direct guidance. I could if you were on level eighteen. Our planes do touch since yours is an ascending spiral . . . It is an ascending ellipse, and therefore I can cross and communicate with you, but not as directly. Once I reach level forty-nine, which I will, I then leave all of this realm of existence. It does not mean I have left this group of seven, this overall group of seven. Imagine, if you will, the seven circles enclosed in an even larger circle upon which seven more circles are stacked, which is in turn in even a greater circle. Then you can have some idea of what infinity is. It does not ever stop."

Monroe concluded from his research that all other intelligent species, excluding humans, either in the physical universe or other energy systems, use a form of communication that is totally and certainly nonverbal. This nonverbal communication is a direct and instant experience. An immediate knowing is transmitted from an intelligent energy system and received by another. The content, he said, can only be a two-digit number, or the actual reliving of an event. He believes before man can communicate with intelligent species at all levels of reality, he must become proficient at nonverbal communications.

After researching OOBEs, Monroe made other conclusions. He said a second body exists in conjunction with the physical body. This body can act independently of the physical body under control of the conscious mind. Some sensory input in the second body registers in the physical body. Some movements in the second body exist in identical space-time as those of the physical counterpart.

Monroe believes that human personality survives the transition of death. Communication between humans can take place above the oral level in the waking or sleeping states. In some humans, the second body separates during sleep. When in the second body, creating a physical effect on a physical living human is possible while the latter is awake. He also believes there is an area of knowledge and concept far beyond the comprehension of the conscious minds of humans.

NEAR-DEATH EXPERIENCES

In 1975, Raymond Moody, M.D., published a book titled *Life after Life*, detailing a phenomenon experienced by people who had almost died, now known as the near-death experience (NDE). Although the book was anecdotal in nature and without academic elitism, the book is credited with inspiring scientists from various disciplines to research this intriguing experience, including two leading researchers, Kenneth Ring, Ph.D., from the University of Connecticut, and Bruce Grayson, M.D., professor of psychiatry at the University of Virginia.

The near-death experience occurs in approximately 30 percent of all near-death instances, whether the cause of death is accidental, illness related, or attempted suicide. In 1992, Ken Ring estimated the number of Americans who had undergone an NDE to be approximately eight million people. Bruce Grayson raised the figure to thirteen million based on a 1994 Gallup Poll.

In her book, *On the Other Side of Life, Exploring the Near Death Experience*, Evelyn Elasae Valarino summarizes NDE research over the past several decades. The NDE experience may include the following stages, but usually not all of them:

- Stage One: **An out-of-body experience.** In an OOBE the subject leaves his or her body and views it from an external vantage point. Often the person is disorientated.
- Stage Two: **Passing through a tunnel.** In this experience, subjects have an impression of weightlessness as they travel through the tunnel. Sometimes they hear a pleasant sound.

- Stage three: **A brilliant light.** At the end of the tunnel, the subject often reports a brilliant light that beckons them.
- Stage Four: **A being of light.** Sometimes the person encounters a being of light that personifies absolute love.
- Stage Five: **Infinite happiness.** Subjects often describe a feeling of infinite happiness, indescribable joy, and infinite peace.
- Stage Six: **Deceased loved ones.** NDE subjects report an encounter with a deceased loved one or an unknown guide.
- Stage Seven: **City of light.** Sometimes subjects report seeing a city of light.
- Stage Eight: **Review of life.** Frequently subjects report a review of their life, which is a timeless three-dimensional vision of the significant events in their life.
- Stage Nine: **Part of the whole.** After the experience, subjects often report being a part of a harmonious universal whole and having a definite place in it.
- Stage Ten: **Absolute knowledge.** People often report having access to absolute knowledge, which is partially or entirely lost upon returning to life.
- Stage Eleven: **A boundary.** Near-death experiencers report a boundary, variously symbolized, such as a bridge, which if crossed would make returning to life impossible.
- Stage Twelve: **A choice.** Subjects are sometimes given the choice of whether to return to life, and sometimes they are told it is not their time.

Rarely does a person experience all these stages in an NDE. However, the stages reported in an experience are nearly identical with other NDEs, and usually people undergo similar emotions.

The being of light encountered in the NDE is described as immersed in a sea of unconditional love that engulfs the subject. This soothing being instills a feeling of absolute safety. The life review takes place in the presence of the being of light who assists the experiencer in understanding his or her good or bad deeds. Subjects report that they experience the emotions of joy and pain that they may have produced in others. The being of light eases the feeling of guilt and remorse of the subject. Judgment of these deeds did not come from the light being, but from the experiencer's own self.

A person who has undergone an NDE often goes through a transformation. Their values usually shift, and often they wish to help others.

After a period of time, their lives take a new direction based on service to others. Most people believe they are stronger and better people after the experience, stronger because they no longer fear death, and better because they now understand the "true meaning" of life. Often NDE survivors have a tremendous thirst for knowledge and understanding. Self-acceptance, self-esteem, and inner peace increase significantly following an NDE. Subjects are usually more tolerant of religions and beliefs that differ from their own. Frequently they develop psychic abilities, including telepathy, prophetic visions, reading thoughts, diagnosing illnesses, and healing.

Experiencers undergo a wide range of emotions, beginning with disorientation and anxiety. As the experience progresses, emotional impressions become increasingly positive and usually culminate in a state of indescribable joy and ecstasy. People leave this state feeling as though they have control over their fate. Many report being angry at having to return to the physical body.

Subjects perceive themselves as either without a body or with an extremely lightweight one. Those who report not having a body during their NDE say they were pure consciousness with a powerful center of energy. All report moving at a very high speed through the tunnel. They could travel to different locations instantaneously by simply willing it, even faraway locations. During an NDE, space and time no longer exist.

Experiencers say they can read the thoughts of others rather than actually hearing sounds. Often they hear the thoughts of others before those thoughts are put into words. Transmission of thoughts occur without words passing between the subject and spiritual beings, from consciousness to consciousness. Many report hearing a member of the medical staff pronouncing them dead. When attempting to communicate with those around them, they find it impossible to make themselves understood.

During an NDE, subjects report they cannot use the sense of touch. A subject may tell of trying to grab someone's arm, often to stop the person from continuing to work on his or her body. Subjects meet with no resistance and pass right through people and objects. Experiencers report that smell and taste play no role.

The return to life may be imposed, requested, or left up to the volition of the NDE subject. Imposed returns outnumber voluntary returns. One reason for an imposed return is to complete unfinished business. Voluntary return often comes from a desire to take care of loved ones dependent on them, usually children. Subjects have the choice of whether to return only if their business on Earth is complete.

Experiencers obediently accept the return to life, but they do so longing for that state of grace they enjoyed during the experience. Once they regain consciousness, they usually dedicate themselves to using the extra time in the physical world in the most generous way possible. Sometimes this acceptance is preceded by a temporary period of anger and revolt. For instance, Morse and Perry recount this from *Transition by the Light*: "Suddenly I felt like I was being pulled down and thrown back into my body. I was angry. I don't think I have ever before felt such a rage! I screamed and screamed in anger and rage because I wanted to go back to that place with the clouds."

Subjects assert they cannot put in words what they have experienced. No one can fully understand them.

After reading Raymond Moody's *Life after Life*, college professor and consciousness researcher Kenneth Ring knew that he wanted to devote the rest of his life to NDE research. In 1980, Ken Ring and Bruce Grayson created an association for studying this phenomenon called the International Association for Near-Death Studies (IANDS) at the University of Connecticut.

One of the first research projects conducted by Ring involved 102 people who had nearly died. They were recruited from hospitals, doctors, and advertising. Of these 102, 49 experienced an NDE, and 53 did not. He found 60 percent of the NDE subjects experienced peace, 37 percent had body separation, 23 percent entered darkness, 16 percent saw the light, and 10 percent entered the light. Most of his researched subjects (28 of 49) experienced a point where they became aware that a decision had to be made about returning to physical life. Twenty of 49 were aware of a spiritual being in their experience, and 8 of 49 were aware of the spirits of loved ones. These spirits usually informed the experiencer that "it was not their time" and "you must go back." Sixteen people willed to return, and five were sent back. Six reported a feeling of loneliness.

Ring's study found the NDE survivors returned to the body with a heightened appreciation for life and a determination to live it to its fullest. They often had a sense of being reborn and a sense of purpose. Following the experience they reported being more adaptable to life situations. They put higher values on love and service to others, and they unconditionally accepted people. Material comforts were no longer important. The NDE subjects most often became religious and the nonexperiencer did not. Experiencers felt closer to God, but were less concerned with organized religion and formal rituals, even though they felt more tolerant. In other words, they became more spiritual rather than more religious. Experiencers' conceptions of death emphasized the peace and beauty of death when compared with the nonexperiencers, and they were more open to a view of reincarnation.

Ring had a difficult time explaining why women were disproportionately likely to have NDEs in connection with illness, and men tended to have them after an accident or suicide attempt.

Ring concluded from his research that the first stages of an NDE represent an out-of-body experience. Two possibilities could account for this early stage: (1) detachment of a person's consciousness, or (2) a second body. Those who have claimed to see this second body call it a replica of the physical body, what Ring called the double. Subjects describe peace, quiet, and lack of pain when they are free from the physical body. Robert Crookall has studied thousands of OOBE cases in which the double left the body. He tells of Estelle Roberts describing her husband's transition: "I saw his spirit leave the body. It emerged from his head and gradually molded itself into an exact replica of the earth-body. It remained suspended about a foot above his body, lying in the same position, i.e., horizontal and attached to by a cord to the head. Then the cord broke and the spirit form floated away, passing through the wall." Muldoon and Carrington report that the Tahitians have described this exact phenomenon. The silver cord is the connection between the physical and spiritual bodies, attached at the occipital protuberance at the base of the skull. Similar cases were described in William Barretti's book regarding deathbed visions, according to Ring.

When the experiencer encounters a presence and hears voices, Ring believes this is a psychological event associated with a shift in consciousness. When consciousness functions independently of the physical body, it becomes aware of another dimension, called the fourth dimension. The conscious becomes free to explore the fourth dimension.

Ring believes this may be explained by the holograph as proposed by Karl Pribram, M.D., Stanford neurosurgeon and holographic theorist. Before we explain this theory, we need to define holography, a method of photography without a lens. The field of light in holography is scattered by an object such as an apple. This wave field scattering is recorded on a plate as an interference pattern. The concept of an interference pattern can be illustrated by the analogy of dropping three pebbles simultaneously into a shallow pan of water. The resultant waves crisscross one another. If one quick-froze the surface ripple, one could record the interference pattern made by the waves. When a laser beam illuminates the interference pattern, the apple reappears as a three-dimensional image, called a hologram. The photographic plate itself is a jumbled pattern of swirls composed of the interference patterns that store the information. It releases the information in response to a coherent light source, the laser beam. An extraordinary property of the interference pattern is that any part of it contains information about the whole. If one broke off a portion of the hologram, the pattern is stored information about the apple, and if only that portion is illuminated, an image of the entire apple would appear.

Karl Pribram claims that the brain itself functions holographically by mathematically analyzing interference wave patterns so that images of objects are seen. Primary reality itself is said to be composed only of frequencies. Different cells of the brain respond to different frequencies. Pribram believes the brain functions like a frequency analyzer and breaks down complex patterns of frequencies into their components. These frequencies are converted into their own familiar object world by a process analogous to the illumination of laser beam interference patterning. Author Marilyn Ferguson states, "Our brains mathematically construct concrete reality by interpreting frequencies from another dimension, a realm of meaningful, pattern-primary reality that transcends time and space."

Pribram believes the frequency domain deals with only the density of occurrence. Time and space collapse. Ordinary boundaries of space and time, such as location, disappear and everything happens synchronously. One can read out what is happening, says Pribram, into a variety of coordinates, of which space and time are most helpful in bringing us into the ordinary domain of appearance.

Pribram believes this helps explain mystical experiences. The people who experience them may be tapping into that order of reality (holographic reality) behind the world of appearance. Spiritual insights fit the description of this domain. The invention of the holograms makes this perfectly plausible.

If mystical experiences are a manifestation of a holographic reality, where time and space collapse and causality can have no meaning, this answers questions about different domains of reality. The act of dying involves a gradual shift of consciousness from the world of appearances to a pure frequency holographic reality. Access to this holographic reality becomes experientially available when our consciousness is free from the dependence on the physical body.

The tunnel effect has been reported in OOBE episodes that are not associated with death, apparently when a transition in consciousness subjectively took place. Researcher Itzhak Bentov also believed the tunnel or darkness was a transitional zone occurring between levels of consciousness. The tunnel is shifting gears from ordinary waking consciousness to direct perception of another frequency domain. What actually moves is awareness, or mind without body. It moves through the gateway to holographic consciousness or to fourth-dimensional consciousness.

Many NDE survivors report seeing a bright light, often at the end of a tunnel. Ring believes this represents the light associated with the state of consciousness one enters after death. In many traditions this is spoken of as the light of the astral world, where most people go following death. In this realm, people are sensitive to a higher range of frequencies that appears as light of extraordinary brilliance.

Ring believes the being of light often seen in the NDE is actually oneself. He believes it is the Higher Self often spoken about in some traditions. It is our total self. Ring explains the individual personality is but a split-off fragment of the total self, which is reunited at the time of death with the Higher Self. During one's lifetime, the individual personality functions in an autonomous way, as though it was a separate entity.

According to Ring, the Higher Self is so awesome and overwhelming with its love, so foreign to one's individual consciousness that one perceives it as separate from oneself. It manifests itself as a brilliant golden light, but is actually itself in a higher form. The Higher Self is a reflection of one's own inherent divine nature.

The Higher Self has total knowledge of the individual personality, both past and future according to Ring. When experienced as a voice, it seems to be an all-knowing one. That is why it can initiate a life review and provide a preview of a person's life events. At this level information is stored holographically and experienced holographically. The whole life review is a holographic phenomenon. Pribram describes holographic consciousness as though "everything is happening at once, synchronously."

An aspect of the Creator is the Higher Self. If the Higher Self has total knowledge of an individual personality, both past and future, that knowledge must include the programmed time of death for the personality. One assumes when an individual is being sent back or when his or her time has not yet come, this reflects their life program. Spirits who pass on this information have access to it. Ring also suggests that some guardian angels may represent an aspect of the Higher Self and not separate entities.

The last stage of the NDE is the world of light where the subject encounters a brilliant golden light. The experiencer perceives a realm of great beauty and splendor and often encounters spirits of deceased relatives and loved ones. Holographically, it is a realm of higher frequencies. Because consciousness continues to function holographically, it interprets the frequencies as objects. Everything in this world of light is enhanced in beauty compared with the physical world. Ring hypothesizes that this world is created by interacting thought structures. These thought forms combine to form patterns, just as interference waves form patterns on a holographic plate. The images produced by these interacting thought forms seem real. If the brain functions holographically to give us a picture of physical reality, Ring believes the mind must function similarly when the physical brain can no longer do so. Because the mind exists independently of the brain, it should function holographically without a brain.

Since individual minds create this world out of thoughts and images, writes Ring, this reality then reflects to a degree the thought structure of individuals from a world of physical reality. Therefore, the forms of the spiritual world are similar to those of the physical world. This world of light is indeed a mind-created world fashioned from interacting thought patterns.

Holographic interpretations can also account for the perception of spirit forms found in this reality and in deathbed visions. A function of interacting mind patterns is encountered with people in spirit bodies. These entities are the product of interacting minds attuned to a holographic domain in which thought alone fashions reality, asserts Ring. Because communication between the NDE survivors and spirit entities is said to be telepathic, this again suggests that thought controls this world of existence.

Most NDE subjects report a paradise world. A few researchers report that their subjects describe a hellish experience. Ring believes individuals passing through a lower frequency experience these hellish experiences, but some get stuck there. This domain is also holographic reality organized in the same way as the paradisiacal realms. The main difference is in the nature of minds that interact to create this reality.

NDE subjects rarely report this hellish domain. Ring believes the tunnel phenomenon serves to shield the individual from awareness of this domain. As mentioned earlier, the tunnel effect represents a shift in consciousness from one level to another. The NDE subject is usually kept from having a direct awareness of this realm. Hell appears to exist at a lower frequency domain and most NDE survivors seem never to encounter it.

From his research, Ring draws some enlightening conclusions. "In the paradigm shift that seems to be leading to a recognition of the primary role of consciousness, the world of modern physics and the spirit world seem to reflect a single reality. If this is true, no scientific account of any phenomenon can be complete without taking its spiritual aspect into account."

EARTH-BOUND SPIRITS

For various reasons, not all souls enter the light after death. A few souls remain in the earth plane because they lack awareness of their passing. Some spirits have the choice of following the direct path to the light but the process may be difficult if it has attached to it an entity that does not want to go to the light. Other souls may become bound to the earth plane by emotions and feelings, often connected with sudden traumatic death. Anger, fear, jealousy, resentment, guilt, and remorse keep the entity attached to the Earth and not to the light. Some people die prematurely and have unfinished business that keeps them earth-bound in the spiritual mode.

Attachments to the physical by some souls cause them not to leave for the light, and they too become earth-bound. Addictions to drugs and alcohol cannot be met in the spiritual realm. They need to experience the drug through the senses of a living person who uses the substance. They accomplish this through parasitic attachment to a physical person.

Incorrect religious beliefs about the afterlife keep many souls from entering the light because the afterlife experience does not coincide with false expectations and preconceived notions.

These earth-bound spirits, the surviving consciousness of

deceased humans, have not gone to the light. These spirits can attach, possess, or obsess a living human. The disembodied consciousness attaches itself and merges fully or partially with the subconscious mind of a living person. They exert some degree of influence on thought, emotions, behavior, and the physical body of a living person. The spiritual entity becomes a parasite in the mind of the host. Most often, the victims of this condition are totally unaware of episodes of complete or partial takeovers.

Spirit possession has been recognized or at least theorized in every era and culture. Approximately 90 percent of societies around the world have records of possession-like phenomena. Contemporary clinical evidence suggests that discarnate beings influence living people by forming a physical or mental connection. Subsequently, they can impose detrimental and/or emotional conditions and symptoms. Names for this condition are possessive state, possession disorder, spirit possession syndrome, spirit obsession, and spirit attachment. Sadly, only a few psychotherapists and religious leaders know about this phenomenon. One exception is William Baldwin, considered one of the leading authorities on spirit releasement. His book titled *Spirit Releasement Therapy* provides guidance for the process of releasing entities into the light. Much of this section of the book is based on Baldwin's research into spirit attachments.

The first written account associated with spirit attachment was found in Assyrian cuneiform tablets dating from 2500 B.C. The tablets describe eloquent incantations and prayers to the tribal gods, interspersed with challenges to the attached demons that imposed disease of every kind. The ancients believed most sickness was caused by evil spirits. Early writings in China, Egypt, Israel, and Greece attributed mental disorders to demons that took possession of an individual. Shamans of most indigenous cultures believed that illness was caused by evil spirits attached to the sick person. It was the shaman's job to rid the sick person of the evil spirit. Once released, the patient often recovered.

In ancient Egypt, a team, composed of a physician to cure the ailment and a priest to drive out the demon, performed exorcism. Zoroaster (sixth century B.C.), the founder of Zoroastrianism in ancient Persia, was also an exorcist. He used prayer, ritual, and the sprinkling of water to drive out evil spirits.

Nearly one-quarter of the healings attributed to Jesus in the New Testament consisted of casting out unclean spirits. He specified more than one type of spirit. The Old Testament also refers to trouble caused by evil spirits.

In the Middle Ages (A.D. 500 to A.D. 1500), there was a revival of the most ancient superstition of demonology modified to agree with theological philosophy. At that time, treatment of mental illness belonged to the clergy, who believed it was caused by evil spirits. The model of exorcism, called the Roman Ritual, was developed by the Catholic Church over a long period of time. The concept of deliverance is based on the explicit command and example of Jesus to "cast out devils."

Today, the religious viewpoint holds that possessive spirits are demons and devils. It does not acknowledge earth-bound spirits of deceased humans. To gain acceptance in Western society, the Catholic Church has played down the role of spirit possession, often ignoring or denying the possibility. Frequently, suspect people are referred to a psychiatrist. A few Catholic priests still perform exorcisms. Between 1970 and 1980, in the United States, priests performed more than 600 exorcisms.

One of the early researchers of spirit possession, Dr. James Hyslop (1854-1920), was a professor of Logic and Ethics at Columbia University. In 1906, he was elected president of the American Society for Psychical Research. His research found that, in many cases, people whose condition would normally be described as due to hysteria, multiple personality, dementia, paranoia, or other mental disturbances showed unmistakable indications of spirit possession. After ten years of investigation, he accepted the fact that discarnate beings could cause mental illness. Hyslop is the true pioneer, writes Baldwin, in the systemic investigation of spirit possession as a cause of mental disorder.

Another pioneer, Carl Wickland, M.D., was chief psychiatrist at the National Psychopathic Institute in Chicago. An avowed spiritualist and exorcist, Wickland found that some people underwent profound changes after practicing with the Ouija board or doing automatic writing. Often they required hospitalization for mental illness. His wife Anna was a gifted medium, and through her, he consulted with discarnate intelligences. He was told that possession of the living by earth-bound spirits of deceased humans caused many mental health problems. By following instructions given by these intelligences, he could alleviate the symptoms of the victims. Following their instructions, Wickland built a device called a "winehurst" machine that generated static electricity. Charges of static electricity were applied with a short wand to the head and spine of the afflicted person. The attached entity would disengage from the patient and incorporate into Anna Wickland and then begin to speak. Dr. Wickland would engage in conversation with the entity, who often turned out to be some deceased person. Wickland's first task was to convince the spirit that physical death had occurred and that it no longer belonged to the earth plane. Most spirits would quickly understand their condition and willingly go with the guiding spirits who came for them. Frequently the guides were loved ones who had died.

Titus Bull, M.D., was the first researcher to suggest that earth-bound spirits could have another earth-bound spirit attached to it. This resulted from possession before death. Baldwin's research also confirmed this.

Wilson Van Deusen was a clinical psychologist at Mendocino State Hospital in California. To understand the mentally ill, Van Deusen developed a relationship with both the patient and the voice (person) who the patient said he heard. Although medical experts call voices hallucinations, patients resent this term and say the voices are real. About 80 percent of the beings (voices) came from the lower order, often vulgar, threatening, malevolent, boastful, antireligious, deceptive, and not very intelligent. High-order hallucinations comprised the other 20 percent of the patient experience. Most were considerate and respected the patient's freedom. They claimed power over the lower order and said the lower beings illustrated the weaknesses and faults of the patient. Van Deusen discovered that the consistencies of the hallucinations, or beings, with whom he communicated were matched almost perfectly with the description of the spirit world. They interacted with humans as described by Emanual Swedenborg two hundred years earlier. Van Deusen hypothesized that the spirit world was the unconscious mind. Most mental experience, claims Van Deusen, is participated in by spirits who do not know anything other than our feelings.

Dr. Edith Fiore, a clinical psychotherapist, discovered during the course of her past-life therapy that past lives described by a person often turned out to be the experience of an attached earth-bound spirit, not at all pertinent to the client. Release of the attached spirit often resolved the present problem, after past-life therapy had proved ineffective. Fiore and others estimate that approximately 70 percent of the population is afflicted with spirit possession. Dr.

Fiore is one of the first therapists to deal with the discarnate spirit directly through the voice of the person afflicted. Others have worked through an intermediary or trance medium.

Dr. William Baldwin, a psychotherapist and former dentist, also speaks directly with the attached spirit through the subject's voice. After placing the patient in a hypnotic state, Baldwin uses a technique that allows him to communicate with the attached entity. After conversing in a loving manner, Baldwin asks the entity if it sees the light, which often the entity does. Baldwin then asks the spirit to leave and enter the light.

Baldwin's research has found that if a recently deceased spirit cannot break away from the attached spirit or does not have enough strength to go to the light, it can also become Earth-bound. Often the newly deceased spirit has an entity attached to it. Sometimes the recently deceased can carry the attached Earth-bound to the light, thereby rescuing the lost soul. Often the deceased can break away from the attached entity and go to the light. The old earthbound spirit becomes lost again and wanders in the lower astral world, often described as the gray place. Here it can await the next incarnation of the being to whom it was attached, or it can quickly attach to another unsuspecting person.

Baldwin claims an attached entity can be benevolent in nature, totally self-serving, malevolent, or completely neutral. Attachment to any person may be completely random or even accidental. Sometimes it occurs simply because the person is in proximity to the dying person. In half of Baldwin's cases, the attachment is random with no prior connection. In the remaining half, connection may include unfinished business in another life time. Most people are vulnerable to spirit attachment on many occasions throughout life.

Mental and physical symptoms, such as strong emotions and repressed negative feelings, can act like a magnet to attract discarnate entities who have similar emotions, needs, or feelings. Anger, fear, terror, sadness, and grief can invite entities with similar feelings. People under severe stress are also susceptible. Altering the consciousness with drugs or alcohol, especially hallucinogens, loosens one's ego boundaries and opens the subconscious mind for discarnates. Sometimes strong analgesics and anesthetics during surgery produce the conditions receptive for possession. Organ transplant recipients are often possessed by the donor's spirit. Both surgery and physical trauma make a person susceptible. Baldwin says the openness and surrender of sexual intercourse can open a person up. Sexual abuse, rape, and incest also make a person vulnerable.

Spirits can attach to the aura or float within the aura outside the body. They can lodge in any of the chakras.

Sometimes a powerful connection between the host and spirit causes the spirit to attach. This emotional bond could have occurred in the present life or in a previous life.

Humans can be affected by attached spirits in many ways. A discarnate entity retains the psychic energy pattern of its own ailment following death. It can produce in the host many mental aberrations or emotional disturbances and any symptom or physical illness. Erratic behavior often results from shifting of control between separate entities.

An attached entity can produce the emotions of anger, fear, sadness, or guilt in the living person. Often the emotional energy leads to inappropriate overreactions to ordinary life situations. Attached entities can alter the path of karmic options and opportunities of the host. Sometimes the planned life line is disrupted by a hastened death or prolonged life. Attached entities of opposite gender can influence sexual preference and gender orientation. Occasionally attached entities can influence the choice of marriage partners and even extramarital affairs.

The host of an entity is usually unaware of the presence of attached spirits. Thoughts, desires, and behavior of an attached entity are experienced as the person's own thoughts, desires, and experiences, according to Baldwin. Acknowledgment of this reality is sometimes experienced months after the entity has been released. The person suddenly notices the absence of a familiar attitude, desire, or behavior. Attached entities always exert some influence, which may range from a minor energy drain to a major degree of control. The earth-bound spirit usurps control from the rightful spirit. A newly formed spirit attachment is usually more obvious to the unsuspecting host.

Attached entities can sometimes cause a sudden onset of drug or alcohol usage, or the host may respond strangely to familiar situations. Often victims experience personality changes, sometimes unusual physical sensations, and perhaps a loss of one's personal identity. The physical appetite for food, sex, alcohol, or drugs may increase drastically following a newly attached spirit. A change in clothing tastes or personal attitude is common.

Baldwin claims spirit entities do not require permission from the host before they attach. However, individual sovereign beings, writes Baldwin, have the right to deny any violation or intrusion by another being. Afflicted hosts may report hearing voices, either internally or externally, or they may have spontaneous visual images of bizarre faces or figures. Symptoms are often similar to hallucinations of schizophrenics. Some report being chased in recurring dreams, and others report being urged to commit suicide by some force. Releasing the entity by Dr. Baldwin's technique often eliminates many unexplained mental aberrations. One can only imagine the number of mental health problems whose real cause is attached entities, a cause unlikely to be diagnosed.

APPARITIONS

Apparitions provide more evidence of the existence of a second body. Commonly called ghosts, these apparitions have been part of folklore since ancient times. Ghostly apparitions are differentiated between luminous ghosts, white ghosts, and unredeemed ghosts, which appear as dark figures. In the majority of cases the apparition obscures the background, but transparency is also attributed to ghosts. Some ghosts resemble living people, and an apparition may be indistinguishable from the person it mirrors. Such apparitions may represent both the living and dead. An apparition of the living is called the double, as found in bilocation discussed earlier. Doubles may be seen in a self-encounter or it may be seen by another person. Often the person is not aware the duplication has taken place.

Frequently, apparitions represent the dying and often appear to a loved one at the moment of death. Apparitions of departed souls are reported most frequently shortly after death. Immediately following death, souls of the deceased are nearer to this world. The *Tibetan Book of the Dead* confirms this and asserts the soul of the dead remains nearby immediately after death. Often the soul does not know what has happened and asks whether it is dead. The departed soul can see relatives as if it were still alive, and can even hear the grieving and wailing. In Tibetan culture, the local spiritual leader must inform the soul of its Earth departure.

In mysticism and folklore tradition, an apparition was called the spiritual body. Alchemists described it as the "star in man," the body of glorification. Religions believe this spiritual body in man is immortal. The idea of a spiritual and immortal body within a person has been an ancient tradition predating Christianity. The Egyptians called it the *ba*, a soul image of man considered man's spiritual double. Gnostics identified this primordial man (spiritual double) clothed in light with the Logos that existed before creation. Adam Kadmon, the spiritual man of Jewish mysticism, was manifested as a quality of light. Jung referred to this inward spiritual man as a daimon. Paracelsus (1493-1541), a Swiss doctor, scientist, and philosopher, claimed a half-corporeal body lives beside the body of flesh as a mirror image. He called it the sidereal body or star body. In death, writes Paracelsus, the elemental body goes to the grave, but the ethereal bodies are consumed in the firmament, and the spirit of the image of God returns to God. Paracelsus said the sidereal body took on the likeness of the dead and could walk through walls. Gradually this sidereal body is consumed by the stars, long after the dissolution of the physical body.

Anieta Jaffe asserts in *Apparitions and Precognition* that the body vacated by the psyche continues to act and behave like a living person. This happens because a residue of actual consciousness remains that bridges the split between body ego and spirit ego (ego of the detached personality).

The American Society for Psychical Research was established in 1882, and their first major study, called the "Census of Hallucinations," under the direction of Professor Henry Sidawick, was formulated at the International Congress of Experimental Psychology. The research examined 1,087 people who had visual hallucinations, another name for apparitions. Out of these 1,087 hallucinations, 283 occurred in the presence of another person. Only 95 of the 283 were actually witnessed by another person; 188 were not. Out of 493 auditory hallucinations, 34 (7 percent) were witnessed by another person.

The researchers asked other subjects, while they were in the awake state, did they ever have a vivid impression of seeing or being touched by a living being or an inanimate object, or did they ever hear a voice that could not be accounted for by external physical causes? Of 17,000 people, 1,684 replied yes (9.9 percent) and the remainder said no.

Studies regarding apparitions show them to be nonphysical for the following reasons:

1. They appear and disappear in locked rooms.

2. They vanish while being watched.
3. Sometimes they become transparent and fade away.
4. Often they are seen and heard by only some of those present.
5. They pass through physical objects, such as walls and closed doors.
6. People have reported walking through them or putting their hands through them.
7. They leave behind no physical traces.Sometimes the central figure appears with other entities and objects. Most often entities appear clothed. Reports of apparitions with hats, sticks, dogs, horses, and carriages have been documented.

People who have experienced an apparition report a feeling of coldness and report no reason for feeling cold. People often reported they had been sleeping and then were awakened suddenly before they saw the apparition. Some woke up and felt a presence in the room.

Researchers divide apparitions into four classes:
1. An experimental apparition occurs as a result of deliberate effort to make the apparition appear.
2. A crisis apparition manifests during a crisis.
3. Postmortem apparitions appear after the death of a subject.
4. Ghostly apparitions are those that haunt locations they were fond of when alive.

The "Census of Hallucinations" attempted to determine whether the hallucinations coincide with an external event. If so, this would provide evidence of a causal connection. If no causal relation was found, the study concluded the apparition would be telepathic, that is, a feeling at a distance. In 1,300 cases studied, 30 death coincidences, that is, an apparition of the recently deceased, appeared to a loved one. This represents a ratio of 1:43. The normal statistical chance of this happening is 1:19,000. The study concluded there was a causal connection.

A poltergeist is a ghost or discarnate entity who makes a variety of sounds, such as whispering, rapping, or singing. They have been known to break household items, such as vases and cups. Sometimes they start fires or move objects from one side of a room to the other. Poltergeist activity has been reported in many countries.

Parapsychologist Dr. Henry Carrington believed that poltergeist activity was associated with juveniles achieving puberty, and that sometimes the combination of sexual maturity and psychological tension produced an energy effect in the home environment. Dr. A.

R. Owen believes there may be some truth to this theory, as he found many poltergeist outbreaks were attributed to the release of emotional tension. Author William G. Roll, in his book, *The Poltergeist,* assumes that poltergeist effects are produced by the mind and psyche of a person, whether or not that person is in the flesh.

The definition of poltergeist is reserved for disturbances of a physical nature, as opposed to typical haunting cases. Poltergeist disturbances are of short duration, rarely lasting more than several months. Hauntings may go on for years. Researchers have found poltergeist activity accompanies a certain person. Activity will follow the individual to different locations, whereas a haunting will remain in a certain locale. Typical poltergeist activity has no reference to apparitions, such as ghosts or hearing footsteps. Poltergeists are considered very sociable and usually nothing happens when the family is away from home. Rarely will the poltergeist perform unless that particular individual it is attached to is at home. Bishop James Pike reports of poltergeist activity following his son's suicide. Objects were moved to different locations, usually when Pike was away. When Pike spoke to his son through a medium, his son said he moved objects to get his dad's attention.

Some of the best evidence for ghosts comes from spirit photographs. Genuine spirit photography did exist at one time, mainly in the nineteenth century. Today it is extremely rare, but under certain circumstances photographing spiritual entities is possible. No one knows how genuine images of spirits find their way onto photographic plates and film. Most often, they would manifest during a portrait setting, frequently when loved ones were being photographed. The spirit figure in a photograph closely resembles the physical appearance that the person had in life, suggesting he or she was surely the surviving spirit of the dead. During the peak of spirit photography, cases of fraud and forgeries gave the phenomenon a bad name, but the number of genuine images vastly outnumbered the deceptive ones.

Hundreds of photographs have been produced. Many photographers who obtained these spirit extras did not have mediumship ability and were frequently at a loss to explain them. Some of the spirit images were in focus, and some were not. Not one of the spirit entities was visible during the time of camera exposure. Researchers believe spirit photography was undoubtedly the work of discarnate beings who wanted to influence human beliefs.

In the early investigation of psychic photography a method called dorchagraphy was developed to produce pictures with the aid of spirit entities, but without the use of ordinary light. However, most spirit pictures taken by nonprofessionals or nonmediumistic photographers were in fact accidental. Spirit photographs were obtained through dorchagraphy, accident, clairvoyance, or ordinary vision. No one has explained them.

Some believe that in the lower regions of the spiritual world, the lower astral region, low-grade spirits dwell who enjoy misleading and manipulating people. Often they are of a harmful and deceptive nature. For some reason these discarnate entities were interested in fostering a spiritual materialism in Europe and America. Author Fred Gettings believed this was the simple truth that lies behind the secret history of spirit photography. Spirit photography was one of the most important factors that led spiritualists in the direction of spiritual materialism.

Many believe spirit photography began in Boston in 1861 with William Mumler. On October 5 an image appeared by accident on his photographic plate. He recognized this extraneous figure as a young girl, the image of his cousin who had died twelve years previously. In 1865, a woman by the name of Mrs. Tyndall came to Mumler for a portrait. A figure of Abraham Lincoln standing behind the woman with his hands on her shoulders appeared on the photograph. The woman then confessed she was really Mrs. Lincoln, a fact completely unknown to Mumler.

In 1971, two young girls took the most famous spirit photograph, now called the "Cottingly Fairies." Elsie Wright, aged 16, and her friend Frances Ealing, aged 10, used to play in Cottingly Beck woods near Elsie's village home in England. Both girls claimed they could see and hear fairies. One day in July, Elsie borrowed a camera from her father and took a picture of Frances with a group of fairies. In September of that year, Frances took a picture of Elsie with a curious "gnome like" creature. The photographic plates themselves were genuine, but skeptics of course debunked the photographs.

As we will discuss in a following chapter, communications between the spiritual world continue today through mediums and electronic means such as television and computers. Communication channels are still open.

Chapter Nine

SPIRIT COMMUNICATION

Describing the Other Side

Communication with spirits has occurred since the most ancient of times. Shamans communicated with spirits that assisted in everyday life circumstances, such as healings and finding food sources. Egyptian priests communicated with gods to placate them. The spiritualism movement of the nineteenth century and early twentieth century involved communication with spirits through mediums. Today, communication with spirits is commonly called channeling. Based on his research, college professor Jon Klimo has written one of the most informative books on the subject titled *Channeling*.

Klimo defines channeling as "the communication of information to or through a physically embodied human being from a source that is said to exist on some other level or dimension of reality than the physical as we know it, and that is not from the normal mind (or self)." Arther Hastings, past president of the California Institute of Transpersonal Psychology, defined channeling as "the process in which a person transmits messages from a presumed discarnate source external to his consciousness." Spirit communication or channeling may include spirits of the deceased, alien intelligences, the Higher Self, or the Universal Mind.

In 1980, a Gallup Poll showed that 71 percent of Americans believed in an afterlife. An amazing 42 percent said they had been in contact with someone who had died. Of these people, 78 percent said they saw the departed ones, 50 percent heard them, and 18 percent actually talked with them. An interesting study found that 30 percent of Americans who did not believe in life after death still claimed they had personal contact with a departed loved one.

Jack Pursel, one of the current popular mediums, channels an entity named "Lazaris." Jon Klimo asked Lazaris how communication takes place between the channel and entity. Lazaris said, "They generate thought–the thoughts are projected through the planes of reality–they are projected into a denser level–they enter in through the star system Sirius into the physical world. Thoughts are down stepped–the mass of energy is aligned. The thought enters the mental plane of activity and then goes to the causal plane of reality where cause and effect hang out. It then steps down to the astral plane and finally into the physical. The energy enters the channel and then comes out through the throat."

HISTORY OF SPIRIT COMMUNICATION

Shamans of Siberia, South America, Tibet, Finland, and America practiced trance channeling, according to Mircea Eliade, a foremost scholar on shamans. While in trance, shamans could communicate with human and nature spirits. They could attract sympathetic spirits to consult with them about mundane matters of life. Often shamans could communicate with a number of discarnate entities at the same time.

Egypt may be where trance communication originated. It enabled the priest to achieve a mystical state that allowed him to talk with gods. While in a trance state, priests could talk directly to the gods, which often animated statutes. Egyptians regarded the afterlife as similar to Earth, where the *ba* (soul) retained the status and qualities it had possessed while embodied.

Emmanuel Swedenborg (1688-1772) is thought to have spent more time communicating with spirits than anyone before him. He was a Swedish scientist, physician, and mystic who had extremely vivid experiences that included prolonged visions, hearing voices, and making sojourns into the spirit world. Often he was visited by spiritual entities, including angels who took him in his spiritual body into the nonphysical realm. Swedenborg wrote sixteen books describing this experience and said, "Today's churchman knows almost nothing about Heaven, Hell, or his own life after death. The spirits were heartsick at the persistence of this ignorance on Earth, especially within the church." Swedenborg cautioned man about spirit communication because some spirits can lie and fabricate information. He claimed he had seen and talked with disembodied spirits a thousand times.

Joseph Smith, during the mid-nineteenth century, claimed to have received material from an angel called Moroni. Information from this experience led him to seek out revelation tablets buried in upstate New York that became the *Book of Mormon*. His interpretation laid the foundation for the Mormon Church.

The Bible often speaks of spirit communication. In I John 4:1, the disciple John emphasized the use in discernment in receiving channeled information: "Beloved, believe not every spirit, but try the spirits whether they are of God: because many false prophets are gone into the world." Today, most agree with John's advice to discriminate and interpret channeled material. A person needs to protect himself or herself against the influence of lower spirits.

Christ also refers to channeling in words similar to others about channeled material during the past 150 years. In Matthew, Christ says, "For it shall be given you in that the same hour what ye shall speak. For it is not ye that speaks, but the spirit of your Father which speaketh in you."

During the mid-nineteenth century, spirit communication became very popular under the name of spiritualism. During this era, the spirit channeling was called mediumship. Almost without exception, the sources were spirits of deceased human beings. The beginning of the spiritualist movement occurred with the loosening of the materialistic world view that had been so dominant since the seventeenth century. Great opposition to spiritualism came from organized religion, the majority of the press, academia, and science. Still, many overcame this opposition to explore this new phenomenon.

During the nineteenth century, a religious group of gentle people called the Shakers formed. In 1837, spirits that claimed to be discarnate American Indians sought periodically to use the Shakers to reestablish contact with Earth life. The spirits asked permission before entering the Shakers' bodies. There are reports of entire tribes taking over Shaker parishioners, who would whoop, sing, dance, eat, and converse with one another in the Native American language.

Abraham Lincoln was reported to have consulted the trance medium Nettie Colburn between 1861-1863. Numerous people witnessed each meeting. Lincoln's spiritual guides told him not to put off action on the Emancipation Proclamation. The channeled spirits also convinced Lincoln the best thing he could do for the low morale of soldiers was to go to the front line at Fredericksburg. He did so with remarkable results.

Peaking shortly after World War I, the spiritualist movement declined for several reasons: reports of fraud and deception, traditional churches claimed contact with the spirit world was demonic, a hostile press made light of it, and insufficient organization with ritual.

Most spiritual information attained by the Theosophical Society was obtained by spirit communication. In 1888, Madame H. P. Blavatsky, who founded the Society, wrote several landmark books including *Isis Unveiled* and *The Secret Doctrine,* claiming the information was channeled under direct inspiration from the "Tibetan" and other Eastern masters. Blavatsky wrote, "There are passages entirely dictated by them and verbatim, but in most cases they only inspire the ideas and leave the literary form to the writer." She believed this material came from evolved spirits.

Alice Baily, another important Theosophist, at the age of 15 first met her spiritual teacher, who later connected her with the mysterious being who channeled volumes of ancient wisdom. In 1919, her chief source, also the "Tibetan," entered her life. She heard a voice: "There are some books which it is desired should be written for the public. You can write them. Will you do so?" Baily said that in no way was it automatic writing. She would assume an attitude of intense, positive attention and then take down the words as she simply listened, registering the thoughts one by one into her brain. Baily said she never changed anything that the "Tibetan" gave her. The "Tibetan" was an ascended master named Djwhal Khul. Baily's work corroborated much of the occult literature about the cosmologic hierarchy regarding physical, ether, astral, mental, causal, and other higher spheres of existence. Baily and the Tibetan master wrote more than twenty books.

Edgar Cayce, known as the sleeping prophet, was the best known clairvoyant of America. Cayce had the ability to lie down and go into a trance, what he called a sleep. He could "see" into the distant bodies of strangers and could diagnose illness and prescribe a cure. Dozens of books were written about Cayce. The Association for Research and Enlightenment, established in Virginia Beach, Virginia, has a library containing records of thousands of readings given by Cayce. Many considered Cayce to be the father of holistic medicine, as he was the first to emphasize the relationship of mind, body, and spirit. Cayce's voice was always his own and no guides came through him. Cayce claimed the information came "by the attuning of self to the divine within, which is a universal or the universal consciousness."

Arther Ford, born in 1896, was a well-known American medium. After entering into a hypnotic sleep, he could accept messages from waiting discarnate entities and transmit them as words and sometimes as thought symbols. Ford relayed information from the spirit of magician Henry Houdini and from Bishop James Pike's son, who had committed suicide.

During the last part of the twentieth century, many people developed the ability to channel and communicate with spirits. Countless books have been written about information from the other side. These channels and their information led Dr. Jon Klimo to research this fascinating phenomenon.

SPIRIT INFORMATION

Research by Klimo found a pattern of subjects the spiritual world communicated to the physical world.

Ageless Wisdom: Nearly all the sources above the lower astral planes, writes Klimo, tell us that from their vantage points, they know the entire universe to be a living spiritual being of which each person is a living part. The sources say that our planet, along with humanity, functions under universal law. We all evolve through a series of embodied and disembodied lives, and eventually after our evolution, we will reunite with God. This truth underlies all that is. The sources say that by virtue of the Higher Self, we are connected to these deepest truths. Various occult, esoteric, and mystery schools repeat this theme, and world religions guise it in different words.

Knowledge of Individuals: The spiritual source claims to have detailed knowledge of the medium's life or the lives of other individuals present during channeling sessions. With certain limits, this information is available to the source, depending on the source's stage of spiritual growth and the purpose for which the information is to be used. These sources can often provide individually tailored advice. For example, Edgar Cayce was responsible for health-related readings to thousands of individuals, with approximately 85 percent accuracy. Personal guidance may teach people how to end old patterns and start new ones, and how to face hardships, illness, and death.

Survival after Death Evidence: An important purpose of the spiritual source is to provide evidence that the human personality survives beyond physical death. Sometimes the source will provide a nickname used by a spouse, the location of lost personal items, or meaningful descriptions of incidents, things that reassure the person that life does continue after physical death.

Description of Nonphysical Realms: Most spiritual communications concur that life in the realms beyond our physical world involves a much closer relationship between the mind and spiritual environment. Information is also provided about the reality experienced by the recently deceased human, as we shall discuss later in the chapter.

Prophetic Information: Some channeled information provides insight about our future, both on personal and global levels. Much of the channeled information during the twentieth century warns about great changes that will occur around the turn of the century. Edgar Cayce predicted great earth changes, including the sinking of parts of the West Coast. Nostradamus, in the sixteenth century, Swedenborg, and the Book of Revelations all predict this great upheaval. Channeled information from space brothers also warns of impending destruction. However, most sources speak in terms of probability, as the exercise of free will can affect the future. Often the message involves raising consciousness and living a loving life, which may soften and delay the predicted changes. Both Edgar Cayce and Ruth Montgomery describe the earth changes that took place in Lemuria, Atlantis, and with the Great Flood.

Creative Inspiration: Some spirit sources are deceased poets, playwrights, painters, dancers, actors, and composers. These creative souls use their natural talents for creative self-expression in the new realms. Through channels, spirits say they occasionally try to impress their creative energies upon their colleagues on Earth, who may experience inspiration and creative ideas. For example, a London homemaker, Rosemary Brown, who had no musical education, wrote an autobiographical book titled *Unfinished Symphonies* that chronicled her lifelong association with the spirits of Beethoven, Liszt, Debussy, Chopin, Schubert, and Bach. Nearly four hundred new compositions came through her in this manner. In the nineteenth century, when Brown was seven, she claims Liszt visited her in a clairvoyant vision and promised that he would work with her as she grew older. A computer study successfully matched Brown's music with known composers.

Science and Healing Information: Klimo's research discovered that disembodied human spirits identified themselves as having been scientists, inventors, engineers, healers, and researchers while on Earth. Through channels, they say they can continue their work in the spiritual realm. Thus, they gain more knowledge and resources without economic restraints. Many communicate that they can tune into a wealth of scientific ideas from the Akashic Records and timeless realms. College Professor James J. Hurtak in *The Book of Knowledge: The Keys of Enoch* claims he received technical information from two nonphysical entities, Enoch and Metatron. Ruth Norman's *Unarius Science* books are filled with detailed descriptions attributed to well-known deceased scientists. They tell how to build devices that operate on virtual-wave energy down-stepped from higher dimensions into our own. Sadly, no one has yet researched this interesting information. A wealth of channeled information comes in the categories of medicine and healing. Most of Edgar Cayce's readings dealt with healing and the role of past lives in a person's health.

SPIRITUAL SOURCES

Klimo has identified a variety of spiritual sources for human channels:

The Channels of Higher Self: Many channelers of spiritual knowledge claim their Higher Selves channel down through an "umbilical cord" to the Lower Selves. They claim constant communication between these levels. However, because of dissociation between the two selves, the earthly counterpart is not usually conscious of its higher aspect. Klimo calls this channeling "expanded self awareness." British channel Stuart Wilde claims the Higher Self takes a greater part of his conscience when channeling, and he believes all channeling is aligning to the Higher Self.

Gods and God: In the 1980s, a Gallup Poll showed 94 percent of Americans believed in God, and 64 percent said God guided them in making decisions. According to 31 percent, God had spoken directly to them. Klimo believes that because of memory loss between Lower Self and Higher Self, the Lower Self often interprets its higher aspect as being godlike. Most channeled information stresses that God is all that is and is the unity that contains all disparate parts. We are all individualizations of the one God, some more evolved in consciousness than others.

Universal Mind and Collective Unconscious: The greater collective conscious has often been called God, All-That-Is, and the Universal Mind. Carl Jung spoke in terms of the collective unconscious, whose contents are composed of various archetypes, which he called racial memories of the most often repeated human beliefs and behavior. Jung said as we contact the archetypes through dreams, myths, meditations, art, or religion, our psyche is engaged by them and we translate them into our individual experiences.

Group Beings: Group entities are sometimes the source of spirit information. A group mind is described as a coherent bundle of individual beings. As these individuals spiritually evolve, they claim to reach a point where further growth means pooling themselves into a larger self. The various *Seth* books, channeled by Jane Roberts, introduced the concept of oversoul. Each personality on Earth is, in fact, a part of a higher entity. The soul evolves by gaining numerous simultaneously incarnating components. Sometimes a person can channel the entity, or the oversoul, to which he or she belongs. Some channels assert they are channeling their own past life reincarnational selves.

Jesus and Ascended Masters: Much of the channeled information is claimed to be from Jesus and other great masters. Most of these highly evolved spirits claim they have experienced incarnations as humans on Earth or similar planets. Some claim they serve in caretaking and teaching roles to heal our planet. The entities claim they have ascended, meaning they no longer have the need to incarnate into physical bodies for further spiritual growth. If they chose to do so, they could manifest in physical form. Ascended masters consciously operate as their Higher Selves.

Nonhumans: This realm consists of angels, devas, elementals, plants, and animals. In the early 1970s, Dorothy Maclean and David Spangler claimed to have channeled angels and devas of entire plant species that helped them with their garden in the northern Scotland community of Findhorn.

Extraterrestrials: The latter half of the twentieth century saw many reports of channeled beings from another planet. Frequently called "space brothers," some claim they reside on planets in the same frequency as ours. However, in the majority of cases, extraterrestrials assert to have come from a vibration higher than our own, saying they have technology to transform the vibrational rate in order to enter ours. Former New Mexico college professor Dr.

Norma Milanovich has channeled, with the aid of her computer, information from entities of the star system Arcturus. Arcturians, according to Milanovich's book *We the Arcturians,* are from the fifth dimension, and their role is to help guide humanity's evolution.

Discarnate Human Souls: Klimo claims more sources for channeling come from this category than any other. The spiritualist movement almost exclusively involved channeling deceased spirits. Most spirits said their principal purpose was to comfort the bereaved and expand the world's view about life after death. Channeled material tells us that after individuals die, they maintain their basic level of understanding and awareness, as well as their personality traits. It also warns those spirits eager to remain in contact with Earth: Too much communication can be hazardous to their spiritual health.

The more evolved souls seek to assist and serve others in their evolution. They strive to raise humanity's consciousness to a new level, where love and harmony reign. These souls call themselves teachers, guides, or guardian angels.

After death, most human souls go to the middle and upper subplanes of the astral world. Of all the disembodied spirits, those in the lower astral domain are most problematic, because they are the least spiritually evolved. After death, they remain near the physical level and can possess other humans. Many are drawn to souls of similar evolvement, such as criminals or addicts. A myriad of these lower evolved entities delights in giving misinformation to channelers.

Some channeled material tells of demons and evil spirits. These entities await every opportunity to tempt and control human souls.

TECHNIQUES OF SPIRIT COMMUNICATION

Klimo describes two basic kinds of channeling: intentional and spontaneous. With intentional channeling, a person controls the phenomenon and can usually produce it at will. In spontaneous channeling, the person cannot control the activity and is at the mercy of the entity. All types of channeling involve a source that communicates from another level of reality through a channel. In some channeling, one can identify the entity source. Other channels cannot, such as when receiving a new idea about a book. Klimo's research has identified a number of spirit communication techniques.

Full Trance: Here, the medium appears to go unconscious or into a trance. Some entity appears to occupy the brain and body and uses it for speaking, writing, or moving about. After the session, the individual regains full consciousness. Sometimes the medium remembers an out-of-body experience. While in trance, the controlling entity has a voice distinctly different from his or her normal voice. Over the past century, most of the well-known channels have been of the trance voice type.

Sleep Channels: Ideas are often imprinted in selected people's minds during sleep. People awaken and feel they have had some knowledge imparted to them while asleep. Sometimes they wake up inspired to start a new project, to visit a foreign country, or to study a new subject.

Dreams: In this technique, the source appears in a dream in some straightforward way. The source chooses the dream period to assure the dreaming channel operates on the same level of reality as the source.

Light Trance: During this technique, the individual has partial or full awareness of the surrounding environment. Purportedly, the transmitting entity co-dwells with the channel.

Clairaudient: During this communication, the medium remains fully conscious or in a mildly altered state. Klimo describes it as gaining attention of the "mind ear" by quieting the self and listening within, which enables the medium to hear a voice. The message of the source is limited by the vocabulary and semantic capability of the channel. This may explain why many writers and polished speakers contend that some of their ideas come from out of the blue.

Clairvoyant: In this case, the clairvoyant claims the information comes in the form of imaging seen with the "mind's eye." They claim to distinguish between material coming from one's own mind and material from outside it.

Automations: Automatic writing has been a popular technique for spirit communication. The medium is usually awake and completely separated from any sense of controlling the writing activity. Automatic writers claim that another entity controls the arm and hand. Automatic writing has transmitted profound information from the spiritual realm. Klimo asserts the *Urantia Book* was transmitted this way.

In Baltimore, in 1892, Elijah Bond and William Fuld invented the Ouija board. The board consists of a flat surface on which is printed a semicircle of alphabet letters, along with numbers zero through nine, the words "yes and no," and sometimes "maybe." Subjects maintain light fingertip contact with a platform on the board surface. Spirits supposedly control the movement of the platform to spell out words. The Ouija board has a reputation for attracting the lowest class of entities. Stokes Hunt writes in *Ouija: The Most Dangerous Game,* that the Ouija board is incredibly seductive because of the information revealed. It can be quite dangerous to a suggestible person.

Open Channeling: In this technique, the medium channels thoughts, images, feelings, and information from another entity. There is no identified source. Open channeling allows anyone to experience the phenomenon of channeling. Creative writers, thinkers, scientists, inventors, and artists have benefitted from open channeling.

Physical Channeling: This category is defined as the human ability to channel unknown energies that affect the physical environment in ways that can be experienced by a person other than a channel. Examples include materializations; dematerializations; levitation; teleportation; table tilting; knocking; rapping; poltergeist activity; and the imprinting of clay, wax, magnetic tape, and photographic film. This activity helped herald the Spiritualist movement of the nineteenth century.

Voices from Spirits: This involves lowering the vibration from the spiritual entity, while at the same time borrowing paranormal energy from the medium, to manifest a presence in the physical world. This enables the vibration of physical air waves to strike ear drums. Those present reported hearing the same external objective voice giving the same message.

Klimo writes, "Virtually all channels and their source tell us that discernment is crucial. As inner information wells up, you may wish to be able to discriminate whether it is coming from the self or from elsewhere, and if from elsewhere, then from what or whom. We need to discern the nature, quality, and trustworthiness of the source. We must guard against the charisma of authority."

LIFE ON THE OTHER SIDE

A strong love existed between Senta Lange and her husband Enne, which continued following Enne's death on August 13, 1983.

After Enne's death, a weekly communication transpired between Enne from the spiritual world to his loving wife Senta in West Germany. This communication gives insight to the life of a soul after the transition from physical life. Senta titled her ten booklets *Enne: Please Continue to Write*. The following is a summary of Enne's communication during the months following his death.

August 23, 1983

Enne said it was lovely there in his new world. When he arrived, many loved ones, acquaintances, and others welcomed him. He needed to rest when he first arrived, but upon awakening, all his friends and relatives returned to fetch him for a celebration to be held in a large hall. He named deceased aunts and uncles in the welcoming party that numbered over one hundred.

His residence was a room in a house he shared with eight other people who were doing the same work that he would be doing. In a later transmission, Enne said that he was given permission to have a house built for himself that he would share with Senta when she made the transition.

Education was important in this new realm. Enne said they were often required to participate in spiritual training. During these sessions, they were shown aspects of the Fall, human evolution, and the creation of the Earth. The teaching process involved being shown events through corresponding pictures and scenes which resulted in a more complete knowingness.

Enne spoke of visitations by others who were from different spheres. His deceased bird and dog were also there, who actually resided in what he called the Animal Kingdom.

Enne spoke of the Realm of Music where he listened to a Mozart concert. He said he felt like joining the violins, but it was not permitted yet.

He also spoke of being around Senta quite frequently, trying to bring her strength and good wishes to help alleviate the pain. Enne felt happy that they were so deeply connected.

Yesterday, he said, seven of them had visited a sick family in England. They sent the family much energy which made them happy, especially if their help and light could radiate into their beings.

August 30, 1983

Enne described his room as having a recliner, table, and a small cupboard. On it stood his wedding picture and a vase with roses. Everyone who lived in this house wore the same kind of garment. A

flower garden and several fir trees were found in front of the house.
Adorning the entrance was a golden arch and a bouquet of white
lilies. Enne said all the houses had the same emblem, the same
emblem found on the robes of heavenly messengers of this Realm
of Compassion. The privilege to wear the emblem had to be earned.
After retiring to their rooms, Enne said they were allowed to visit
loved ones on Earth. This is when he sends his strength and blessings to Senta. Once it is time for their spiritual work, a special bell
rings that calls them together.

Things are much simpler there than Enne would have imagined.
He said everything was so simple, according to God's law, and he
was surprised how difficult Earth beings make it.

When called upon to do spiritual work, they are shown specific
families and towns, and are told why these people are afflicted so
they can better understand the situation. Their teachers instruct
them how they can give help, relief, and strength. Today, they were
to visit a prison camp in Russia.

Enne describes his realm as being enormously large. Repeatedly
he is shown a new part of it, where he met a multitude of souls.
Millions of spirit missionaries reside here to help humankind overcome the very hard Earth school. Tomorrow he was to go to Italy.

September 6, 1983

Enne said he needed to let go of many things which still bind
him to life on Earth. Much is no longer needed in the realm of spirit. His main objective in his new life was to do all and everything
from the premise of love and compassion. One's position in the
spiritual world, either in the Darkness or the Light, depended on
their association and awareness of God and Christ. He said that
those who never went to church on Earth are soon in the light, since
their souls are more attuned to the God essence. Those who are the
most religiously devout are often so bitterly disappointed. He said
often their prayers were only a mouthing and did not come from
the heart. They were shown that repetitive prayers alone would not
help, as deeds are foremost in God's eyes. They need to learn much
before they could enter the sphere of light.

Everyone in this realm is repeatedly shown their own life pictures.
He said good and bad is illuminated so one can realize their impact.

In a visitation to Argentina, they were asked to help a family
who had lost many of their belongings in a fire. Now they are filled
with new-found courage and are beginning to rebuild. Enne was

shown that it was a payment of a debt for them. In a former life, they had greatly hurt some people by deliberately setting a fire. Enne said the cause would always be shown in the kind of effects that surface later in the course of one's life.

September 13, 1983

During this transmission, Enne talked about his spiritual education. A course was taught explaining the development of the soul after the Great Fall, including pictures of what happened afterwards. There is a course where they are taught certain life episodes and what they could learn from them.

His course taught him about a soul, while on Earth, who did many bad deeds. In the spirit world, the soul resided in a very dark sphere. It took a long time until she repented. After prolonged repentance, the soul incarnated again on Earth. She then married a man who treated her badly, drank a lot, and even beat her. She stayed with him because of her thirteen children and her love for him. The soul gave her children much love and raised them appropriately, with all entering respected professions. After twenty-eight years of marriage, her husband died. Within her soul, she had already forgiven her husband. When she made the transition, she was welcomed with love on the other side, and she moved into a sphere of light. She was told she had paid her debt and now she could advance further. In the next life, she was told, "You will be born as a man and will marry a woman. Your marriage will bring you many blessings to you in the eyes of God, due to his great mercy." In this way, souls clear themselves, since everyone shall eventually fully return to the light.

September 20, 1983

Enne said their work in his new world is based on the premise of compassion and love. When working in his realm, they often visit rest homes for the sick souls. Here, they care for the awakening souls and inform them the reason they are there and the work to be done on Earth after they feel like participating.

Yesterday they had gone to Italy to aid a sick and poor family. They had received this mission of mercy because of the many requests received from relatives.

Enne said in this spiritual realm, they could read the thoughts of everyone and see their actions and deeds. By letting their entire love force radiate, they were able to prevent much suffering. "Otherwise," said Enne, "life there resembles that on Earth, only expressing on an etheric level and not as materialized as on Earth."

After returning from an Earth mission, Enne describes a little celebration they had with the children who came from the heavenly Children's Realm. The children sang, danced, and recited short poems. Then a heavenly messenger talked to them and thanked them for their work.

September 27, 1983

Enne was told the Earth is the lowest world and is one of the toughest schools for every soul. It stretches over many Earth incarnations for everyone and must be experienced until everyone is ready once again to inhabit higher worlds.

Only through the realization concerning the acts of Christ, who imparts his redemptive spark to everyone, are we allowed to call ourselves again the children of God. Enne said that through Christ all would again advance to the sphere of light in order to live once again in divine harmony. This alone is the primary goal which everyone must achieve.

"All other worlds," he said, "are only schools that help souls develop and mature. As man becomes spirit again, so does Earth. Eventually, all material aspects will dissolve and vanish. Therefore, man has the obligation in each lifetime to let go of all evil, vanity, greed, self-centeredness, and vice. All these create disease, difficulties, and life destinies which manifest throughout many life times. God does not punish."

Everything in a person's life was created by the soul, by the person alone, according to how far one has strayed from the divine path. Everyone is and remains his or her own judge. Each creates the cause and experiences the effect for which it ultimately pays. There is no damnation, as a soul creates its own hell. However, God's mercy always rules above everything.

October 4, 1983

Enne was told when man, the soul, is allowed to reincarnate, he is shown his new Earth life with its established segments, all of which leads toward spirit evolution. The soul is usually interested in this and is ready to walk the new path. God gave man the merciful gift of free will. Man can create his life as he wishes, either for the good or for the bad. The will of man will be the gauge of each life's maturation.

Enne said they had gone to Burma, assisting people who were blind, wretched, and poor. Upon returning, they were shown these people's life pictures. Some of them had been great leaders at one time, but they had thought only of themselves and were blind to the

misery of their subjects. Others were illustrious dignitaries who sub-
jugated everyone and rejected all divine spirituality. They demanded
money, even from the poorest subjects, by promising them entry into
Heaven. Now they were experiencing what it meant to be blind and
poor themselves.

October 11, 1983

Many souls of the deceased frequently say to everyone, "Now I
feel free, I am so happy." They are happy they left the Earth school
behind. Now they are surrounded by light, peace, and harmony.

"Those who are already in spiritual matters," said Enne, "usually
need no prolonged rest in the new realm. They are soon introduced
to their new spiritual work."

Those souls who had little knowledge about spiritual matters and
never inquired about them but lived a normal Earth life, are taken to
a beautiful place of tranquility or rest home. In this setting they are
lovingly cared for during a short or long rest period. Here they are
carefully introduced to the laws and mode of divine, spiritual life.
Always, they are surrounded by a world of beauty, peace, and harmony. It is a place of peace amid beautiful parks, gardens, temples,
and homes, an environment they share with birds and animals. All
this makes the soul feel happy, evoking a sense of unending greatness
of the heavenly world.

Those souls, far removed from God, who created misery on Earth
are taken to sad places of darkness by compassionate missionary spirits. There is a law that "like attracts like." Even in the time of deepest
darkness, heavenly messengers care for these souls. If any ask for
God's help, these spirits will shine their light.

Enne says not to be afraid of death because everyone continues to
live. One door closes and another one opens, bringing the joy of freedom and peace, health, and happiness in reunion with loved ones.

Loved ones on Earth should be thankful to leave earth school
behind. All those who leave first will create a home for themselves and
their loved ones.

Work in this realm is primarily in form of thought. Whatever the
soul wishes, happens. Enne says when he wants to be around Senta,
he can do it in a flash. During sleep, he can walk with Senta's soul
through the sphere there, and they can do many things together.

If one wants to create or beautify one's home, wishes come true
only if one has completed one's work well. It is a reward in a sense.
For those who want to gain specific knowledge, there are large

libraries and scientific establishments available. If one wishes to listen to harmonious music, the wish is fulfilled.

In this realm, games such as soccer, tennis, and chess do not exist. Enne was told there are spheres that exist for those souls who cannot adjust and are bound by their hobbies. In these spheres, spiritual advancement is not as possible, as the path toward the light is much harder. This is why people should enjoy everything, but not bind themselves to anything fanatically.

They do eat and drink in this realm, including spiritual fruit and refreshing spiritualized wine. Inhabitants do not have excretory organs nor do they sleep. If they wish, they do rest surrounded by a twilight. Otherwise, it is always bright and warm. Speech is always expressed by thought, since everyone knows at once what the other thinks and wishes.

Enne tells Senta that before sending the reports to her, they are discussed with Konrad and Boduin, the helpers and protectors of their circles.

October 18, 1983

"Things in this realm are so similar to Earth," says Enne, "yet they are completely different. The spirit world has great beauty, and is endless in its breadth and size. All souls encountered are seen as they really are, with no disguise possible. It is a great surprise to many since man on Earth portrays himself or herself quite differently from whom he or she really is in soul. Lies, deceit, and disguise are totally impossible in this realm, since everyone can see into another's soul instantly."

The one who loves and acts according to true love can give it abundantly. Love is very powerful and is the Alpha and Omega for everyone. The more one can let this radiate, the easier the spiritual work can be accomplished. Love is the agent which helps one let go of faults and weaknesses. Letting go of one's faults in the spiritual world is much harder to do. Enne says he works on letting go of his constantly. Often they receive the task to help those on Earth who show the same faults and weaknesses.

Enne said he was astonished to experience how much the power of human thought will create either misery or blessings for each individualized soul. This is why each person should pay great attention to their thoughts. Thoughts of hate and anger fly like sparks toward a person who creates consequential effects, showing up in the form of restlessness or illness.

Freedom of action is another thing that is so different in this realm. If one wants to walk, one walks. If one wants to fly, one can fly. This is all possible because of the power of thought. When one wants to visit someone, one is instantly with them. The power of thought creates great joy, and loving thought creates an endless blessing, said Enne.

Enne just visited Afghanistan, and he said, "The people were so caught up in hate that it intensified their misery even more." He believed conflicts are so senseless.

October 23, 1983

In this session, Enne talked about his spirit plane. Upon arrival they were led to the boundaries of a meadow which was formed like an amphitheater. The newcomers were told, "This is the Sphere of Arrivals called the Land of Surprises." Enne recognized two distinct groups of people present. One group wore garments of different colors, but the other group, the minority, were new arrivals being welcomed by the heavenly hosts.

In the distance Enne discerned a high, thick bank of fog. As the heavenly hosts approached the fog bank, their garments took on the hue of light gray. When they returned, their garments shone again in brightness. Continuously new souls emerged from the fog bank with their guardian angels as every deceased person passed through this fogbank. Enne called it the Gate of Admission.

When souls pass through this fog region, they are stripped of all attributes of the fleshly bodies. All falsehoods and all facades fade away. The purpose of this fog is to dissolve everything except the spiritual attributes of the soul. What is hidden will be revealed as their "book of life," which is open to everyone. The term they use for the Earth is "the last judgment day."

Souls emerged from the fog in great astonishment as they were met by their loved ones. Some souls were quite exhausted and weak, and their loved ones greeted them from afar. Many were just carried to their place of rest.

Enne was told the color of the soul's garment reveals the just sentence which the soul has proclaimed about itself because of the unerring power of God's law, as deeds correspond to belief in the same way as the body does to the spirit. Faith is nothing without deeds. God forgives everyone according to one's deeds, so Jesus taught, and not according to one's faith. All forms of faith will remain in the fog bank.

Only love and good deeds allow the soul to progress to the light. Proclamation of the verdict is not final, since God leaves the way for repentance and mercy. Enne was told as long one is willing, one can learn everything here very rapidly. Everyone has a distinct mission, the more one does right, the faster the soul will mature.

Enne described a journey with an angel of death who radiated a warm light, much love, and mercy. As they passed through the fog bank, they approached the cot of an old man who turned to his sleeping comrade and said, "Look, Jan, I am going home now. But all this radiance is not for me!" Then the silver cord was severed and the soul left the body. The heavenly messenger said, "Now, brother, come home once again." The old man replied, "This must be a mistake because I have not been a good person. What did I ever do for God?" The messenger said, "You have helped the poorest, the hungry." But the man denied he had done anything good. "You once gave a hungry boy your very sparse meal. You gave a pair of shoes to a wino which you could hardly spare yourself. You gave an old woman glasses you could hardly spare yourself. You held watch at the bed of a sick comrade. You bore with patience your assigned poverty. You encouraged others and made them accept their fate. . . . Just deeds will never be forgotten. Now come home." They passed through the fog bank and the old man was dressed in his new garment, and he already started to look much younger.

November 1, 1983

Often the connection of a deceased person to the loved one is very strong, especially if the bereaved one is weeping a lot and mourning. They are constantly drawn back through the fog bank toward Earth. Often, after time, their effort to make themselves known is unsuccessful, and they are ready to follow the heavenly messenger.

Everyone retains his or her own free will, Enne was told. Souls can fall in their progression or advance.

Enne was taken to a meadow by his teacher and climbed the hill behind the meadow which overlooked a deep valley of blooming splendor. At the foot of the hill he saw hundreds of different paths which branched off in all directions. The light paths led up the hill according to specific color, and the dark path branched off in the foreground. In the middle was an immaculate white path, which was exceedingly bright, that led to a glowing arch. The teacher told Enne, "Now you can understand the full meaning of the garment since you will see that each soul will unquestionably take the path which corresponds to their soul garment. Only the heavenly messenger will retain his light robe on all the paths. . . . Over all paths rules and rests the divine power of love."

The teacher told Enne, "In this case (the idea of Heaven), as in many other earthly affairs, Bible interpretations, Bible translations about mortality, etc., created such a false view in the consciousness of man. And yet, each transition from death to immortality is always a step in the development of the soul. There are many places for all souls, Enne was told, depending on their evolution. Jesus taught, "In my Father's house are many mansions."

November 8, 1983

Enne said that spiritual knowledge gained on the physical plane usually resulted in a quick awakening on the other side. Then the integration follows, the schooling, and the retrospective view of the life to look at it objectively. Everything is subject to the all-encompassing law of cause and effect. Every person has his or her own star from birth until the return back to spirit, which course he or she must follow without fail. If the soul has passed its test and done well, it proceeds and receives new tasks.

Some receive tasks to help souls in the dark worlds to come to the light. Many souls live in varying degrees of unknowingness in the dark spheres. Some have no cognizance that they have died, and are wandering in the vastness of the other side. Some sense their life has changed, but they now live in a dream state. Heavenly hosts cannot enlighten them, as the law commands that all striving must originate from within.

The predominant thought of individuals in the physical revolves around their livelihood. In spirit they may continue their pursuits. There are all kinds of earthly endeavors such as office work, mining, construction, etc. Souls often remain stuck in this state for a long time before they awaken and long to come into the light.

Enne was taken into a dark sphere in the land of Low Thought Forms. Here, the souls looked haggard, gray, gloomy, and worn out; their thoughts radiated hate. He observed that these souls lived in filthy shacks, often one hundred to a dwelling. He saw frequent altercations between the inhabitants who said they held little hope for their future. The heavenly messenger told Enne, "Poor souls, their stay here corresponds to their earthly life. Their thoughts and feelings created the strange peculiarity, whereby their soul, once in the spirit world, drew to them this place according to the law. There is never a mistake in this! . . . It is always self which is the judge and executioner."

Enne was then shown the Land of Repentance. Souls that harmed many people on Earth must pass through this land. Dark gray garments are worn here. In the spirit world the soul forms its clothing according to its state of mind or spirit. The burdens of their deeds seem to wear them down. Because the soul lacks selfless feelings, it now lives in a barren place. All misery caused to others on Earth, passes by them continuously until the soul bows down in shame and repents. Heavenly messengers are then allowed to intervene.

Enne was then shown the Land of Rest. Everything there is similar to the earthly existence. It is made simple and infused with love, peace, and happiness. Landscaping is magnificent. Here, souls are allowed to rest until they are awakened, strengthened, and ready to move on. That is why the guardians of the fog bank test every soul garment, not to pass judgment, but in order to lead each newcomer to its assigned messenger.

Enne advises Senta, "Please remember your shortcomings already while on Earth and endeavor to get rid of them, as your stay here will be more beautiful."

November 16, 1983

Enne said that when they are busy with work, they are continually being guided where they are allowed to view life destinies of many people. They could understand why different things show themselves during a life span. Constantly, they recognize God's immeasurable mercy in all of them.

Enne tells of one troubled family of ten who were very poor that he visited. At one time the ten people lived together, at the court of King Louis the XIV, in great abundance that they took for granted, never thinking about the poor and misery of others. After being called home, they repented their thoughtless way of life and asked to clear this immediately in their next lifetime. Enne was told if they fell back in opulence or discord in their next life, a much worse situation would arise than they are experiencing now. He was told, "If one regrets one's mistakes and strives to live a better life, if one cleans up one's weaknesses, one can mitigate one's karma or even erase it." Whatever individuals suffer, they have laid the cause for themselves. The spiritual radiates positive thoughts to them, said Enne, so they may turn their souls toward the light.

November 23, 1983

Enne says it is a wonderful experience when the spiritual group visits a country in order to radiate all their energy of peace, directed to all souls. In daily life on Earth, those who are already peaceful within can accomplish much for peace. They live in harmony and radiate much love.

Enne was shown the souls of men in the Arab region that instigated the holy wars. They now reap what they sow, though they vowed while in spirit to dedicate themselves to peace. They have not matured spiritually and are accruing new burdens when they are not able to become peaceful in the human forms. Enne was told why it is always so important to strive for peace within and without and to live peacefully, because peace will bring God. He said if you could see this spiritual picture, you would see countless groups from the spirit world who are working for peace on Earth.

Enne was shown a village connected to God and Christ. These villagers were satisfied, happy, and at one with nature in a loving way. No one was suffering any deprivation. All were working thankfully, and very few got sick. His teacher told Enne that all these people paid their karmic debt and when they return home, they need not return to Earth again. When in the spirit world, they may help others to advance. In the last incarnation, Enne was told, they were all physicians, nurses, and helpers in a leper colony where they helped the unfortunate with infinite love and great sacrifice. Only small weaknesses and mistakes are still there to clear up.

November 29, 1983

Enne was taken to a lower sphere where he found many souls huddled together, complaining and lamenting. They were in great agitation, and some were quiet and weeping. From their life picture, they had slandered people and used the mistakes of others to their own advantage. They now regretted those actions and promised to atone for them. The heavenly messenger said, "They shall be forgiven," and told them, "This Christmas they shall go down to Earth with our helpers and ask forgiveness of all those whom they had hurt knowingly and unknowingly. After that they will be educated so that they may advance."

December 6, 1983

Enne told Senta that in his sphere everything was being prepared for the holidays. There was an immense peace hovering over everything. Every soul was happy and filled with expectations to see Christ. Everywhere candles were burning because on the day when Christ comes, there will be a celebration.

Enne was told during that week he may begin to build a new home after the holidays. He wanted to arrange everything with great beauty so that Senta might have a surprise when he was allowed to receive her on that side. He looked forward to their reunion.

Many who die unexpectedly are unable to grasp the situation and are clinging to their earthly ways. Sometimes they needed to be induced with sleep. Many souls came there after the conflict in Arabia. Many of those who had war experiences needed to be put in a convalescent home, as they could not bear the heavenly glow and peace.

December 13, 1983

"They had called everyone," said Enne, "and a long column proceeded to the big temple in the green valley. Everything was festively decorated with candles everywhere, and ringing of bells permeated the entire atmosphere."

Then Emanuel appeared before them and delivered a speech about the birth of Christ and His act of Redemption. After songs of thanksgiving, a brilliant light appeared, followed by an immense stillness, because of the powerful radiation of peace that emanated from Christ. His whole being radiated in unending love and mercy, but there was a profound seriousness surrounding Him. Enne said, "His voice penetrated so deeply into them that they could only listen attentively. He spoke of love, peace, harmony, and the vast mercy of God. Christ proceeded to bless everyone, and long after He left, there was a deep silence. From now on," said Enne, "our love for our Heavenly Father and the Christ was deeply anchored within their souls, that a yearning springs up in each who saw Him to emulate Him."

December 20, 1983

Many in the divine sphere, reported Enne, are allowed to go down to Earth at Christmas to be with their loved ones in order to give blessings. Ernie's teacher told him that God's mercy is without measure, for everything the soul or man does against the law of God will reap the consequences of that law. Everything will be forgiven and annulled, if man places himself under God's will and accepts the love of Christ.

December 27, 1983

Enne talked again about their task of radiating energy and peace to all Arabic nations. They were dismayed with the hate, distress, and misery that showed up there in certain individuals. Many lives in the Arab world need to pay for something and, therefore, they must walk through these life situations. They brought everything onto themselves. Enne says this is why they are being shown again and again the life pictures of certain people.

Enne was shown a life picture of a blind professor who asked himself, "Why me? I am so well liked." His past life picture showed that he burned out the eyes of people.

Another life picture was of a paralyzed young woman. In a former life she had cut people into pieces as a fanatic priest.

He was shown another person who was spending his golden years in harmony and thanksgiving. The teacher told Enne, "This child of Earth helped so many people in his last lifetimes and spread happiness all around. Now God's blessings are flowing his way in double measure."

Enne said, "Through these life pictures, they recognize how good and bad are forever balanced. It also helps them to act accordingly and to try to patiently emulate the laws of the divine."

Chapter Ten

ELECTRONIC SPIRIT COMMUNICATION
A Direct Line to Spirit

Since the advent of electronic communication, innovative scientists have attempted to use it for communication with the spirit world. Three of the world's greatest inventors individually attempted to invent a device that could communicate with the spiritual realm. Nikola Tesla, G. Marconi, and Thomas Edison all attempted in the last years of their physical life to develop such a device, but none of them succeeded. Theosophist Alice Baily in 1936 predicted that those who died would communicate with people on Earth, and this communication will be "reduced to a true science. . . . Death will lose its terror and that particular fear will come to an end." Forty years later, Yogi Sant Kesharvadas said at a lecture in India that "we would be able to pick up a phone and call friends, loved ones, and colleagues who have died." Fulfillment of these predictions was not far off.

In the 1950s a new generation of researchers in Europe and America attempted this remarkable feat of communicating electronically with the spirit world. They used various techniques for recording on magnetic tape words, phrases, and complete sentences of purported spirits who had died. Research was conducted by thousands of people, much of it under strict laboratory conditions. Hundreds of thousands of these short, faint spirit voices were recorded over the years. A few of these spirit voices were proven to have come from the experimenter's own unconsciousness by way of mind-over-matter, or psychokinesis.

Beginning in 1967, Latvian psychologist Konstantin Raudive collected on tape more than 75,000 voices, of which 15,000 are documented. He heard the voice of his deceased mother, who called him by his own boyhood name. Using an ordinary tape recorder, Raudive would sit quietly alone and address departed friends and loved ones. After asking questions, he would let the tape recorder run for several hours in his laboratory. Recorded on the tape were responses to the questions from the dead, who explained they could modulate sound waves with their thoughts that would simulate voice patterns. Raudive discovered that spirits needed a white noise that they could modulate into voice patterns. He found that the white noise between radio stations produced a rich spectrum of frequencies that spirit voices could manipulate into voices. His book *Breakthrough* described his research, but startled the scientific community. Later studies of Raudive's recordings found that they lasted an average of 1.8 seconds. A most powerful communication was received in a Latvian voice saying, "There is no death here. The Earth is death."

Swedish film producer Fredrich Juergenson taped hundreds of paranormal voices and published a book about them in 1964. Like Raudive, Juergenson heard the voice of his deceased mother. Being a good friend of Pope Paul VI, he shared his pioneer research with the Pontiff. The Vatican was so impressed that it authorized its own research team. A leading Jesuit researcher, Swiss theologian Reverend Father Leo Schmidt, was given permission by his superiors to collect the voices of spirits. Since 1969 he had collected more than 10,000 of them. An interesting article appeared in *Transmissions* (1999) stating, "Roman Catholics were given the Church's blessing to contact loved ones beyond the grave. Leading Vatican theologian Father Gino Concetti said it was no longer a sin, as long as mediums, fortune tellers, and palmists are not included."

The next breakthrough came in the 1970s when electronic technician Bill O'Neil was visited by a spiritual being named Dr. George Jeffries Mueller, a former university professor and NASA scientist. Doc Nick, another spirit, accompanied Mueller, and together they proceeded to instruct Bill O'Neil how to design a new piece of electromagnetic equipment that would convert spirit voices into audio voices.

George Meek, an engineer and retired president of a refrigerator and air-conditioning firm, had established the Metascience Foundation. Meek financed Bill O'Neil's development of the spirit communication machine they called the Spiricom. Under Mueller's guidance, this thirteen-tone generator produced a mixture of tones in the human male voice range. The Spiricom served as Dr. Mueller's voice box. The voice of Mueller sounded robotlike in the beginning, but with much tinkering, the Spiricom became smoother and more controlled. Mueller could communicate his social security number, unlisted phone numbers, and much personal information to validate his authenticity. On October 27, 1977, the voice of Doc Nick came through the Spiricom. By the fall of 1980, the technology had advanced to the point that the spirit voice was easily understood, although still quite fuzzy. On Easter Sunday in 1982, George Meek held a press conference at the National Press Club in Washington, D.C., to announce the success of the Spiricom. For the first time in history, the Spiricom system allowed extended instrument dialogue with the spiritual realm.

As director of the Metascience Foundation, George Meek published a newsletter, *Unlimited Horizons*, sent to readers in twenty-three countries. Meek's successor, Mark Macy of Continuing Life Research, published the newsletters *Contact!* and *Transmissions*, updating readers on spirit electronic communication. Macy and Pat Kubis coauthored a book titled *Conversations Beyond the Light* based on information received from electronic communication used as a major source of material for this chapter.

The spirit world used another medium, the telephone. American parapsychologists D. Scott Rogo and Raymond Bayliss were major researchers in this arena. Since 1976, they investigated more than fifty cases of paranormal phone calls by interviewing witnesses. These paranormal phone calls lasted only a few seconds, usually with the name of the caller given and a quick hello and goodbye. The researchers surmised that deceased relatives wanted only to prove they were still alive, but lacked sufficient energy for a conversation. Many recently deceased callers were not aware they were in the spirit world. Often they appeared confused, and the calls were short. Callers who had been dead for some time had clearer voices and longer calls. When recipients realized that the caller was dead, they often experienced a physical shock that shortened the call. Rogo and Bayliss hypothesized the released emotions interrupted the flow of energies necessary to maintain the contact. Spirit callers occasionally try to identify themselves through statements nobody else would use. Research showed the telephone company's long-distance lines and repeater-amplifiers had been bypassed.

A new science of electronic communication between the physical and spiritual worlds was emerging, called the science of Instrumental Transcommunication (ITC). The undisputed leaders of this new science of ITC are Jules and Maggy Harsch-Fischbach, who administer the Transcommunication Study Circle of Luxembourg, commonly called CETL. CETL is the main receiving lab on Earth and is primarily a research facility where researchers are committed to opening the line of communication between Earth and the astral planes. The universal message that CETL hopes to convey is that "We are all one. Our souls, our spirits are not to be separated from each other. Higher souls do not see us as separate individuals." Maggy, a school teacher, and Jules, a government employee, have dedicated their lives to this new paradigm research. Today, CETL and a growing number of other sound labs throughout the world engage in ITC experiments with the spiritual worlds.

Since the late 1980s, Maggy and Jules have been receiving messages from the dead by way of tape recorder, telephone, radio, television, fax, and computer. CETL has received images, text, and simulated voices from spirits, who say they can manufacture voices reminiscent of their Earth voices by using apparatuses from their side of the veil. These apparatuses can "soak up" noise on Earth, such as the static between radio stations and turn it into artificial voices.

On October 4, 1986, CETL received its first video image from the spirit world. Maggy and Jules recorded it with a VHS recorder and a Panasonic A-Z video camera. For about one-tenth of a second, the image of a man named Pierre K. appeared on the television screen. The image was quite distorted and hazy but had enough clarity for Pierre's family to identify him immediately. Shortly afterward, CETL began receiving many paranormal video images from the spirit realm, including one from Hanna Buschbeck, who had been working with audio transmissions while she was alive on Earth. Spiritual colleagues made suggestions about how to improve the quality of images, which led to the development of new equipment that held longer picture sequences. Television pictures beamed to Earth showed the spirit landscape and people interacting in those landscapes. Deceased scientists were now able to speak via television to a roomful of Earth scientists.

With every experiment, Maggy and Jules turned on both radios and their small television set. Shortly after Konstantin Raudive's death, a voice came over the speaker of one of the radios. The intelligence behind the deep voice identified himself as Raudive.

CETL soon discovered that the biggest obstacle to ITC contact was not technical in nature, but involved the energy field created when two or more beings became aware of each other. CETL scientists called this a contact field, a field strengthened when beings collaborate in a close psychic and spiritual rapport. They found real success could not be achieved in ITC contacts until they firmly established this contact field across dimensions. Scientists in the spiritual world warned that the reception of their message could be seriously affected by humankind because clarity of transmission depended upon the contact field, the thoughts of those receiving the transmission. Negative-thinking people could seriously affect vibrations coming from the astral plane.

By 1993, television transmission was playing a less important role in the overall ITC project. Research teams in the spiritual world were now able to access the hard drives of Earth computers. They could leave detailed computer-scanned images and several pages of text. Computer images were less subject to distortions compared with video images.

One of the first messages received via the computer came in November, 1987, signed by Richard Francis Burton, who had lived in the nineteenth century. Following that message came many others. For safety reasons, Maggy and Jules would turn off the computer when they left. Upon their return, they would find the computer turned on whenever a message had been left.

By the end of 1987, the Luxembourg group had recorded about two dozen voices, all of deceased individuals, except one called the Technician who had never incarnated on Earth. Many spirits could be identified by the manner of their voices. From 1986 to 1993, fifty different male and female voices have spoken through technical equipment at Luxembourg. Sound labs have been established in the United States, Australia, Austria, Belgium, England, Germany, France, Italy, Netherlands, Spain, Sweden, and Switzerland.

The late 1980s presented a history of negative forces interfering with CETL. The threat came from deceased low-level earth-bound beings in the lower astral planes. Many ITC researchers became ill, and George Meek escaped a life-threatening situation. ITC researcher Klaus Schreiber reported trouble with negative forces, and within the following year he was dead. Reports from spirit scientists said the ITC stations came under control of low-level beings who could imitate the voices of higher beings. ITC investigators were instructed to control their fear, pray, think positively, and develop inner peace. They were told that negative beings would always try to destroy transcommunication. Because of the negative interference, ITC research shut down for a time.

Spiritual beings on the third astral plane told ITC researchers that their purpose was to contribute to the evolution of mankind's view on eternal life. Their findings provide hard evidence of life after death through spirit voices and spirit images by electronic means. As expected, traditional scientists have totally discounted this new paradigm research.

TIMESTREAM

Earth investigators and spiritual world scientists who call themselves Timestream have developed a joint ITC venture. Facilities in the spiritual realm are located in the astral world third plane on a planet Marduk. Spirit workers describe Timestream's facility as the size of a large cathedral containing advanced video and sound equipment, more advanced compared than primitive Earth equipment. The purpose of Timestream is to communicate with Earth.

The director of Timestream is Swejen Salter, a scientist who lived on Earth's parallel planet Varid. She died in 1987 at the age of thirty-eight and has since been living on the astral planet Marduk. She compares Timestream's building to a huge post office or large bank building. Salter leads a small team of scientists that include Thomas Alva Edison, Marie Curie, and Wernher von Braum who are part of a large group of spirit colleagues in Timestream. ITC researchers Konstantin Raudive, Frederick Juergenson, and Klaus Schreiber joined the team after their deaths. Other members of the team include writers Conan Dogal and Jules Verne. George and Hal Roach of Hollywood fame provided artistic consideration in television transmission. In 1989, four hundred spirit colleagues were involved in the research project at Timestream; this number grew to one thousand by 1994. The main criterion among the scientists is compatibility, even more important than knowledge and intelligence. These spirit scientists believe that as more powerful equipment is developed, the contact field will not be nearly as important as it is now.

In 1986, Maggy and Jules received on their FM tuner a high-pitched voice who identified himself as a higher being without a name. They were to call him Technician and his assignment was Earth. Technician is multilingual, with great knowledge about the past and future. His extraordinary knowledge of physics, math, astronomy, and electronics has greatly helped the project. He instructed Maggy and Jules on modifying equipment for better reception at the Luxembourg lab. Maggy said Technician had a memory like a computer. CETL regard Technician, who never incarnated on Earth, as an angelic being who is the doorkeeper between the two dimensions, guiding all contact but leaving the dialogue to human spirits. Technician modestly admits he, too, is always learning.

Technician described the difficulties the spirit workers have had in building a mediumistic bridge, or contact field to those on Earth. This endeavor has been going on for many years. Building this bridge has involved a growing relationship of love, trust, and unity of thought between the workers on Earth and those in the spirit world. With advances in ITC, Technician said, "Earth is gaining easier access to current descriptions of the afterworld, complete with hard evidence to supplement rich religious descriptions of human heritage. A new electronic system will function when a unity of thought has been reached among experimenters on your side."

Sir Richard Francis Burton, another key member of the Timestream team, lived a life filled with world travel and exploration from 1821 to 1891. He and his companion, Swejen Salter, discovered a plane of transition to the fourth level. He also helped develop the Burton Bridge, enabling voice contact with Earth via radio, television, telephone, computer, and video.

Salter often complained of lacking cooperation from scientists on their side. During the summer of 1988, she and Burton embarked by ship for a research expedition on Marduk. One mission was to recruit scientists who had an interest and willingness to assist in ITC development. Both Marie Curie and Albert Einstein promised such cooperation. One scientist whom they hoped to recruit but could not was Alexander Graham Bell, the inventor of the telephone.

THE ASTRAL PLANET

Located on the third level of the astral plane, the planet Marduk has three suns. It orbits one sun and is illuminated by the other two, so that total darkness never occurs. Marduk has one moon larger than the Earth's moon. The circumference of Marduk is 76,000 miles. Deceased colleagues say the landscape reminds them of Earth, with rivers, lakes, stars, vegetation, mountains, and even polar caps.

A single large river, the River of Eternity, winds across the entire planet. The deepest part of the river is more than one mile deep and the widest part stretches more than two miles across. The river is described as a snake circling the entire planet stretching over thousands upon thousands of miles. With no ground layers, there seems to be no seepage of the river

Most of Marduk's 60 billion inhabitants live scattered along the river. Communities of people cluster along the river and include many peoples who lived ages ago, such as the Vikings and Stone Age people. They wear the same clothes that they wore in their Earth lifetimes. In each community, people share a particular religion or nationality, and share similar cultures and similar spirit interests. Different religious faiths remain segregated and secure in their particular beliefs. Any type of house the mind can imagine is found there, including houses with thatched roofs, magnificent palaces with glass towers, and houses with roofs of gold. Schools and universities are found throughout the cities of Marduk.

New arrivals in spirit usually join the nationality group closest to their original roots. They receive the living quarters they ask for, and some join already established spiritual families. Generally, newly arrived spirits gravitate toward those who shared similar interests. For example, there are communities of artists and musicians.

The longer people live on Marduk, the more feelings of divisiveness between various groups fade. Individuals begin to feel at home with all the other races and beliefs. Life on Marduk is safe and secure, free of misery and suffering. Some people have lived there for hundreds of years without reincarnation.

Swejen Salter said from the third plane, individuals can travel mentally in space. With the mind, they can visit other dimensions and other planets. Traditional transportation is also available. Airplane enthusiasts are excited about the availability of airplanes. Many people use ziocopters, similar to helicopters but they fly with different physical principles. Electric automobiles and solar-powered vehicles are available for surface travel. Timestream said that people were allowed to construct cars and planes to their own preference.

Bodies of Marduk's inhabitants are similar to earthlings', but of finer matter and faster vibration. Those who had missing limbs while on Earth have regenerated new appendages. Disfigured Earth bodies become perfected here. People who die at an old age will each choose the body of the age they were most healthy and handsome or beautiful. If eyeglasses were part of their image, they may still wear them. Masters often choose to portray themselves as older to maintain an image for their disciples. Color of hair and skin cannot be changed and will remain as it was on Earth. The average age that a person chooses is between twenty-five and thirty.

People who die of old age on Earth undergo a regenerative sleep on Marduk, lasting approximately six weeks of Earth time. Children arriving on the third level receive care from their relatives who already reside there or from people who love children. After time, children will develop into adults. The personality and character of humans who arrive here do not change in the process of dying. Neither do people awaken all-knowing, as there is plenty of opportunity to learn. Psychological problems and conflicts are not eliminated on this plane. Neither is sexuality, because sex is part of human nature, if both partners harmonize and desire it. Pregnancy is impossible here, an advantage for some. Spiritual beings eat and drink as Earth beings do, but nourishment is synthetic. Earth food materializes, including meat, which is reproduced without the need to kill.

Timestream scientists say that communication on the astral plane occurs through telepathy, and spiritual beings do not need larynxes or other speech equipment necessary to human beings. Because of their lack of speech organs, communication with Earth has been difficult. Technician commented on their language, "We all speak one language which is comparative to telepathy. When we speak to you, we translate it into your Earth language. Our language according to your human terms consists of 27,000 characters. . . . Our language is immediately usable after bodily death." Technician also commented on communication from mediums. He said that material from mediums was based four-fifths on the human psyche and one-fifth from spirit sources. Conversely, ITC transmission contains four-fifths from spirit and one-fifth from the psyche of the experimenter.

A variety of life forms inhabit Marduk. In addition to humans who inhabited other planets, dwarfs, giants, gnomes, and formless beings share this planet of 60 billion humanoids. Friendships and partnerships among all continue to be nourished here.

Many animals are found on Marduk, at an age of vitality and well being. Animals lack nothing and are cared for by animal-loving humans or by their owners. Just as our spirit relatives wait for us, so often do our family pets if a love bond has been formed. Spirit relatives often take pets, and if the pet wishes to see us, that wish is granted. Often a grand reunion ensues between a newly deceased person and his or her beloved pet who has waited so patiently for the reunion. Timestream is very much against animal experimentation on Earth because animals are evolving into a higher life form. Their treatment on Earth will influence their existence as a higher life force. If treated cruelly, an animal may also become cruel.

Eventually, a person becomes aware of lessons that he or she has failed to learn while on Earth, and a time comes to learn new things. This is a time for a reality change, a time to reincarnate. Whatever lessons not learned on Earth will hold back a soul's progress. Timestream said living on Earth puts one's ideas to practice. Life, they said, is the acid test of what a person really believes. One purpose of the astral plane is to wean humans away from patriotism and nationalism. On the higher planes one finds a universal understanding, with no separation by time, space, and dimension. Each soul is part of the whole.

An irony arises with the name of Marduk. On Earth, Marduk was the son of the Sumer god Enki in ancient Mesopotamia. Marduk eventually became the leader and the primary god of ancient Babylonia. The ancient Sumerian cuneiform writings told of the earliest inhabitants of Earth, gods that came from the planet Nibiru. These gods, called the Anunnaki, genetically engineered humans with DNA from *homo erectus* and genetic material from the gods. The created humans were to serve as workers for the Anunnaki. According to the research of Zecharia Sitchin, Nibiru was considered the twelfth planet of our solar system as determined from the cuneiform writings of Sumer. Its elliptical orbit around the sun took 3,600 years and it would come relatively close to Earth during its orbit. It was the god Marduk who renamed the Nibiru planet "Marduk" after himself. Is there a connection with the astral planet Marduk?

SPIRITUAL KNOWLEDGE FROM THE THIRD PLANE

Swejen Salter reminds Earth people that the midastral dimension is neither Heaven nor Hell. The third plane is not a permanent place. It is only an interim place where the soul either reincarnates to Earth, moves to another planet, or proceeds through an evolutionary process into the fourth plane or perhaps into the celestial planes nearer to God. Deceased scientists in Timestream say that we do indeed have a soul, which is a small beam of undying light residing in the heart. This corresponds to the ancient mystics' knowledge of the soul as the "seed atom" residing in the left ventricle of the heart.

Spirit scientists describe five stages of the soul's evolution into the human body. It begins as a small beam of light that evolves into a Light Being on the mental-causal plane. Next, an astral body forms of a heavier vibration and begins to assume a shape similar to a physical body. In the next stage, the etheric body develops, sometimes called the electric body. The final stage is the physical body in which matter vibrates at its lowest level and has the densest shape. Following death, the eternal soul sheds its physical body, etheric body, astral body, and finally the mental body, moving back through the planes toward light. After it has completed its evolution, it returns to its source, the creator.

A soul does not return to its creator until it is ready: each soul has its own path of evolution. The soul has its own inner direction and its own free will. Some people do not advance to the midastral planes. They remain trapped for a time in the lower astral planes, a dark and dismal place called Hell and Purgatory in Western thought. No one stays there permanently. At any time, an entrapped person may call for help to be released from this bondage.

Timestream communication says each individual sentences himself or herself according to desires. The deep desires and wants act like a magnetic attraction to a plane where those things exist. Thought, attitude, belief, and behavior raises or lowers the frequency of the astral body. At death, we simply go to the dimension compatible with our spirit.

Factors that raise the vibration of the astral body include (1) love, (2) compassion, (3) service to others, (4) an air of calm detachment, (5) eating fresh fruits and vegetables, (6) drinking pure water and breathing clean air, and (7) a realistic concept of spiritual existence.

Factors that lower astral body frequency are (1) fear, (2) hatred, (3) resentment, (4) egotism and selfishness, (5) attachment to worldly things, (6) regular use of alcohol, tobacco, and drugs, (7) eating heavier foods such as red meat, (8) hurting people and animals with malicious intent, and (9) spiritual ignorance. Any combination of these attributes chains one to a lower plane. Timestream says the lower astral realms are overpopulated.

All messages from Timestream originate from the third astral plane. On this level the decision is made to move onto a higher plane or return to Earth for more experience. The higher astral planes are

wonderful realms called Heaven by Christians. Many spirit colleagues of the ITC research team descend to the midastral plane to
lower their vibrations and participate in ITC.

On the higher mental-causal plane originates divine inspiration,
free of Earth desires and conflicts. Beings on this plane cause many
artistic and technical breakthroughs by sending telepathic messages to
artists and inventors. Many light beings send messages of love and wisdom to project leaders at Timestream that are then relayed to Earth.

In the higher celestial planes live various Earth gods and deities
whose wisdom, understanding, and unconditional loving nature are
beyond human comprehension. These personalities include Jesus
Christ or Yeshua Ben Yussuf, Muhammad, and Buddha, each of whom
moved directly to the higher plane after their earthly sojourn. The
Bible refers to these various planes metaphysically as "Jacob's Ladder."

Spiritual colleagues speak of reincarnation as part of the path of
evolution, a spiritual law. Technician said that every being on Earth
and in higher dimensions can postpone reincarnation for awhile or
reject it. However, one cannot forever escape it. One communication
from Timestream states: "The life of a spirit is an eternal life composed
of many, many experiences on many planets, in many dimensions,
that help us evolve into a higher state of being in which we become a
fit being to live in God's presence." Technician adds, "The human soul
returns to Earth often enough to learn all human life experiences
before moving onto other dimensions."

At the moment of death, we carry our thoughts, attitudes, and
desires with us in our astral bodies. However, the astral plane has no
time, and to the people on the astral plane a human life is only a short
dream, barely remembered.

According to Timestream, reincarnation is not forced onto spiritual beings. A spiritual being willingly undertakes it for his or her knowledge and wisdom. Many Timestream spirit colleagues did not believe
in reincarnation when they lived on Earth. On the astral plane, they
discovered it to be a fact. Swejen Salter explains that some people
decide for themselves about reincarnating. In some cases, higher
beings tell them to reincarnate. However, nobody is forced to return.
For many, the process is like an inner voice that reminds them of their
duties and lessons still waiting on Earth. Some meet with spiritually
evolved beings who tell them it is time to return to earth.

After deciding to reincarnate, the person is led to a special building for the process of reincarnation. Salter describes the process: "The

procedure is similar to people's arrival here. Only this time it is going back. The person is placed in what looks like a tub. The body which takes on an average of twenty-five to thirty years begins to change and becomes increasingly younger and smaller. It returns to the state of a child, then to a baby, and finally to a small cell. By the time the body has become a cell, it is no longer present here among us. The cell has meanwhile arrived in the female body of a human being. When the body has disappeared on the third plane, conception has taken place, and the soul is in the cell. Other research suggests that the soul may not immediately enter the cell but remains close to the cell and may enter anywhere between conception and birth."

Salter speaks about abortion: "To an aborted fetus, its memory of that painful time is as fleeting as a dark part of a dream. No one can extinguish the life of a soul. However, the mother may suffer great guilt from the act which can torment her for a lifetime." Higher beings may decide about the karmic consequence of an abortion, which depends on the motive. If for convenience sake, the mother may have to repent and make up for what she avoided. Because of the millions of abortions, the soul may have to wait several lifetimes to finally get a suitable body that will give the particular experiences the soul needs.

Technician comments on the end to reincarnation: "When a man (or woman) has experienced all facets of earthly life, grief, joy, happiness, pain, suffering, and exhaustion, when all search for knowledge was satisfied, and he (or she) explored all corners of the Earth; when the wheel of life comes to a conclusion after many incarnations, then the time has come to look for new horizons."

The next horizon is the fourth plane and above. According to the higher being Technician, when a person reaches the fourth plane, the person is freed from the law of reincarnation. How many reincarnations are necessary to reach that state of consciousness? The answer: how much do you want to experience? There are many galaxies in which to play and learn. The adventurous, who love sensation, may undergo millions. For the single-focus spiritual person who wants to know God, the evolutionary path might be very short and quick. According to Timestream, the individual soul decides.

An evolutionary process also takes place on the third plane that enables the inhabitants to move to a higher dimension or to return to Earth. The final step in the third plane is to live in harmony and peace with others. One must attain this knowledge before progressing higher.

Timestream scientists compare the higher Beings of Light to humans. A human is one personality, whereas a higher being incorporates the attributes and knowledge of many human personalities in one. Some are very close to the principal source (God) and far from the existence of man. Salter says what is amazing about celestial beings is their sincerity: "They have no secrets from one another. They interact like a network of computers, exchanging information as fast as a computer bank. If you speak to one of the higher beings, then all of the others simultaneously are aware of the conversation. All of them are aware of your entire personality, too." Insincerity is foreign to these higher beings, as nothing remains hidden in their dimension. Higher beings most often take the attitude of a grown-up toward a little child. Salter learned to approach higher beings by convincing them she was really sincere in wanting to communicate with them. Human reactions, she said, are very frequently alien to them. Salter felt higher beings often held things back from her, as they felt humans do not need to know everything "because the background of events and some information would go beyond their comprehension." Some events, she said, are tied up with past lives and future experience. A great deal of confusion might occur if humans were given too much information.

Technician adds that many higher beings are not interested in humans and remain far removed from them. Many are not informed about our way of life. These higher beings may manifest in many different forms, ranging from angels to human forms.

Jesus, on the planet Marduk, is only one personality among many others who belong to the entity Pescator. According to both Salter and Technician, he is one of the few higher beings who has access to all the planes, and who still maintains contact with people on Earth. They say he can appear in a human body, but he is not human and he has a differently structured personality. Salter said she was assigned to the Timestream project by Pescator (Jesus). She meets with him and six other higher beings periodically to review the lab's progress. Salter observes that when celestial beings speak among themselves, following them with her mind is difficult. Communication with celestial beings is difficult, as they have a non-human perspective.

According to Technician, there are parallel worlds where some sort of double of ourselves is living right now. Existence of these material worlds is triggered by our thoughts, wishes, imaginations, and actions. Doubles continue separately with their physical and spiritual development, and they, too, will pass on to spiritual worlds as we do. In the spiritual realm they do not live with their double counterpart, but in Marduk each lives in different areas of the river bank. For every three-dimensional world, claims Technician, there can be an infinite number of material parallel worlds.

Parallel worlds often spin off in separate physical dimensions during crucial events. During these times, new physical dimensions and new time lines break out. This reality moves in a slightly different direction. Timestream reports the Earth has many parallel worlds, all very similar but with their own slightly unique history. They describe Earth 1651 where Newton died of measles and never formed his theory. They refer to Earth 1933 where Hitler came to power and changed the course of history. A parallel world also exists where he did not come to power.

Timestream says that death is a great adventure. After arrival on the third plane, the newly deceased souls rest for a few days or weeks, and then are free to travel on the third plane and see the sights. They are usually very happy to reunite with old friends and relatives on this midplane. Following death, the entire memory of the individual's past lives is restored. After arriving, people may seek out friends and relatives of former past lives. Frequently people wake up after death in shock. Few find that the third plane corresponds to their expectations. They are surprised to find on this plane petty thieves, adulterers, liars, and fraudulent business people. Timestream says these individuals are segregated into their respective groups and cannot harm the more respected spirits.

One of the principal tasks on the third plane is to find those lost souls who are entitled to live on this plane, but for some reason have not found their way there. Often people do not realize they have died, and others reject the idea of life after death. Many souls remain in a confused state, wandering around in their homes and among their friends. Reaching them is difficult. People who have died a violent death also remain in a confused state for awhile, and they linger around the scene of their accident or murder.

Information from Timestream explains that dying does not make one omniscient because greater mysteries remain to be understood. Dying does not eliminate emotional problems on the astral plane. They say on this plane, one creates one's own reality, as this is a dream world reality. Heaven is a dream world, but is as real to the people who live there as our world is to us. Heaven is what you believe it is. The time people spend on the astral plane may be only a few weeks or hundreds of years. Those who reject the idea of life after death or never thought about it usually reincarnate very quickly. If their Earth life evolved around material things, they will usually return to Earth. Those who think of only money and golf usually get bored very easily because there is no competition on this plane. If additional lessons need to be learned, one may reincarnate on Earth or perhaps another inhabited planet. Earth, they said, is the school of hard knocks, which confronts each individual with the consequence of actions.

Technician says religion is good if it helps a person to progress spiritually. Many people during their lifetime follow the instructions of their church, but could not find God after death. "There are many who have died and crossed the threshold to the plane of light without help from religion," said Technician. Prayer is not useful if it does not come from the heart. He said faithful Christians like to believe in angels and other higher beings, but when confronted with them, many turn away disappointed because they are too much like human beings.

Technician said, "You may not like it. It is as I have told you, reincarnation exists. There are parallel worlds. Mankind evolves in a forever moving wheel of life. Reincarnation means progression forward, not backward. Animals are subject to the cycle of incarnation. . . . There is a purpose for sickness and infirmity. Do not judge the fate of other people. . . . Many of those individuals have selected a life of suffering for their incarnation. . . . We refuse to ask questions about people's karma. Knowing about individuals' karma, our own or those of others, does not serve the purpose of progression and cannot be of use to us."

Timestream emphasizes that the astral plane is only an interim place. People have the opportunity to experience a heavenly refuge here, patterned after their expectation of heaven. Many astral planets comprise the astral plane where most people awaken after death. The third plane is a construct of the mind. All worlds throughout the immense universe are composed of pure consciousness, and the principal axiom of life everywhere is that thought creates reality. On the third plane all possibilities are also realities, because one has total freedom and total choice. In fact, Timestream emphasizes that our mental attitudes about life are creating our spiritual environment right now. We are responsible for the environment we go to after death. Thoughts have no limits and reach across all dimensions. After death, the astral body, which contains our thoughts and emotions, is released to the plane in the astral world that resonates with those thoughts and emotions. Salter says that negative thoughts attract one to lower planes where people act out their dreams of lust, greed, and selfishness. We choose which plane we will reside on. Most people arrive on the third plane, but the spiritually mature person can attain the fourth plane.

Timestream reports that the Akashic Records are located on the fourth plane. These are records of people's lives who have lived on Earth and all the events that have occurred or will occur on Earth. Reflections of the Akashic Record can be seen on the third plane, though not a true record because it is distorted. Most psychics can access only the third plane and the reflective Akashic Record. As a result, their predictions are only half-truths. Those clairvoyants who can access the fourth plane are more accurate.

After souls pass into the fourth plane, only a few of them are interested in contacting the Earth plane. Technician says, "Beings on the fourth plane have feelings, but they are no longer comparable with human feelings." The fourth plane is a plane of timeless truth, what Carl Jung called the archetype.

What a gift the ITC researchers and timestream have given us! If traditional science and religion became involved with this research, the potential would be enormous. A direct communication and cooperation between Earth scientists and spirit scientists could accomplish wonderful things for the well-being of our planet. Religious leaders could correct many misconceptions regarding their teachings. If people realized the spiritual truth about the evolution of their souls, their thoughts and actions would probably be reflected in a more harmonious planet.

Chapter Eleven

THE SACRED SCIENCE OF SPIRIT AND MATTER
A Unified Theory of Reality

The principles of sacred science are based on the premise that one cannot separate science from spirit. Spirit operates under universal laws that we are just beginning to understand scientifically. If the sacred concepts introduced in this book are true, they should obey the laws of the universe and operate under sacred principles. Does this mean that God the Creator operates with certain scientific principles? The most probable answer is yes. Because the soul is one with God, the soul's journey of involution and evolution must likewise obey universal scientific principles. If the axiom "As above, so below" has truth, then spiritual planes also operate under universal sacred law.

Traditional scientific evidence supports the concept of rebirth, destiny, the soul, spirit communication, near-death experiences, and astral travel. Yet, we are still missing a unified theory about the relationship of the spiritual world to the physical world. The research of pioneer theorists has made this important connection between these very different worlds of spirit, mind, and matter. Two scientists, David Bohm and Karl Pribram, while seeking answers to unexplainable events, came up with the same theoretical model about the universe, the holographic theory of reality. This model explains concepts of reality that traditional science has not. Science has avoided investigating the paranormal realm. Because the paranormal falls outside the paradigm of orthodox science, little research has been done. The holographic model takes into account aspects of both the spiritual and physical worlds. It can explain the evolution of the soul, destiny, reincarnation, telepathy, psychokinesis, and the concept of time and space. This model supports the teaching of Eastern mysticism that we are all connected. Every action has a reaction, and every cause an effect.

266

Albert Einstein was unable to discover the unifying field theory of physics. However, he held quantum physicist David Bohm in such high esteem that he predicted Bohm would one day be the first to discover this unifying field theory. Bohm's holographic theory may not be the explanation Einstein had in mind, but it may in fact be the "holy grail" of physics.

THE IMPLICATE ORDER

David Bohm grew up in Wilkes-Barre, Pennsylvania, graduated from Penn State University, and became a quantum physicist and protégé of Dr. Albert Einstein. During the McCarthyism days of the early 1950s, Bohm was asked to testify against John Oppenheimer, project coordinator for the first atomic bomb. Bohm's refusal to testify resulted in the loss of his position at Princeton University, eventually leading to an academic life at the University of London in England.

Bohm's research showed that if matter is broken into smaller and smaller pieces, it reaches a point when those subatomic components no longer possess the traits of the original object. For example, physicists have found that electrons sometimes behave as if they were compact little particles with no dimension. An electron is not an object as we know it, but can manifest itself as a particle or wave. When manifested as a wave, an electron cannot do things as a particle. If fired at a barrier with two slits, it can go through both slits simultaneously. When wavelike, electrons collide with one another creating interference patterns. The ability to behave as a wave or particle is common to all subatomic particles. Light, gamma rays, radio waves, and x-rays can transform from waves into particles and back again. Physicists classify this subatomic phenomenon as quanta, the basic component of the etheric universe. They discovered that quanta manifested as particles when they were observed and as waves when they were not observed.

Bohm found an interesting aspect of quantum reality regarding a strange state of interconnectedness between unrelated subatomic events: Subatomic procedures could create a pair of particles with identical properties. No matter how far apart photons travel, they would always have identical angles of polarization. They were in correspondence. Bohm's hallmark research began with plasma, which is a gas containing a density of negatively charged electrons and positive ions, atoms with a positive charge. Once in a plasma, electrons stopped behaving like individuals and started behaving as if they were part of a larger interconnected whole. They produced well-organized effects. Bohm found that entire oceans of subatomic particles behaved as if they knew what untold trillions of others were doing.

After reading a classic textbook by Bohm on quantum physics, Einstein said this book allowed him to understand quantum physics for the first time. On the other hand, after writing the book, Bohm said, the more he knew about quantum physics the more he did not understand, and he became dissatisfied with the then current interpretation of quantum theory. Bohm then proposed the existence of a new subquantum field to explain the findings of quantum physics. Calling this new field "quantum potential," Bohm theorized that it pervades all space, and that its influence does not diminish with distance. At the subquantum level where quantum potential operates, location ceases to exist. All points in space become equal to all other points in space, suggesting it is meaningless to speak of anything as separate from anything else. Physicists call this property nonlocality. This theory allowed Bohm to explain the interconnectedness of two particles without violating the theory of relativity's ban against traveling faster than light speed. Because the quantum potential permeates all of space, Bohm said all particles were nonlocally interconnected. He asserted that all things were part of an unbroken whole, embedded in a space that was as real and rich in process as the matter that moved through it.

When Bohm used the holographic model, it became possible to understand this new order of physics. The hologram possessed an order hidden or enfolded, the same way that the order in a plasma is enfolded in the seemingly random behavior of its electrons. The interference pattern on a piece of holographic film appeared disordered to the naked eye. Bohm realized that the universe employed holographic principles in its operation, and that it was itself a giant flowing hologram. This model explained Bohm's revolutionary ideas of the quantum world. In 1980, Bohm published a book, titled *Wholeness and the Implicate Order*, to explain his revolutionary idea of the quantum world.

Bohm believed that the tangible reality of everyday life is really an illusion, similar to a holographic image. Beneath reality lies a deeper order of existence, a vast and more primary level of reality. This gives rise to all objects and appearances of our physical world, much like a piece of holographic film gives rise to a hologram. Bohm termed this deeper level of reality the implicate, or enfolded order, which he later likened to the spiritual world. He referred to our own level of existence in the physical as the explicate, or unfolded order, and Bohm saw manifestations of all forms in the universe resulting from countless enfoldings and unfoldings between these two orders.

Bohm said the electron was not one thing but a totality or ensemble enfolded throughout all of space. A continuous series of unfoldments and enfoldments creates the appearance of a moving electron. A constant influx from the implicate order sustains particles, and when a particle appears to be destroyed, it is not lost, but merely enfolded into the deeper implicate order from which it sprang.

Bohm used a piece of holographic film and the image it generates as analogous to an example of the implicate and explicate order. The film symbolizes the implicate order because the image encoded in its interference pattern is a hidden totality enfolded throughout the whole. The hologram projected from the film symbolizes the explicate order, which represents the unfolded and perceptible version of the image.

The constantly flowing exchange between the two orders explains how particles, such as electrons and positrons, can shape shift from one kind of particle to another. Shifting of a particle like an electron enfolds back into the implicate order whereas another, such as a proton, unfolds and takes its place. Bohm's theory also explains how a quantum manifests as either a particle or wave. The way an observer interacts with the ensemble determines which aspect unfolds and which remains hidden. Essentially, the observer determines the form a quantum takes.

Unlike a static hologram, Bohm described the universe as a "holomovement," conveying its dynamic, constant, enfolding and unfolding nature, which moment by moment creates our universe. In the implicate order, movement is described as one degree of enfoldment related to another form of the present, or a different degree of enfoldment. All these different "presents" unfold together at any moment.

Bohm used another analogy to describe implicate order properties that describe wholeness as a flowing movement. A drop of dye is placed in a viscous liquid, such as glycerine, encased between two cylinders, one inside the other, and while rotating the outer cylinder, the dye drop threads into the liquid. The original ordered state, in which the drop is at one place in the liquid, can be viewed as the explicate order. Following a number of turns of the cylinder, the dye appears to disappear totally. The distribution of dye in the liquid appears random throughout the liquid. After the cylinder rotates, a higher order of entropy or disorder takes place, and information about the dye is lost and the explicate order destroyed. When the cylinder is rotated backward and has reconstituted itself, the drop reappears. This apparent random state of the dye is not disordered, but of a hidden or implicit order. Bohm claims this order pervades the universe. This hidden order, spread throughout the whole, is the implicate order. When it evolves into form, where it can be seen, it becomes explicit. Implicit/explicit orders are different expressions of the same order.

The implicate order, according to Bohm, is not made of parts. In this order, things enfold each other and provide the basis for the explicate order that we call particles and planets. This is the physics of the holomovement universe, which carries the implicate order and allows us to see and experience our fourth-dimensional space-time world. Beneath each explicate order is an implicate order. With Bohm's model, the electron is a total set of ensembles enfolded throughout the whole and not localized in any particular location in space. In one sense, the particle is not one thing at all, but successive unfoldments. In another sense, because everything enfolds into everything else, the particle is always the same.

Bohm says our universe goes beyond our concept of only three-dimensions. A universe of countless dimensions, it embodies whole-ness. Quantum mechanic mathematics relies on the concept of a multidimensional reality. For Bohm, the multidimensional reality is one unbroken whole that extends through the universe, including all particles and fields of physics. The holomovement enfolds and unfolds in a multidimensional order. Both time and space are projected from a higher-dimensional reality. Space and time become subtotals that unfold the way the dye drop particles unfold in the cylinders.

In Bohm's holistic universe, there are no random events. Life is implicit in inanimate matter. The principle must be included in the holomovement itself. Life is no accident, and it is a subtotal, as is nonliving inanimate matter. Life and nonlife constantly intermingle and enrich each other. According to Bohm, distinctions between the animate and inanimate are only abstractions, suggesting that everything in the universe is alive. Even a rock is in some way alive, says Bohm, for life and intelligence are present not only in all of matter, but in energy, space, time, and the fabric of the whole universe. Bohm believes the holomovement is the life energy, as living organisms are particular unfoldings of what the inner depth of the holomovement contains. When an organism dies, it sinks back into the implicate where there is no time.

Bohm sees consciousness and matter as tightly linked. Consciousness is implicit in the holomovement and therefore implicit in all matter and therefore contained in all matter. All of consciousness is enfolded in matter, and matter is the unfolding of all consciousness. Consciousness is a more subtle form of matter, and the basis for the relationship between the two lies deep in the implicate order. It is present in various degrees of enfoldment and unfoldment in all matter. Bohm believed brain and mind, mind and body as enfolding each other. They are neither separate nor the same, but projections of a higher-dimensional reality.

Insight, says Bohm, comes from the holomovement. The movement of the whole, it expresses itself through the explicate forms. Both consciousness and life are ensembles enfolded throughout the universe.

Just as every portion of a hologram contains the image of the whole, every portion of the universe enfolds the whole. This has great implications. If we knew how to access it, we could access all knowledge of the past and future. Enfolded in small regions of space and time are the whole past and the whole future. This means that every cell in our body enfolds the entire cosmos, as does each blade of grass and every speck of dust.

The implicate order gives birth to everything in our universe, containing within it every subatomic particle that has been and will be. It contains every configuration of matter, life, consciousness, and energy, including the forces that control the size and shape of galaxies.

According to contemporary physics, every region of space contains different kinds of fields composed of waves of various lengths. Each wave has at least some energy. After calculating the minimum amount of energy a wave can possess, physicists have found that every cubic centimeter of "empty" space contains more energy than the total energy of all matter in the known universe! (Some call this zero-point energy.) Bohm also believes this infinite ocean of energy exists. Matter does not exist independently from this sea of empty space, but is a part of space. If matter, such as a crystal, is cooled to absolute zero, a stream of electrons can pass through it without being scattered. Once the temperature is raised, the crystal scatters the electrons. Bohm believes space is the ground for the existence of everything, including ourselves. The universe is but a ripple resulting from the "Big Bang" explosion on the surface of this cosmic sea of energy found in empty space. It is a comparatively small, autonomous pattern of excitation that gives rise to recurrent, stable, and separable projections into a three-dimensional order of manifestation. In other words, materiality and the enormous size of the universe do not exist alone, but are a by-product of something much vaster. The sea of energy in "empty" space is, in fact, the multidimensional implicate order.

In 1982, physicist Alan Aspect led a research team proving Bohm's quantum theory that each photon could correlate its angle of polarization with that of its twin, meaning the two photons were nonlocally connected. Physicist Paul Davies said, "The nonlocal aspect of quantum systems is therefore a general property of nature." Aspect's findings provide great support for Bohm's model of the universe. Even Bohm admits that his theory only approximates the truth. The 1982, Nobel Prize laureate in physics, Brian Josephson, believed that Bohm's implicate order may someday lead to the inclusion of God and mind.

Not long after, Robert John Russell wrote in *Zygon, Journal of Religion and Science* that Bohm's theory relates to religion. He believed the holomovement allowed Christians to connect with Bohm's theory. He asks the question and even suggests that the holomovement is the Creator God. Bohm himself does not believe God is the holomovement, but thinks the Divine is beyond the holomovement and implicate order. The holomovement, he believed, is part of the created order. Bohm's theory suggests a pantheistic image of God, meaning God is the universe.

Kevin Sharpe suggests in his book, *David Bohm's World, New Physics and New Religion,* that the holomovement is an image of God. Sharpe tries to weave in Bohm's theory with Christian doctrine and believes the universe and everything in the universe depends on God for its existence, paralleling a holomovement theology. He writes, "The holomovement God is continually making each item, relation, feeling, etc. in the world. God does it moment by moment by unfolding the potential of the implicate holomovement, which itself is God. Everything depends on the continual activity of God as creator in Christianity."

However, God is not the only creator, because humans and other beings take part in the holomovement. They create the explicate only with God. Sharpe writes, "We participate in the divine creativity by reaching into the holomovement in our creative acts." Scientific laws describe the way God works, and a holomovement theology describes how God brings each moment into existence. Everything bears the mark of the holomovement and everything is in God. Sharpe believes the immanence and transcendence of this holomovement God are the root of spirituality.

The attributes of the holomovement, says Sharpe, equate with a personal God. Our emotions, thoughts, feelings, hopes, fears, and relationships are part of the explicate order we experience, coming from the holomovement. Both the subjective and objective unfold from the implicate order. These two categories of experience are both partial views of reality. The whole God includes these human attributes, and humans are only parts of the whole. In summary, the holomovement God is the source of all our objective and subjective experience.

The domain of the sacred, the spirit, and the Holy God lie beyond the holomovement, asserts Bohm. From this beyond come compassion, intelligence, love, and insight. Insight from the beyond, claims Bohm, can pierce through and change brain matter. Chaos arises from fragmented thought, the source of which is human deception caused by human consciousness folded into the holomovement. Bohm calls this corruption of the holomovement the sorrow of humankind. By removing the mind's fragmentary blockage, insight allows one to perceive reality differently. Our ideas entirely shape our reality, claims Bohm. For Bohm, insight is the supreme intelligence. We needed it to reorder our minds and eliminate the chaos of fragmentation. Fragmentation, says Bohm, is the source of locality. Embedded in the implicit order, fragmentation could unfold into the explicit to cause separation and locality.

In the early stages after the "Big Bang," nonlocality locked together all the particles in the universe. Once expansion of the universe began, the particles collided and caused locality. Locality and separation go hand in hand. The movement from nonlocality to locality has gone so far in the universe that we understand little of nonlocality. Almost everything is related in a local manner, except at the quantum level.

The relationship of cause and effect is one of the greatest implications derived from Bohm's holographic theory of the implicate

order. Bohm's theory states that all objects in the universe are connected with one another. Everything causes everything else. What
happens anywhere affects what happens everywhere. For Bohm, a
cause is a condition or event that when copied, will always cause the
same effect. The cause is necessary to produce those effects. Bohm's
theory explains the law of cause and effect, the law of Karma.

Bohm's implicate order resolves most paradoxes and dualities that
have plagued modern science and ancient philosophy. Perhaps the
implicate order theory of Bohm is the elusive unified field theory of
physics that Einstein thought Bohm might discover. It solves the par-
ticle-wave dilemma, the duality of which began the quantum evolution. Bohm's theory explains the puzzle of continuity and
discontinuity posed in quantum physics. Some ensembles unfold
into the explicate order giving the appearance of continuity, and
others unfold differently to appear discontinuous. This answers the
question of locality verses nonlocality. A local event in the explicate
order has its nonlocal root in the implicate holomovement. The paradox of time also can be explained. Time is enfolded in the whole
and is an aspect of the timeless holomovement. Newtonian physics
said the world was as it appears, but quantum physics says the world
is different from the way it appears. Bohm's model claims matter
and mind enfold each other. The brain is not separate from mind,
and mind is not limited to the brain. Neurophysiologist Karl Pribram
also arrived at this conclusion.

THE HOLOGRAPHIC BRAIN

Though no one knew what an engram was made of, scientists
thought it would be a matter of time before they were discovered. In
1946, Karl Pribram worked for Karl Lashley at the Yerkes Laboratory
of Primate Biology in Orange Park, Florida. Lashley trained rats to
perform a variety of tasks, such as running through a maze. After
removing various portions of the brain, Lashley retested them. To his
astonishment, he found that no matter what portion of the brain he
cut out, he was unable to eradicate their memories. Motor skills were
impaired, but not memory. Pribram concluded that memory was not
localized at specific brain sites, but was somehow distributed
throughout the brain as a whole. Each memory has a specific location in the brain cells. These memory traces are called engrams

Lashley had also discovered that after removing 90 percent of a rat's visual cortex, the rat could still perform tasks requiring complex visual skills. When 98 percent of a cat's optic nerve was severed, the cat could still perform complex visual skills. Supported by scientific studies, Pribram later hypothesized that vision was an aspect of holograms. Additional research on cats, monkeys, and rats has shown that visual holographs are not, in fact, spread evenly across the visual cortex. A holograph forms and is projected in the cortex for every five degrees of the visual field. The entire field is built up of a series of overlapping holographic parts.

In 1948, Pribram accepted a position at Yale University where his research found patients who had portions of their brain removed for medical reasons never suffered loss of specific memories. Partial temporal lobe removal did not create gaps in a person's memory. The discovery of the principle of the hologram allowed him to understand how memory could be distributed, rather than localized in the brain. If every portion of holographic film contained all the information necessary to create a whole image, Pribram thought it equally possible for every part of the brain to contain all of the information necessary to recall a whole memory.

Pribram did not find one-to-one correspondence between the external world and the brain's electrical activity. Because neurons are packed so densely, their expanding ripples of electricity create a wavelength phenomenon and constantly crisscross one another. Pribram thought this gave the brain its holographic properties, that is, the wave front nature of brain cells connecting to others to give the hologram of memory. A hologram can store large amounts of information. A one-inch square of film can store as much information as found in fifty books the size of the Bible.

Brain cell synapses contain thousands of holographic images, hypothesized Pribram. With millions of synapses in the brain, the model could account for the phenomenon of association, that is, how one image, experience, or idea recalls another similar to it. It could explain how perception leads to thought in the stream of consciousness, an unfolding and constant refolding of holographically stored memory.

Pribram believed if the hologram model were taken to its logical conclusion, it could open a new paradigm regarding objective reality. The physical world of trees, automobiles, mountains, and so forth may not exist the way we believe it to exist. He wondered whether mystics might be right, that reality was *maya,* only an illusion! What was really out there was a vast resonating symphony of wave forms that is only a frequency domain transformed into the world as we know it after it enters our senses.

Bohm's and Pribram's theories provide a profound new way of looking at the world. Our brains mathematically construct objective reality by interpreting frequencies that are ultimately projected from another dimension. This dimension, a deeper order of existence, lies beyond space and time. The brain is a hologram enfolded in a holographic universe, writes Michael Talbot in *The Holographic Universe*. Pribram realized that reality looks concrete to us because our brains can take the holographic blur created by vast waves and frequencies and convert it to familiar objects that make up our world. Bohm believes our brains even construct space and time. For example, a cup has two different aspects to its reality. The brain, which acts as a lens, filters and manifests a cup. Take away the lens, and the cup is an interference pattern. "Which is real and which is illusion?" asks Talbot.

FORMATIVE CAUSATION

Lending support to Bohm's implicate theory is former Cambridge University scholar Rupert Sheldrake's theory on formative causation. Sheldrake's theory involves morphogenetic fields that are aspects of Bohm's implicate order. These fields spread out over time and space to guide members of species in particular behaviors, an example of the all-encompassing holomovement. Just as Bohm's quantum potential guides a particle's nonlocality, Sheldrake's morphogenetic fields guide atoms and cells to form structures similar to their previous forms. As we will see, the morphogenic field is like the quantum potential, a sort of memory wave.

In explaining the theory in his book, *A New Science of Life: The Hypothesis of Morphic Resonance*, Sheldrake states that the orthodox approach to biology is found in the mechanistic theory of life in which living organisms are regarded as physiochemical machines. His organismic or holistic philosophy provides a context for a radical revision of the mechanistic theory. Encompassed in his organism theory are plants, animals, organs, tissues, cells, crystals, molecules, atoms, and subatomic particles.

Morphogenetic fields describe how the characteristic forms of embryos and other developing systems come into being. Sheldrake believes these fields have measurable physical effects. They are responsible for the characteristic form and organization of systems at all levels of complexity, not only in biology but also in the realms of chemistry and physics. Morphogenetic fields are associated with previous similar systems, and every field of a past system becomes part of a subsequent system that crosses both space and time. Particular systems are organized today because they were organized that way in the past. A plant takes up its form because past members of that species took that form.

Morphogenetic fields also explain animal behavior, and they explain why animals act instinctively, because similar animals acted in the same way. If a rat learned to carry out a new pattern of behavior, a subsequent rat would learn the task more quickly because of the morphogenetic field. The more rats that have learned the task, the easier for subsequent rats to learn it. Scientific evidence has shown this to be true. Sheldrake calls this hypothesis "formative causation."

A biological morphogenetic field is the blueprint defining specific forms in living organisms. It explains regenerative abilities. For example, if a flatworm is cut into several pieces, each piece regenerates into a complete worm. The morphogenetic theory helps explain the regulation of developmental systems that produce structures that characterize a species. It helps explain why spiders spin similar web designs without learning from other spiders.

Formative causation is the process by which morphogenetic fields play a causal role in the development and maintenance of all complex forms. Morphogenetic fields are not themselves energetic but can order physical changes, although they cannot be observed directly. Each system has its own specific morphogenetic field. It can be thought of as a structure surrounding and embedding the morphogenetic germ that contains the virtual final form of the system. This field orders events within a range of influence in such a way to actualize virtual form. The morphogenetic field reveals itself only through its ordering effect, corresponding to the potential state of a developing system already present before it takes its final form. If part of the physical system is removed, the final form will be actualized again. This is regeneration. Transformation takes place when a new form replaces the original high-level morphic unit.

When atoms come under the influence of the higher-level morphogenic field of a molecule, the electron orbit is modified to enhance the probability of events leading to actualization of the final form. Probabilities of other forms are diminished. Morphogenetic fields of molecules restrict the possible number of atomic configurations based on expected calculations that start from free atom probability structure.

Formative causation works at all levels of manifestation. Sheldrake says that when atoms come into existence, electrons fill the same orbitals around the nucleus. Atoms repeatedly combine to give the same molecules form. Seeds of a given specie produce similarly appearing plants, and spiders spin the same type of web. According to the formative causation theory, the known laws of physics do not uniquely determine forms of complex chemical and biological systems. These laws permit a range of possibilities from which formative causes select.

The particular form of the morphogenic field, according to Sheldrake, is due to chemical and biological forms caused by influences from previous similar forms that require action across space and time. Sheldrake said a resonant effect of form upon form across spatial time would resemble energetic resonance. He called this process morphic resonance. Atoms, molecules, crystals, cells, organs, and so forth each has their own characteristic pattern of vibration. Through morphic resonance the form develops, with its characteristic internal structure and its vibrational frequency. Morphic resonance takes place through morphogenic fields and gives rise to a characteristic structure. A given system could be influenced by all past systems with a similar form and pattern of vibrations. An automatic averaging of past forms results in a spatial probability distribution within the morphogenic field. The form of a system depends on the cumulative morphic influence of previous similar systems. For example, chemists who have synthesized entirely new crystals often have greater difficulty in getting substances to crystallize for the first time. Nevertheless, as time passes, these substances tend to crystallize with greater ease.

Sheldrake writes that inorganic morphogenesis is rapid, but biological morphogenesis is relatively slow and passes through a succession of intermediate stages. The development of multicellular organisms takes place through a series of stages controlled by a succession of morphogenic fields. In the case of biological forms, the successions of fields work with the DNA to guide cell growth and direction.

The hypothesis of formative causation also applies to all aspects of animal and human behavior in which patterns of movement repeat. Sheldrake sees behavior as coming from three causes: (1) genetic inheritance, (2) morphogenetic fields of the nervous system, and (3) motor fields that shape behavior patterns.

Morphogenic fields depict a universe in which laws of nature are built. Laws are, in effect, habits reinforced by repetition. Sheldrake does not believe these laws of nature are eternal but that they evolve. Fields are continually modified, such as a field of clover. The expression of an individual clover as it develops in the presence of its environment is transmitted to the field of clover. A field in turn transmits this total experience to the forms of every individual clover. This sounds almost like the principle of group souls associated with plants and animals. Some fields have been around so long and have been reinforced so often by events that they are essentially changeless. Once a field comes into existence, it does not die, although the objects it created may become extinct.

In a 1982 meeting with Bohm, both Sheldrake and Bohm agreed that morphogenic fields are an aspect of the implicate order. Sheldrake's theory is holographic. Bohm called the morphogenic field a guide wave that receives its energy from the implicate order. The guide wave exists in a multidimensional reality beyond three-dimensional space and time, and guides whatever is unfolding in those moments of space-time. If what is unfolding in space-time are cells, it guides them into place to form, for instance, an individual clover. Once the clover has formed, the guide wave remains in place to give it continued shape. This works because the implicate and explicate forms and the entity it shapes are not really separated but are different dimensions of the same thing.

Sheldrake believes the appearance of new forms could result from creative principles that are unknown and inherent in life in the universe. He also conjectured that a conscious agent oversees the whole universe and creates new forms. Bohm equates the creation of a new form to a flash of insight by the universe. With an insight, Bohm said, "You realize the whole in the mind." The movement of the whole universe creates a new form.

Both Bohm and Sheldrake agree on the unity of consciousness, and that the consciousness of each person forms its own field, including memories and experience. The morphogenic field that is the whole of consciousness gives the individual its general shape.

Arising from the holomovement, the individual consciousness changes the whole, thus affecting the consciousness of people in the future.

Sheldrake's hypothesis helps explain the classical anecdote of the hundredth monkey, as told by Lyale Watson in *Lifetide: The Biology of Consciousness*. When a monkey tribe on an island near Japan was introduced to freshly dug sweet potatoes, the monkeys were reluctant to eat them because they were dirty. One female discovered the potatoes could be washed. This discovery was monumental, like discovering fire. Shortly afterward, the female taught this behavior to a few monkeys of the colony, who in turn taught it to some others. Quite suddenly, the behavior became universal. Watson believed at a certain point when enough monkeys, say the hundredth monkey, carried the consciousness over a threshold by pushing it to a critical mass, the behavior became universal. At that time almost every monkey in the colony washed the sweet potatoes. Not only did monkeys wash sweet potatoes on that island, but monkeys on other islands and on the mainland, such as the colony of monkeys in Takasakiyama, also washed the potatoes.

Another example of formative causation lies in bacterial behavior. When a new antibiotic is introduced to counteract bacteria, bacteria change to become resistant to the new drug. The morphogenic field of bacterial consciousness causes this behavior.

The peace meditation held on December 31, 1986 organized by John Randolph Price also exemplifies the morphogenetic fields regarding consciousness. Worldwide, millions of people prayed at the same time on December 31 at 12:00 Greenwich time for world peace. Around the world, communities held local gatherings to participate in this cosmic experiment. The effect was monumental! Within a relatively short time, the iron curtain between West and East Germany came down and the Cold War ended. Countries around the world made peace. Headlines in the newspaper literally read, "Peace is breaking out around the world." Perhaps the morphogenic field of world peace created by the mind raised the consciousness regarding world peace. Of course, skeptics call this a coincidence, but those who participated know that the world peace meditation created this remarkable change in consciousness.

EASTERN MYSTICISM AND PHYSICS

One of the first people to draw a comparison between the teachings of Eastern mysticism and quantum physics was University of California professor Fritjof Capra in his book, the *Tao of Physics*. Capra said Eastern mysticism was based on direct insights into the nature of reality, whereas physics is based on observation of natural phenomenon in scientific experiments. Eastern mysticism emphasizes the basic unity of the universe. The highest aim of Hindu, Buddhist, or Taoist followers is to become aware of the unity and the mutual interrelation of all things. This belief transcends the idea of an isolated individual self, and these philosophies teach that one needs to identify with the ultimate reality of interconnectedness.

The Eastern world view is intrinsically dynamic; time and change are essential features. The cosmos is one inseparable reality, forever in motion, alive, and organic. It is spiritual and material at the same time. The force causing this motion is an intrinsic property of matter. This image of the Divine controls everything from within, not as a ruler who directs the world from above. Ironically, Capra believes the world view of Eastern mysticism is the same view emerging from modern physics. Mystical thought provides a relevant philosophical background to the theories of contemporary science. Capra believes an essential harmony exists between the spirit of Eastern wisdom and Western science. Two foundations of modern physics, quantum theory and relativity theory, allow us to see the world very much as the Hindus, Buddhists, and Taoists do.

Einstein strongly believed in nature's inherent harmony, and the greatest goal in his scientific life was to find a unified foundation of physics. While trying to achieve that goal, he developed the special theory of relativity, which provided a common framework for electro-dynamics and mechanics. It unified and completed the structure of classical physics. At the same time, it involved drastic changes in the concept of space and time that undermine the foundations of Newtonian physics. According to the relativity theory, space is not three-dimensional and time is not a separate entity. Both are connected with a fourth-dimensional continuum of space-time. We can never talk about space without talking about time and vice versa. Different observers will order events differently in time, if they move with different velocities relative to the observed events. All measurements involving space and time lose their absolute significance in relativity theory. Mass is nothing more than a form of energy. An object at rest has stored energy in its mass as given by the famous equation $E = MC^2$. E = energy, M = mass, C = speed of light. When describing phenomenon involving velocities approaching the speed of light, the description needs to allow for the effects of relativity.

Gravity force, said Einstein, curves space and time. Traditional geometry is no longer valid in curved space. Three-dimensional space is also curved, according to Einstein's theory, the curvature caused by the gravitational fields of massive bodies. Wherever there is a massive object, such as a star or planet, the space around it is curved, the degree of curvature depending on the mass of the object. The whole structure of space-time depends on the distribution of matter in the universe, and the concept of empty space loses its meaning.

Einstein made scientists realize that geometry is not inherent in nature, but is imposed upon it by the mind. Unlike Greek philosophy, Eastern philosophy has always maintained that space and time are constructed by the mind. They do not derive abstract and eternal truths from geometry.

Quantum physics has shown that for every particle, there exists an antiparticle with equal mass and opposite charge. The antiparticle of the electron is called the positron. Pairs of electrons and positrons can be created spontaneously from photons and can be made to return to the photon state by a reverse process, called annihilation. In the process of scattering electrons and photons, particles move forward in time, and in another process they move backward in time. For every process, there is an equivalent process with the direction of time reversed and particles replaced by antiparticles. All particles can move forward and backward in time. Time and space are fully equivalent. They are unified into a four-dimensional interaction and can stretch in any direction. Particle interaction can be interpreted in terms of cause and effect only when space-time diagrams are read in a definite direction. When taken as four-dimensional patterns without any definite direction of time attached to them, there is no before and after, and therefore no causality. Eastern mystics assert that in transcending time, they also transcend the world of cause and effect.

The main purpose of Eastern mysticism is to express all phenomena in the world as manifestations of the same ultimate reality, the essence of the universe. This reality underlies and unifies the multitude of things and events we observe. Hindus call it Brahman, Buddhists call it Tathata (suchness), and Taoists call it Tao.

The word "Brahman" means growth and suggests life, motion, and progress. Chinese mystics see the world in terms of flow and change. Karma expresses the dynamic interplay of all things and events, meaning action, denoting the dynamic interaction of all phenomena. In Buddhism, karma signifies the never-ending chain of cause and effect in human life. Eastern mysticism has no place for static shape or material substance. According to quantum theory, matter is never quiet, but always in a state of motion.

In Eastern philosophy, the reality underlying all phenomena is beyond all form and defies all description. Often it is described as formless, empty, or void. This emptiness is not mere nothingness, but is the essence of all forms and the source of all life. Buddhists call this ultimate reality *sunyata* meaning the *void*. Bohm calls this living void the implicate order that gives birth to all forms in the physical world. The void has infinite creative potential. This void of Eastern mysticism can easily be compared with the quantum field of subatomic physics that gives birth to an infinite variety of forms. Like the subatomic world, the phenomenon world of the Eastern mystic is a world of continuous birth and death. In Chinese philosophy, this field is implicate in the notion of the Tao as empty and formless, yet producing all forms. This is expressed explicitly in the concept of *Chi*. Chi means ether, and was used in ancient China to denote the vital breath or energy that animates the cosmos. Chi is a nonperceptible form of matter present throughout space that can condense into solid material objects that Bohm would call the explicate. Chi condenses and dispenses rhythmically, bringing forth all forms and eventually dissolving into the void. Chi underlies the essence of all material objects and carries their mutual interactions in the form of waves. Mystics assert that the presence of matter is merely a disturbance of the perfect state of the fields at that place. Similarly, the quantum field is a continuum present everywhere in space, yet in its particle aspect has a discontinuous granular structure.

The distinction between matter and empty space must be abandoned when it becomes evident that virtual particles can manifest simultaneously out of the void, and again vanish into the void without any nucleon or interacting particle present. The vacuum is not empty and contains an unlimited number of particles that come into being and vanish without end. Like the Eastern void, the physical vacuum contains the potentiality for all forms of the particle world. Forms are merely transient manifestations of the underlying void. Capra states that many physicists see the discovery of the vacuum's dynamic quality as one of the most important findings of modern physics. A Chinese sage named Tsai said, "When one knows that great void is full of Chi, one realizes there is no such thing as nothingness."

Modern physics has shown that movement and rhythm are essential properties of matter. All matter is involved in a continual cosmic dance. Hindu belief maintains all life is a great rhythmic process of creation and destruction, of death and rebirth. Eastern mystics teach that all the things and events we perceive are creations of the mind arising from a particular state of consciousness, and when transcended they dissolve. Attaching deep significance to shape and structure is the basic human illusion. Both modern physicists and Eastern mystics have realized that all phenomena are dynamically interrelated. Eastern philosophy calls this interrelationship the law of karma.

THE SCIENCE OF PRAYER

Mind creates our reality. What we most often think we often get, depending upon the intensity of the desire behind the thought. As we have seen in our discussions about the astral realm, thoughts shape the reality of the astral planes. Perhaps this explains the principle behind prayer, a focus of one's desires and thoughts. The effect becomes even stronger if one believes the intended result will occur. This is called faith. Norman Vincent Peale, in his classic book *The Power of Positive Thinking*, demonstrates how the power of prayer and positive thoughts can create a positive outcome. If these principles are correct, the results of prayer should stand up to the rigors of science. As we will see, scientists have proven very clearly the effects of prayer.

One of the pioneer researchers of prayer was Franklin Loehr, who in the late 1940s demonstrated that prayer influenced plant growth. Since Loehr's early research, many scientifically controlled studies have shown that prayer can positively affect health conditions, physiological functions, and mental well-being. Prayer has also been shown scientifically to influence enzyme activity, bacteria growth, healing rates, and seed germination. Today, traditional science totally ignores more than one hundred well-controlled experiments of prayer.

Research has demonstrated that the effects of prayer are nonlocal, meaning distance is not a factor. It makes no difference whether the person or object being prayed for is nearby or far away. Prayer can function at any distance to change physical processes in a variety of organisms, ranging from bacteria to humans. Nothing seems to block the power of prayer. When objects are placed in a lead-lined room or in a cage shielded from all forms of electromagnetic energy, the prayer effects get through.

Theologian Richard J. Foster describes twenty-one separate categories of prayers. Prayers may be for confession, the acknowledgment of wrongdoing, or to ask for forgiveness. Thanksgiving prayers offer gratitude. They may be for adoration, to give honor, and to praise. Prayers of lamentations or crying in distress ask for vindication. Two of the most common prayers are for petition, asking something for oneself, or for intercession, asking something for others. Prayers may be individual or communal, private or public.

Prayer take many forms. They can be explicit for specific events to occur, called direct prayers. Practitioners of directed prayer have a specific goal, image, or outcome in mind. They attempt to steer the process in a precise direction. Other prayers may be more generic, called nondirected prayer. Nondirected prayer is an open-ended approach in which no specific outcome is held. Since the 1980s, the Spindrift organization in Salem, Oregon, has performed simple lab experiments that prove prayer does work. Their research discovered which type of prayer technique gets the best results, the directed or nondirected prayer. Results of their experiments showed that both methods are effective, but that the nondirected technique appeared quantitatively more effective. The technique frequently yielded results twice as great as the direct approach.

One of Spindrift's experiments involved growing mold on the surface of a rice agar plate. An alcohol rinse stressed the mold, damaging it and retarding its growth, but did not kill it. A string was placed across the mold, dividing it into side A (the control side), and side B (the treated or prayed-for side). When prayer was directed to side B, nothing happened, as the growth remained static. When directed prayer was replaced by nondirected prayer with no goal, side B began to multiply and formed additional concentric growth rings. Spindrift concluded from this and similar experiments that healing will be most effective if the prayer is free of visualization, association, or specific goals. They suggested that emotional and personality characteristics should be excluded from thought and replaced by a pure and holy qualitative consciousness of the prayed for person.

They refer to this method of healing as genuinely spiritual healing. Methods that rely on directed prayer are referred to as psychic healing, faith healing, mental healing, or the placebo effect. These methods depend on suggestions to the patient that he or she will improve.

If one does not pray for a specific result, how does one tell if the prayer has been answered? Spindrift believes that when a nondirected prayer is answered, the outcome is always in the direction of "what is the best for the organization." Answered nondirected prayer moves the organism toward those states of form and function that are healthiest for it. Spindrift demonstrated this in a series of germination experiments in which the researcher did not know what was best for the seed involved.

One batch of seeds was oversoaked, making it heavier than it should be for proper germination to occur. Another batch was undersoaked, making it lighter than optimal. The seeds were evaluated early in the germination process according to change in weight. Not knowing which batch was which, the practitioner could not tell the seeds what to do. They had faith the seeds would simply move toward the norm, according to what was best for each seed. When compared with a control, the oversoaked beans eliminated water and lost weight, and the undersoaked beans gained water and increased their weight. Spindrift concluded that a nondirect prayer moves the organism toward the healthiest state. Sometimes, what is best for the organism may be death, such as for a person suffering from intense pain. One needs to pray only for what is best, according to Spindrift.

Larry Dossey, M.D., author of Healing Words, writes, "Empirical evidence for prayer power, then, is indirect evidence for the soul. . . . It is also evidence for shared qualities with the Divine, 'the Divine within,' since infinitude, omnipresence, and eternal are qualities that we have attributed to the Absolute." Larry Dossey has concluded from his prayer observations that nondirected prayer works best for those who are introverted, and directed prayer for those who are extroverted.

Studies by Yujio Ikemi at Kyushu University School of Medicine in Japan involved patients who had spontaneous regression of cancer. The research found these patients had a prayer-like attitude of devotion and acceptance of their condition that preceded the cure. The patients did not pray aggressively for a specific outcome. Ikemi's research suggested that cancers sometimes regress spontaneously when all specific requests are abandoned as in direct prayer. The key to disease regression may simply lie in being true to oneself. One must go beyond all ulterior wishes, perhaps even excluding the hope that the cancer will disappear. Larry Dossey defines a cure as "The realization that physical illness, no matter how painful or grotesque, is at some level of secondary importance in the total scheme of our existence." Jesus implied in his teachings that there may be a higher purpose to the illness that we do not understand. In other words, the meaning of a particular disease may be known only to the Divine. There is no linear relationship between health and spiritual attainment, as there are sickly saints and healthy sinners.

Other researchers have found the opposite, directed prayer is more effective. In research with 126 cancer patients, psychophysiologist Jeanne Achterberg and G. Frank Lewis found that improvement directly related to the specificity, strength, and clarity of the patient's mental images. Achterberg also examined the ability of subjects to specifically affect the number of certain types of white cells, neutrophils, and lymphocytes, which make up 85 to 90 percent of the total white blood cells. Thirty subjects were randomly assigned to pray for or to image either neutrophils or lymphocytes. Counts were made before and after their imaging sessions. The results showed that the neutrophils significantly decreased in the neutrophil group and lymphocytes decreased in the lymphocyte group. The researchers concluded that highly directed imagery was cell specific.

Cardiologist Randolph Burd, M.D., a practicing Christian, designed a scientific study of the role of prayer on healing. For a ten-month period, a computer randomly assigned 393 patients (those admitted to the coronary unit at San Francisco General Hospital) either to a group prayed for by a home-prayer group (192 patients) or to a group that was not prayed for (201 patients). Neither patient nor doctor knew to which group the patient had been assigned. The prayer group was given the first name of the patient to be prayed for, and they prayed each day for the person. Significant results followed. The prayed-for group was five times less likely than the control group to require antibiotics. They were three times less likely to develop pulmonary edema. No patients in the prayed-for group required endotracheal intubation compared with twelve in the control group. Fewer patients died in the prayer group, although this was not statistically significant. Dossey commented that if this had been a drug study, it would have been heralded as a medical breakthrough.

Spindrift also demonstrated that prayer is more effective if the praying person is familiar with the object of the prayer.

Studies have researched the effect of prayer on healing, fungus, yeast, and bacteria. Ten subjects tried to inhibit fungus culture growth by concentrating on them for fifteen minutes at a distance of one and one-half yards. Of 194 cultural dishes, 151 showed retarded growth. Another study found that sixty subjects without known healing abilities could impede or stimulate significantly the growth of cultured bacteria. Sixty university volunteers in yet another study could alter the genetic abilities of the *E.coli* bacteria. The bacteria mutated in the direction desired by the subjects. The studies suggested that ordinary people through prayer or imaging could cause biological changes in other living organisms.

There have been 131 controlled experiments on prayer based on spiritual healing. Of these, 77 experiments have shown a statistically significant effect by prayer. Science has proven that prayer is effective, but how does prayer work?

As we have discussed with the morphogenetic field, perhaps thought forms in the astral field creates physical reality. As discussed in *Keepers of the Secrets*, volume two of the *Sacred Science Chronicles*, human actions and thoughts are immortal and preserved in the astral field. This astral world parallels the physical world, one dimension removed. One can project any image into the astral field that essentially contains the first principle of substance. This astral light is sometimes referred to as the soul of the world, symbolized in ancient time by the serpent devouring its tail. Everything that we confirm by our actions remains in the astral light, and its reflection continually influences our thoughts, which are also preserved in the astral field. Prayer is a thought form also recorded in the astral realm.

Both passion and strong will project into the astral light. To accomplish anything, one must believe that it is possible to do and then act on it. Faith begins with the certainty of finishing the act. The secret power of prayer is to think and will. Results are manifested when one wills well, wills long, and wills always. A skillful person knows how to direct his or her will and can influence natural tendencies. Successful direct prayer also depends on will and faith that the prayed-for event will happen.

Eliphias Levi asserts that in modern magic, spirits assist in accomplishing a ritual purpose. Spirits take instruction literally and have trouble with logic. Most spirits have no intention of deception and usually have difficulty in distinguishing between mental and physical reality. One can take this a step further and assume that spirits are under the influence of prayer, and if the will is strong enough, spirits can assist the praying individual. Souls that inhabit the astral light, according to Levi, have imperfect wills that can be governed by more powerful wills or direct prayers. On the other hand, perhaps our guardian spirits know our higher life purpose and assist in our nondirect prayers, which are often for the soul's best interest.

Centuries ago, the border between religion, prayer, and magic was difficult to discern. Magicians tried to manipulate spirits through mechanical rituals, whereas religion worked on spirits through submission and honor. In the sixteenth century, opposition to magic developed partly because it presented an alternative to Christian prayer. Protestants claimed that Catholics perform magic in their many rituals and liturgies. One might conclude that prayer and magic are one and the same, operating under similar principles.

THE HOLOGRAPHIC SOUL

As we have seen, the purpose of the soul is to evolve so it can return to its source, God. Evolution of the soul involves experience, both in the physical and spiritual worlds. The holographic model appears to have answered many mysteries raised regarding the journey of the soul. Traditional science has avoided investigating many experiential phenomena that do not fit within its narrow paradigm of reality. Because these mysteries cannot be explained by conventional knowledge, most scientists have ignored them, often maintaining the condescending attitude that these phenomena are figments of a person's imagination. However, these are paranormal and mystical experiences that can be explained by the holographic model. The model explains telepathy, precognition, psychokinesis, and what mystics describe as the unity of everything. It can explain the near-death experience, the out-of-body experience, and lucid dreaming. Carl Jung's theories on archetypes, synchronicities, and coincidences are easily explained using the holographic umbrella as a model. Other mysteries such as karma, past lives, Heaven and Hell, apparitions, and the concept of evolution all are consistent with holographic principles. All these holographic mysteries describe the path of the soul!

Dr. Stan Grof, former assistant professor of psychiatry at Johns Hopkins School of Medicine, said only a holographic model can explain such things as archetypal experiences, the collective uncon-scious, and other unusual phenomenon experienced by altered states of consciousness. Grof, an early researcher on the psychic effects of the drug LSD, guided more than three thousand LSD sessions during his investigations. His subjects reported that after an LSD experiment, they knew what it was like to be an animal, a plant, or even a blood cell. Some could experience the consciousness of the entire planet. Sometimes on these cerebral trips, they encountered discarnate spir-its and spirit guides from higher planes of consciousness. On occa-sion, they could travel to other universes on other levels of reality. Grof claimed that "LSD gave the human consciousness access to an infinite subway system that existed in the subterranean reaches of the unconscious." Grof coined the term "transpersonal" to describe the experiences in which consciousness transcends the customary bound-aries of the personality. Grof believed the essential characteristic of a transpersonal experience is holographic, as with feeling that all boundaries are illusory and with the lack of distinction between part and whole. He believes a deep connection exists between the holo-graphic process and the way archetypes are produced.

F. David Peat believes that Carl Jung's "synchronicities" are flaws in the fabric of reality. Momentary fusion allows us a brief glimpse of the immense and unitary order underlying all of nature. Synchronicities, claimed Peat, reveal the absence of divisions between the physical world and our inner psychological world of reality.

The holographic model is based on the interconnectedness of all things. Montague Ullman, professor emeritus at the Albert Einstein College of Medicine, performed numerous ESP dream experiments. He found we could communicate with one another in our dreams, suggesting an underlying state of interconnectedness. Ullman's research found that no matter how spiritually unevolved a person is, dreams depict his or her failings by containing metaphors to prod him or her into a greater state of self-awareness. He concluded this was nature's way of ensuring survival of the species. Dreams are nature's way of counteracting the unending compulsion to fragment the world. Ullman believes dreams represent a natural transformation from the implicate into the explicate.

Lucid dreaming is the process by which a dreamer maintains full waking consciousness during the dream and can control events in the dream. Fred Alan Wolf, Ph.D., author and physicist, believes lucid dreams can be explained by the holographic model. All dreams, claims Wolf, are internal holograms, and ordinary dreams are less vivid because they are virtual images. He believes the brain can generate real images, as happens in lucid dreaming.

Psychologist Robert Anderson of the Renssalar Polytechnic Institute in Troy, New York, believes we can tap into information in the implicate order that is directly relevant to our memories. He calls this process personal resonance and likens it to a tuning fork. In a sea of an almost infinite variety of images in the implicate holographic structure of the universe, these images are available to personal consciousness by personal resonance.

In 1987, Princeton physicist Robert Jahn and clinical psychologist Brenda Dunne revealed in the results of ten years of rigorous experimentation that mind can psychically interact with physical reality. They proved that through mental concentration, humans can affect the way certain kinds of machines operate. Only the holographic model and standard reality could explain these results. Jahn and Dunne concluded that reality is itself the result of the interface between the wavelike aspects of consciousness and the wave patterns of matter. Because all physical processes possess a wave/particle duality, we can assume consciousness does, as well.

They believe psychokinesis involves the exchange of information between consciousness and physical reality, creating a resonance between the two. Jahn and Dunne believe subatomic particles do not possess a distinct reality until consciousness enters the picture. Instead of discovering particles, they believe physicists may actually create them. They cite evidence about a subatomic particle called the anomalon whose properties vary from lab to lab.

If mind affects physical matter, this gives great implication for the relationship between mind and physical health. Holistic healers confirm that physical health often reflects the state of mind. The term holistic refers to the whole person, mind, body, and spirit, a perfect example that everything is connected. Holistic practitioners claim that by changing the mind set, one can change physical health. As we have seen, psychologist Jeanne Achterberg, Director of Research and Rehabilitation at the University Texas Health Science Center, trained individuals to increase only one particular white blood cell in the body. She concluded that belief can affect a person's health. Imagery is an important tool for the holographic mind and for improved health.

Precognition can also be explained by the holographic model. Michael Talbot writes about nineteen documented cases of people who had precognitive glimpses of the sinking of the *Titanic*. Some were experienced by passengers who paid attention and survived, whereas others ignored the vision and drowned. Professors Jahn and Dunne at Princeton University conducted 334 formal trials on research with precognition. Volunteers experienced accurate precognitive information 62 percent of the time.

Researcher David Loye, writes Michael Talbot, believes that reality is a giant hologram. In this hologram the past, present, and future are fixed up to a certain point. He claims more than one hologram floats in the "spaceless water of the implicate." He believes these multiple entities could also be visualized as parallel worlds. The future of any given holographic universe is predetermined. When a person has a precognitive glimpse of the future, he or she is looking into the future of only that particular hologram. However, like amoebas, these holograms occasionally swallow and engulf each other, melding and bifurcating into a new hologram. When one acts on a premonition to alter the future, one actually leaps from one hologram to another. Choosing one holographic feature over another is like creating the future.

Bohm describes the precognitive hologram differently. He said when people dream of accidents that later occur, and do not take the plane or ship, they have not seen the actual future. They have seen something in the present that is implicate and moving toward making that future. The actual future was different from the dreamed of future because they altered it.

The holographic paradigm can explain remembrance of past lives. Joel Whitton, M.D., professor of psychiatry at the University of Toronto Medical School, used hypnosis to study what people unconsciously know about themselves. About 90 percent of Whitton's hypnotizable subjects could recall past life memories. His most remarkable discovery involved the information received when regressed subjects went to the interim between lives. Subjects reported there was no such thing as time and space. Part of their purpose was to plan for the next life, deciding important events and circumstances to be experienced in the next life. In the interim life, Whitton found these individuals to be actually self-aware and to possess a heightened moral and ethical sense. A moral obligation accompanied the plan of the future. They saw themselves with total honesty.

Whitton called this conscious state of mind the "meta conscious-ness." Subjects chose to be reborn with people they knew in a previous life so they could make amends for past actions. Planned encounters with soul mates allowed reunions with loving relationships experienced in previous lives. Accidental events were scheduled that allowed for personal growth. Some chose to experience a rape at a certain age, and some chose to experience a serious disease. Often the subjects asked Whitton to censor their memories with post-hypnotic suggestions because they did not want to know their futures. Whitton concluded that the unconscious mind is aware of the rough outline of one's destiny and actually steers one toward its future.

The out-of-body experience also exemplifies a holographic phenomenon. Individuals experiencing OBEs affirm that location is an illusion, as in the holographic model. Everything is nonlocal, including consciousness. Another striking holographic feature is the plasticity of the form a person assumes in an out-of-body state. Some describe their phantom double as naked; others say it is fully clothed. The body is a kind of hologram that can assume many shapes. Robert Monroe claims that thought habit creates the OBE form. This gives additional credence to the idea that consciousness is contained not in the brain, but in a plasmic holographic energy field that permeates the physical body. For instance, being able to see in all directions without turning one's head is normal during an OBE.

Supporting the holograph model is evidence provided by David Eisenberg, M.D., of the Harvard Medical School, who published an account of two school age children in Beijing who, with the skin of their armpits, could see enough to read notes and identify colors. In the 1960s, the Soviet Academy of Science investigated a Russian peasant woman who could see photographs and read newspapers with the tips of her fingers.

Another holographic aspect of the OBE involves blurring between past and future that occasionally occurs during the OBE. During an OBE experience, Dr. Alex Tanous described objects lying on a table. Three days later Tanous was able to place the objects, not present at the time of the OBE, in the same position they had held during the OBE, suggesting a holographic paradigm of time. This helped confirm Bohm's reality of the implicate where the past, present, and future cease to exist.

Talbot writes about Heaven as a hologram, saying our innermost feelings are responsible for creating the form we assume in the afterlife, as experienced by people in near-death experiences. People confined to wheelchairs in the physical world find themselves running and dancing in their NDEs. Those with amputated limbs are whole again. The elderly are young again, and children see themselves as adults. When Whitton hypnotized patients to the between-life state, subjects reported the classical NDE features, such as passing through a tunnel. He also concluded that thought forms created the shape and structure of subjects in this realm. As they experienced this between-life state, they gradually became a hologram composite of all their past lives. They even had names different from those used in past physical incarnations.

Reviewing one's entire life and reexperiencing all emotions that accompanied it gives further evidence of a holographic NDE. Information of the life review is displayed in amazing detail, suggesting a holographic model. Most who experience NDE are usually very honest in their self-reflection, stressing two things: to love more and to learn forgiveness. They also stressed knowledge, saying knowledge can accompany them after death. Some experiencers of near-death said they had access to all knowledge, whereas others, upon their return, had a strong thirst for knowledge. Some report that they did not have to ask questions to access this infinite library of information. Others report that instead of acquiring knowledge, they remembered it. After their return, they soon forgot it. Often they said information arrived in chunks that registered instantly in their thoughts. They used all forms of communication, including sounds, holographic images, and telepathy.

Some who experience NDE support Loye's hypothesis about parallel universes. Occasionally they see a future that will come to pass only if they continue on the current path. A few receive a vision of what life would be like today if certain events had not occurred thousands of years ago.

In Swedenborg's travel to the spiritual world, he referred to holographic traits. He also reported that humans are connected in a cosmic unity. Swedenborg said that each person is Heaven in miniature and that every person is a microcosm of the macrocosm. He believed "the universe is constantly created by two wavelike flows, one coming from Heaven and one coming from our own soul and spirit." Putting them together we get a resemblance to the hologram. From all his spiritual travels, Swedenborg concluded that Heaven is actually a more fundamental level of reality than our physical world.

All appearances are illusions in a holographic universe. Holographic images are constructed by the interaction of the consciousness present, but are illusion-based. Our mind constructs holographic images in the afterlife realm. Philosophy professor Michael Grosso, Ph.D., after studying apparitions of the Virgin Mary, believes that such visions are not of the true historical Mary, but are actually psyche holographic projections created by the collective unconscious.

Bohm's holographic universe is composed of two orders, the implicate and the explicate, also called the void and nonvoid by Tibetan Buddhists. The void is the birthplace of all visual objects, and the nonvoid is the reality of visible objects. Hindus call the implicate order Brahman, which is formless and the birthplace of all forms in visible reality. What comes out of Brahman enfolds back into it in an endless flux. Bohm calls the implicate order spirit, whereas the Hindus say it is pure consciousness. Because the material universe is only a second-generation reality, a creation of veiled consciousness, the Hindus call the physical unreal or illusion. Brahman is the illusion maker, and nature is the illusion (*maya*). *Maya* keeps us from realizing that there is no such thing as separateness. It separates the united consciousness so that each object in the physical is seen as separate from ourselves. Implicate and explicate ideas can be found in virtually all shamanic traditions, be they in Hawaiian Kuhunas, Native American medicine men, or Aborigines of Australia. Spiritual light bearers tell us repeatedly that the purpose of life is to learn, and the soul learns best in the explicate order where it evolves through the lessons of life.

Quantum physics and the holographic model both explain the concept of the soul's evolution. Entropy (chaos and disorganization) is produced as locality originates from a state of nonlocality. Locality is generally at a lower energy level than is nonlocality because it is less organized. In the explicate universe there is movement over time from nonlocality to locality associated with the expanding universe. This first movement from nonlocality to locality has gone so far in the explicate world that there is little nonlocality in the explicate world except at the quantum level. Increasing entropy is the second movement of the universe through time. In other words, we have locality, separateness, and entropy on one side balanced by nonlocality on the other side.

Balancing increased entropy is the increase in complexity described by the term evolution. The concept of evolution states that some parts of the world are building up rather than running down. The work of Nobel Prize laureate Ilya Prigogene is important in describing evolution. According to Prigogene, the universe began with extremely high energy, which it has a tendency to lose. The universe produces more complex objects, such as the sun and planets that store and spend energy, which also run down. At the same time we see biological, social, chemical, and physical systems that increase in energy and operate under physical laws. A system that uses energy is at first unstable and chaotic, but finally settles in and stabilizes at a higher energy level. A system can become more complex, and as it does so, it satisfies the second law of thermodynamics at the expense of its environment. Entropy always increases. The environment takes on more entropy to make up for the system's energy growth and stability. Therefore, net entropy plus its environment increases.

The key characteristic of evolution, which is the increase in complexity of a system, is greater internal connection. The universe is becoming more complex, which means some of its parts are connecting more with one another. Different elements come together to form wholes or systems, and systems unite to form supersystems. When these parts compose a system, they are more connected than when they are not in a system. This is like the implicate order. Complex systems involve their parts, not only in connections and movement as in the holomovement, but they also reflect in qualities in their self-regulation, life, maintenance, defense, and so on. Thus the implicate holomovement makes its appearance in the explicate order. A system is more nonlocal than its parts because the whole causes elements to behave in special ways, whether in clusters, together, or as individuals.

The universe has developed in two directions. It has increased in entropy and locality, reflecting the increase of separation between objects and the winding down of the universe. The other direction is toward evolution, which leads to increased complexity and the gradual increase in internal connection, reflecting the advent and development of life and complex systems. In summary, there are two opposite and related movements of the universe. The first is evolutionary toward complexity with an increasing number of connections among the universe parts (nonlocality), and the second is toward locality and increased entropy.

After studying the concept of the holographic universe, one

might conclude that the soul is holographic. Mystics have said the soul unfolds from the spiritual to the physical and enfolds back to the spirit. This involution and evolution of the soul can be described as the soul originating from the implicate, unfolding to the explicate, and enfolding back to the implicate. The holographic model describes the repeated process of unfolding and enfolding in terms of past lives. As we have seen, the soul has been equated to consciousness, and some quantum theorists believe that evolving consciousness displays the principles of the holomovement. Nearly all aspects of the soul's evolutionary path are included in the holographic paradigm.

We are one with everything, according to Eastern mysticism that teaches that once we realize this sacred truth, we can return to God. Perhaps sacred truth lies in the teachings of Jesus about love and forgiveness, two examples showing oneness, and two principles taught in the spiritual world to people who have had a near-death experience. With unconditional love, judgments cannot be made about others because we are all one. The judged individual experiences what is necessary for his or her soul growth in its hologram of reality. Judgment will draw us back to the explicate until we realize we are one with the universe and with the person we are judging. Forgiveness is the other key to returning to the implicate. Anger attaches us to separation and locality, while forgiveness releases us from the wheel of rebirth that brings us back to the explicate. Love is the common thread that connects us all, and once we realize this, both Western and Eastern religion teach that we will return to God.

RESURRECTION

As we complete our inquiry about the human soul, trying to understand resurrection might be appropriate, one of the great mysteries of religion. Christians believe for those who have gained salvation, the physical body will resurrect from the grave during end times. Others say this is a misinterpretation, and there will be a spiritual resurrection. Author Greg Braden has tried to address this dilemma with a hypothesis in his book *Awakening to Zero Point: The Collective Initiation.* He has based his resurrection theory on science and ancient mystical teachings.

Resurrection, as defined by Braden in biblical terms, is the act of consciously vibrating from one state-space to another. The Earth's acceleration through a course of evolutionary change causes this shift of consciousness. Humans, claims Braden, are linked to the changing electromagnetic magnetic fields of Earth, which causes a cellular change. The human aspect of the shift can be consciously facilitated through free will and right choice. Healing of the Earth is the purpose of this shift, and the shift will result in a new way of experiencing of the human form. Braden believes this shift will happen when we awaken to "zero point," resulting in a collective initiation. Christian names for this shift are the Second Coming, the Rapture, Armageddon, the Day of Judgment, Planetary Resurrection, and the Tribulation. Contemporary thought may describe it as the New Age, Polar Reversal, the Fourth Dimension, and the Age of Aquarius. Indigenous people describe it as the closing of a cycle, the Sixth World.

The shift in planetary consciousness, explains Braden, will occur with a low intensity magnetic field of Earth and a higher frequency of Earth's vibration. Scientists have acknowledged that the intensity of Earth's magnetic field is presently dropping rapidly, now 38 percent lower than it was two thousand years ago. Lower magnetic fields, says Braden, provide the opportunity for change through the rapid manifestation of thought and feeling. Over the period between 1986 and 1993, the vibration of the earth has increased from 7.8 to approximately 8.6 cycles per second. Braden believes the shift will transpire when the threshold resonance reaches 13 cycles per second and the magnetic field approaches zero. Thirteen is a number found in the Fibonacci series of numbers discussed in the first book of the *Sacred Science Chronicles, In the Beginning.* At this time there will be a sustained electromagnetic null-state for approximately seventy-two hours.

When this happens, there will be a polar-reversed field. The last time the Earth experienced a 180-degree magnetic reversal was approximately 11,000 to 13,000 years ago. Physicists would call this time an electromagnetic null-zone or a time of zero point. At this time, claims Braden, Earth will begin a new cycle of awareness, the fourth dimension. This transition will take approximately twelve years and will last until approximately A.D. 2012, corresponding with the end of the Mayan calendar. Earth will continue to express in three-dimensional space while experiencing resonance to fourth-dimensional space. At this point of time, Earth will begin the ascension process, identified in Mayan and biblical writings. For approximately a thousand years, Earth will be in a stable fourth-dimensional experience. Revelations 20:5 states, "This is the first resurrection. Blessed and holy is he who shares in the first resurrection! Over such the second death has no power, but they shall be priests of God and Christ, and they shall reign with him a thousand years."

Braden believes each cell within the physical body of each human is presently becoming aligned to a higher range of frequency than that which has been experienced during the last two thousand years. This zone of higher frequency information represents an evolved awareness that each individual strives to attain. Braden believes this is the state of awareness that the Universal Christ attained during his thirty-three years on Earth.

The timing of the magnetic shift coincides with the dimensional shift to allow us direct access to heal ourselves and successfully accomplish the dimensional shift. The idea of vibrating each cell of the mind/spirit/body complex into a higher form of expression is not new. A good example is the three-day process modeled by Christ during the time of crucifixion, burial, and subsequent resurrection.

Resurrection results from the conscious vibration of all mind/spirit/body aspects into a higher expression of the same body. Braden says resurrection is not about the soul essence of life leaving the body, meaning death. It is through the body that the soul may express the wisdom attained in the life experience. Resurrection is the conscious access to the next relative zone of experience ascending from the present. This means that from a third-dimensional experience, resurrection may begin as resonance to fourth-dimensional information. When vibrating at a high pitch, explains Braden, third-dimensional matter no longer has the same meaning or function from the same point of reference as preresurrection. All patterns of energy within the physical body balance through the conscious shifting of each aspect into harmony with the new reference point. Braden believes this energy of reference is love, the purest frequency of expression that may be generated and sustained within each cell of the body. The purpose of resurrection is the new expression of love energy, the gift of Christ. This forms the bridge between the third-dimension low frequency/high magnetics to the optimized experience of high frequency/low magnetics.

Resurrection and the subsequent ascension are the goals of the life experience. As a resurrected being, the person resonates with the energy of fourth-dimensional grids while still expressing the context of the third-dimensional world. Through life experience, we learn the process of resurrection. Each activity we do provides us a tool for assimilation and for generating a higher and greater frequency of energy. With each experience is a thought and feeling that can never be forgotten or erased. Awakening is the beginning of the shift, the collective initiation into the time of new wisdom.

Braden believes, prior to the time of the collective initiation, an opportunity will be presented to some individuals to experience the resurrection process early, maybe days before the shift. This event will occur at the close of the cycle and is known as the Rapture. It will be the beginning of a new experience for those who have loved both the Earth and people of the Earth, and who have given lifetimes of themselves to the process of the conscious cycle. The Rapture marks the completion of that period at the beginning of the resurrection/ascension process into the higher dimensional experience. Those souls who have accelerated their evolution will have the opportunity to complete their process early, before the Earth shift.

According to Braden, biblical texts tell of 12,000 star seeds that incarnated into each of the twelve Israel tribes, carrying different families, customs, and vocations to various world geographic locations. The 144,000 individual seeds each anchored a unique experience of a common body of information. They successfully manifested a Christed vibration. Most seeds are without heavy karmic debt. They have returned to make use of the holographic nature of the conscious matrix and again anchor the memories of purpose at a time close to the end of the cycle. For those individual seeds, the Rapture becomes meaningful. The Rapture allows these 144,000 individuals the experience of simultaneous resurrection and ascension. Individuals that will experience the Rapture are preconditioned to recognize the codes of certain tones. These tones will allow specific fields surrounding the body, those of the human Mer-ka-ba, to move into speeds and key ratios of vibration that will accelerate the experience of the dimensional shift for those individuals. The Mer-ka-ba fields will allow them to access the vibration of the fourth-dimensional state preceding the collective Earth experience. The book of Revelations states, "No one could learn that song except the 144,000 who had been redeemed from the Earth." At the close of the cycle, some individuals who have fulfilled their commitment will choose to stay and usher the Earth into a new era. For others, the

Rapture will signal an opportunity to "return home" to other dimensions. The remainder of the people will not hear the tones; they are programmed to complete the cycle with Earth.

The Rapture, explains Braden, is designed to retrieve those seeds who have completed their tasks within the great cycle of experience, available to all those who know the tone, consciously responding to the familiar vibration ages ago. Biblical writings refer to multiple resurrections over a period in Earth's progress up to and through the shift. Revelation 20:4 states, "They came to life and reigned with Christ a thousand years. The rest of the dead did not come to life until the thousand years were ended. This is the first resurrection."

The concept of the Mer-ka-ba has been deleted from most of the open religious literature but has been preserved through the esoteric teachings of the mystery schools, shamanistic initiations, and hidden in religious doctrine. Mer-ka-ba may be thought of as a vehicle, sometimes called the Light Body of Time Space, writes Braden. It is an aspect of the body with specific direction that entrains each cell of the body to a specific key resonance. Ancient texts refer to a field of energy, information and light radiation from a specific point. The name in both Egyptian and Hebrew vocabulary is Mer-ka-ba. In Egyptian it translates literally to Mer=light, ka=spirit, and ba=body.

The Mer-ka-ba seed forms and remains a point at the root of the first chakra, located at the base of the spine. Mer-ka-ba energy surrounds each individual cell and the entire body as a composite field radiation. Electrical impulses radiate from the first eight cells immediately following conception, and the cells form a star tetrahedron. From this pattern of the star tetrahedron, we approach and understand the human relationship within itself, specifically within creation in general. In two dimensions, the star tetrahedron appears as the Star of David. The star tetrahedron is deeply rooted in the memory of human consciousness, including that of the natives of South America, North America, and Egypt. Patterns of the star tetrahedron reflect codes that are deeply etched into each soul at a level much deeper than that of the conscious knowing.

When rotating, the dynamic plane of the Mer-ka-ba assumes a flattened saucer like expression. At key speeds and ratios, the top and bottom of the tetrahedron begin to move toward each other, and the edges of the form expand outward. When rotation becomes faster than the speed of light, the extremes of polarity neutralize one another and express themselves as unity. The form of a dynamic

Mer-ka-ba represents a constant on varying scales, which are similar in form for an atom, cell, galaxy, extraterrestrial craft, and universal field of a human.

Ancient texts refer to the sphere as consciousness perfected, the clearest form of geometry that a human may hope to attain within the Earth experience. Each individual soul progresses through successively complex forms of geometry represented by Platonic solids, approximating the sphere. They include the tetrahedron, hexahedron, octahedron, dodecahedron, and finally the icosahedron, which is the geometry of perfection for the Earth experience. Each time an individual form ascends, all fields of that form also ascend through resonance into the grid/matrix lattice. This is the science of the Mer-ka-ba. Through the specific ratios and rates of rotation the fields of the Mer-ka-ba wrinkle the grid, allowing the experiences of varied dimensionality consciousness to resonate with the field.

We have described the journey of the soul that originates from God, and whose destiny is to return to God. With the help of quantum physics, the holographic model, and ancient wisdom, we find that all souls are connected on some level. As the ancient mystics have taught, we are all one with God. The common denominator that unites us all is love, another name for God.

REFERENCES

*Listed below the reference material are the subheadings of the chapter
with the reference numbers indicated*

CHAPTER ONE: THE SOUL AND RELIGION

(1) Aristotle, *On the Soul*, Harvard University Press, Cambridge, MA, 1975 (1936).

(2) Badham, Paul and Linda (editors), *Death and Immortality in the Religions of the World*, Paragon House, New York, 1987.

(3) Bremmer, Jan, *The Early Greek Concept of the Soul*, Princeton Press, Princeton, NJ, 1981.

(4) Burgoyne, Thomas H., *The Light of Egypt or The Science of the Soul and the Stars*, Sun Books, Santa Fe, NM, 1980 (1889).

(5) Drury, Nevill, *Dictionary of Mysticism and the Occult*, Harper and Row, Publishers, San Francisco, 1985.

(6) Eliade, Mircea, *Shamanism: Archaic Techniques of Ecstasy*, Princeton University Press, 1964.

(7) Furst, Jill Leslie McKeever, *The Natural History of the Soul in Ancient Mexico*, Yale University Press, New Haven, CT, 1995.

(8) Harner, Michael, *The Way of the Shaman*, Bantom Books, New York, 1980.

(9) Johnson, Christopher Jay, and McGee, Marsha G., *How Different Religions View Death and Afterlife*, The Charles Press Publishers, Philadelphia, 1991.

(10) *Merriam Websters Collegiate Dictionary*, tenth edition, Merriam Webster, Springfield, MA, 1993.

(11) Sharma, I. C., *Cayce, Karma, and Reincarnation*, The Theosophical Publishing House, Wheaton, IL, 1975.

(12) Shaw, Gregory, *Theurgy and the Soul: The Neoplatonism of Imblichus*, The Pennsylvania State University Press, Princeton, NJ, 1981.

(13) Siblerud, Robert, *Keepers of the Secrets: Unveiling the Mystical Societies*, Sacred Science Publications, Wellington, CO, 1999.

(14) Wolf, Fred Alan, *The Spirtual Universe: How Quantum Physics Proves the Existence of the Soul*, Simon and Schuster, New York, 1996.

(15) Zukav, Gary, *The Seat of the Soul*, Simon and Schuster, New York, 1989.

Other references used that are mentioned in listed references:

(16) Plato, *Timeaus*

(17) *Bhagavad Gita*

(18) *Corpus Hermetica*

(19) *Poimandres*

Introduction (4) (6) (7) (11) (15)
The Soul and Native People (2) (5) (7) (8) (13)
The Early Egyptian Concept of the Soul (14)
Greek Philosophy of the Soul (1) (3) (10)

Mathematics of the Soul (5) (10) (12) (16)
Religions of Soul Resurrection (2) (7) (9) (17)
Religions of Soul Reincarnation (2) (9) (11)
Mystical Societies' Deep Knowledge of the Soul (13) (18) (19)

CHAPTER TWO: INVOLUTION AND EVOLUTION OF THE SOUL

(1) Burgoyne, Thomas H., *The Light of Egypt or the Science of the Soul and the Stars*, Sun Books, Santa Fe, NM, 1980 (1889).

(2) Heindel, Max, *The Rosicrucian Cosmo - Conception or Mystic Christianity*, The Rosicrucian Fellowship Press, Oceanside, CA 1943.

(3) Sharma, I. C., *Cayce, Karma, and Reincarnation*, The Theosophical Publishing House, Wheaton, IL, 1975.

(4) Siblerud, Robert, *Keepers of the Secrets: Unveiling the Mystical Societies*, Sacred Science Publications, Wellington, CO, 1999.

Introduction (1)
Involution (1) (2) (3)
Evolution (1) (4)
The Law of Action and Reaction (2) (4)

CHAPTER THREE: THE SPIRITUAL PLANES

(1) Besant, Annie, *The Ancient Wisdom: An Outline of Theosophical Teachings*, The Theosophical Publishing House, Wheaton, IL, 1977

(2) Besant, Annie, *Man and His Bodies*, The Theosophical Publishing House, Adyar, India, 1960 (1896).

(3) Drury, Nevill, *Dictionary of Mysticism and the Occult*, Harper and Row, Publishers, San Francisco, 1985.

(4) Jinarajadasa, C., *First Principles of Theosophy*, The Theosophical Publishing House, Adjar, India, 1960.

(5) Leadbeater, Charles W., *A Textbook of Theosophy*, The Theosophical Press, Adyar, IL, 1946.

God and Creation (1) (3) (4) (5)
The Physical Plane (1) (2) (5)
The Astral Plane (1) (2) (3) (5)
The Mental Plane (1) (2) (5)
The Causal Plane (1) (2) (5)
The Higher Planes (1) (2)

CHAPTER FOUR: REBIRTH

(1) Besant, Annie, *The Ancient Wisdom*, The Theosophical Publishing House, Wheaton, IL, 1977 (1897).

(2) Cooper, Irving, *Reincarnation, The Hope of the World*, The Theosophical Press, Wheaton, IL, 1964 (1920).

(3) Cranston, Sylvia, and Williams, Carey, *Reincarnation: A New Horizon in Science, Religion, and Society*, Julian Press, New York, 1984.

(4) Sharma, I. C., *Cayce, Karma, and Reincarnation*, The Theosophical Publishing House, Wheaton, IL, 1975.

(5) Stevenson, Ian, *Children Who Remember Previous Lives*, University Press of Virginia, 1987.

(6) Wambach, Helen, *Reliving Past Lives*, Arrow Books, London, 1978.

(7) Wambach, Helen, *Life Before Live*, Bantom Books, Toronto, 1979.

Other references used that are mentioned in listed references:

(8) Bernstein, Morey, *In Search of Bridey Murphy*.

(9) *Talmud*.

(10) *Kabbalah*.

    Introduction (2) (3) (5) (7) (8) (9) (10)

    The Concept of Rebirth (1)

    Karma (1) (2) (4)

    Scientific Evidence for Reincarnation (3) (5) (6)

    Past Lives (6) (7)

    Edgar Cayce (3) (4)

    Other Evidence for Reincarnation (2) (5)

CHAPTER FIVE: DESTINY AND FREE WILL

(1) Avery, Kevin Quinn, *The Numbers of Life*, Dolphin Books, Garden City, NY, 1974.

(2) Burmester, Helen S., *The Seven Rays Made Visual*, DeVorss, Marina del Rey, CA, 1986

(3) Butler, Christopher, *Number Symbolism*, Barnes and Noble, Inc., New York, 1970.

(4) Dobbins, Michael, *Tapestry of the Gods*, University of the Seven Rays Publishing House, Jersey City Heights, NJ, 1988.

(5) Drury, Nevill, *Dictionary of Mysticism and the Occult*, Harper and Row, Publishers, San Francisco, 1985.

(6) Eysenck, H. J. and Nias, D., *Astrology: Science or Superstition?* St. Martin's Press, New York, 1969.

(7) Gauquelin, Michael, *Birth Times: A Scientific Investigation of the Secrets of Astrology*, Hill and Wang, New York, 1983.

(8) Hopper, Vincent Foster, *Medieval Number Symbolism*, Cooper Square Publishers, New York, 1969.

(9) Jones, Marc Edmund, *Astrology: How and Why It Works*, Penguin Books, New York, 1945, 1969.

(10) Lansdowne, Zachary F., *The Rays and Esoteric Psychology*, Samuel Weiser, York Beach, Maine, 1989.

(11) MacNaughton, Robin, *Sun Sign Personality Guide*, Bantom Books, New York, 1978.

(12) Mayo, Jeff, *The Planets and Human Behavior*, CRCS Publications, Reno, NV, 1972.

(13) McIntosh, Christopher, *The Astrologers and Their Creed: A Historic Outline*, Frederick A. Draeger, New York, 1969.

(14) Millman, Dan, *The Life You Were Born to Live*, H. J. Kramer,Tiburon, CA, 1993.

(15) Oken, Alan, *Soul Centered Astrology: Science or Superstition?*, St. Martin's Press, New York, 1982.

(16) Parker, Derek and Julia, *The Compleat Astrologer*, Bantam Books, Toronto, 1971.

(17) Polansky, Joseph, *Sun Sign Success*, Destiny Books, New York, 1977.

(18) Stearn, Jess, *A Time for Astrology*, Signet of New American Library, New York, 1971.

(19) *The Urantia Book*, Urantia Foundation, Chicago, 1955.

(20) Van Deusen, Edmund, *Astro-Genetics*, Pocket Books, New York, 1976.

(21) Wedel, Theodore Otto, *The Mediaeval Attitude toward Astrology*, Archon Books, Yale University Press, 1920.

(22) Wood, Ernest, *The Seven Rays*, Theosophical Publishing House, Wheaton, IL,1925.

Other references used that are mentioned in listed references.

(23) Baily, Alice, *Initiation, Human and Solar*

(24) Baily, Alice, *Esoteric Psychology*

(25) Blavatsky, Helen, *The Secret Doctrine*

(26) Ganivet, Jean, *Amicus Medicorum*

(27) Plato, *Timaeus*

(28) Plato, *The Republic*

(29) *Pistis Sophia*

(30) *Rig Veda*

History (13) (18) (21) (26) (28) (29)
The Principals of Astrology (5) (6) (11) (16) (17)
Theories of How Astrology Works (9) (12) (16) (20) (21)
The Science of Astrology (7) (13) (16) (20) (21)
Numerology (1) (3) (8) (14) (27)
The Seven Rays (2) (4) (10) (19) (22) (23) (24) (25) (29) (30)
The Soul's Influence by Astrology and the Seven Rays (15)

CHAPTER SIX: CELESTIAL INHABITANTS

(1) Connolly, David, *In Search of Angels*, Putnam Publishing Group, New York, 1993.

(2) Davidson, Gustav, *A Dictionary of Angels*, The Free Press, New York, 1967.

(3) Drury, Nevill, *Dictionary of Mysticism and the Occult*, Harper and Row, San Francisco, 1985.

(4) Jonanovic, Pierre, *An Inquiry into the Existence of Guardian Angels*, M. Evans and Company, New York, 1993.

(5) Marsello, Robert, *Fallen Angels . . And Spirits of the Dark*, The Berkeley Publishing Group, New York, 1993.

(6) Moolenburgh, H. C., *A Handbook of Angels*, Safron Walden, Essex, England, 1988.

(7) Siblerud, Robert, *In the Beginning: Mysteries of Ancient Civilizations*, Sacred Science Publications, Wellington, CO, 1999.

(8) Siblerud, Robert, *Keepers of the Secrets: Unveiling the Mystical Societies*, Sacred Science Publications, Wellington, CO, 1999

Other references used that are mentioned in listed references:

(9) Aquinas, Thomas, *Summa Theologia*.

(10) Kaplan, Ayreh, *Meditation and Kabbalah*.

(11) Oesterly, W. O. E., *Angelology and Demonology in Early Judaism*.

(12) Pope Gregory, *Homila*.

(13) Pope Gregory, *Moralia*.

(14) *Book of the Angel Raziel*.

(15) *Book of Enoch*.

(16) *Book of Jubilee*.

(17) *Enoch I*.

(18) *Enoch II*.

(19) *A Genesis Apocryphan*.

(20) *Kabbalah*.

(21) *Koran*.

(22) *Levi 3*.

(23) *Secrets of Enoch*.

(24) *Talmud*.

(25) *Testament of Levi*.

(26) *Testament of Nephali*.

(27) *Zohar*.

(28) Moody, Raymond, *Life After Life*.

        Introduction (1)

        Early Chronicles of Angels (1) (2) (7) (8) (26) (16)

        Functions and Nature of Angels (1) (2) (7) (15) (27)

        The Hierarchy (2) (6) (9) (11) (12) (14) (20) (25)

        Celestial Personalities (1) (2) (3) (6) (10) (15) (16) (17) (19) (20) (21) (24) (27)

        The Fallen Angels (2) (3) (5) (13) (18) (22) (23)

        The Seven Heavens (2) (12) (16) (25) (27)

        Other Beings (5)

        The Science of Angels (1) (4) (6) (28)

CHAPTER SEVEN: THE SPIRITUAL HIERARCHY

(1) *The Urantia Book*, Urantia Foundation, Chicago, 1955.

CHAPTER EIGHT: THE SOUL AFTER DEATH

(1) Baldwin, William J., *Spirit Releasement Therapy*, Human Potential Foundation Press, Falls Church, VA, 1993.

(2) Drury, Nevill, *Dictionary of Mysticism and the Occult*, Harper and Row, Publishers, San Francisco, 1985.

(3) Fiore, Edith, *You Have Been Here Before*, Ballentine, NY, 1978.

(4) Fiore, Edith, *The Unquiet Dead*, Doubleday (Dolphin), New York, 1987.

(5) Foulks, E., *Investigations:* Research Bulletin of the Institute of Noetic Sciences, Vol. I, No. 314, Sausalito, CA, 1985.

(6) Gettings, Fred, *Ghosts in Photographs*, Harmony Books, New York, 1978.

(7) Jaffe, Anieta, *Apparitions and Precognition*, University Books, New Hyde Park, New York, 1963.

(8) Monroe, Robert A., *Journeys Out of the Body*, Anchor Books, Doubleday, New York, 1971.

(9) Monroe, Robert A., *Far Journeys*, Doubleday and Company, Inc., Garden City, New York, 1985.

(10) Moody, Raymond A., *The Light Beyond*, Bantam Books, Toronto, 1988.

(11) Muldoon, Sylvan and Carrington, Hereward, *The Phenomenon of Astral Projection*, Century, London, 1969.

(12) Pike, James A., *The Other Side; An Account of My Experiences with Psychic Phenomena*, Doubleday, Garden City, NY, 1968.

(13) Ring, Kenneth, *Life at Death, A Scientific Investigation of the Near-Death Experience*, Coward, McCann, and Geoghagen, New York, 1990.

(14) Roll, William G., *The Poltergeist*, The Scarecrow Press, Inc., Metuchen, NJ, 1976.

(15) Tyrrell, G.N.M., *Apparitions,* Gerald Duckworth and Co. Ltd., London, 1943.

Other references used that are mentioned in listed references:

(16) Bousfield, W. R., *The Basis of Memory.*

(17) Durville, Hector, *Le Fairtome des Vivants.*

(18) Moody, Raymond, *Life After Life.*

(19) Morse and Perry, *Transition by the Light.*

(20) Valarino, Elasase, *On the Other Side of Life, Exploring the Near Death Experience.*

(21) *Egyptian Book of the Dead.*

(22) *Tibetan Book of the Dead.*

> Out of Body Experience (8) (9) (11) (16) (17) (21)
> Near Death Experience (10) (11) (13) (16) (18) (19) (20)
> Earth Bound Spirits (1) (3) (4) (5)
> Apparitions (2) (6) (7) (12) (14) (15) (22)

CHAPTER NINE: SPIRIT COMMUNICATION

(1) Blavatsky, H.P., *The Secret Doctrine*, Theosophical University Press, Pasadena, CA, 1963.

(2) Brown, Michael F., *The Channeling Zone*, Harvard University Press, Cambridge, MA, 1997.

(3) Brown, Rosemary, *Unfinished Symphonies, Voices from Beyond*, W. Morrow, New York, 1971.

(4) Eliade, Mircea, *Shamanism: Archaic Techniques of Ecstasy*, Princeton University Press, 1964.

(5) Klimo, Jon, *Channeling,* Jeremy P. Tarcher, Inc., Los Angeles, 1987.

(6) Lange, Sente, *Enne: Please Continue to Write*, Book I, Hauptstrasse, West Germany, 1984.

(7) Milanovich, Norma, *We the Arcturians*, Athena Publishing, Albuquerque, NM, 1990.

Other references used that are mentioned in listed references:

(8) Hurtak, James J., *The Book of Knowledge: The Keys of Enoch*, The Academy for Future Science, Los Gatos, CA, 1977.

(9) Norman, Ruth, *Unarius Science*.

(10) *Book of Mormon*.

> Introduction (5) (10)
> History of Spirit Communication (1) (2) (4) (5)
> Spirit Information (3) (5) (8) (9)
> Spiritual Sources (5) (7)
> Techniques of Spirit Communication (5)
> Life on the Other Side (6)

CHAPTER TEN: ELECTRONIC SPIRIT COMMUNICATION

(1) Kubis, Pat and Macy, Mark, *Conversations Beyond the Light*, Griffen Publishing, Boulder, CO, 1995.

(2) Locher, Theo and Harsch-Fischbach, Maggy, *Breakthroughs in Technical Spirit Communication*, Continuing Life Research, Boulder, 1997.

(3) Meek, George W., *After We Die, What Then?*, Metascience Corporation, Franklin, NC, 1980.

Other references used that are mentioned in listed references:

(4) Raudive, Konstantin, *Breakthrough*.

> Introduction (1) (2) (3) (4)
> Timestream (1) (2)
> Marduk (1) (2)
> Spiritual Knowledge From the Third Plane (1) (2)

CHAPTER ELEVEN: THE SACRED SCIENCE OF SPIRIT AND MATTER

(1) Bohm, David, *Wholeness and the Implicate Order*, Routledge and Kegan Paul, London, 1980.

(2) Braden, Gregg, *Awakening to Zero Point: The Collective Initiation*, LL Productions, Bellevue, WA, 1993.

(3) Briggs, John P. And Peat, F. David, *Looking Glass Universe: The Emerging Science of Wholeness*, Simon and Schuster, New York, 1984.

(4) Capra, Fritjof, *The Tao of Physics*, Shambhala Publications, Boulder, CO, 1975.

(5) Dossey, Larry, *Healing Words: The Power of Prayer and the Practice of Medicine*, Harper Paperbacks, New York, 1993.

(6) Foster, Richard J., *Prayer: Finding the Heart's True Home*, Harper, San Francisco, 1992.

(7) Levi, Eliphas, *Transcendental Magic*, Bracken Books, London, 1995.

(8) Peale, Norman Vincent, *The Power of Positive Thinking*, Prentice Hall Press, New York, 1987.

(9) Russell, John Robert, *Zygon,* Journal of Religion and Science

(10) Sharpe, Kevin J., *David Bohm's World, New Physics and New Religion*, Bucknell University Press, London, 1993.

(11) Sheldrake, Rupert, *A New Science of Life: The Hypothesis of Morphic Resonance*, Park Street Press, Rochester, Vermont, 1981.

(12) Siblerud, Robert, *Keepers of the Secrets: Unveiling the Mystical Societies*, Sacred Science Publications, Wellington, CO, 1999.

(13) Talbot, Michael, *The Holographic Universe*, Harper Perennial, New York, 1991.

Other references used that are mentioned in listed references:

(14) Watson, Lyale, *Lifetide the Biology of Consciousness*.

The Implicate Order (1) (3) (9) (10) (13)
The Holographic Brain (3) (13)
Formative Causation (3) (11) (13) (14)
Eastern Mysticism and Physics (4)
The Science of Prayer (5) (6) (7) (8) (12)
The Holographic Soul (9) (13)
Resurrection (2)

INDEX

Aaron 160
Ab 6
Abaddon 195
Abel 159
Aborigines 75,295
Abortion 154,183,261
Abraham 16,141-2,146,
152-3
Absolute 2,3,10,18,46,
78,137,169,286
Abstract Thought
45,65,68
Abyssinia 151
Achterberg, Jean 287,291
Acupuncture 55
Adam Kadmon 221
Adam 6,34,157,159
Addey, John 121,128
Adriel 158
Aeons 147,157
Africa 5,6,76,91,97
Age of Aquarius 298
Ahmad, Mirza 143
Air Signs 116
Akashic Record 101,231,
265
Akh 8
Alchemist 24,153,220
Alcmaeon 8
Alexander the Great 108
Allah 1,7,46
American Society for
Psychical Research 226
American 75,92-3,225,
228,249
American Indians 226-7,
295
An 150
Anafiel 155

Anael 30,149
Ancient of Days 195,197,
160,172,178,180,185,188
Anderson, Robert 290
Angel of Death 243
Angels 12,34,47,59,
141-64,185-6,190,195,
197-8,232,243,264
Animal 3,20,26,51,53-4,
236,257,264,279
Annunaki 155,258
Antigravity 169
Anubis 152
Aphrodite 109
Apocalypse 153
Apostles Creed 16
Apparition 201,220-24
Aquarius 115,117
Aquinas,Thomas
111,143-4, 146-147
Aramaic 141
Archangels 12,29,47,139,
147,149
Archetypes 38,42,47-8,
65,72,140,291,289
Architect of Universe
178
Archons 12,23-4,108,157
Arcturians 232
Ares 109
Argentina 237
Aries 113-4,117
Aristotle 8,107
Ark of the Covenant
148
Armageddon 298
Aryans 110
Ascendant 107,124,
127-8,192

Ascendant Masters 232
Ascension 300
Asia 3,75,91
Aspect, Alan 272
Association for
Research and
Enlightenment 228
Assyrian 106,142,148,
215
Astral Body 7,38,56,
58-9, 60,62-5,67,
200-01,81-3,86,259,265
Astral Plane 50,56-64,
203,254,257,260,263
Astral Projection 200-03
Astral World 38,40,45,
48,52-3,60,62,66-7,
70,80,84,86,224,226,
229,233,288
Astrology 11,13,23,27,
44,86,101
Atma 73
Atman 18,19
Australia 3,70,253,295
Austria 253
Automatic Writing 234
Avidya 18,19
Avonal 174,184,187
Azazael 156-8
Aztec 5

Ba 6,8,221,226
Babylonia 14,106-
7,141,150,258
Bach 230
Baily, Alice
135,228,249
Balaam 141
Baldwin, William
215-220

Barbiel 149
Barque 8
Barretti, William 210
Barzakh 17
Basilides 159
Bayliss, Raymond 251
Beelzebub 158,195
Beethoven 230
Belgium 76,124,253
Bell, Alexander G 265
Belphegor 158
Bernstein, Morey 89
Berossus 106
Besant, Annie 46,78,203
Beshter 150
Bhagavad Gita 17,20
Bible 2,16,77,100,141,
227,243,260
Big Bang 272-73
Bilocation 9,201,220
Binsfield, Peter 158
Biorhythms 120
Birthmarks 91-2
Bisexual 34,44,190
Blavatsky, Helena 46,
134-5,228
Bohm, David 266, 267-
276,292,295
Bok, Bart 124
Bond, Elijah 234
Book of Mormon 154,227
Bousfield, W. R. 200-01
Bozacano, Professor 201
Braden, Greg 128,297-
302
Brahman 19,19,47,
282,295
Bridey Murphy 89
Britain 76
Brown, Rosemary 230
Brown, Frank 122
Buddhic Body 203
Buddhic Plane 48,73-4,83

Buddhism 17,20,59,
75,90,102,118,260,
281,283,295
Bull, Titus 217
Burd, Randolph 287
Burgoyne, Thomas
28,35
Burma 91,239
Burton, Richard
253,255

Caligasta 195-7
Camael 149
Cancer 115,117
Capra, Fritjaf 281-4
Capricorn 115,117
Cardinal Sign 117
Carrington, Henry 222
Cassiel 30,160
Cathars 77
Catholic 16,77,145,156,
158,161,216,250,289
Causal Body 19,45,65,
67,69,70-4,79,80-1,
83,203
Causal Plane 45,65,68,
70-4,79
Cayce, Edgar 99-102,
228-9,230-1
Celestial Recorders 176
Celts 76
Census Directors 176
Central Axis 4
Cerviel 149
Chakra 56,138-140,
200, 219,301
Chaldean 8,10,106,141,
151-3
Chamuel 150
Channeling 225-6,229,
231,233,235
Cherubim 47,141,146-8,
153,185-6

Chi 118,283-4
China 98,109,201,215
Chinese Astrology 117
Choisnard, Paul 123
Chopin 236
Christianity 15,16,47,
57,63,76,91,100,102,
109-11,135,141,144,
148,151-2,163,221,
259,264,272,287,289,
297
Clairaudient 230
Clairvoyant 88
Clark, Vernon 128
Clement of Alexandria
16,143
Colburn, Nettie 227
Collective Unconscious
232,290,295
Concetti, Gino 250
Connolly, David 143-4
Consciousness 3,5,19,
39,48,58,71-3,82-3,
102,131,136,139,140,
170,205,208-15,221,
229,244,261,264,
271,273,279,280,284,
289,291,295,297-8,
301-2
Cooper, Irving 103
Coordinate Trinity 173
Corps of Finality
177,190
Corpus Hermetica 26
Cosmic Consciousness 3
Cottingly Fairies 224
Creator Daughters 175,
178-9
Creator Sons 174-5,178-
183-4,188,190
Crookal, Robert 210
Curie, Marie 254-5
Cycles 120,140

Daimons 10-13,151,221
Dalai Lama 59,91
Danes 75
Daniel 141-2,145-6,
152,155
David 141
Davidson, Gustav
144-45,150,156
Davies, Paul 272
Day of Judgment 16,77,
298
Debussy 230
Deity 2,5,46-7,165-68,
173,175
Demiurge 11,12,14,22-6,
47,157
Demon 110,149,155-8,
215,228
Dense Body 39,43,55,
56,60
Descendant 107,127-8
Desire World 38-40
Desire Body 38-41,58
Destiny 20,102,104,
105-40,110,155-6,158,
166,170,177,182,187,
189,195,197,266,293
Deva 47,232
Devachan 65-71,80
Devil 20,110,155,158,
195,197
Diogenes 8
Dionysius 147,149,150,
157
DNA 278
Dominations 47,147,149
Dominions 147,153
Dorchagraphy 224
Dossey, Larry 286-7
Dreams 4-5,9,90-1,203,
232,234,289-92
Dualism 22,35,47,73,
274,291

Dunne, Brenda 291-92
Durville, Hector 202

Ea 150
Earth Signs 116
Earth-Bound Spirits
214-220
Eden 148
Edentia 173
Edison, Thomas
249,254
Egypt 6,8,10,13,24,35,
46,76,97,106,108,122,
201,215,225-6,301
Einstein, Albert 255,
267-8,279,281-2
Eisenberg, David 293
Elementals 58-9,66,81,
164,232
Eliade, Mircea 4
Elijah 76,141,154
Elohim 157
Elves 59,163
Emotional Soul 39
Enfolded Order 269
England 236,253,267
Engrams 200,274
Enki 258
Enlil 150
Enoch 143,145,147,154,
157,160,231
Entropy 295-6
Eskimo 76
Essenes 77,142
Eternal Son 166,167-8,
170-1,173-4,180,187
Ether 55,58,201
Etheric Body 40,61-2,
138,200-02,221,259
Etheric Double 7,55-6,
81,203
Europe 75,77,91,98,249
Eve 6,34,157-9

Evil Spirits 3,4,110,215-
16,233
Evolution 15,25,28-44,
46,47,50-3,58,62,65,
67-8,70,72,74,78-80,
82,87,112,134,139-40,
176,178-9,181,183,
185,189,193,229,
239,259,265,266,
289,295-7,300
Exodus 146,154
Exorcism 215,216
Explicate Order 267-
274, 295,297
Extraterrestrials 232
Ezekiel 146,148

Fairies 59,163,224
Fall 2,5,238
Fallen Angels 155,157,
159,163
Fate 11,14,25,27,104,
108-10,112,264
Father, God the 166-67,
173,175,178-9,187-8
Feminine Signs 117
Ferguson, Marilyn 211
Fibonacci Numbers
35,298
Ficino, Marsilio 35,298
Finalitiers Corp 191-195
Findhorn 232
Finland 25,226
Fiore, Edith 217,218
Fire Signs 116
First Heaven 40,69,140-
150,152,159
Fixed Signs 117
Fleiss, Wilhelm 120
Flood 24,110,154,230
Ford, Arther 229
Formative Causation
277-280

Foster, Richard 285
Fourth Dimension 32,
    210,298-9,300
France 75,77,124,143,253
Freemasons 111
Free Will 18,40,42,
    105-140
Fuld, William 234

Gabriel 30,141,143,
    148,150-2,159,180-5,
    187,196
Gallop Poll 75,160,206,
    225,231
Ganivet, Jean 111
Garden of Eden 141,148,
    158-9
Gauls 71
Gauquelin, Michael
    124-6
Gemini 115,117
Genesis 141,143,146
Germany 124,253
Gethsemane 142
Gettings, Fred 224
Ghosts 6,56,199,201,
    220,222-3
Gita 18
Gnomes 58,163,224
Gnostic 22-4,47,76-7,
    108-9,134,221
Goblins 163
God 22-7,45-51,72-3,
    76-7,88, 101-2,108-10,
    130,137,139,141-159,
    165-9,170,177,180,
    187-8,192-3,198,210,
    221,231,237,240,242,
    245-7,258,260-1,264,
    266,272-3,289,297,
    299,302
Gods 79,106,144,146,
    225-6,231

Grace 88,209
Grand Universe
    165,167-170,173,177,
    188,190,194
Gravity160,170,177,282
Grayson, Bruce 206,209
Great White
    Brotherhood 52
Greeks 8,10,24,46,
    76,106-9,129,141,215
Gremlins 163
Grigori 155
Grof, Stan 289
Grosso, Michael 295
Group Soul 51-4,79
Guardian Spirits 3,4,13,
    289
Guardian Angels 26,146,
    150,153,160,233

Hades 9
Hallucinations 217,220-1
Harmonics 121,128-9
Harsch-Fishback, Jules
    & Maggy 252-5
Hastings, Arther 225
Havona 165-6,169-172,
    174,176-9,188,190
Hawaii 75
Heaven 5,15-17,19,24-5,
    40-1,43,60,64,67-9,
    88, 142,144-5,148,
    155-7,174,226,243,
    259,263-5,289,293-4
Hebrew 15,47,141,143,
    147-8,151,301
Heindle, Max 37,42,44
Hell 5,16,19,40,45,60,
    62,94,155,157-8,213-
    14,226,239,258,289
Hemi-sync 162,204
Heracleitus 8

Hermeticism 24-28,
    32-3,35,37,44,46,
    109,135
Herod, King 142
Hezekiah's Pillars 111
High Authority 176
Higher Self 69,71,112,
    139,212-13,225,229,
    231-2
Hindu 17,20,46-7,75,90,
    110,134,161,281-2,
    284,295
Hipparchus 108
Hoffer, Abram 119
Holland 163
Hologram 210,211-13,
    268-69,275-6,292,
    294-5,297
Holographic Theory
    266-67,289-91,293,
    297
Holomovement 272-4,
    276,280,295
Holy Spirit (Ghost) 16,
    46,135,137,151,154
Homer 8
Homosexuality 104
Hopi 76
Horoscope 108-9,112,
    114,116,123,125,
    127-8,138,140
Hosts 147
Houdini, Henry 229
Houses (Astrological)
    107,108,114,116
Huna 76
Hundredth Monkey 280
Huntington, Ellsworth
    120
Hurt, Stokes 235
Hypnosis 89,95-99,100
Hyslop, James 206

Iadalbaoth 157
Iamblichus 10,11,13,14
Iblis 156
Iceland 75
Ikemi, Yujio 286
Illusion 268,275-6,284, 293-5
Immortality 1,6,8,15, 17-21,25,70,195,192, 221,244
Implicate Order 267-274,279,283, 291,296
Incubus 163
India 91-3,103,109-110, 201
Indians 4,5
Infinite Soul 29
Infinite Spirit 167-8, 170-1,173-4,178-181, 185,187
Instrumental Transcommunications (ITC) 251,253-4,257, 260,265
Intuition 71,82,136,139
Inuit 75
Involution 28-44,79, 266,297
Iraq 105
Ireland 75,89,163
Irenaeus 156
Isaiah 146-7
Isial 8
Islam 15-17,75,77-8, 141,143-4,151,159-60
Isle of Paradise 168,170-1
Israel 22,150,152,215,300
Italy 75

Jacob 141
Japan 120-1
Jaffe, Anieta 221

Jahn, Robert 291-2
Jehoel 148
Jehovah 26
Jerusalem 25,159
Jerusem 172,178-9,183, 189,190-1
Jesus Christ 16,22-3,78, 90,106,108,111, 141-2,159,174,178,197, 215-6,227,232,237, 239,246-7,260,262, 287,297,299,301
Jewish 30,75,77,104, 106,142,144,151-2, 157-9,161,221
Joan of Arc 143
John the Baptist 22,76, 141-2,152,159
Jonas, Eugene 119
Jophiel 150
Joseph 141
Josephus 77
Josephson, Brian 272
Judaism 15,16,46,75,148
Juergenson, Fredrich 250,254
Jung, Carl 109,127,221, 232,265
Jupiter 46,109,114,124-6
Justi 146
Justinian 10

Ka 7,8,201
Kaaishim Angels 160
Kabbalah 30,33,47,135, 141,149,150-1,153-4, 156,165
Kabbalists 35,75,145
Kamaloka 60-1,63-4,80
Kaplan, Aryeh 159
Karma 19,20-1,25,37, 70,81,83-8,100,131, 140,144,241,261,264, 274,283,289,300

Kepler, Johann 121,125, 130
Kersharvadas, Yogi 249
Khaibut 7
Khat 7
Khul, Djwhal 135,228
Klimo,Jon 225-6,229, 231,233-4
Koran 16,17,141,143, 145,151,159
Krafft, Karl 123
Kronus 109
Kubis, Pat 251
Kahunas 295

Lamech 155
Lammars, Arthur 100
Lange, Enne 235-248
Lange, Senta 235-248
Lanonandek Sons 174,182-3,194-6
Lapland 75
Lashley, Karl 274
Lasson, Leon 127
Lateren Council 155
Lazaris 225
Leadbetter, Charles 46,48
Lebanon 94
Leo 115,117
Levi, Eliphias 288-9
Leviathian 158
Lewis, G. Frank 287
Libra 113,115,117
Life Carriers 174,184
Lilit 157
Lincoln, Abraham 224,227
Liszt 230
Lithuanians 76
Locality 268,272,273-4, 295,297
Loehr, Franklin 284

Logos 10,13,46-8,50-1,
54,73,148,221
Lord of the Day 137
Lords of Karma 85,86
Lorrain, Perre le 111
Lower World 3,4,5
Lower Selves 231
Loye, David 292,294
LSD 289
Lucifer 155-6,158,163,
183,194-7
Luther, Martin 144
Luxembourg 252-3
Luxor Temple 35

MacLean, Dorothy 232
Macy, Mark 251
Magi 13,111
Magic 7,24,136-7,145,
149,156,163,288-9
Magistral Sons 174
Mammon 159
Manichaenism 157
Marconi, G. 249
Marduk 254-8,262-3
Mars 109,114,123-7
Marsello, Robert 156
Martyrs 147
Mary Magdalene 77,
109,142
Masculine Signs 117
Master Universe 169,178
Mathematics of Soul
13,14
Maya 275,295
Mayan Calendar 298
Mayo, Jeff 120
McDougall, Duncan
202
Mead, Margaret 76
Mecca 182
Mediumship 225,227,
229

Meek, George 250-1
Melchizedek
154,174,181-3,186,
190-1
Memory 200
Menos 9
Mental Plane 45-6,50,
52,54,64-9,80,259
Mental Body 45,64-69,
82,86,203
Mer-ka-ba 154,155,
300-2
Mercury 109,113
Mermaids 163
Mesopotamia 80,97,
106,109,146,258
Metascience
Foundation 250
Metatron 148,150,152-4,
158,231
Methodist Church 144
Mexica 5
Mexico 5
Michael 30,142-3,
148-151,157,159,167,
172,174-5,178-9,180-2,
184,194-7
Mictlan 5
Midheaven 107,124
Mighty Messengers
175,189
Milanovich, Norma 232
Milky Way 35,122,172
Millman, Dan 133
Mirandola, Picodella 10
Monadic 48,50-1,54,
79,112,129,134
Monroe Institute 203
Monroe, Robert 162,
203-6,293
Montgomery, Ruth 230
Moody, Raymond
161,206,209

Moolenburgh, H. C.
146,149,160
Moon 113,119,120,123,
125-7
Morontia 166,171,173,
176,178,180,186-9,
191-3
Morphic Resonance
276-280
Morphogenic Field
276-280,288
Moses 141,143,152,154,
159
Mother Spirit 180-1,
185,188
Mozart 231
Mueller, George 250
Muhammad 17,78,143,
152,160,260
Muldoon, Sylvan
200-4,210
Mumler, William 224
Muslim 17,46,63,104
Mutable Signes 117
Mysticism 21,37,46,
281-4,297

Nag Hammadi 76
Nature Spirits 58
Near Death Experience
(NDE) 7,141,160-1,
199,206-214,294
Nebadon 165,167,170,
173,178-186,193,195,
197
Nelson, John 119
Neoplatonism
10,109,121
Nephilim 146,155
Neptune 114
Nether World 7
Netherlands 76,124

New Testament 15,16,40, 76,147,150,155, 200,215
New Jerusalem 63,145
New Age 298
Nibiru 146,150,155,258
Nicene Creed 16
Nirvana 20,21,44,258
Noah 143,153,155
Nonlocality 268,272-4, 284
Noos 9
Norlatiadek 172,194
Normon, Ruth 231
North America 3,75,91
Norwegian 75
Nostradamus 230
Numerology 129-134
Nuriel 159

Oesterly, W.O. 150
Ogdoad 14,25
Oken, Alan 138-139
Olcott, Henry 46
Old Testament 15,16, 141-2,146,148,156,216
Omniphim Angel 176
Ophaniel 148
Ophanim 148
Origen 143-145
Orvonton 165,170-2,174, 178-9,181
Osiris 6,9
Ouija Board 216,234-5
Out of Body Experience (OBE) 162,199-206, 289,293
Oversoul 232
Owen, A.R. 223
O'Neil, Bill 250
Panorama of Life 40, 42,60
Paracelus 221

Paradise Trinity 174-5, 178,180
Paradise 63,166,168-180, 182,185-190,192-4,213
Paradise Creator Sons 166-7,178-9
Paradise Sons 175,195-196
Parallel Worlds 262-3, 292,294
Particle 267-276,283-284
Past Lives 72,80-1,89, 95-99,100,231
Past Life Therapy 217
Pauling, Linus 124
Peale, Norman V. 284
Peat, F. David 290
Persia 106,141,151,159
Personality 2,5,7,112, 125-6,133,136,139, 166-7,170,173,178, 187-8,191,262
Peter 146,150
Phantom Limb 201
Pharaoh 6,8
Phi 35
Philo of Alexandria 144
Philolaus 130
Physical World 41,49, 51,56,63,65,67,85
Pike, Bishop James 223, 229
Pisces 115,117
Pistis Sophia 77,108,134
Pixies 163
Plato 8,10,12,107,109, 130
Platonic Solids 302
Plotinus 10,109
Pluto 114
Polarity 29,31-2,40
Poltergeist 93,222-3,235
Polynesia 76
Pope Paul II 111

Pope Gregory 147,149, 156
Pope Paul VI 250
Porphyry 10
Possession (Spirit) 215
Power Directors 178
Powers 47,147,149,153, 185
Prana 55,60,61
Prayer 264,284-89
Precession of Equinox 108
Precognition 292
Pribram, Karl 210-12, 266,274-6
Price, John Randolph 280
Prigogene, Ilya 296
Principalities 47,147,149
Proclus 14
Protestants 16,161,289
Prussians 76
Psyche 8,20,112,221
Psychokinesis 266,291
Pueblo Indians 75
Pursel, Jack 225
Purgatory 40,45,57, 60,63,64,80,258
Pyramid 6,35
Pythagoras 9,13,122, 129,139

Quanta 267-276
Quantum Physics 267-8, 270,281-4

Ra 6,8,46
Raphael 148-151,153,159
Rapture 298,300-01
Raquel 149
Raudive, Konstantin 249,250,252,254
Ravitz, Leonard 118

Rebirth 11,12,14,18-26, 37,43-44,50,56,59, 69,75-104,140,266, 284,297

Reincarnation 6,17,18, 20,75-105,232,238, 258,260-1,264

Relativity Theory 281, 268

Ren 7

Resurrection 15-17,192, 195,297-302,232

Rig Veda 135

Ring, Kenneth 206, 209-10,212-213

Rishi 110

Roberts, Jane 232

Rogo, D. Scott 251

Roll, William 223

Romans 10,76,107

Rosicrucian 37,39, 40,44,46,75,78,111

Russell, John Robert 272

Saccas, Ammonius 10

Sacred Geometry 13,35

Sagan, Carl 124

Sagittarius 115,117

Sahu 7

Salamanders 58,164

Salter, Swejen 254-6, 258,260-1,265

Salvington 173,178, 179,180-1,183-7,190, 193,196

Sammael 149,154, 156-58

Samuel 30

Sandalphon 154,159,160

Sanobim 185-86

Sanskrit 60,73,83,101

Sariel 157

Satan 142,148,152, 154-8,183,194-7

Satania 172,178,179,181, 183,189,191,194-5,197

Saturn 109,113,124-126

Schizophrenia 220

Schubert 230

Schreiber, Klaus 253-54

Scotland 75,232

Second Heaven 42,69, 148-49,157,159

Second Coming 298

Seconoaphim Angels 177

Seed Atom 39,43,259

Sekham 7

Sephiroth 30,33,135, 147,151,153,157

Seraphiel 148

Seraphim 47,147-48, 156-58,160,176-177, 182-89,190,196

Seraphs 34,153,196

Seedahely, William 161

Seth 232

Seven Master Spirits 166, 168,171-73,176

Seven Rays 29,134-140

Seventh Heaven 72,152, 154,159-60

Shakers 227

Shaman 3,4,5,59,201, 215,225-26,295,301

Shapeshift 269

Shekinah 150,154

Sheldrake, Rupert 276-280

Sheol 15

Shining Ones 66

Shiva 46

Siberia 201

Sidawick, Henry 221

Sidereal Body 221

Silver Cord 39,202,210, 243

Simmons, Ruth Mills 89

Sioux 76

Sitchin, Zecharia 146, 155,258

Sky 3,4,5

Smith, Joseph 227

Sodom 152

Solitary Messenger 176

Solomon 153

Son 166,178,179,188

Soul Mate 293

South America 3,226

South Pacific 76

Space Brothers 232

Spain 253

Spangler, David 232

Spindrift 285-87

Spiricom 250-1

Spirit Possession 199, 215-216

Spirit Attachment 215, 219

Spiritual Guides 363, 144,289

Spiritualism 225

Spiritualist 226-28,233, 235

Sprites 163

St. Francis 9

St. Paul 15,142,147,149, 151,200

Star Body 221

Star Tetrahedron 301

Steiner, Rudolf 149

Stevenson, Ian 89-95, 102-104

Stoicism 107

Subtle Body 19

Succubus 164

Sufis 75,78

Sumer 80,105,109,141, 146,150,155,248
Sun 113,123,127,138
Supernaphim Angels 176
Supreme God 23,24,27, 157,166
Sweden 226,253
Swedenborg, Emanuel 145,217,226,230,294
Swedes 76,90
Switzerland 76,252
Swoboda, Herman 120
Sylphs 58,164
Synchronicity 109,289, 290

Talbot, Michael 276, 292-3
Talmud 77,151,154
Tanous, Alex 293
Taoist 281,282
Tart, Charles 199
Tartatus 158
Tathata 28
Taurus 113,114,117
Telepathic 88,96,208, 213,222,266,289
Teltscher, Alfred 120
Tesla, Nikola 249
Tetragrammaton 47,154
Tetrakyts 130
Thailand 91
Theosophist 46,48, 65,73,88,134,228,249
Theurgy 11,12
Third Heaven 42,69,154, 159
Thoth 24
Thought Adjusters 180, 182,187-88,196
Thought, Concrete 38,65
Thought World 38

Thrones 47,147-49,153
Thymos 9
Timestream 254,255-65
Tibet 91,201,220,226, 295
Tighe, Ruth Mills 89
Timeaus 14,130
Tlingit Indians 91,92,94
Tomaschek, Rudolf 119
Torah 15,160
Transmigration 20,23, 78,102
Transpersonal 289
Tree of Life 4,30,148, 154
Tribulations 298
Trinitized Sons 173-76
Trisagon 147
Tsai 24
Turel 157
Twin Soul 34,36,37,44
Twining, Professor 39

Ullman, Montague 290
Undines 58,164
Unfolded Order 269
Union of Days 171
United States 91,216, 253
Universal Father 166, 168,170-74,178-79, 182,188,194-95
Universal Mind 3,29,47, 48,65,101,168,225, 231
Upanishads 19
Ur 146,153
Urantia 165,234
Uranus 113,114,134
Uriel 148,151,153,158
Ursa Major 110
Uversa 172-3,178,180, 197

Uzziel 149

Valarino, Evelyn 206
Van Deusen, Edmund 126
Van Deusen, Wilson 217
Van Zelst, Zaalberg 201
Vatican 250
Vedas 110
Vedic 20
Venus 109,113,125,127
Virgin Mary 141-2,152, 295
Virgo 115,117
Virtues 147,149,151-2, 156
Vishnu 47
Vital Body 38,40,42-3
Vitality 55,56,60,62
Void 282-84,295
Volquire, Alexandre 123
Von Braum, Wernher 254
Vorondadek Sons 174, 182-3

Wambach, Helen 95-99
Watchers 141,155,159
Water Signs 116
Watson, Lyale 280
Watters, R. A. 202
Wave 267-276,283,291
Wesley, John 144
West Germany 234
Whitton, Joel 292-294
Wickland, Carl 216-217
Wilde, Stuart 231
Witch 111,158
Wolf, Fred Alan 290
World Soul 10-14,130

Xenoglossy 89

Yahweh 46,47,147
Yam 19
Yamahaki, Dr. 119
Yang 117,118
Yeshua Ben Yussuf 260
Yin117,118
Yogi 201

Zadkiel 149,150
Zacharial 30,159
Zachiel 149
Zagzagal 160
Zaphkiel 149
Zechariah 146,152
Zero Point 297,298
Zero Point Energy 271
Zeus 46,109
Zodiac 22,26,44,106,
    108,110,112-114,
    118-119,130,137-38,
    140
Zohar 145-47,153-4,
    159,165
Zoroaster 215
Zukav, Gary 2
Zuni 76